A guide to the cathedrals of Britain

Acknowledgments

Cinnabar
235 West 56th Street,
New York, NY 10019
*Jade Bliss, p 12, and Global
Blossom, p 50
(both invented by Jerri Banks)*

Daddy O
44 Bedford Street,
New York, NY 10014
*The Horny Latte, p 28
(invented by Philip Casaceli)*

The Dining Room
154 East 79th Street,
New York, NY 10021
*The Columbian, p 15
(invented by Jennifer Joseph),
and Shirley Temple Black, p 19*

DYLAN Prime
62 Laight Street,
New York, NY 10013
*St Croix Cocktail, p 45
(invented by Michael
Waterhouse)*

Madame X
94 West Houston Street,
New York, NY 10012
*Chocolate-Covered Strawberry,
p 16 (invented by Heather
Culton), and First Kiss, p 34*

Pop
127 4th Avenue,
New York, NY 10003
Mojito, p 14

Town
The Chambers Hotel,
15 West 56th Street,
New York, NY 10019
*Mother's Day Martini, p 10,
The Rossini, p 17, and Town
Passion, p 17 (all invented by
Albert Trummer)*

Union Bar
204 Park Avenue South,
between 17th and 18th Street,
New York, NY 10003
Caramel Martini, p 9

V-Bar
3355 Las Vegas Boulevard,
Las Vegas, NV 89109
Blueberry Mojito, p 51

Drinks
Climax, p 27, adapted from
The Bartender's Black Book,
5th Edition, Stephen Kittredge
Cunningham, The Black Book
Co., 2000

Waltzing Matilda, p 54, Mocha
Mint, p 67, Casino, p 72, and
Sonic Blaster, p 74, adapted
from **www.mixed-drink.com**

Thanks to:
Mixed-drink.com,
Mojo Magazine, Piff,
Greg Chow, The Bartender's
Black Book, Stephen Kittredge
Cunningham, The Black Book
Co., 2000.

A guide to the cathedrals of Britain

Anthony S. B. New

Constable London

First published in Great Britain 1980
by Constable & Company Ltd
10 Orange Street London WC2H 7EG
Copyright © 1980 Anthony S. B. New
Set in Monophoto Times New Roman 9pt
Printed in Great Britain by
BAS Printers Limited, Over Wallop,
Hampshire

British Library Cataloguing in Publication data
New, Anthony Sherwood Brooks
A guide to the cathedrals of Britain
1 Cathedrals – Great Britain – Guide-books
I. Title
914.1′04′857   DA660

ISBN 0 09 462350 3

For Susannah and Nicholas
who came to some of them

Birsay +✠ Kirkwall

Medieval foundations or earlier {
✠ Cathedrals of the CHURCH of ENGLAND & the CHURCH in WALES

+ Former cathedrals either in ruins or used by parishes (including those of the CHURCH of SCOTLAND)

Later foundations {
▲ Cathedrals of the SCOTTISH EPISCOPAL CHURCH

⚔ Former ditto.

⊕ Cathedrals of the ROMAN CATHOLIC CHURCH

• Cathedrals of Eastern Churches

Peel Cathedral and the former cathedrals of Birsay, Iona, Lismore and Millport are on small islands

Monastic foundations have the name underlined

+ Dornoch

Fortrose +✠ +Elgin
Inverness ▲ +Birnie

⊕ Aberdeen

+ Brechin

Dunkeld +
Lismore ✠
Iona + ▲ Oban

Perth ⊕▲ Dundee
+ St Andrew's
+ Dunblane

Glasgow
Paisley ✠⊕
Millport ▲ ✠
Edinburgh

Motherwell ⊕

⊕ Ayr

Hexham + ✠ Newcastle
✠ Carlisle ✠ Durham

Whithorn

Middlesbrough ⊕

Peel ✠

Lancaster ⊕
✠ Ripon
Bradford ✠ ✠ York
Blackburn ✠ ✠ Leeds
Liverpool ✠ Wakefield
St Asaph ✠✠⊕ ✠ Manchester
Bangor Salford ⊕ ✠ Sheffield
Chester ⊕ ✠ Lincoln
Wrexham ⊕ Southwell ✠
Derby ⊕ ✠ Nottingham
Shrewsbury ⊕ Lichfield ✠ North Elmham +
Birmingham ✠⊕⊕ ✠ Leicester ✠ Peterborough Norwich ⊕
✠ Coventry Ely ✠
Worcester Northampton ⊕ Bury St Edmunds ✠
Belmont ⊕✠ Hereford
St Davids Brecon ✠ ✠ Gloucester St Alban's ✠ ✠ Chelmsford
Llandaff ✠ Newport ⊕ Oxford ✠⊕ Brentwood ⊕
Cardiff ⊕ Clifton ⊕ Bristol Westminster ✠⊕⊕ London ✠
Wells ✠ Southwark ✠
Old Sarum + Guildford ✠ Rochester ✠ Canterbury
Salisbury ✠ ✠ Winchester
Exeter ✠ Portsmouth ✠⊕ Arundel ⊕
Plymouth ⊕ Chichester ✠
✠ Truro

Contents

Illustrations

Maps and diagrams

Illustrations

Readers will quickly discover that this book goes beyond the usual run of forty or so 'ancient' English and Welsh cathedrals and into the less familiar field of Scottish and Roman Catholic ones. Quite a number of abandoned ruins are included, and a considerable array of 19th and 20th c. buildings

Exact criteria for inclusion proved impossible to define, and in the end some 'ins' and 'outs' were dictated more by the heart than the head. St Giles' at Edinburgh (in) was a cathedral only for a few years in the 17th c. But then so were Holy Trinity Kirk at St Andrews (out) and – so far as records can prove – Iona Abbey (in). Exactly similar is the case for (or against) Westminster Abbey (out), briefly the seat of a bishop in the 16th c.

Churches on the sites of former cathedrals but subsequently so much rebuilt that they retain no authenticated vestige of the original (e.g. Crediton, St Germans, St John's at Chester) are out. So are those which were begun but never progressed far enough to be consecrated (Leicester's Church at Denbigh, the Pugin Cathedral of Everton at Liverpool). Those which were full cathedrals but were superseded (Belmont, Millport, Old Sarum) are in. Pro-cathedrals, of which there have been many (Holy Apostles Clifton, Holy Trinity Guildford, Bishop's Court in the Isle of Man), are out.

The method of description will quickly become evident: a general historical note, followed by a 'walk round' inside, then outside, in logical sequence. First impressions of an exterior are very important but a real understanding usually depends on seeing the interior first. Mostly a simple clockwise sequence is followed; in a few instances, however, the visitors' route is somewhat regimented and not necessarily the best. In every case there are of course rooms and passages that are private, and I have a duty to deans and administrators to emphasize that even responsible adult visitors must be discouraged from venturing beyond the 'straight and narrow' – not only for reasons of security and privacy but sometimes also for their own personal safety.

Equally, however, the the serious student of any age is likely to find a generous reception to a request to be allowed to see 'behind the scenes' at any cathedral, though obviously this must depend on whether there is someone free to unlock and lock, and it must be remembered that the time of paid staff is costly. Even in parts of buildings indicated as open, occasional disappointments are unavoidable, because of services, maintenance works or staff shortages.

It should be remembered that cathedrals are, first and foremost, places of Christian worship and reverence. That many have become national monuments of architecture and art is, in a sense, their misfortune. Yet their role as tourist attractions means that present-day pilgrims can share the ever-increasing cost of maintaining them and guarding their precious contents.

Whatever the following pages may suggest, they are not museums: they are 'living' buildings and all sorts of changes are constantly happening. This particularly applies to movable things like chests and works of art, and even to monuments and glass which sometimes turn up in unexpectedly different places. In a few cases the text has been adjusted in anticipation of such alterations.

The diagrammatic plans are to a uniform scale of 1:2000. All are drawn as though the N. point were at the top of the page, and throughout the text the liturgical points of the compass (altar at the E. end) are used, even in the uncommon cases where the building's orientation is greatly misplaced. A single arrow indicates the point on the plan where the tour starts, by no means always at the principal entrance.

In the text the differences between great and small are somewhat ironed out by devoting disproportionately more space to the lesser-known buildings. Whilst the great ones need no advocate and can be visited over and over again for a lifetime, the humbler will always reward a special journey.

In the checking of my text I have had such invaluable help from deans, administrators, archivists, churchwardens and others with expert local knowledge that I find it distinctly embarrassing not to be able to mention every person by name with an individual 'thank you' to each. Out of over a hundred I do however single out with special gratitude the Dean of Peterborough, who gave me the right sort of encouragement at the very start with a model criticism of what I had written about his own cathedral, and Mr Ian Fisher of the Royal Commission on the Ancient and Historical Monuments of Scotland, who helped me with no fewer than eight in Scotland. I very much hope that everyone else, whether they submitted (as in many cases) pages of detailed scholarly comment or merely gave an approving 'imprimatur', will accept this inadequate paragraph as something more than a mere formal acknowledgement. If I seem to have ignored some of their suggestions it is almost certainly through lack of space.

A.S.B.N.

A note on church history

Through the centuries, Church doctrines have flowed and ebbed
with racial, social and political changes. Even within the limited area
of Britain, many separate branches of the Church have existed. In
earlier centuries the divisions between them were largely
geographical. The new tenets that came with and after the
Reformation found themselves in constant conflict with the old and
with one another, but latterly they have existed side by side in
mutual respect. Only those branches of the Church with bishops,
and therefore with cathedrals, need concern us here: not the many
types of Nonconformity.

Apart from the Scottish Episcopal cathedrals, the Anglican ones
of Guildford and Liverpool, and the Greek cathedral in London, all
the buildings in this book – or their immediate predecessors on their
sites – have at some time been Roman Catholic, though it is true
that the links of the early Celtic, Norse and Irish Churches with
Rome were often extremely tenuous. At the Reformation the
English (Anglican) Church was separated from Rome (1535) and
linked instead with the state, with the Sovereign as its head; its
strength was to lie in its wide range of permitted tenets, from near-
Roman Catholic to 'low' or Evangelical. In Wales the state link was
severed in 1920, the Church of Wales thus becoming disestablished.
The Isle of Man remains within the Anglican Church.

In Scotland the jurisdiction of Rome ended abruptly in 1560, and
there followed a long tussle between the Presbyterians who wanted
merely priests and the Episcopalians who wanted bishops as well.
During about half of the period up to 1690 there were Protestant
bishops (and therefore cathedrals) intermittently, but in that year
the Presbyterians were finally recognized as the Church of Scotland.
Except where they had already fallen into ruin, the cathedrals
continued in use as parish churches, sometimes divided to house
more than one congregation. After a period of toleration, the
Episcopalians (colloquially known as 'Piskies') were from 1746 to
1792 suppressed by penal laws; eventually these were relaxed and in
1864 the present Scottish Episcopal Church was formed under the
impetus of the English Anglo-Catholic revival.

In England, Scotland and Wales pockets of Roman Catholic
adherents survived persecutions of greater or lesser degrees of
severity for nearly three centuries until the Relief Act of 1790, which
was followed by the Catholic Emancipation Act of 1829, and the
establishment of new hierarchies of bishops in 1850 (England and
Wales) and 1878 (Scotland).

Many medieval cathedral establishments (e.g. Durham) were monastic and thus had a prior as well as a bishop, and were served by monks. At the Reformation in England their priors became deans and their monastic buildings were turned to other uses; their number (and that of the non-monastic cathedrals like Wells) was added to by making eight other great monastic churches (e.g. Peterborough) into cathedrals. Subsequent new Anglican cathedrals have mostly been formed from parish churches, though several of these (e.g. St Albans) were themselves monastic in origin. Of the 'modern' Roman Catholic cathedrals only one (Belmont) is monastic, but it has ceased to be a cathedral: all the others throughout Britain were either founded as cathedrals or were formed from parish churches.

It follows from the above that in England and Wales two main categories of cathedral exist: a) Church of England, or Church in Wales, and b) Roman Catholic. A third category includes predecessors – abandoned and ruined (e.g. North Elmham) or surviving fragmentarily in churches (e.g. Hexham).

In Scotland the position is somewhat different. In simplest terms there are three categories: a) ancient cathedrals, b) Roman Catholic, and c) Scottish Episcopal. In the first category, however, some are abandoned and ruined (e.g. Whithorn) and some have continued in use by the Church of Scotland which still calls them cathedrals (e.g. Dornoch). There is again a small category of predecessors – abandoned (e.g. Birsay) or surviving parochially (Birnie).

Abbey A monastery having an abbot at its head. The traditional definition requires there to be at least twelve monks. An example of an abbey church which has become a cathedral is St Albans. See Priory.

Aisle An outer part of the body of a church, separated by an arcade and usually less tall. The colloquial meaning, a walkway between pews, is misleading.

Altarpiece An ornamental panel, particularly one containing a painting, behind an altar.

Ambo A reading or preaching desk, usually one of a pair and less elaborate than a normal lectern or pulpit. Plural = ambones.

Ambulatory A passageway, especially for processions, particularly one leading from one side of a church to the other behind the high altar.

Apse A semicircular or polygonal (usually semi-octagonal) termination to a church or chapel, particularly common in Norman work. Examples are at Norwich and Peterborough but traces frequently exist even where later builders have extended churches eastwards, e.g. at Bangor and Hexham. Adjective = apsidal.

Arcade A row of arches, either free-standing to separate an aisle or walkway, or attached to a wall as ornament or strengthening.

Archbishop Ecclesiastical head of a province or group of dioceses.

Archdeacon Head of a subdivision of a diocese, with special responsibilities such as parish church maintenance, He has a stall in his cathedral.

Archdiocese A group of dioceses, or province.

Armature A patterned metal framework in a big window to steady the glass.

Art Nouveau An art phase at its height in the first decade of the 20th century, characterized by deliberate rejection of traditional forms and by a swirling style of ornament. In cathedrals it occurs chiefly in memorials, e.g. at Gloucester.

Arts and Crafts Movement An art philosophy prevalent towards the end of the 19th century, led by William Morris and based on the dignity of the craftsman, and bringing a new life to the Gothic Revival. Leeds Cathedral is an example.

Ashlar Finely squared stonework.

Aumbry A cupboard or recess for sacred vessels, often in the wall to the N. of an altar.

Baldacchino A large ornamental canopy, e.g. over the altar at St Paul's.

Ball-flower A common ornament of the English Decorated style, for instance in the chapter house at Wells.

Baptistry The enclosure or part of a church in which a font stands.

Baroque A phase of the Renaissance or Classical Revival in which designers invented freer forms instead of sticking rigidly to Greek or Roman precedents. St Paul's and Birmingham Cathedral are examples.

Battlements Interruptions in the line of a parapet, originally for defensive purposes (e.g. arrow-shooting) but later usually for ornament.

Bay A unit of building, consisting for example of one arch of an arcade, one window or set of windows at each level, and one set of vault ribs.

Belfry A part of a tower where bells are hung (not where they are rung from, which is the ringing chamber).

Bishop The chief church dignitary of a diocese, having his official seat or throne in a cathedral.

Boss A piece of wood or stone, often carved, covering an intersection of vault ribs or roof timbers.

Brass A flat metal memorial plaque with incised effigy, heraldry, inscription, etc., usually originally filled with enamel and let into a stone. St Albans and Hereford have many examples.

Buttress A projection from a wall to stiffen it and to help support particular loads, especially side-thrusts from roofs.

Byzantine A style of architecture derived from Near Eastern but ultimately from Roman models and characterized by the use of domes and flat ornament, especially mosaics. Westminster Cathedral is the principal example in Britain.

Cadaver An effigy in the form of an emaciated corpse.

Cames Grooved strips of lead dividing and securing small panes of glass in a window.

Campanile A bell-tower: usually a detached one, as at Chichester.

Candelabrum A hanging multiple candle-holder. Fine examples are at Bristol and Southwark (C. of E.).

Canon A cathedral dignitary entitled to a stall in the quire. The same word also means a church decree, a metal loop on a bell, or a piece of music in which one subject is repeated by different parts.

Canopy A covering or hood, used to add dignity to seats, pulpits, memorials, etc.

Capital, cap The uppermost part of a column; in classical architecture carved in one of a number of set patterns (Tuscan, Greek or Roman Doric, Ionic, Corinthian, Composite), in Romanesque or Gothic more freely.

Carillon A mechanism for playing tunes on bells. Derby has an example.

Cartouche An imitation rolled-up scroll: used particularly to describe wall-monuments of similar informal shapes.

Chancel The eastern part of a church (not usually applied to cathedrals).

Chantry A very small chapel endowed for a priest to say masses for a dead person.

Chapter House The meeting room for business of a cathedral chapter, consisting of the dean and canons.

Chevet An E. end comprising a series of apses.

Choir *See Quire*

Ciborium A canopy, usually over an altar.

Cinquefoil A cusped decoration, dividing an arch or a circle into five lobes.

Classical Descriptive of ancient Greek and Roman architecture in general and the styles derived from them.

Clerestory Upper windows letting light in over the roof of an aisle or other lower building.

Cloister A covered passage around a quadrangle or garth at the side of a (usually monastic) church.

Close The precinct of a cathedral, usually containing the bishop's palace, deanery and canons' houses, and stretches of greensward.

Collegiate church One with a college of priests or chapter but no bishop.

Columbarium A hallowed place for the depositing of cremated remains.

Communion rail The low rail or wall in front of an altar at which communion is taken.

Composite An order of Classical architecture. The capitals are a combination of Corinthian and Ionic.

Confessional A small compartment in which confessions are made in private to a priest.

Consistory court A bishop's court dealing with Church matters. Ancient examples are at Chester and Leicester.

Corbel A projection from a wall, usually of stone, supporting a roof member or a jutting wall.

Corinthian An order of Classical architecture, with bell-shaped capitals decked with acanthus leaves.

Cornice The projecting upper part of a wall, particularly on a Classical building. See Entablature.

Corona A circular chandelier or hanging ornament or (at Canterbury) termination to a building.

Credence A shelf for sacramental vessels.

Cresting An ornamented, often openwork, band along the top of a wall or fitting.

Crocket A small repetitive leafy ornament, particularly on the side of a pinnacle or spire.

Crossing The part of a church where the nave and chancel (or quire) and the transepts intersect, often crowned with a tower.

Cruciform Cross-shaped: particularly applied to a church plan. Dornoch and Winchester Cathedrals are good examples.

Crypt A substructure, often vaulted and sometimes used for burials.

Culdee A devotee of the later Celtic Church in Scotland till about the 14th century.

Cupola A little ornamental dome, usually Classical in detail, as at Portsmouth (C. of E.).

Cusp A pointed projection in Gothic tracery.

Dean The head of a cathedral chapter.

Decorated The second principal style of English Gothic *c.* 1250–1360. Tracery is either Geometric (E. end of Lincoln, N. transept of Hereford) or Curvilinear (Exeter, E. end of Carlisle). Columns and arches are richly moulded. Carving is luxuriant and often naturalistic (Wells, Southwell). Vaults have tiercerons and sometimes lierne ribs. Smaller arches are often ogee-shaped.

Diocese The territory served by one cathedral and its bishop.

Dissolution Of monasteries, the act of dissolving or breaking up, with particular reference to that carried out under Henry VIII. See Reformation.

Dog-tooth A little repetitive pyramidal ornament common in Early English work.

Dome A part-spherical vault or roof.

Doric An order of Classical architecture (differing somewhat in Greek and Roman) with plain capitals.

Dormitory or Dorter A monastic sleeping-hall. The finest in Britain is at Durham.

Dossal A hanging behind an altar.

Early English The first principal style of English Gothic, *c.* 1140–1260. Windows are mostly simple lancets or combinations of them with, sometimes, elementary tracery (Salisbury, Worcester). Columns and openings often have attached shafts of darker stone such as Purbeck marble, and capitals of springing or 'stiff leaf' foliage (Lincoln). Dog-tooth was the favourite ornamental moulding (Ely W. porch) but naturalistic or figure carving is common. Vaults are usually quadripartite.

Effigy A statue, usually of stone and often horizontal on a tomb.

Embattled With battlements.

Entablature The element of Classical design above the columns, consisting of cornice, frieze and architrave.

Episcopal Of a bishop.

Façade A principal front of a building.

Fan vault A type of vault invented in the 14th c., in the form of inverted concave half-cones (Gloucester cloister, Peterborough retro-quire).

Feretory The setting of the principal shrine of a church, usually behind the high altar.

Ferramenta Ironwork, especially in window glazing.

Flamboyant The final phase of French Gothic, contemporary with English Perpendicular and found in less ornate form in Scotland.

Flèche A small spire mounted on a roof.

Flying buttress A buttress in the form of a part-arch, especially one transferring the thrust from a high vault across the roof of an aisle.

Font A ceremonial basin for baptism.

Four-centred arch A shallow, pointed arch based on arcs of circles described from four centres, the end ones having a smaller radius than the middle ones.

Frater A monastic refectory or dining hall.

Fretted Pierced with a pattern.

Frosterley 'marble' A dark marble-like stone from County Durham used in the Middle Ages as a substitute for Purbeck, q.v.

Galilee A large porch (usually W.), often enlarged into a chapel. Durham's is the best known.

Gallery An upper floor overlooking the main one, for congregational use, for organ or musicians, or for maintenance.

Gargoyle A fancifully carved water spout.

Garth A garden, especially inside a cloister.

Geometric A kind of tracery: see Decorated.

Gothic The pointed-arched style of architecture. Gothic Survival refers to 17th c. work (as at Durham), Gothick to late 18th c., and Gothic Revival to 19th and 20th c.

Grisaille A greyish patterned glass, as at Salisbury.

Groin The intersection between planes of a vault. A groin vault (typical of early Norman work) has no ribs.

Grotesque Fanciful carving, e.g. of dragons or monsters.

Hagioscope An opening in a wall or pier to give a view of an altar (also called a squint).

Hall-church One in which the aisles are similar in height to the nave, as at Bristol.

Hammer-beam A projecting bracket giving support clear of the side walls to the main trusses of a timber roof. Bury St Edmunds has a good example of such a roof.

Indent The hollow in a stone to receive a memorial brass.

Ionic An order of Classical architecture with twin-volute (spiral) capitals.

Italianate Italian in character, particularly in imitation of medieval styles. Westminster and the Ukrainian Cathedral are examples.

Jesse Tree A family tree showing the descent of Jesus from Jesse: a favourite subject for glass.

Lady Chapel A chapel dedicated to the Virgin Mary, usually at the E. end of a cathedral.

Lancet A single tall pointed window of the Early English style.

Lantern-tower A tower with clerestory or similar windows above the surrounding roofs.

Lean-to A single-sloping roof, as over an aisle.

Lectern A reading desk on a stand, often in the form of a brass eagle.

Ledger-stone A flat grave-slab in a floor, usually with deeply incised lettering.

Lierne A linking rib in a vault, not a tierceron or ridge rib. Lierne vaults were first built late in the 13th c.

Light A subdivision of a multiple window.

Lucarne A little gabled opening in a spire.

Majestas A representation of the Risen Christ.

Matrix The hollow or indent in which a memorial brass is fixed.

Metropolitan cathedral The cathedral of an archbishop.

Minster An inexact term not necessarily meaning a cathedral but usually at least a collegiate church.

Misericord A ledge on the tip-up seat of a stall, intended to provide rest for infirm clergy during long periods of standing. The undersides often have fanciful and humorous carvings.

Mouldings The continuous contours of the stones of arches and other parts of buildings.

Mullion The vertical 'post' separating the lights of a window.

Narthex A western compartment of a church, bigger than a porch and like a galilee. Motherwell and Newport have examples.

Nave The main congregational part of a church.

Niche A recess for a statue.

Norman The Romanesque, round-arched style of 1066–*c*. 1190. Window, doorway and other arches are usually semicircular (or sometimes semi-elliptical) and, especially in later work, ornamented with zigzag and other repetitive patterns. Vaults are quadripartite, groined in early work and ribbed in later. Ornamental sculpture contains a high proportion of grotesque and often semi-barbaric elements.

Ogee A wave-like shape formed by alternate convex and concave curves, either in small arches (with two such curves meeting at the apex), frequent in Decorated work, or in mouldings.

Order A standard unit of Classical design, consisting of entablature, column and base (see Capital). Also used to describe one of several arches round a doorway.

Orientation The placing of a building in relation to the points of the compass. Traditionally a church altar is at the E. end.

Pax A small representation (usually of the Crucifixion) kissed by the celebrant at Mass and then by others as a token of peace.

Pediment A triangular gable-end or feature over an opening in Classical architecture.

Pelican in her Piety A carving of a legendary bird, feeding her young with her own blood, used as an allegory of sacrifice.

Pendentive One of the triangular spandrels below a dome when it is supported on a square base.

Perpendicular The last principal phase of English Gothic, *c*. 1340 onwards, characterized by vertical patterns in tracery and wall-panelling and a general impression of height and light (Canterbury nave, York quire). Windows are large. Arches are often four-centred. Ornament is often conventionalized: foliage, flowers and heraldry. Vaulting is usually complex, either broken into small compartments by liernes (Gloucester quire) or of fan type (Gloucester cloister, Peterborough retro-quire). Timber roofs are often almost flat (Manchester).

Pier A mass of masonry supporting part of a building and not necessarily joined to a wall.

Pietà A representation of the Dead Christ in the arms of his Mother.

Pilaster A projection from a wall in the form of a flattened 'column'.

Pinnacle A common Gothic upward termination, sometimes provided to add weight and stability.

Piscina A stone basin for washing consecrated vessels.

Podium A base or platform on which a building stands.

Poppyhead An ornamental top to a seat-end, usually carved with foliage (not with poppies, the word being a corruption of *poupée*).

Precinct Surrounding roads and buildings, in the case of a cathedral often the property of the dean and chapter.

Pre-Raphaelite An art movement founded in 1848, deriving inspiration from early medieval Italian work.

Presbytery Either (Church of England) the E. part of a cathedral containing the altar, or (Roman Catholic) the priest's residence.

Priest's doorway That on the S. side of a chancel.

Priory A monastery having a prior as its head. Many monastic cathedrals had priors (e.g. Ely, Worcester).

Pro-cathedral A church or chapel serving temporarily as a cathedral, as at Bishop's Court in the Isle of Man.

Province An archdiocese or group of dioceses, headed by an archbishop.

Provost In certain comparatively newly constituted Church of England and Scottish Episcopal cathedrals, the head of a chapter or cathedral council, equivalent to a dean.

Pulpit An enclosed platform for preaching.

Pulpitum A heavy stone screen to the W. of a quire, often containing small chapels or other rooms, and often supporting an organ.

Purbeck 'marble' A dark marble-like stone from Dorset used throughout Southern England, especially in the late 12th and early 13th cc., for small ornamental shafts and other architectural detail.

Pyx A small vessel for consecrated bread.

Quadripartite The simplest type of vault over a square bay, divided into four segments.

Quatrefoil A cusped decoration dividing a circle into four.

Quire or **Choir** Architecturally the part of a cathedral intended to contain the stalls of dignitaries and singers. In this book the spelling 'choir' is reserved for those who sing; in Scotland, however, the version 'quire' is regarded as archaic. In many cathedrals especially those still with Norman E. ends like Norwich and Peterborough, the 'ritual' quire has been extended beyond the architectural one.

Refectory Monastic dining hall, also called a **Frater**

Renaissance Rebirth: particularly applied to Classical architecture as revived in Britain in the 16th to 19th cc.

Reredorter An annexe to a monastic dormitory containing

garderobes and therefore built over a drain or stream.

Reredos A screen or panelling behind an altar.

Respond A corbel at the end of an arcade instead of a pilaster or half-column.

Retro-quire The part of a cathedral immediately behind the quire.

Rib One unit of the main framework of a vault.

Riddel-post One of the (usually four) posts supporting curtains around an altar.

Ridge The apex-line of a double-sloping roof or ceiling.

Reformation The change in Church doctrines and organization in Britain and elsewhere early in the 16th c., when the authority of Rome was increasingly rejected by the so-called Protestants. The Dissolution of the Monasteries was part of this process.

Romanesque One of the round-arched styles derived from Classical Roman architecture, in England principally Norman.

Rood Crucifix, especially one hanging at a chancel or quire entrance or set on a rood screen.

Rusticated Cut into strongly marked blocks to give an effect of strength, especially around openings and at corners. The 18th c. work at Derby includes instances.

Sacristy Room close to an altar, where sacramental vessels are kept.

Sanctuary The part of a church or cathedral within a communion rail and containing an altar.

Saxon The pre-Conquest style or styles, usually Romanesque and generally primitive in detail. Distinctions between Saxon and early Norman work are not always easy. North Elmham and the crypt of Ripon are the main examples amongst cathedrals.

Sedilia Priests' seats within a sanctuary, usually of stone.

See Bishopric.

Sexpartite A French form of vaulting in which one unit of six segments covers two bays. Several instances occur in England, notably at Canterbury.

Shaft A small column, especially one attached or partially attached to a larger member.

Shrine A housing of a saint's body or relics.

Slype A passage out of a cloister, particularly one between a transept and a chapter house.

Spandrel A space between two shapes, especially between an arch and its enclosing rectangle, often used for ornament.

Spire A pointed termination, usually on a tower, and usually either of stone or framed in wood. A broach spire is an octagonal one with broaches or part-pyramidal corner supports where it rises from a square base.

Springing The level at which the curve of an arch commences.

Stalls Dignitaries' or singers' seats in a quire.

Steeple A tower and/or spire.

Stoup A basin for holy water at a church entrance.

Tester A suspended canopy, especially over an altar or pulpit.

Throne In a cathedral, the bishop's ceremonial seat.

Tierceron One of a group of ribs rising from the base of a vault and reaching the ridge.

Tomb-chest A box-like structure, usually of stone, often highly ornamented and carrying an effigy of the person commemorated, and ostensibly containing his or her body.

Tracery Patterns in the heads of Gothic windows and elsewhere.

Transept A cross-arm of a church, projecting N. and/or S. from a crossing, and usually of similar height to the nave and chancel or quire.

Transitional An architectural style between two clearly defined ones; particularly applied to that between Norman and Early English when round and pointed arches occur together. In Scotland the use of round arches continued much later.

Trefoil A cusped decoration of three lobes.

Triforium A gallery below an aisle roof, or the arcade screening it from the nave. The gallery is also called a tribune.

Triptych A three-panelled picture, with the outer panels often hinged to fold over the centre.

Trumeau An ornamented column dividing the parts of a twin doorway.

Truss A single unit of a roof frame, usually triangular in form.

Tudor The last phase of Perpendicular architecture in England, characterized by four-centred arches, fan and similar vaulting, and over-all panelling of surfaces. Many chantries and tombs are in this style.

Tuscan The simplest form of Roman Classical architecture.

Tympanum A semicircular panel, especially one within a Norman door-arch.

Undercroft Basement or crypt.

Vault A stone roof on the arch principle, usually rectangular in plan, or an imitation in wood and plaster.

Vesica A two-pointed shape formed by the intersecting arcs of two equal circles.

Vestry A robing room for clergy or choir.

Voussoir One stone of an arch.

Walk One side of a square cloister.

Wall-arcade A low blank arcade usually at the base of a wall, either ornamental or for strengthening or to form a series of canopies over seats.

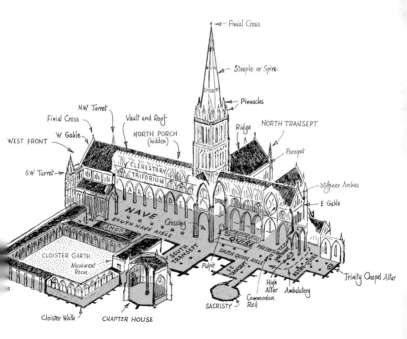

Salisbury, showing the names of the principal parts

S. Porch of St Machar's Cathedral, Aberdeen (14th c.)

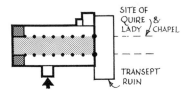

SITE OF
QUIRE) &
LADY) CHAPEL

TRANSEPT
RUIN

The first bishop's seat at Old Aberdeen was established in 1136 by David I, in a church traditionally said to have been founded by Machar, a friend of St Columba, in the 6th c. It was rebuilt from the early 14th c. onwards. When complete in 1532 it had an aisleless quire, transepts and central tower about 150 ft high, and a Lady chapel, but all the E. parts fell into disuse after 1560. The central tower and transepts collapsed in 1688, probably as an indirect result of the removal of the remains of the E. end by Cromwell's men.

The remaining parts of the building continued as a parish church and were restored by Sir George Gilbert Scott in 1869–71.

The most unusual feature of the **interior** is the Romanesque character of the massive round piers. These and their arches are in fact early 15th c. The tiny clerestory incorporates a passage in the wall thickness and the flat timber ceiling has a series of heraldic bosses – arms of contemporary kings, princes, bishops and earls and, astonishingly still in their central place at the E. end, those of Pope Leo X which establish its date as *c.* 1520.

In the **S. aisle**, towards the W. end, hang colours of the Scots Guards and Gordon Highlanders. The window over the war memorial is one of three by Douglas Strachan in this aisle. The rather ponderous monument on the W. wall, with emblems of mortality crowded in, is to Bishop Scougall (d. 1682). The W. end of the **nave** has a gallery and an unusual, almost styleless window occupying nearly the whole wall; its glass is of 1867. In the NW. corner of the nave a boldly lettered ledger-stone of 1610 attracts attention. Looking E., the unbalanced clerestory – eight windows on the N. and ten on the S. – is noticeable. The present E. window and the wall that blocks the crossing arch are of 1953.

At the W. end of the **N. aisle** are various old memorials: an effigy of Bishop Lichtoun, an inscribed tablet propped against it, and an effigy of a canon wearing an almuce or head-and-shoulders hood of a kind unknown in England. On the N. wall is a big tablet to the Paton family; then a recess with the effigy of another cathedral dignitary, Walter Ydil, *c.* 1470, also with almuce. The glass in this aisle is all of the 1940s, the first two windows by Marjorie Kemp and the next three by Margaret Chilton.

The font, towards the E. end of the arcade, is a tapering granite cylinder by Hew Lorimer (1954). The E. window glass, more clearly seen from here, is by William Wilson (1953).

Now across to the **S. chapel**, passing the undistinguished 19th c. pulpit. The glass here is by Daniel Cottier, of Pre-Raphaelite type. The small memorial to the right of the altar commemorates William Strachan (d. 1666) but is dated 1754. On the S. wall is an unusual tablet with bas-relief effigy and inscription to Canon Dods (d. 1496) and beneath it a smaller one to Alexander de Rynd (d. 1492). The window just before the aisle wall-clock is another by Douglas Strachan (1913). Back at the **S. porch**, a wooden stair leads to the Charter Room on the upper floor where an interesting collection of books, documents, charters, prints and other records is exhibited; a small charge is made, and it is not open on Thursdays or Sundays (except after services). The inner doorway of the porch is of an unusual form, with a pointed arch surrounding one of later form.

Finally the **exterior**, starting to the left with the path leading to the S. transept. As in most ancient Scottish churchyards, there is a vast number of showy tombs, and a full description would be impracticable. The two transepts, walled round together as a single rectangle, contain a number of interesting ones. Just inside on the right, i.e. on the W. wall of the S. transept, is a good tablet to William Blake (d. 1714) flanked by Corinthian columns. The first tomb recess on the S. wall is of Bishop Dunbar (d. 1532). The further one is attributed to Bishop Stewart (the early 19th c. plaque on its back wall has nothing to do with it). A number of 17th and 18th c. tomb-slabs are worth looking at for their good lettering, but most are broken. On the W. side two moulded piers mark the start of the destroyed crossing and at the N. end, under a 19th c. brick arch, is a tablet to Bishop Lichtoun (d. 1440); his effigy is one of those now inside, in the N. aisle.

Through the central E. opening there is now no sign of the quire or Lady chapel – only more big tombs. Turn left then and go along the N. side of the cathedral where the churchyard wall has an array of monumental lettering of the 19th and 20th cc., good, bad and indifferent. The path leads to the W. front, the finest feature of the cathedral. Its seven-light window contrasts strongly with the fortified character of the towers, almost windowless and with machicolated parapets. It is all of c. 1400, except the stone spires with their bands of embattled ornament which were added early in the 16th c. The round-headed twin doorway has lost the figure of the Virgin and Child which is believed to have stood in the vesica-shaped niche; the Roman Catholic cathedral of Aberdeen has what is considered to be a replica.

Aberdeen, St Andrew (Scottish Episcopal Church, Grampian)

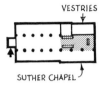

The roots of the Episcopalian congregation in Aberdeen go back to 1717, to a meeting-house at the back of the Tolbooth. Later an upper room of Bishop John Skinner's house was used, and there the historic consecration of Samuel Seabury as first Anglican bishop of the Church in America took place in 1784, consecration in England not being legally possible at that time. The present cathedral was begun in 1817 to the design of Archibald Simpson (planner of Edinburgh new town). G. E. Street built a bigger chancel in 1880. This was demolished and rebuilt under Sir Ninian Comper in 1935–48, the original intention having been a complete new cathedral as an expression of thanksgiving from the American Church.

An immediate impression of space and light is created by tall arcades and tall aisle windows, all in the Tudor style typical of the early Gothic Revival. There is no clerestory, and galleries originally ran down both sides. These were removed in 1909 without detriment to the design, for the arcades have no capitals except where one shaft of each column runs up to meet the plaster vault. Into the aisle vaults, which are also plaster, shields were affixed in 1935, eight to each bay and every one within an angel-held wreath. Those over the N. aisle are of the (then) 48 states of the U.S.A.: those on the S. of 48 traditionally Episcopalian families of the diocese. With only five bays available, eight extra shields have been slipped in at the E. end of each. Though of undoubted interest, these are an unfortunate distraction aesthetically.

Ahead is the typically Comper ciborium on columns of burnished gold and with a 'crown' of a form familiar to him from the nearby

King's College Chapel (his father had been an Episcopalian priest in
Aberdeen). Behind is his E. window (1942) of blues and yellows,
with the top of the tracery opened out for a Majestas.

In the **N. aisle** the octagonal font is of *c.* 1865, with Evangelists'
emblems in four panels, and on the W. wall is a monument to Lt.-
Col. Gordon (d. 1885) with standing figure by Stevens of Bayswater.
The flags include one of American combat regiments presented by
President Eisenhower. At the E. end, the Lady chapel reredos is by
Sir Robert Lorimer (1917) and the Madonna by Maxine Duff.

Now into the **quire**, passing the 19th c. Gothic pulpit and the
undistinguished Gothic stalls. Here the plaster vault has big star
ornaments with more shields, royal and episcopal, and one can have
a closer look at the ciborium and the great silver candlesticks. On its
N. is a foundation stone of the extension, laid by the U.S.
ambassador Joseph Kennedy in 1938.

The S. or **Suther chapel** contains the E. window and plain green
altar from Street's quire of 1880, also a carved chair, and Lorimer's
screen of 1909 that till 1963 stood at the quire entrance. It has been
'folded' to fit the narrower width. In the **S. aisle** is a very strange
memorial window to the Rev. William Browning (d. 1843); and two
display cases, one with a set of communion plate of 1811 and the
second with various relics. At the W. end is a memorial to Bishop
Skinner (d. 1816) with standing figure by John Flaxman. Behind is a
plaque brought from the previous church and recording its
consecration by him in 1795.

The Tudor-style façade ornamented with four pinnacled turrets is
typical of its period, but unusual in Aberdeen in being of sandstone
and not granite. The other three sides are granite and can be seen by
walking through the side passages right round the building, though
little is to be gained by doing so. There is no tower, though
Comper's design for rebuilding on a more spacious site did of course
include one.

Aberdeen, St Mary of the Assumption (Roman Catholic, Grampian)

This was built in 1858–60 to the design of Alex Ellis, but the tower
and spire (by Ellis's partner R. G. Wilson) were not added till
1876–7. It became a cathedral in 1878 but many of the enrichments
added at that time were swept away again in 1960 leaving the white
interior now exceptionally plain though some recent embellishments
have been added.

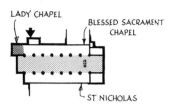

The general style is Decorated, with arcades on plain octagonal
columns without capitals, and a curiously thin roof with diagonal
rafters and intermediate trusses. The aisles, painted pale blue, have
lean-to roofs on a network of struts forming what would nowadays
be called a 'space frame'. In the **N. aisle** the mosaic Stations of the
Cross are by Gabriel Loire of Chartres (1969). At the E. end of the
aisle, the chapel of the Blessed Sacrament, the reredos painting of
Our Lord – its green reminiscent of Coventry – is by Felix
McCullough. The oak-panelled **quire** has the bishop's throne against
the E. wall, backed by a red curtain; the glass-fibre rood above,
hanging beneath the rose window, is by Charles Blakeman. Also of
interest are the open iron-framed ambones and the altar on three
granite legs (1960). The SE chapel, to St Nicholas, has another
McCullough reredos, on the theme of the City Patrons.

From this end of the cathedral the iron-balustraded W. gallery
can be seen, with the Connacher organ of 1887 in two halves flanking
the W. window. Beneath it is the shrine to St John Ogilvie, with
engraved glass by David Gulland (1978). The grey-green granite
font standing centrally at the end of the nave has a brass cover by
Gunning. Finally, the little **Lady chapel** in the NW. corner beneath
the tower: this has a plaster vault but is of particular interest for the
statue of Our Lady of Aberdeen, a replica of the medieval figure
believed to have come from the W. doorway of St Machar's
Cathedral, Old Aberdeen, and now in the church of Finistre in
Brussels.

The **exterior**, hemmed in by other buildings, is dominated by the
slender granite tower with recessed belfry and spire (200 feet high,
the tallest in the city). It can be better appreciated than from the
narrow Huntly Street by going all the way round into Crimon Place;
this provides an E. view and incidentally contains the presbytery
entrance.

Arundel, St Philip Neri (Roman Catholic, West Sussex)

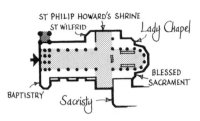

The diocese of Arundel and Brighton was founded in 1965. Its
cathedral is the former parish church founded by the 15th Duke of
Norfolk and built in 1870–73 by Joseph A. Hansom (inventor of the
hansom cab) to replace a temporary chapel in Arundel Priory
adjacent to the Anglican church. His French Gothic style, imitative
rather than inventive, has been likened to Beauvais for its
comparative shortness and height and to Bourges for some of its
details.

Inside the W. entrance the height and lightness of the **interior**
make an immediate impact. High clustered columns with springing
foliage capitals, a band of quatrefoils in place of a triforium, and a
tall clerestory with pairs of two-light double windows support a
quadripartite vault 71 ft high. The whole building is in fact vaulted.
Much of the stained glass is to Hansom's own design.

The **N. transept** contains the shrine of St Philip Howard, Earl of
Arundel (d. 1595), designed by Malcolm Lawson-Paul (1971) and
bright with heraldry. The limewood figure of St Philip with his dog
is by Ivor Hursey. On its left is a tablet to five Maxwell-Stuart
brothers, only one of whom survived active service, and on the right
a plaque of 1973 commemorates the cathedral's centenary. The
chapel leading off the transept is St Wilfrid's and contains a war
memorial. The NE. one is the Lady chapel.

Hansom's intention was to give the apsidal **E. end**, which is
similar in design to the nave, a radiating series of chapels in the
manner of a French *chevet*, but foundation and other problems
prevented both its fulfilment and the completion of the NW. tower.
The windows in the ambulatory, intended to connect the unbuilt
chapels, came from Derwent Hall in Derbyshire; those of the
clerestory, representing choirs of angels and archangels, are by
Hardman. Liturgical re-ordering has brought the altar forward into
the crossing so that one can no longer stand here to appreciate the

transept windows – of which those in the clerestory are again the best.

The Blessed Sacrament chapel at the SE. was originally St Joseph's and has allusions to him in its glass and roof bosses. In the S. transept the wall tablet to Bishop Cashman, first bishop (d. 1971), is by Lawson-Paul, and the statue under the very tall pinnacled canopy on its E. wall is of St Philip Neri. Looking now W.: the organ and gallery are in full view, and the fine rose window above. Along the S. aisle, the arrangement of the wall-arcading is governed by the positions of confessionals. Past these is the vaulted baptistry with a plain octagonal stone font.

Finally the outside, starting at the W. front with its gabled doorway and row of niches with figures of Christ and the Apostles, and the rose window. Along the S. side one can only go as far as the sacristy. On the N. there is the unfinished tower, forming a *porte-cochère* at the N. entrance. It is then worth walking along the road to look up at the impressive apse and at the flèche (which has somehow missed being centrally over the crossing), and then a little way down Parsons Hill to see Cathedral House – but much the best views are the distant ones from beside and across the river. The placing and the general massing of the building with its very French shape and its flying buttresses are so much more successful than the rather mechanical detail one sees at close quarters.

Ayr, The Good Shepherd (Roman Catholic, Strathclyde)

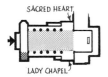

The diocese of Galloway was revived in 1878 and based on Dumfries, where the pro-cathedral was burnt down in 1962. However, the bishop's throne had been moved to Ayr the previous year, to an ordinary brick church built in 1955 in the suburb beyond the racecourse. The architect was John Torry.

What defines a cathedral is the bishop's throne within it and one cannot always have soaring arches and rich woodwork. Long, low and unambitious, with standard metal windows and a low tower capped by a chimney-like turret, it is reminiscent of post-1945 schools in style. To the NE. are domestic buildings; to the E. a somewhat later hall which is much more distinguished.

The inner W. vestibule (at the geographical E. end) leads on the left to the wood-screened baptistry with green marble font, by three doors to the nave and aisles, and on the right to the gallery stair. The main structural system comprises very low brick arcades and seatless aisles, wide plastered ceiling, and white-lined transept and quire arches, the latter in a mock-Tudor shape. The bishop's throne on the N. side of the quire has a curiously angular, mitre-like canopy, light and varnished like the remainder of the woodwork.

Bangor, St Deiniol (Church in Wales, Gwynedd)

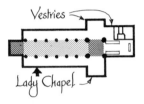

St Deiniol founded a cell here in 525. He became a bishop and his church a cathedral about 546. Nothing remains of pre-Conquest buildings, the last of which was destroyed in a Norman assault in 1071. The present transepts and presbytery contain traces of its successor, begun about 1120. Frequent and extensive damage was caused during rebellion and invasion in the course of the 13th c., and much of the present walling can be attributed to that period. Further extensive damage was caused in 1402 by Owain Glyn Dŵr and another rebuilding involving the nave arcades, W. tower and much of the E. end took place around 1500. In 1868–84 Sir George Gilbert Scott did extensive restoration and rebuilt the crossing to receive a great new tower which was subsequently decided to be too heavy for the available foundation.

Just inside the S. doorway is the 15th c. octagonal font, with a 20th c. cover by Thompson, signed with his 'mouse' carving. Its platform is a good place to stand to see the **nave**, with early 16th c. four-centred arcades, clerestory and restored low-pitched timber roof. The aisle roofs are similar. On the left pier of the W. tower, facing E., are seven small brasses; opposite, against the end pier of the N. arcade, stands the carved wood Mostyn Christ (1518), a rare portrayal, showing Christ seated and wearing the Crown of Thorns. The tower window glass, and that at the W. end of the aisles, is early 19th c. by David Evans and was originally in the E. window.

At the W. end of the **N. aisle** is a small 'museum' area containing various stone fragments, pieces of carved crosses, panels of 16th c. tomb-chests, a pair of 18th c. dog tongs (for ejecting fierce dogs), a splendid 14th c. bas-relief tomb-slab of a lady, a number of 14th c. ornamental floor tiles from the presbytery floor (reproduced there and in the S. transept by Scott), five wooden carvings of saints thought to be 15th or 16th c. Flemish, two headless busts of bishops, a misericord and a number of old documents, prints, etc. In the second bay is a wall tablet to Charles Allinson (d. 1729) and there are several later ones further along the aisle. The screen at its E. end is of 1954.

The N. transept is occupied by vestries, so one must now step back into the nave in front of the nave altar. The frontal (normally in use except in Advent and Lent) is by Iris Martin (1975). The beautiful chairs, two on each side flanking bigger Victorian ones, are late 17th c. The quire screen behind the altar is by J. Oldrid Scott (1908) and the hanging Rood above by Alban Caroe (1950, sculptor Harold Youngman). Above that, the E. bay of the nave roof has been canted so as to clear Scott's enlarged tower arch. The stone pulpit (1880) is also by Scott (senior); the brass eagle lectern (1905) is enhanced by its wrought-iron stair balustrade.

Now across into the S. aisle, where a 16th c. Flemish Madonna stands against the left pier of the arch into the S. transept or **Lady chapel**. The screen is of 1960. Though what is now visible is very largely Scott's work, including the typical high-pitched roof, the transept is fundamentally Norman but was lengthened late in the 13th c. Internally it is dominated by the big 'hoop' light fitting. A credence niche and tomb recess are built into the S. wall. If the latter is of Owain the Great (d. 1169), as is supposed, it must have been re-made a century later; in front stands a 17th c. chair and in its back wall is a small Crucifixion. To the right of the altar is a good wall tablet to Bishop Jones (d. 1956); that to the 17th c. psalmist Edmund Prys on the same wall is 19th c. The chapel reredos, containing another medieval Crucifixion, is by Alban Caroe (1950), with a painting of the Journey to Emmaus (with Disciples in modern dress) by Brian Thomas (1955).

A narrow curtained opening now leads into the **crossing**. The two banks of stalls with pinnacled canopies by Scott senior (1879) were moved to their present rather cramped position by J. Oldrid Scott in 1908 when he extended the quire into this tower space and added the screen. The whole N. transept is taken up with the vestries and organ and is not open to visitors; thus one must now turn right into the **presbytery**, where the stalls and bishop's throne are also by Scott senior. This part of the building was early 13th c. but was largely reconstructed about 1500 and again by Scott. The 19th c. wooden roof is of very curious design, a kind of cross between a lierne vault and a waggon roof with diagonal ribs – some of which spring from the wall-plate and some from corbels. The figure of Christ on the sill of the blocked window on the N. side is Dutch, 17th c. The E. and S. windows are by Clayton & Bell, *c.* 1870.

From the quire the centre arch of the screen leads back into the nave behind the nave altar. Now turn left into the S. aisle again where there is a curious double wall tablet to Humphrey Humphreys, (d. 1699) and Robert Morgan (d. 1682). Many of the other memorials, mostly 17th and 18th c., are unfortunately more or less illegible; by the door lobby is a plain one to Dean Jones (d. 1727).

Now the **exterior**, starting outside the S. doorway which, with the niche over, and indeed most of the aisle itself, is of *c.* 1300. The S. transept, as seen from outside, is largely Scott's work, and so is the stump of his ill-conceived central tower, eventually capped with a low pyramidal spire and battlements, *c.* 1970. The simple W. tower is dated by a (renewed) inscription of 1532 clearly visible on a string course over the W. doorway. Continuing round the N. side, the white house quite close to the tower is the Deanery, mostly of 1863; the N. aisle with its old doorway and Geometric tracery is very much a repeat of the S.; then come Scott's N. transept and vestries, the former with vestiges of Norman walling on its E. side, and the latter with equally scanty 13th c. work and an upper storey that, in origin at least, is of 1776–81. Scott's too is the reconstructed E. end with odd pipe-like shafts at the angles of his buttresses. In spite of Scott, however, the outside of the presbytery and S. transept are archaeologically the most interesting part of the cathedral, for in the E. wall of the latter is a blocked arch to the Norman apse (foundations of which have been traced) and in the S. wall of the presbytery a shallow Norman buttress set at such an angle that it obviously marked the beginning of the curve of the chancel apse. Just W. of it is a blocked Norman window.

The almshouses in the SE. corner of the churchyard were built in 1805.

Belmont, St Andrew (Roman Catholic Abbey Church, Hereford and Worcester)

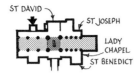

The Benedictine abbey of Belmont was founded in 1853 on his own estate by a convert, F. R. Wegg-Prosser, as a token of his disagreement with the affairs of Hereford Cathedral, two miles to the NE. The church to Edward Pugin's design was already partially built when the design of the E. end had to be quickly amended so that it could serve as a cathedral itself, from 1855 for the whole diocese of Menevia, i.e. Wales, and from 1895 to 1920 for Glamorgan, Monmouthshire and Herefordshire only. Cardiff Cathedral replaced it and it reverted to being purely monastic.

The wayside church in an unassuming country churchyard certainly has a rather grander central tower and E. end than one would ordinarily expect, but its true nature is only revealed inside. The arrangement with, at the time of writing, monks' quire in the nave, is however to be altered so that it reverts to a position E. of the tower. The nave, scholarly Decorated with dark high-pitched roof and twin clerestory windows over each bay, is part of the original design. The more ornate quire, with roof panels now alternately blue and dark blue, is of c. 1860; the vaulted tower was not finished till 1882.

Inside (in the N. transept, to the left on entering) the principal thing to see is the richly pinnacled tomb of the first bishop, Thomas Brown (d. 1880), designed by Peter Paul Pugin. The tomb-chest in the N. quire aisle with Renaissance detail is of Bishop Hedley (d. 1915). Continuing anti-clockwise round the E. end: the three chapels all have original Gothic altarpieces; at the E. end itself, however, the altar has been taken out. Off the S. transept a doorway (private) leads into the abbey buildings, the front terrace of which can be seen outside by going past the W. front. The shafted W. doorway of three orders and the fine Decorated W. window should be seen from there too, as well as the well-proportioned tower with its double belfry windows.

Birmingham, St Philip (Church of England, West Midlands)

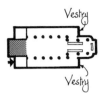

The history of St Philip's goes back only to 1708 when a second parish was created in Birmingham, centred on the High Town. Its church was designed by Thomas Archer, equally well known for his St John, Smith Square, in London, and it was consecrated in 1715, though then still incomplete. King George II gave £600 in 1725 towards the final stages. In 1884 the E. end was taken down and rebuilt in a new position to make space for a lengthened chancel. The architect was J. A. Chatwin.

St Philip's became a cathedral in 1905, on the formation of the diocese. In 1940 it was considerably damaged by fire bombs, the entire main roof being made open to the sky. The churchyard is virtually a public park, crossed and recrossed by paths, so that the building can readily be seen from many angles: perhaps the SE. view is best. Its Baroque style of architecture owes more to the Italian Borromini than to Wren, especially in the tower which grows steadily more fanciful as it goes upwards to the leaded cupola with its gilded boar's head vane; the concave-sided belfry stage is both unusual and dignified. The tower stonework was entirely renewed in 1958–59, as that of the remainder had been a century earlier.

Entry by the SW. doorway leads first into a **vestibule** containing a graceful wooden stair which leads to the gallery. The tablet half-way up, seen through the wrought-iron balustrade, is to David Owen (d. 1823) and an inscription over the door records the King's gift.

The **nave and chancel** are so modest in scale that they can be considered as a single unit. Chatwin's contribution was the three Corinthian columns on either side of the chancel, and the extra length that they represent. These seemingly rather random-placed columns obscure the curved side portions of the E. wall, but their great merit lies in their definition of the chancel, where a screen would have been an intrusion and an impediment. The eastern ceiling is also distinguished by coffering. The arcades and galleries are virtually as Archer left them, except that the pier bases, as in many churches of the period, were designed to rest, visually, on the

Anglican Cathedral, Birmingham (1715)

top of box pews: as now exposed they are less satisfactory. As also frequently happens in 18th c. town churches the galleries themselves cut arbitrarily across the arcade columns and the outer windows; here, however, the memorials affixed to each pier at gallery level help to alleviate the effect. Also the W. gallery has been removed so as to open out the tower space as a baptistry. There are many minor wall tablets.

Behind the grey and white marble font of *c.* 1890 is one of Sir Edward Burne-Jones's windows which are the glory of the cathedral. This, the last of the four (1897), is a Last Judgement. All have in effect two tiers of figures and take full advantage of the large untraceried areas available for glowing colour. All were made by William Morris.

Turning E. again to the chancel windows, only the centre one tells from the nave: the red, blue and white Ascension (1884). Some of its colouring is echoed in the varied banners hanging above the galleries.

In the **N. aisle**, beneath the gallery, are many more wall tablets, including, at the W. end, Moses Haughton the artist (d. 1804), and on the N. wall Beatrix Outram (d. 1810) by Westmacott. The altarpiece in this aisle is of the Art Nouveau period (1907) and somewhat reminiscent of a four-poster bed.

Turning back into the nave at its E. end: the unusual cylindrical pulpit was given in 1960. The low wrought-iron **chancel** screen is of such quality that it has been attributed to Jean Tijou or to Robert Bakewell of Derby; it may well have been the original communion rail. The organ case, originally in the W. gallery, is the original, by Thomas Schwarbrick of Warwick; its mechanisms, however, have been repeatedly renewed. The stalls and the bishop's throne date from the 1905 reorganization, but the silver and crystal Cross and candlesticks are recent work by John Donald (1963).

From here the other three Burne-Jones windows can be appreciated: the central Ascension put in when the chancel was enlarged, and the Nativity and Crucifixion (NE. and SE.), 1887. Pevsner describes them as 'shouting triumphantly from behind the altar'. In the **S. aisle** more brilliant colour is provided by the Creation tapestry at the E. end by Carole Raymond (1975).

Outside, the prominent statue close to the tower is that of Dr Gore, first bishop of the diocese, erected in his lifetime (1914). Amongst a great number of churchyard memorials the most prominent is the tall obelisk to the traveller Frederick Burnaby (d. 1885), dominating the S. side. Perhaps the most interesting, however, is that to two workmen, John Heap and William Badger, killed in 1833 in an accident whilst building the town hall; it consists of an actual piece of broken column meant for the building, and is close to Cherry Street.

Birmingham, St Chad (Roman Catholic, West Midlands)

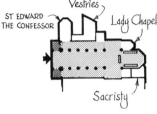

Built as a parish church and replacing a less ambitious one of 1806, this was one of Augustus Pugin's earliest works and unusual in being largely of brick. It dates from 1839–41, except that one tower was unfinished until 1856, six years after the building became a cathedral. The NW. chapel was added in 1933 by S. P. Powell. Subsequent changes have been indirect but far-reaching: the fundamental replanning of the whole of the surrounding streets, and the removal one by one of fitments which seem to have been integral with the design and which were, according to a 19th c. writer, 'wrought with marvellous refinement'.

The cathedral's new setting on the brink of the Ringway is, in an entirely different manner, as dramatic as Pugin intended. The best general view is now across this traffic artery. The style is that of the Gothic churches of NE. Germany, with twin W. towers and spires, double main doorway, and sculpture which appears something of an afterthought. One looks in vain for Pugin's ironwork which adorned the W. doors.

The **interior** is dominated by stone arcades even taller than the outside might suggest, with the usual thin Pugin roofs enlivened by gilded chamfers on the main beams and by red, blue and gold stencilled patterns which in the E. parts become more varied. The crossing is defined by stouter columns, those flanking the sanctuary being picked out with gilded enrichment in a barley-sugar pattern; the transepts project hardly at all. 'Re-ordering' brought about by the new liturgy has involved raising most of the crossing floor to an

Roman Catholic Cathedral, Birmingham (1839–56)

unnatural height to accommodate the nave altar, and accounts for the very regrettable demise of Pugin's rood screen.

The NW. **Chapel of St Edward the Confessor** (1933) is as Gothic as the remainder but tame compared with real Pugin. Two Dürer paintings which hung each side of its altarpiece have gone.

Off the centre of the **N. aisle** opens the former baptistry, with wrought-iron screen and tiled floor and a stair leading to a side entrance and to the crypt, which are normally locked. The present font is outside the baptistry, an inverted tetrahedron with rounded corners. Close to it is the hexagonal wooden pulpit, early 16th c. and believed to have been brought from St Gertrude's Abbey, Louvain. It is richly carved, with four figures in niches representing Fathers of the Church. In the **N. transept** the canopied monument of Bishop Walsh (d. 1849) was designed by Pugin. The window above, a grand composition based on large and small vesica shapes, is by Hardman & Co. (1868). That of the S. transept, which can conveniently be examined at the same time, is similar but less satisfying.

Opening off the N. transept is the **Lady chapel** which does still contain Pugin fittings: glass, reredos, altar, and wooden screen with gables steeply pointed like the roofs of the building itself. The Madonna on the left is 15th c. German, coloured to Pugin's instructions. Just outside is a floor-slab with ornamental brass cross to John Hardman (d. 1903).

Now the **quire**, reached by the new steps. The stalls are a strange mixture of Pugin Gothic and flimsy modern. The former incorporate a good deal of 15th c. carving from the church of St Maria in Capitol in Cologne: beasts and figures of the first quality. Best of all is the exquisite group on the desk-end nearest the bishop's throne. Pugin's tall canopied throne has itself vanished, leaving behind just a plain chair and two stools against a background of more Cologne panels depicting the Virgin Mary flanked by Apostles. The chancel's three original apse windows remain, and the canopied high altar, richly coloured and gilded.

The **S. transept** is like the N. E. of it is a passage leading to vestries. Upwards is an impressive view of the eastern roofs. The S. aisle, too, is impressive, looking along the outside of the great arcade. To its right is the W. organ gallery with its odd arrangement of boxed and unboxed pipes. Towards the W. end of the S. aisle a doorway leads to the adjacent bookshop.

Outside, there is not a great deal else to see. On the N. side the ground begins to fall away steeply, so that St Edward's chapel stands on a great plinth of curved steps. From the lower end,

beneath the Lady chapel, the sheer height of brickwork is quite
overwhelming at close quarters. Under these E. parts is a series of
crypt chapels and oratories in the form of a chancel and side
chapels, which Pugin designed in a style more akin to Norman, as
though they were earlier in date than the church itself; they contain
more brasses and other memorials, and have some original
painted decoration, but are not normally open.

Birnie, St Brendan (Church of Scotland, Grampian)

The early records of Moray diocese perished when Elgin cathedral
was burnt in 1390. It is however known to have been established in
1107; its seat was at Birnie *c.* 1160–90, at Kinnedar for a short time,
and then at Spynie till 1224. At Spynie the cathedral foundations, 74
feet by 35 feet, were formerly visible. At Birnie there still stands the
even smaller early 12th c. Romanesque building, now a picturesque
country church, the foundation of which is ascribed by legend to
St Brendan, reputed discoverer of America, *c.* 500.

Alterations in 1794 included enlargement of the nave windows
and rebuilding of the W. wall, and on the outside it is now very hard
to distinguish which masonry is original: most undoubtedly is. In
1962–3 the nave windows were restored to resemble the original.
Internally, the ashlar on the N. side and the plain chancel arch with
its half shafts and scalloped caps are certainly superior to the rubble
W. wall. The open timber roof is 19th c.

On the N wall, is a crude tablet to a minister, William Sanders
(d. 1670). Nearer the chancel arch is the font, of which the plain
bowl may well be 12th c. The N. chancel window (St Brendan) and
that over the priest's doorway are by Crear Macartney. Behind a
grille on the S. side is kept Brendan's bell, called a ronnel bell, said
to be of silver and copper and to have been blessed by the Pope:
also a Spanish goat bell for comparison, and a 'hairy' Bible bound
in undressed calfskin. Bishop de Tonei is said to lie buried beneath
the floor.

Outside, the circular form of the churchyard shows its early,
probably pre-Christian, origin (the northward extension is modern).
A sundial on the S. wall of the church is dated 1793 and the bellcote
must be of the same date. Otherwise the windows are the main

Interior of the former Cathedral of Moray at Birnie (early 12th c.)

interest: remains of a cinquefoil head over the priest's doorway, a little 12th c. opening in the chancel N. wall, and the Georgian-type W. window with a one-piece arch-shaped lintel which could well be much older.

By the glebe field gate on the left, at the point where the gravel path begins on the way back to the road, is a Pictish carved stone; others have also been identified in the churchyard wall.

Birsay, Christ Church [Scottish Development Department] (Orkney)

The first church on the tidal island of the Brough of Birsay was probably founded in connection with a Celtic monastery *c*. 600. After a pagan period the see of Orkney was re-established by the Norwegian Earl Thorfinn *c*. 1050 and Christ Church, Birsay, was its cathedral from the early years of the 12th c. until *c*. 1160, when the see was transferred to Kirkwall. Probably it did not fall into disuse till the Reformation. Only in very recent years has the ruin been tentatively identified; hitherto it was known as St Peter's and a site near the parish church on Orkney mainland was thought likely for the cathedral. It is in the care of the Secretary of State for Scotland and subject to a small entrance fee.

It is reached by a causeway covered for six hours at each tide. A steep path leads to the custodian's office and museum, the tiny 11th c. cathedral being to the right, with a courtyard building identified as the bishop's palace immediately beyond. Only low walling remains, but the outline of both buildings is clear and complete and the lower courses of the S. wall are considered to be part of the earlier church.

From the W. entrance the opening to the quire can be seen to have been narrowed, probably in the 12th c., to allow the introduction of part-circular recesses in the E. corner of the nave. In each of these the base of an altar can still be seen. The altar in the quire is a reconstruction: it is thought that originally it was further W. and that a shrine stood in the apse. A grave in the centre of the nave is conjectured to have originally been that of St Magnus.

Around the cathedral lies a Pictish cemetery overlaid with a Norse one. This, with the bishop's palace and the numerous other early building remains, are described in the official guide book.

Blackburn, St Mary (Church of England, Lancashire)

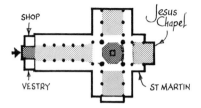

The diocese was formed in 1926 and the parish church of 1820–6 became a cathedral. Very little is known of earlier buildings, though a church certainly existed before the Conquest and there are records and slight remains of the medieval building.

The architect was John Palmer. A fire in 1831 occasioned another partial rebuilding with the help of Thomas Rickman. In 1933 a big eastward extension was begun under W. A. Forsythe, comprising the crossing and aisled transepts and a new quire (which subsequently became the Jesus chapel). Completion of his design with its great lantern-tower had to be abandoned and Laurence King designed the present lantern and flèche (1961) and most of the internal fittings and finishes. Some parts of the E. end still remained unfinished at the final consecration in 1977.

The vaulted tower space is an immediate introduction to the mixture of styles – pre-Victorian Gothic into which have been added a classical doorcase and bright new colouring in the medieval spirit. The effect of space and light in the **nave**, due initially to the height of the arcades and the breadth between them, is accentuated by Forsythe's subtle widening of the last bay and by the shining Derbyshire 'fossil marble' floor and the clear window glazing. Those more used to faded, muted colours may at first find the striping of the plaster vault a little assertive, perhaps distracting from the splendour of the heraldic bosses. The attractive aisle vaults, grey-blue with gilded ribs, are flat-topped so as not to resemble real stone. Ahead is the crossing with its hanging 'corona' over the altar; behind, on the W. wall, a great figure of Christ the Worker by John Hayward, with a loom-like background in wrought iron.

Off the **N. aisle** the NW. porch is now the cathedral shop. In the view up the aisle the 'ring' light fittings are prominent; even more so the bright star pattern of Florentine derivation on the ceiling of the junction bay with the transept: it is repeated in the other three. On the right of this bay is a gate to the choir stalls. The Forsythe extension commences here, though its embellishment is due to Laurence King. The big **N. transept** has more striped decoration on its low-pitched roof. The glass in its main window is 18th c. Flemish. In the transept aisles are medieval stalls with miserere seats, four on each side. In the NE. corner stands a sculptured Madonna bathing her Child by Josephena de Vasconcellos.

Back at the **crossing** a closer look at the metal 'corona' is possible, and the square Portland stone altar beneath it. At the four corners of the sanctuary are tall wood and metal candlesticks; behind it stands the new bishop's throne, backed by a screen of wood and iron and flanked by stalls. The lantern high above contains glass panels of blazing colour designed by John Hayward. The eight-ribbed ceiling that crowns it has a symbolic representation of the Trinity, while metal seraphim occupy the pendentives below. From here too can be seen the angled bay added by Forsythe at the end of each arcade, followed by a short one with a plain instead of vaulted ceiling; from the nave these are hardly noticeable.

In the **N. quire aisle** steps lead to the crypt rooms (not open to the public). A right turn instead leads into the **Jesus chapel** occupying the first bay of the intended quire. Here the colour scheme is mostly red and yellow, with a striking reredos picture of Our Lord under a rectangular tester. High above the arch a detached classical canopy crowns a brightly coloured Crucifixion group and on the right an engraved glass screen separates **St Martin's chapel** which is reached by returning to the N. side and passing between the cranked open fence-like screens behind the bishop's throne. In effect this passage also links the two halves of the organ which stand above the two E. corner bays of the crossing; it also provides westward glimpses down the nave.

St Martin's is the chapel of the East Lancashire Regiment and contains its roll of honour as well as regimental colours. The flat blue ceiling displays the arms of St Martin and of Tours his bishopric, and the abstract E. window provides yet more colour.

In the **S. transept** the little coat-of-arms on the left is all that remains of a big monument to Sir Thomas Walmsley (d. 1612). Beyond it is a big glass-fibre Madonna, an enlarged interpretation of the figure on a 15th c. pax found in the churchyard. The transept itself matches the N. one except that its ceiling is panelled with oak instead of plaster, the N. side having been roofed later. The font is here: based symbolically on an egg shape, it has a bronze cover with a delicate sculptured Baptism of Christ by John Hayward and a memorial inscription to Bishop Claxton's family. The big S. window above is also by Hayward and was made from 19th c. glass taken out of various nave aisle windows, reduced to pieces and reassembled; the bottom lights however are of 1830. In the W. wall of the transept the right-hand window contains scattered fragments of 16th c. glass.

Before passing into the **S. nave aisle** it is worth looking up at the organ (1969), without a case in the traditional sense. On the right of the aisle is White's Gothic-style pulpit of 1940, and in the nave itself are Laurence King's choir stalls in contrasting style. On the left of the aisle is another stair to the crypt, and ahead at the end the vestry doorway with a little angel above.

Outside, Palmer's W. doorway has had big bright diocesan and cathedral arms added to the doors and a Majestas and angels added to the fanlight. Round to the left, the S. doorway of the vestry has similarly been embellished with a Nativity. From down the slope one can see the octagonal lantern with its graceful crowning spire and Cross – also the grandiose and unfinished S. transept front with a covered loggia and outside pulpit and a strong architectural axis at one time intended to relate to a future road layout. From the E. end the outside of the crypt rooms can be seen. A pleasant path through trees leads back up the N. side where, at the top of the churchyard, are two prominent tombs of the Feilden and Petre families. To the NW. is a pretty pair of cast-iron gates, no doubt by Palmer, with reticulated tracery and set between pinnacled stone piers. Though rather blocked by fine trees, the most attractive external view of the cathedral is from this direction.

Bradford, St Peter (Church of England, West Yorkshire)

The parish church of St Peter became a cathedral in 1919. It originated as a chapel to Dewsbury at an unknown date and part of the S. arcade of the early 13th c. church still exists. That was burnt down in 1327 and rebuilt apparently piecemeal from 1360 onwards. The nave and its aisles were completed in 1411 and the clerestory later in the 15th c.; till 1724 its roof was thatched. The W. tower is of 1493–1508. The S. or Bolling chapel collapsed in 1615 and was

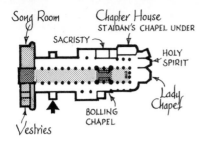

Song Room
Chapter House
ST AIDAN'S CHAPEL UNDER
SACRISTY
HOLY SPIRIT
Lady Chapel
BOLLING CHAPEL
Vestries

rebuilt with Jacobean windows. The S. porch was built when the aisle was re-faced in 1833. Later restorations were done in 1860 and under T. H. & F. Healey in 1896–9. In 1951–5 the song room and choir vestries were added N. of the tower, and in 1955–8 the balancing wing on the S. In 1961–5 the chancel was demolished (leaving the outer walls of the chapels) and the E. end rebuilt and extended. All this was under Sir Edward Maufe.

Maufe designed new fittings within the old buildings too; of these the most prominent is the **nave** organ on four columns at the W. end. The main arcades are early 15th c. with plain capitals on columns of quatrefoil section; the four E. bays of the S. arcade, however, have earlier columns, possibly early 13th c. but with 14th c. caps. The shields above the columns are of dioceses and civic authorities. The clerestory is 15th c., and the roof partly 18th and partly 19th c. with many old bosses newly coloured. The chancel arch is 19th c. Beyond it is Maufe's central tower, with the main organ to its N., and then his arch to the new quire. Turning about, his W. additions are evident too, at the end of each aisle.

The low-pitched **S. aisle** roof is 19th c. Many minor wall tablets are grouped around the S. door and around the W. end of the aisle, including some on the arcade. There is also an excellent model of the church as it was in 1898. The steps at the end lead to vestries. The font, standing under the last arch, is of 1841 but its pinnacled wooden cover is mostly early 16th c.

On the S. pier of the **tower** arch hangs a large early 19th c. tablet to the Stead and Mawson families, unusual in being of wood. Within the tower are numerous other memorials, mostly 18th and 19th c., some unfortunately 'skied' and too high to see. The hot-coloured Victorian W. window is by Heaton, Butler and Bayne.

The steps at the W. end of the **N. aisle** lead to Maufe's song room. A headstone brought inside commemorates Hannah Barwick

(d. 1788) and refers to the battle of Waterloo. On the N. wall a good tablet is to Isaac Hollings (d. 1734). Another on the arcade pier just E. of the screen is to William Rawson (d. 1737), a curiously elongated design to fit the space. Bay 2 is a war memorial corner with five banners and a busy window by A. L. Davies (1921); carved on its sill are traces of a sword, helmet and inscription, probably a 15th c. memorial. The arms of Queen Anne hang over the N. door and the rest of the wall is lined with wall tablets of which the following deserve notice: Joseph Priestley (d. 1817), with sculpture of canal building by William Pistell; Faith Sawrey, (d. 1767); Faith Sharp (d. 1710); two nice cartouches, unfortunately re-lettered; Abraham Sharp (d. 1742), by Peter Scheemakers; and a bronze tablet of 1951 commemorating local anniversaries.

The **N. transept**, added by Healey in 1899, contains more memorials: on the W. wall the bust of William Sharp, surgeon (d. 1833) by Joseph Gott (the upper part with female figure is missing); on the N., Abraham Balme (d. 1796), a teacher and pupils group by John Flaxman; and on the E. two more re-coloured and inappropriately re-lettered early 18th c. cartouches.

Back in the **N. aisle**, the square opening above the end of the arcade gave access to the rood loft, the stair to which can be seen beyond the arch in the former Leventhorpe chapel. On the right are Maufe's stall-backs within his new tower; in the wall on the left a fragment of interlace carving, perhaps 10th c., a vestry doorway, and a 17th c. table. Two more steps lead into the 1961–5 extension. To the left a lobby and stair give access to a library and a small muniment room, the latter with a little window towards the altar, reproducing the former arrangement of a priest's watching loft. Tall arches on the right flank the **quire**, with small clerestory and boldly coloured roof with unmoulded beams. The three arches behind the high altar screen the E. Lady chapel. Turning now W., the comfortably solid bishop's throne is on the left. This and most of the other fittings are Maufe's, but stalls of 1899 have been re-used except in the back row. They occupy the space beneath the new lantern tower, which has high windows on three sides and the organ in the fourth. The head stops at the ends of the organ arch are portraits of the then Provost and of Maufe himself.

At the E. end of the quire are two different, more lightly framed oak chairs and desks of 1955, attractively coloured and gilded. Go past these, back to the N. quire aisle (which forms part of a continuous ambulatory around the quire) and left into St Aidan's chapel with its plain marble floor at a somewhat lower level; the simple ceiling with plain beams supports the chapter house above. At the chapel entrance are re-set a piscina from the old chancel, another Saxon carved stone, and one carved with sheep shears.

Steps on the left of the aisle lead up to the chapter house and NE. porch. At the end of the aisle are glass doors to the simple **Chapel of the Holy Spirit**, reserved for private prayer. Its E. window tracery contains a dove. Then the ambulatory leads across to the S. side; to the right is an impressive view down the quire and nave, to the left the simplified Gothic Lady chapel. The three coloured E. windows are early work (1863) by William Morris in collaboration with Sir Edward Burne-Jones, Dante Gabriel Rossetti and possibly Albert Moore and F. M. Brown; they have been adapted from the former main E. window.

The S. section of the ambulatory is curved because of the restricted site. It contains a World War II book of honour, and further along are banners and other relics of the West Yorkshire Regiment, as well as a tablet commemorating the consecration of the E. end, 1963.

Back now into the old part of the cathedral, the 17th c. former Bolling chapel. The big plain tomb-chest on the left is of Margaret Mason (d. 1829). Amongst many wall memorials are an oval brass inscription to Thomas Wood (d. 1712), and a big tablet to Thomas Clapham (d. 1719) with coat-of-arms. Pass the steps to the organ console, go down into the nave aisle and turn aside to look at the brass eagle lectern (c. 1910) and the pulpit which, though mostly of 1860 and 1899, incorporates panelling from the earlier 'three-decker'.

The **S. transept**, like the N., is of 1899. On its E. side is a new SE. porch with a blocked doorway bearing the Bolling family arms which was the private entrance to their chapel.

Along the main **S. nave aisle** are many more tablets, some 'skied'. Prominent are those to John Rand (d. 1873) with marble bust, and John Smyth (d. 1686), re-lettered and with a multiplicity of cherubs' heads and skulls.

In the vaulted S. porch, built in 1833, is a quaint incised grave slab bearing dates of three uses, in 1617, 1728 and 1732. Finally, a **circuit** starting round the W. end, where the tower completed in 1508 is now flanked by Maufe's two vestry wings. Beyond the lawns to the N. is a close of cathedral houses. A path leads round the N. side of the cathedral, past a doorway of 1681 on the E. face of the choir vestries, re-set there after the 'bone house' on the site was pulled down. The path past the N. porch is paved with grave slabs and leads up and out into Stott Hill. In Church Bank the new SE. corner is built right up to the pavement and it is a good idea to cross the road to see the S. side better – the sanctus bellcote and Alan Collins's Majestas on the side of the Lady chapel, the new lantern tower, and finally the long low embattled old walls which date largely from the 1830s.

Brechin, Holy Trinity (Church of Scotland, Tayside)

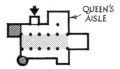

QUEEN'S AISLE

Near an earlier Columban one, a Culdee (Celtic) community was founded by Kenneth II *c*. 980 and its round tower still stands. A bishop was first mentioned *c*. 1150. Of his church a few carved stones have been found; it was rebuilt early in the 13th c. 'Improvements' in 1806–08 resulted in demolition of the transepts and rebuilding the aisles with roofs flush with the nave. In the 'restoration' of *c*. 1900 under John Honeyman the S. transept was rebuilt as it had been but the N. one was replaced by an outer aisle. The nave and aisle roofs resumed their original form with clerestory, and the quire was rebuilt from a ruin.

The N. porch (by Honeyman) leads into the N. aisle with its markedly leaning arcade of alternately round and octagonal columns; the S. arcade has all octagonal columns and other irregularities can be noticed. The high open nave roof is Honeyman's. At the W. end of the **N. aisle** is a benefaction board of 1683. The doorway here leads into the tower base, now a vestry but formerly the chapter house; close by is an Adam window by William Wilson (1952), one of the many examples of good modern glass throughout the building. The second, Prophets, is by Douglas Strachan (1949). The outer or **Queen's aisle** has an arcade by Honeyman but the wrought-iron screen was added in 1951. It contains the 19th c. font; its *Magnificat* W. window is by Gordon Webster (1978), and the two N. windows are by Wilson, as well as the *Benedicite* in the rose window.

At the E. end of the N. aisle various carved stones are collected: a coffin-lid of *c*. 1200; the St Mary stone, a Pictish cross-slab of

Northumbrian character of *c.* 900; and a shallow-arcaded circular font bowl, possibly 12th c., originally in Aldbar church and now on a 19th c. stem. The **quire**, now fitted with Gothic panelling, table and pulpit, not over elaborate, has glass by Henry Holiday (1902), of which that in the side windows, without any Gothic detail, is specially good. In the centre of the quire hangs a brass 'hearse' or candelabrum believed to be early 16th c. Flemish. In the **S. aisle** the centre window (Apostles) is by Herbert Hendrie (1932); the other two, also Apostles, are in the totally different idiom of Hugh Easton (1952). At the W. end is a bronze Art Nouveau tablet to David Carnegie (d. 1900) with bas-relief bust. A glass case contains an interesting collection of plate. In the SW. corner the round tower projects into the aisle and shows a doorway formed in 1806 and later blocked. There is also another group of old carved stones: the Aldbar Stone, a standing Celtic cross with interlace work; the Brechin Hogback, a grave cover with Norse animal carving and heads of about 11th c.; and several minor ones. Finally the main W. window (*Te Deum*) by Wilson (1958) can be seen to advantage; the organ is divided into two halves on its gallery to avoid hiding it.

The **outside** is here taken clockwise, starting with Honeyman's N. transept and the quire, which has some 13th c. stonework in its base. The E. churchyard is a crowded necropolis; below the E. window is the curious Speid 'Isle or tomb' with its explanatory inscription under glass like a garden frame. The S. transept and aisle are 19th c., but the nave clerestory is not and it is instructive to compare the latter's splendid corbel-table with the mechanically carved grotesques of the aisle below.

Then the round tower, chimney-like, minaret-like, almost unique in Britain (a less good one is at Abernethy, but in Ireland they are comparatively common). It is thought to be of Kenneth II's time, *c.* 980, though the extreme top is 14th c. Perfectly circular throughout, it tapers uniformly outside but the internal diameter of 7′ 8″ is constant. Much above ground level, confirming the defensive origin, is a strange doorway with saints (or bishops) at the sides, a Crucifix above, and beasts at the bottom corners.

The W. front of the nave has a fine, though decayed, 13th c. doorway. The window and gable above are 15th c. The tower, also badly weatherworn, is 13th c. too at the base, though it was probably not completed till the next century or even later; it is one of the best of its kind in Scotland. Beneath the W. window are two medieval stone coffins.

Between October and March weekday opening is from 2 p.m. to 4 p.m. only (not Wednesdays).

Brecon, St John the Evangelist (Church in Wales, Powys)

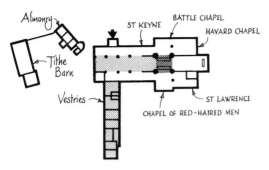

Standing somewhat away from the centre of the town, this is a priory church that became a cathedral in 1923. Its known history began with the establishment of the priory by Bernard de Neufmarche, a follower of William the Conqueror – but no doubt there was a church here already. Shortly afterwards it became subservient to Battle Abbey in Sussex. In the first quarter of the 13th c. the chancel, tower and transepts were rebuilt. The nave and aisles followed 100 years later, and the N. and S. chapels were added towards the end of the 14th c. So nothing remains of the Norman building except the font and some walling at the tower end of the nave.

Though the priory was dissolved and most of the monastic buildings gradually disappeared, the church survived for parish use and was eventually restored by Sir George Gilbert Scott in 1860–75. Further restoration work, particularly on St Lawrence's chapel and the remaining monastic buildings has been done under W. D. Caröe and his son Alban Caroe.

Inside the lychgate the first view is of the short sturdy central tower and the N. transept, both 13th c. The 15th c. N. porch, the normal **entry**, is two-storeyed. The two large stones just inside are querns for grinding corn; the upper storey is a muniment room.

Straight ahead inside the main door is the font, older than the building itself and with unusual sculpture. From it can be seen most of the interior of the cathedral, grand in its proportions but darkened by a great deal of coloured glass. Above the font is a brass chandelier of 1722. The arcades, slightly different on the two sides, are 14th c. E. of them, leading up to the arches of the 13th c. central tower, are the short lengths of remaining Norman walling, and

Cathedral interior, Brecon (13th and 14th cc.)

beyond the tower the dignified 13th c. chancel. The big clerestory windows occur unusually over the arcade columns. Behind, the big 14th c. W. window has glass of 1898.

The **N. aisle** is still the Corvizors' (Cordwainers' or Shoemakers') aisle and has a display of books and pictures, old roof bosses and other relics. St Keyne's chapel at its E. end is separated from the nave by a medieval screen which originally stood between the nave and quire and from the aisle by a modern copy of it. The 14th c. tomb on the left, rich with ball-flower ornament, is supposed to be that of the 'builder of the nave'.

In the E. part of the **nave** the high-level doors which once led on to the rood loft are prominent (anciently the church was commonly called after the great Holy Rood that stood here). The pulpit is less ancient than it appears; its medieval panels were taken from another screen. The tomb-slab of David Vaughan (1689) in the floor close by is worth inspection for its robust lettering.

Next the **crossing**, with the stalls of 1874 and the small bishop's throne made in 1915 for the enthronement of a suffragan bishop of Swansea. The intention of vaulting the tower space was never realized; from here the walls above can be seen to have passages in their thickness. The effect of sturdiness is rather misleading, and the five bells can no longer be safely rung.

The **N. transept**, too, has an upper passage. This transept is the Battle chapel. Battle being a hamlet three miles from Brecon, as well as the name of the Sussex abbey, there is a tangle of associations, and since there were battles at both Battles no one really knows which was named after what. An array of monuments here includes several in marble to the Watkins family by a local sculptor, J. E. Thomas.

Two arches lead to the banner-hung Havard chapel, once the Lady chapel and now dedicated as the memorial chapel of the South Wales Borderers. The old tomb-slabs that here cover the entire floor have a wealth of interest in their local history and no-nonsense lettering. This is a 14th c. addition to the church, as can be seen from the ball-flower ornamented doorway near the far end of the S. wall. Ancient houseling benches form the communion rail, but most of the oak furnishings were given after either the First or the Second World War. The small reredos painting of the Baptism of Our Lord is by Francesco Albani. The tomb N. of the altar is of Walter and Christina Awbrey, 1312.

A rich 13th c. doorway of four orders leads into the **chancel**. Its vaulting, Scott's 1862 completion of the original scheme, is unusual in that the spandrel stones lie, French fashion, parallel to the ridges. Otherwise this is all Early English, with shafted lancet windows, triple sedilia and, most unusual, triple piscinae. The reredos is of 1937; a worn stone Crucifixion on the N. wall may be part of an earlier one, and the Mockery picture nearby is attributed to Honthorst.

Another four-order doorway leads to the **S. transept**, the chapel of the Red-haired Men. It contains numerous things of interest, including a very elaborate domestic cupboard, a copy of a Raphael Madonna, the tomb of Edward Bevan the first bishop, an 18th c. chamber organ by Henry Bevington, and many memorials. The little chapel of St Lawrence opening off it was rescued from ruins in the late 1920s and is set aside for private prayer.

Just inside the **S. aisle** a doorway leads into the garden. Passing it for the time being, one comes to the curious wooden effigy of a 16th c. lady of the Games family, an ornately carved cupboard, and the 17th c. monument to David Wilkins and his wife. Near the W. end is the largest cresset stone in the country; this is a kind of multiple candle-holder. Another door in the S. aisle leads into one of the surviving monastic wings, still retaining a somewhat domestic character with irregular passages leading to vestries and similar small rooms in two, three and four storeys.

Now back to the garden door, leading into the railed part of the churchyard which is open between 9 a.m. and 5 p.m. To the right is the vestry wing. Turning left, however, so as to skirt the cathedral anti-clockwise, the way passes the Deanery garden on the right, then the E. end of the cathedral which is flanked by a fine cedar, and finally the N. side. Just before regaining the porch it is worth looking at the 14th c. dormer window of the Corvizors' aisle, built on top of an earlier one with the object of admitting more light. Past the W. end, on the left before the lychgate, is the monastic almonry, and behind it the tithe-barn: both are now restored to church use, but not normally accessible to the public.

Brentwood, The Sacred Heart and St Helen (Roman Catholic, Essex)

The original church, at Pilgrim's Hatch, was built in 1814. The first in Brentwood itself was built in 1837 and still stands as a social centre. Its successor nearby was designed by Gilbert Blount (1858–61) and became a cathedral, of very modest size, in 1917. In 1972–4 it was drastically enlarged by John Newton, who turned its

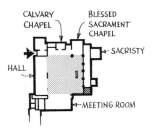

axis, demolished the N. aisle, and converted the former nave into a sanctuary at right angles to the old. To the W. and S. of his new nave are halls which on great occasions can be opened out into one large space. The old S. aisle is retained as sacristy and vestry and so the external appearance from the S. is virtually unaltered.

The doors from the covered porch on the new W. wide lead to an inner lobby with narthex and stall to the left, hall to the right, and nave ahead. The Gothic arches prominent on entering the nave are the old S. arcade, now blocked by panel walls and painted grey and white. Straight ahead is the square spiky tabernacle on a round stone stem, designed by Michael Clark. This corner, the former chancel, is now the Blessed Sacrament chapel; the old chancel arch rests on typical Victorian responds with foliage and angels, and the E. and W. window glass by Mayer of Munich is original; the high-pitched roof has been painted brown and white. The 19th c. font, also re-coloured, stands just inside the old nave.

Back now up the new N. 'aisle', re-passing first the Lady chapel with its Gothic window, then the new Calvary chapel with carved reredos from the old building, and lastly the confessionals, to the back of the new nave. Behind, and over on the other side, are big sliding doors to the hall and the meeting room. The clerestory round three sides includes coloured glazing in semi-abstract form and below it are new Stations of the Cross. The stone pulpit with Chi-Rho emblem and the altar with Last Supper were carved by J. Poole; above hangs a new Rood by David Johns and behind are three rather pallid paintings.

To the left outside the main door, at the end of the courtyard, is Cathedral House, which is the original priest's house of 1836 – Tudor-arched white brick with attractive fretted eaves and a newly added porch. Back in the main road, the statue of St Helen is Italian, by Ferdinand Stuflesser and that of the Risen Christ on the corner is by Tina Madden. Harmony between old and new has been achieved by using similar ragstone; conversely, however, the old building has unfortunately been re-roofed in lifeless concrete tiles to match the new. Blount's SW. tower, square with octagonal top and spire, is also not specially attractive.

Bristol, Holy Trinity (Church of England, Avon)

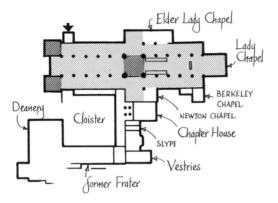

Bristol was among the six cathedrals established in 1542 in what had been abbeys. This one was Augustinian and had been founded in 1140. Little remains of that date except the abbey gatehouse and the chapter house. A Lady chapel E. of the N. transept of the church was added about 1220, and that too remains.

The quire and its aisles were rebuilt, with what is now called the Eastern Lady chapel, about 1298 to 1330 in a Gothic style unlike any elsewhere. Work – and probably money – petered out at the stage when re-modelling of the S. transept was hardly started, and the crossing-tower and transepts were only resumed *c*. 1470 and completed *c*. 1515. Rebuilding of the nave was stopped at the Reformation and it fell to ruin; with the W. towers it was eventually completed in 1868–88 by G. E. Street. Meanwhile Sir George Gilbert Scott had carried out a restoration of the older parts around 1860.

The diocese by a strange anomaly long consisted mainly of Bristol City and the distant county of Dorset. It was united with Gloucester in 1836 but set up again in 1897 in more logical form with the newly completed cathedral.

As seen from College Green, therefore, the central tower and transepts and all to the left is medieval, and all to the right 19th c. Entry is by the N. porch; the rose window over the inner doorway, looking into the high aisle interior, is a hint of the building's unusual form, with vaulted aisles as tall as the nave. But it is simplest to defer examination of Street's work for the time being.

Looking E. from the W. end of the **nave**, J. L. Pearson's five-arched screen is prominent, and the quire beyond. Close by, in the W. nave bay on the S. side, is the alert reclining figure of Sir Charles Vaughan (d. 1630) and on the N. the recumbent effigy of Joan Young, (d. 1603). Central in the nave stands the small medieval font.

Still deferring a look at architectural details, go next up the **N. aisle**, where the last bay has some hanging banners and, in the wall recess, an effigy of Dean Elliot (d. 1891). On the right (in the nave) the brass eagle lectern is of 1863.

The **N. transept** in its present form is of about 1500 and has a lierne vault with richly carved and re-coloured bosses and foliage capitals. The base of the N. wall is Norman. In the big window above, the glass is of 1890, in memory of Edward Colston the merchant-philanthropist – but that on the E. side has medieval fragments of various dates. On the N. wall is a monument to William Gore (d. 1814) flanked by soldiers, and (centrally) one to Bishop Butler (d. 1752), a typical early Gothic Revival piece of 1834. Beside the arch on the E. side is the worn tomb-slab of Abbot David (d. 1253).

This opening with a scrolly screen leads to the **Elder Lady Chapel**, built by Abbot David before the Norman E. end was replaced, and now set aside for private prayer. It is fully developed Early English, so clean and fresh in its details as to seem newly built. Notice particularly the use of Purbeck marble, detached window shafts, wall arcading, foliage capitals and spirited spandrel carvings of animals. But the E. window (with Hardman glass) is Geometric Decorated and the vault is probably later 13th c. too. Fragments of older glass are in the N. windows. The arches in the S. wall were made in the 14th c.; under the further one is the tomb of Maurice, Lord Berkeley (d. 1368), with effigies of him and his mother.

Now the **N. quire aisle** with many wall tablets on the left, and the rear of the organ on the right. Past these, one can begin to savour Bristol's special form of early 14th c. Gothic. The quire is a 'hall-church', i.e. with aisles as tall as the 'nave', and no triforium or clerestory. The arcades (but not of course the vault) are the tallest in

View into Lady Chapel from S. Quire Aisle, Bristol, with 'star' memorial to an abbot

England. Moreover, instead of by external flying buttresses, the thrust of the main vault is countered by internal ones in the form of openwork stone bridges on which the aisle vaults (running transversely) are poised. It is a unique, ingenious and fascinating form of construction. The quire itself, broad rather than high, has the earliest form of lierne vaulting, unusual in having cusped top panels and no ridge-rib. The window tracery, too, is of distinctive character.

The E. window of the aisle has late 17th c. glass said to have been given by Nell Gwyn. On the N. wall are more wall tablets than can be mentioned individually, including some above the stone gallery. Prominent is a big one to William Powell (d. 1769), by J. Paine. Just beyond is the first of the spectacular star-shaped wall recesses which are another of Bristol's unique features. This one has the broken 13th c. coffin lid of Viliam le Someter; the second contains a bust of the poet Robert Southey (d. 1843). On the E. wall is a 15th c. reredos sadly mauled to receive later memorials, particularly that of Robert Codrington (d. 1618), with kneeling figures under angel-held curtains. On the right the stone cadaver under a slab with six squat Ionic columns is Paul Bush (d. 1558), the first bishop, deposed by Mary I because he was a married man.

The **Eastern Lady chapel** is short and wide and structurally a continuation of the quire; indeed it was the sanctuary until the 19th c. So the big complex end window is the E. window of the whole building; some of the Jesse Tree glass in it is 14th c. Below, the elaborate reredos is substantially original. It and the much renewed sedilia and the three more star recesses were plastered over during the Commonwealth, so preserving much of the original colouring, now seen fully restored. The stars, taken clockwise, have the effigies of Abbot Hunt (d. 1481), Abbot Newbery (d. 1473), and Abbot Newland or Nailheart (d. 1515), all well-preserved. The altar candlesticks are of 1712, given in thanks for the return of two Bristol ships from a world voyage during which 'Robinson Crusoe' was rescued. Parts of the glazing in the side windows are 14th c. too: note particularly the (restored) St Edmund window on the extreme right.

The back of the reredos forms the W. wall of the Lady chapel. It continues with a stone screen brought from the Whitefriars' church at the Reformation; 17th c. doors lead into the **S. quire aisle**. Straight ahead is another star which originally contained the effigy of Thomas, Lord Berkeley (d. 1321). In this aisle the full splendour of the arch and vault system can be enjoyed, its elaborate monochrome interplay of shapes and spaces enlivened by regimental and other banners and by Keith New's brilliant Holy Spirit E. window (1962). In the window to the right of that is early 16th c. German glass, and amongst many memorials in the E. bay may be singled out that to Harriet Middleton (d. 1826), by E. H. Baily, with a mourning woman. A doorway in the S. wall leads into a passage which is the sacristy or ante-chapel to the early 14th c. **Berkeley chapel**. Even this passage has a unique roof – a miniature stone vault with ribs and bosses but no infilling, supporting a flat stone roof. It is like a demonstration model of how a Gothic vault works. In the S. wall are three recesses, one with a flue up to a pinnacle outside; this is thought to have been for baking communion bread. Over them are collected fragments of 14th c. glass. At the W. end is a 17th c. chest and in the E. wall an unusual diagonal niche and a doorway uniquely enriched with carved seed-pods and spiral ammonites. The chapel itself, two vaulted bays with two altars and two piscinae, is much more ordinary. Its glass dates from a restoration of 1924–5. Three niches on the S. wall are unorthodox in detail. In the centre hangs a superb 15th c. brass candelabrum from Bristol's Temple Church; probably the finest in England, it has figures of the Virgin Mary and St George.

Now back into the S. quire aisle. One each side of the chapel doorway are two heraldic stone brackets which once supported the organ. Then a monument to Bishop Searchfield (d. 1622), and, in another star, one probably to Maurice, Lord Berkeley, (d. 1326). Opposite is a way into the **quire**, the traditional arrangement of which was restored by Pearson after completion of the nave. Contrary to their new appearance, the stalls incorporate many 16th c. traceried panels, remounted, and a fine set of playful misericords. A good example, readily seen, is the mermaid on the fourth stall from the E. on the N. side. The quire pulpit also has panels of the same date. The rich stone quire screen is of 1905 and the delicate reredos of 1899. The screens from the Whitefriars church, now at the sides of the quire, were previously used as a pulpitum, dividing what is now the quire into two; the fine Renatus Harris organ of *c.* 1685, now over the N. quire stalls, stood on it with its two cases facing E. and W. Note Pearson's delicate brass altar rail before returning to the S. quire aisle.

Continuing W., a last star recess contains the supposed effigy of another Lord Berkeley, Thomas (d. 1243). More wall tablets, then on the left an iron screen to the **Newton chapel**, which is mid-14th c. and quite ordinary. On its E. wall is a chantry tomb with kneeling space for a priest, early 16th c.; a prominent insciption records its repair in 1748. On the S. side the big tombs are of Sir Henry Newton (d. 1599) and (with the canopy) Sir John Newton (d. 1661). At the W. end, which has a simple 15th c. wooden screen, are a Sir Richard Westmacott memorial to Elizabeth Stanhope (d. 1816), and Alfred Drury's modern plaque to the 17th c. Bishop Trelawny.

Back in the S. quire aisle, the last bay has a different vault, with the treasury above it. By the transept entry, on the left, is a monument by Sir Francis Chantrey to Mary Elwyn (d. 1818).

The **S. transept** has a rather earlier, plainer vault than the N. and is also Norman in its basic form. A more obvious difference lies in the shorter main window, where the monastic buildings joined on, and the night stair (private) beneath it which led to the dormitory. Against the E. wall is a carving of the Harrowing of Hell, thought to be pre-Conquest; the columns under it probably came from the Norman cloister. Then the Newton chapel screen, already noted, and on the S. wall a further group of early 19th c. memorials.

The small stair in the SW. corner leads to the **cloister**. Only the E. walk is left, with Tudor windows to the garth, a curious 14th c. doorway at the S. end, and on the left essentially Norman walling. The windows contain collected fragments of 14th and 15th c. glass. On the left at the foot of the stair is a good monument by John Bacon to Sterne's 'Eliza', Elizabeth Draper (d. 1778). The three round arches lead into a graceful rib-vaulted vestibule and thence to the **chapter house**, all late Norman. Its E. wall had to be rebuilt after the 1831 riots; the plate glass windows beautifully incised with historical lists of dignitaries shed a new harsh light on the rich and unusual wall patterns.

The rest of the cloister is not open to the public. Beyond the chapter house are some smaller rooms and more minor memorials. The S. walk has gone and what is old on that side is absorbed into the Cathedral School. The short piece of N. walk is modern reconstruction. Turn back now to the transept through the same doorway (19th c.) and go to the **crossing** to see the tower vault, also late 15th c., and the W. side of the quire screen.

After seeing the medieval work it is now easier to understand the Street **nave and aisles**, which can very conveniently be taken in from this point. They are little more than an unadventurous adaptation of the E. parts – modified in many details, such as the earlier-style window tracery and the more orthodox main piers and capitals. It is still a hall-church, without clerestory, and it is that which gives Bristol its own special dignity.

Returning W. along the **S. aisle**: a large brass on the first pier is to Jordan Palmer-Palmer (d. 1885) and the figure in the wall recess is of Dean Pigou (d. 1916). The nave pulpit close to it is of 1903 – not the most handsome stonework in the building.

Externally the chief interest is in the other abbey remains. Though so much reduced, they are the most extensive in Britain of an Augustinian monastery. The tall gatehouse (to the left on leaving the N. porch) is 12th c. at the base, with separate ways for wheeled and foot traffic, and 15th c. in its upper parts. Past Street's twin W. towers is the now open-ended cloister, with on the right a prominent cinquefoil-headed doorway. It is worth going a little way down the hill for the sake of an impressive diagonal view of the W. front. What is now the Deanery and school grouped against the S. side of the cloister is a jumble of Norman and (mostly) later buildings. Little is gained by going along Anchor Road below and back up the Trinity Street steps: the alternative is to reach the E. end of the cathedral on the level from College Green. Here the imposing central tower, late Perpendicular but rebuilt by Pearson, can be appreciated in isolation; several of its bells are medieval. The Bishop's Palace, visible through the churchyard gates, was left in ruins after the 1831 riots.

Bury St Edmunds, St James (Church of England, Suffolk)

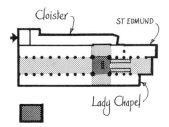

The ecclesiastical renown of Bury rested on its abbey, founded about 903 in honour of King Edmund, but its great church was in ruins long before 1913 when the diocese of St Edmundsbury and Ipswich was created. One of the two Perpendicular parish churches in its precincts was chosen as the cathedral. It had been mostly built about 1510–30, and Edward VI gave money towards its completion. Sir George Gilbert Scott's restoration of 1865–9 included replacing a

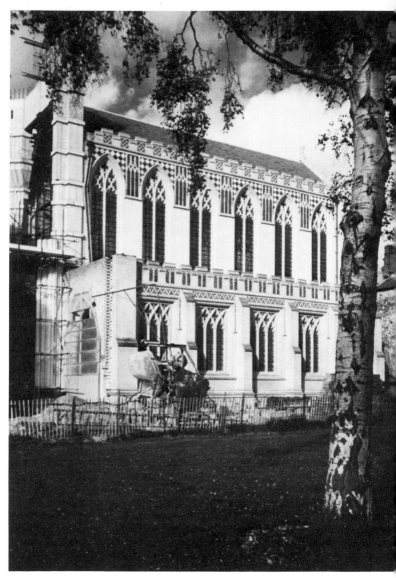

Quire under construction, Bury St Edmunds (1956)

chancel of 1711; his chancel has now itself been replaced.

The enlargement to cathedral form began with the cloister and NW. porch, opened in 1960, and continued with the new crossing, quire and chapels (1967–70). The architect was Stephen Dykes Bower, and his choice of style was a fully-fledged Gothic somewhere between Decorated and Perpendicular. The crossing-tower and a series of chapter rooms to the NE. have yet to be built.

The Norman gatehouse tower of the abbey came to serve as a **campanile** to St James's and is in effect a detached part of the cathedral. It was built in the second half of the 12th c. and is quite richly decorated, especially on the side facing the street and town. Its proportions are somewhat spoilt by the raising of the general ground level to counter flooding, the original level within the tower being clearly visible.

Similarly, steps lead down from the street through the new NW. porch into the cathedral. Over it is the library. Straight ahead is the cloister, and to the right the **entrance** newly made in what was a blank bay in the N. wall. First to catch the eye is the 19th c. font with its splendid pinnacled canopy, a 1914–18 war memorial; both were coloured and gilded in East Anglian style in 1960.

The **nave** arcades are tall, even for East Anglia, and typical of the early 16th c. From each pier a stone shaft runs up to the roof corbels, past the doubled clerestory windows. But the wooden roof itself, of hammer-beam type, is by Scott, coloured and gilded in 1948–9. Beyond are the new arches of the crossing, and past them the new quire. Behind, on either side of the W. doorway, are monuments to Chief Justice James Reynolds (d. 1738), a bewigged seated figure with three cherubs, and Mary Reynolds (d. 1736). The W. window is a Last Judgement, by Hardman.

A special feature of the interior, their prominence depending on their arrangement, is the series of a thousand blue kneelers made throughout Suffolk. They may be in their 'display' positions in the aisles only. The **N. aisle** has a series of 19th c. Old Testament windows by Clayton & Bell, and a number of minor wall tablets. The low-pitched roof is the original. The pendant lights with black hoops and golden balls, recurring in different forms throughout the building, are by Dykes Bower. The octagonal canopied pulpit, best seen from the E. end of the aisle, was designed by Scott.

The **N. transept** is the start of the new building. Here the nave altar is in full view, with its new, rather Jacobean, communion rail and, above, the temporary roof of the crossing where in due course a lantern-tower will be built. The transept roof itself has a busy

floral pattern. On its N. wall are steps which will lead to an upper
floor over the cloister, and beneath them is an explanatory model of
the whole project. The organ case over the arch to the N. quire aisle
is also unfinished.

On the left in the **N. quire aisle** a doorway leads into the cloister.
Beside it stands a little chamber organ by Thomas Casson (1905),
made for the crypt chapel of St Paul's Cathedral. Over it is a
fragmentary 16th c. Spanish painting of Christ carrying the Cross
restored by Tom Keating. The ceiling has another lively floral
pattern.

A double arch leads into St Edmund's chapel, with a temporary
N. wall until the hall alongside can be built. The nine tapestries on
this wall relate the story of St Edmund and were made by
schoolchildren (1970). The brass eagle lectern is 19th c.

In the **quire** the full length splendour of the new work is all
around: piers and pointed arcades only slightly different from
traditional design, a blind 'triforium' with arches just clear of the
wall, tall clerestory, and another richly panelled ceiling with typical
Dykes Bower patterning in pale blue and gold, black and white. The
gaily painted shields above the arcades represent the arms of the
barons who took an oath at the abbey in 1214 to force King John to
sign Magna Carta. The light oak furnishings harmonize perfectly:
Gothic stalls, low in contrast with the building, and simple in
contrast with the pinnacled bishop's throne. The animals on the
offsets of the throne are the wolves which traditionally guarded the
head of St Edmund after his martyrdom. Above the NW. part of the
quire is a second portion of organ case, also unfinished.

In the **sanctuary** the three E. windows and one on the S. are by
Charles Kempe (1867–70) and were in the old chancel. The stone
sedilia, transferred from Scott's chancel, are richly carved in
Decorated style, and a simple brass in the floor commemorates
Bishop Hodgson, first bishop of the diocese (d. 1944).

The **S. chapel**, which is the Lady chapel and reserved for private
prayer, has plain dignified furnishings, a simple low-pitched roof
of entirely traditional type, and a splendid blue and gilded screen.
The **S. transept** echoes the design of the N. transept and has a
similarly patterned ceiling; but there is a S. window with,
unfortunately, glass of indifferent quality, a memorial of 1847. The
wall tablets are again of minor interest. The chamber organ is of
1790.

Likewise the **S. aisle** is very similar to the N.: roof, coloured
kneelers, and windows. This side the Clayton & Bell glass depicts

New Testament scenes. The last window on the left, however, has early 16th c. Flemish glass with the story of Susanna and the Elders in the lower lights and parts of a Jesse Tree in the upper.

Prominent over the N. doorway is a gilded trumpeting cherub which once belonged to the church's organ case and found its way to a Belgian antique shop. Below it are the arms of Charles II. The **cloister** is reached through this doorway by turning right down the ingenious circular steps through the wrought-iron screen (1978). It will lead to the future chapter house. The wall on the right contains the only remains of pre-14th c. work still visible; on it are a number of wall tablets, some early 19th c., some mid-20th c.

Finally the **exterior**. The W. front was altered by Scott to accommodate his nave roof. The fleur-de-lys foot scrapers by the W. doorway are an unusually pretty detail. Past the tower lies the abbey precinct, now a great churchyard, with St Mary's Church away on the right, the ruined W. front of the abbey church straight ahead (incredibly filled up with doors and windows of real houses) and on the greensward an Elizabeth Frink sculpture of civic, not ecclesiastical significance. From here the cathedral's run-of-the-mill Perpendicular of the older parts can be contrasted with the rich tracery and flint flushwork of the new; at their junction is the stump of the tower-to-be. Further exploration towards the S. and NE. will reveal many more remnants of the abbey.

Canterbury, Christ Church (Church of England, Kent)

In all probability a church already existed in Canterbury when St Augustine arrived from Rome in 597. The present cathedral's story begins with a complete rebuilding by Lanfranc, the first Norman archbishop, in 1070–6. The present nave, aisles and transepts are on his foundations and pieces of his work are traceable in the transepts; his NW. tower was only replaced in 1832. His quire gave way in 1096–1130 to a much bigger one on a high crypt, built by his successor Anselm. There remains the whole of this crypt as well as all the outer walls of quire and aisles as far as the beginning of the E. (Trinity) chapel. Some of the monastic buildings to the N. are also fundamentally either Lanfranc's or Anselm's.

All this was before Archbishop Becket's murder in 1170. That and a fire which destroyed the inside of the quire in 1174 prompted fresh activity. By 1184 new quire arcades and vaults were completed and the Trinity chapel and the Corona at the extreme E. had been built;

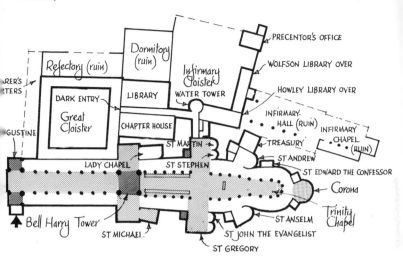

two stages of this work can be distinguished, the first under William
of Sens, the second under William the Englishman. After a long
pause the nave and aisles and most of the cloisters were rebuilt in
1378–1405 and the main transepts and their E. chapels during the
period up to 1468. The SW. tower was rebuilt in 1424–34; the
central one ('Bell Harry') was not begun till 1496. Restorations have
been under George Austin, 1832–41, W. D. Caröe in the 1920s and
Peter Marsh currently.

The following perambulation takes the usual kind of route but,
because of the richness and complexity of so much of the
architecture and fittings, individual descriptions can be little more
than a catalogue. That particularly applies to the glass and the
monuments, both of which justify separate and prolonged tours.

Just inside Christ Church Gate (1507–17) one of the finest views
of the cathedral immediately opens up; but it is one which
emphasizes the Perpendicular at the expense of the earlier work.
Nave aisles and clerestory with big windows, pinnacles and deep
buttresses are all standard for their date. The SW. tower is much
more elaborate, especially towards its top. So is the porch with its
tiers of niches: these and their statues, continuing around the W.
front, were renewed in 1862. The NW. tower is of 1832, matching
the SW. Bell Harry tower owes much of its dignity and strength to

Central Tower vault, Canterbury, as seen from below (c. 1500)

the octagonal corner turrets; it was the culmination of the medieval work and not finished till after 1500.

The SW. porch has a 15th c. lierne vault and heraldic bosses. So has the interior of the **nave**. The clerestory is so high that its glass hardly tells, and the triforium is insignificant. The whole effect is of verticality, and the upward sweep of the pier shafts, some into the arcade arches, some into the clerestory arches and some into the vault, has a breathtaking logic. Eastward is a strainer arch across the tower. Westward, the great window has glass mostly of *c.* 1400 but with some 12th c. figures at the base.

In the arch to the **NW. tower** stands the great Baroque canopy of an archbishop's throne of 1704, carved by Grinling Gibbons and probably designed by Nicholas Hawksmoor. The chapel of

St Augustine beyond has the tomb of Archbishop Benson (d. 1896), by Sir Thomas Jackson. The painting on the SE. pier of the tower is St Christopher by Garofalo.

The aisles have high lierne vaults too. In the **N. aisle** the tracery lights have a little old glass. Starting at the W. end are a tablet to Hadrian de Saravia (d. 1612), the canopied tomb of Dean Lyall (d. 1857), and a tablet to Sir Alfred Lyall (d. 1911). On the right stands the black and white marble font of 1639, with marble steps and a blue, white and gold cover; the ironwork of the pulley system displays the 1662 royal arms. In the third bay is an Indian campaign memorial by George Nelson (1848), and in the fourth the marble Gothic tomb of Bishop Parry (d. 1890). Then a wall tablet by Nicholas Stone to the musician Orlando Gibbons (d. 1625), the tomb-chest with effigy of Archbishop Sumner (d. 1862), and two more memorials to Indian campaigns, those of 1895–8 and 1845–6. On the right, the coloured and gilded Gothic pulpit is by G. F. Bodley (1898).

On the N. wall again is the reclining figure of Sir John Boys (d. 1612); then a small tablet to John Turner (d. 1720), and a double monument of the late 16th c. to members of the Hales family, with the mother's kneeling figure and representations of a burial at sea and a river scene. One more tablet, to Richard Colf (d. 1613), then seven steps up and down again into the **N. transept**. This, the scene of Becket's martyrdom, was probably kept at its original low level in deference to his memory when it was rebuilt in 1448–68. In design it follows the nave, but some of the 1070 masonry can be seen at, for example, the base of the W. wall. The glass in the main N. window was given by Edward IV and finished in 1482, but much of it was destroyed by a Puritan in 1642. In the floor are some big matrices of brasses and on the left (W.) wall a nice cartouche to John Clerke (d. 1700). The canopied tomb on the N. side is of Archbishop Peckham (d. 1292), with oak effigy. The even bigger one with a great vaulted canopy is to Archbishop Warham (d. 1532). Sir Ninian Comper's W. window of the Royal Family (1954) is the very antithesis of all that is outstanding in Canterbury's glass.

Next the tall fan-vaulted **Lady chapel** (Deans' chapel), reserved for private prayer. The stone screen and the E. window surround are specially noteworthy, and the heraldic E. window mostly original. The monuments, taken from left to right, are to Deans Rogers, Boys and Fotherby. Dean Boys's (d. 1625) on the right of the altar, shows him at his library desk where he is supposed to have died. The portrait on copper is of Dean Bargrave (d. 1643). To the left outside the chapel is the spot where Becket fell, marked by a modern wall inscription.

Ten steps lead down into the **crypt** through a restored 12th c. doorway. The entire W. part of the crypt is of *c.* 1100, almost unaltered since, with groined vaults on short columns and cushion capitals. Almost every capital is carved, with vigorous creatures and foliage in astonishing variety, the finest sculpture of its period in England. The windows are mostly Perpendicular enlargements.

Parts of the crypt are used for exhibitions, and some chapels may not be accessible. However, the following route is likely to be feasible, starting along the N. aisle which presently widens to the N. transept with two apsidal chapels. St Mary Magdalen's has a 14th c. Nottingham alabaster Entombment, and a panel of 13th c. French glass. St Nicholas's has four more such panels, scenes from the saint's life.

Continuing up the N. aisle, Holy Innocents' chapel, also apsidal, is on the left. Here the columns and capitals are specially rich. The small marble font is probably 18th c. Next follows the taller, later 12th c. Trinity chapel crypt. Now the vaults are ribbed, with pointed arches, slenderer columns and a restrained use of Purbeck marble. Beneath the high altar and looking down into the E. part of the crypt is the watching chamber for Becket's tomb, now called the Wax Chamber. At the NE. is a little 18th c. organ. At the E. end is the circular Corona undercroft with radiating vault and a big floral boss; its sanctuary has old tiles and its E. window 13th c. glass.

The roundels of glass adorning some of the windows beneath the S. side of the Trinity chapel are all 19th c. At its W. end are 7th c. stones of unique archaeological interest from the Saxon church of Reculver on the N. coast of Kent, including two tall columns. The stalls nearby are of 1932 and were originally in the nave.

Back in the main crypt, the two much larger piers near the E. end were added later in the 12th c. where the re-planned quire did not quite fit the older substructure. Continuing along the S. side, St Gabriel's chapel is on the left. This not only has superb columns and capitals like Holy Innocents' opposite, but also an almost unparalleled series of early 12th c. paintings, as well as some 13th and 14th c. glass. The effigy on the left of it may be of Lady Elizabeth Tryvet (d. 1431).

In the centre of the crypt is the chapel of Our Lady Undercroft, with delicate stone screens on three sides, *c.* 1400. At the W. end are stone seats and at the E. an original reredos with a 17th c. Portuguese ivory Madonna. Its vault too has some medieval

painting. Turning S. again, the tomb under a decrepit canopy is of
Lady Mohun (d. 1404), and the canopied monument filling a whole
arch is the cenotaph of Archbishop Morton, *c*. 1500. The S. transept
crypt is the Black Prince's chantry, fitted out by him in 1363 with a
veneer of Perpendicular detail. It is used by the Huguenot church
and only open to the public for services. By its arches stands a copy
of a medieval Swedish statue of Becket.

Then the main W. area of the crypt, with a wealth of further
carved capitals, and so back to the N. transept again (there is a
similar stair to the S. transept), and to the crossing with its
impressive view upwards into the lantern stage and the fan-vault of
Bell Harry tower. The tower arches have stiffening 'strainers' on
three sides, the fourth being perhaps omitted to leave free the view
of the 'Martyrdom' window. On the E. the stone pulpitum acts as a
stiffener; its main artistic importance lies in the six original early
15th c. statues of kings and the hexagonally patterned gates into the
quire.

Up to the E. transept the quire piers (1175–9) are round and
octagonal alternately: beyond, round and clustered. Further E. still,
the narrowing at the start of the Trinity chapel is due to the
preservation (following the 1174 fire) of the outer chapel each side,
with of course its crypt. The triforium of two twin openings is
known to have been directly derived from Sens cathedral; the tall,
closely spaced piers with almost Corinthian capitals and the main
sexpartite vaults are also of pure French character. The clerestory has
single big windows with triple openings inside, and the whole system
continues with little change into and around the Trinity chapel
(1180–4), with an increasing use of Purbeck marble.

The stone screen around the quire is of 1304–5. At the W. end it is
hidden by rich stalls and screenwork of 1682. The N. and S. stalls in
three banks are by Sir George Gilbert Scott (1879).

Now the view back to the W. down the nave should be enjoyed
before turning right into the **N. quire aisle**. The bust on the right is
of Alexander Chapman (d. 1629); three paintings opposite include a
17th c. interior possibly by Peter Neefs. Just beyond is a picture of
King Charles the Martyr, done *c*. 1660. Wall-arcading marks the
start of the early 12th c. outer walls. In the third and fourth bays are
what is left of the supremely important so-called Theological
windows, the 'Bible of the Poor', *c*. 1200: a description is opposite.
Then in a blank arch a 15th c. wall-painting of the life of
St Eustace, also described opposite.

The **NE. transept** is not unlike the quire, but with a very irregular

Quire window and 16th c. monument, Canterbury

triforium, and extra wall-arcade below it. Here the early 12th c. work is disguised by added Purbeck marble and dog-tooth ornament. The round N. window has late 12th c. glass in its centre. The door below leads to a passage where the inside of the upper storey of the 12th c. water tower can be seen; on its right is a way out to the library undercroft. A wall plan explains the ancient waterworks system. Back in the transept, the tomb is of Archbishop Tait, d. 1882 (figure by Sir Edgar Boehm). The left chapel, St Martin's, has a framed 15th c. painting of the Saxon Queen Ediva and a 13th c. glass panel of St Martin and the Beggar.

Reverting to the N. quire aisle, ahead under the arcade is the wonderfully rich (but restored) canopied tomb of Archbishop Chichele (d. 1443). The **quire** is worth entering again at this point, to see Austin's archbishop's throne of 1844 and to its right the brass eagle lectern of 1663. The clerestory windows are 19th c. copies, but from here can be seen the eight splendid Genealogical figures of the late 12th c. in the E. clerestory of both transepts, recently restored and replaced. The other tombs and monuments around can be seen presently from the aisles.

Continuing along the N. side, the effigy of Archbishop Howley (d. 1848) is by Richard Westmacott junior. Opposite is a chained Bible of 1572. The brown stone of the next tomb with its tall canopy (Archbishop Bourchier, d. 1486) is Bethersden marble. On the left, the chapel of St Andrew is used as a vestry and thus not accessible, but through the stone screen and scrolly gate one can glimpse the rib vault and wall-paintings and the clock with jacks on the N. wall.

The **Trinity chapel**, sixteen steps up, can now be seen in detail, with its round and pointed arches, zigzag on the vault ribs and window arches, double main columns, and lavish use of Purbeck marble. The geometrical marble floor is of the pattern called *opus alexandrinum*, of *c.* 1220; to the E. of this stood St Thomas à Becket's shrine, the spot now being marked with a brass inscription let into the floor. The ambulatory has the finest array of glass in the cathedral, eight out of the twelve windows being original and all twelve having their iron armatures – which contribute much to the appearance, for they are exceptionally large untraceried areas. The subjects are all miracles worked by St Thomas.

Off the second bay is the little fan-vaulted chapel of St Edward the Confessor with a double, wood and iron screen of 1439, a 16th c. canopied seat and some 15th c. glass. Of the two main windows above it the left one is 19th c. by Clayton & Bell. Opposite stands the great alabaster tomb of Henry IV (d. 1413), and Queen Joan of

Navarre, with painted oak canopy. In the third bay are two splendid windows and the delightful figure at prayer of Dean Wootton (d. 1567). The bronze figure is of Archbishop Davidson (d. 1930). The window in the fourth bay contains picture-stories of five separate miracles.

Then comes the **Corona**, built at the same time as the Trinity chapel. A stair each side leads to a roof gallery, open in summer on payment. The windows, in order, are: first, part of a 12th c. Jesse Tree, then an 1861 Jesse Tree, centrally a complete original window devoted to the Crucifixion and Resurrection, then another 19th c. window, then a 13th c. Majestas. The altar here is dedicated to the Saints and Martyrs of the Twentieth Century. The plain memorial of Cardinal Pole, (d. 1558) on the N. faces Caröe's ornate canopy and kneeling figure (by F. W. Pomeroy) of Archbishop Temple (d. 1902). From this point there is an excellent view to the W. showing the Petworth marble chair of the archbishops with the high altar below, both replaced in their original positions in 1977 – also of the quire and pulpitum to the W., and the nave beyond.

On the S. side the first window has more miracles; above the shapeless tomb opposite is an explanatory modern cartouche to the Cardinal de Coligny-Chatillon (d. 1571). In the second bay is the once splendid tomb of Archbishop Walter (d. 1205) with a little medieval glass above. The alabaster tomb under the arcade is of Archbishop Courtenay (d. 1396). Under the next arch lies the gilded bronze figure of the Black Prince (d. 1376), under a painted wooden canopy; the pieces of armour above are replicas of his original. The miracles series is continued by one of the two windows in this bay, and by a final one just before the top of the steps. Above the steps the little window of the watching chamber should be noticed.

The next chapel on the left is St Anselm's and the strangely canopied monument within its double stone screen is Archbishop Meopham's (d. 1333). To the left of the groin-vaulted apse is a 12th c. painting of St Paul in Malta. The glass is by Harry Stammers (1959).

Now the **S. quire aisle** and, on the right, three sumptuous canopied tombs of archbishops: Simon Sudbury (d. 1381), John Stratford (d. 1348) (alabaster), and John Kempe, (d. 1454). The **SE. transept** contains, first, St John the Evangelist's chapel with altar and rails in memory of Archbishop Temple (d. 1944), and then St Gregory's chapel, furnished in memory of Archbishop Dr Geoffrey Fisher (d. 1961). The distinctive S. windows are by Erwin Bossanyi (1956–62). Continuing down the aisle, the damaged

monument in a niche in the outer wall is that of Dean Nevil
(d. 1615) and his brother; the effigy in the following bay is of Prior
Henry (d. 1331). The glass above and in the next two windows is
largely 13th c. but French; the last effigy is of Archbishop Reynolds
(d. 1328). A door on the left leads to steps up to All Saints' chapel,
not open to the public. Steps down now lead past a nice group of
18th c. wall tablets on the left, and a larger one on the right, into the
S. transept. Passing the head of another flight which goes through a
15th c. doorway to the crypt, and then the bell of H.M.S.
Canterbury with a model of her 1744 namesake, one comes to the
banner-hung St Michael's chapel (Chapel of the Buffs).

This is a 15th c. rebuilding of one of Lanfranc's chapels and has
a lierne vault. Under the altar is the simple stone tomb of
Archbishop Langton (d. 1228), the extremity of which can be seen
outside protruding into the churchyard! Though not open to the
public, its profusion of re-coloured monuments can be seen quite
well. The central tomb is of Margaret Holland (d. 1437), and her
two husbands the Earl of Somerset and the Duke of Clarence. The
others are taken in order, starting on the left inside the gates:
William Prude (d. 1632), a kneeling figure; Sir Thomas Thornhurst
(d. 1627), reclining; Lady Thornhurst (d. 1609), with two figures;
Dorothy Thornhurst (d. 1620), kneeling; Sir George Rooke
(d. 1708), of Gibraltar fame; and, near right, Francis Godfrey
(d. 1712).

The main S. transept is like the N. In the huge S. window are 24
of the Genealogical figures made for the quire clerestory in 1178–90
and moved here in 1792. With the later glass in the tracery, they
have all been recently restored. The W. window is by Christopher
Whall (1903).

Lastly the **S. nave aisle**, where the monuments are mostly 19th c.
A 17th c. one in the second bay is to Robert Berkeley and in the
third is one by Michael Rysbrack to John Sympson (d. 1752). Those
in the last three bays before the porch all have Australian
connections: a governor, a bishop and a philanthropist.

The **cloister** can be reached by turning right outside the porch and
right again, past the tower and (with the Archbishop's Palace
straight ahead) through a doorway into its SW. angle. The arcades
and vaults are of 1390–1411; renewal of the badly decayed
stonework has been in progress for about twenty years. The big ogee
arch-frames are remarkable; so are the many hundreds of bosses,
mostly heraldic, in the lierne vaults. Look first along the S. walk,
but go up the W. walk. From here there is a view across to the

chapter house, with the library on its left and the N. transept on its right. In the fourth bay is a late 17th c. memorial, and at the end a little hatch into the cellarer's quarters for handing out refreshment. On the N. side early 13th c. arcading is broken into by the later vault shafts and by a doorway to the refectory (now to the Archdeacon's House garden). The enlarged bays opposite were the monks' washplace. The E. wall is more complex, with first a Norman doorway to the dormitory undercroft (now library), then a 15th c. one to the groin-vaulted passage called Dark Entry, then early 14th c. windows and doorway to the chapter house (superimposed on walling with 12th c. arches still visible), then 15th c. doorways to the slype and finally to the N. transept.

Now back to the **chapter house**. Though the walls are mostly early 12th c., the furthest one represents a 14th c. extension, and the wooden roof and window tracery are 15th c. It is rectangular and plain, with less ornament in the 14th c. seat arcading than is normal.

Back again to the Dark Entry, which is a late 11th c. passage under the end of the dormitory. By going through into the **Infirmary Cloister** and turning left (under three rebuilt bays) one can see the original vast extent of the whole undercroft, and thus of the dormitory. The rebuilt part above is the main library (by John Denman, 1954). Looking back towards the cathedral, four Norman arches support a passage that led from the dormitory to the NE. transept; in it are two inserted 15th c. windows. There is also ground-level access at this point into the crypt transept. To the left is the water tower, a unique Norman structure also with 15th c. windows above, and behind it rises the eight-storeyed Norman stair tower.

E. of the water tower is another open undercroft, 13th c. It once supported the Prior's chapel. In its place at the upper level is now the 17th c. brick Howley Library. Steps also lead from this undercroft to the upper transept. Going off to the N., i.e. forming the E. arm of the Infirmary Cloister, is another Norman undercroft; above that is the brick Wolfson Library by Harold Anderson (1966). The alley leads on northwards through the late 15th c. Prior's Gateway into Green Court, which is now really part of King's School, and here can be seen the great Norman staircase of the monks' almonry close by the fine 12th c. gatehouse to this side of the priory, and the monastic brewery, bakehouse and granary, as well as the Tudor façade of the Deanery.

Turning back towards the cathedral, the third 15th c. doorway on the left leads out into the infirmary hall, with the treasury,

projecting from St Andrew's chapel, on the right. The roofless hall
with its chapel at the far end retains its stately S. arcade. To the
right now is Edward the Confessor's chapel perched on the side of
the Trinity chapel, and a view right through the crypt below. Still
moving E., the 14th c. flint building on the left is Table Hall (the
infirmary), now the choir school. The chancel arch of the infirmary
chapel stands, and the roadway actually goes right through the
chancel and out on the S. side; in the N. wall are examples of the
14th c. tracery patterns peculiar to Kent. Ahead is the former priory
guest house, called Meister Omers (*c.* 1400).

Finally back down the S. side of the cathedral, a walk not to be
hurried. First are the Corona and the Trinity chapel, wholly late
12th c., then St Anselm's with another stair tower, the SE. transept
with the Huguenot church entrance, and the S. quire aisle: all early
12th c. from crypt upwards except that the clerestory was rebuilt
with the interior later in the same century. The wall-arcading and
the strong patterns of the window ironwork are especially
noteworthy. Then comes the S. transept with its E. chapels, and the
nave, all 15th c., and lastly the S. porch again.

Cardiff, St David (Roman Catholic, South Glamorgan)

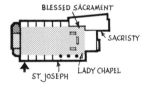

The diocese was formerly that of Newport, although its cathedral
was at Belmont in Herefordshire. Peter Paul Pugin's church in
Cardiff, built in 1884–7 to replace one of the 1840s became a co-
cathedral in 1916 and replaced Belmont altogether in 1920. It was
badly damaged by bombs in 1941 and restored by F. R. Bates in
1959.

The extremely wide nave, though traditional Gothic in detail, has
an advanced plan for its date, giving everyone a clear view of the
altar without obstructing arcades; instead, individual arches beneath
the tall windows lead to confessionals, porches and side chapels. The
new timber roof trusses, fully exposed, are of hammer-beam form
with ties added – all except the hammer-beams being of quite flimsy

appearance. The big chancel arch and the gallery arches are of buff stone, the remainder mostly light grey-painted stone and rough-cast. The net-like tracery of the circular E. window is by Bates; the clerestory windows retain Pugin's Geometric patterns and have alternate clear and coloured glazing, the latter being restorations, no doubt of Hardman originals. Modern again are the ring light-fittings with pendant cylinders, the tiara-like baldacchino at the E. end, and the ceramic Stations of the Cross by Adam Kossowski.

The baptistry is still in the NW. corner under the tower, past the doors to the main W. lobby; the font repeats the 'net' motif of the E. window (both being probably inspired by the varied tracery of the stone communion rail). The N. side is taken up largely with confessionals, but one bay is formed into a chapel in memory of Father Stephen Bruno. The E. end, again re-ordered since the post-war rebuilding, now has the archbishop's throne under the baldacchino (the former throne from Belmont). The Blessed Sacrament chapel on the N., separated by an iron screen, has a modern altar with sharply pointed reredos. Access to the Lady chapel, corresponding on the S. side, and to the areas beyond has been sacrificed to the needs of the extended raised quire. A brass eagle lectern has been discarded there.

In the third bay from the E. is a Pietà; in the fourth, the chapel of St Joseph with an ineffective Gothic reredos. The angular stone pulpit is post-war, with banal zigzag ornament. From this angle the excellent W. window can be well seen, evidently another work of Hardman & Co.

An external tour can start along the S. side where new ancillary buildings are to be erected. At the time of writing large areas to both E. and N. (the cathedral's orientation is reversed) were also cleared for rebuilding and a general NE. view of the rock-faced exterior was being opened up – grey-brown stone with redder dressings. To go round the whole backland of shops and thence into Charles Street is hardly worth while; quicker to retrace one's steps to the W. front, an uninspired grouping with asymmetrical tower (the statue below the belfry is naturally St David), big main W. window and insignificant doorway.

Carlisle, Holy Trinity (Church of England, Cumbria)

The bishopric was set up in 1133 in a priory which had been founded in 1102. Only ten years before that Carlisle had been re-

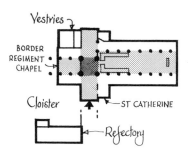

Vestries

BORDER
REGIMENT
CHAPEL

Cloister

ST CATHERINE

Refectory

taken from the Scots. The now truncated nave and much of the transepts are early 12th c. The quire is partly early 13th c., but a fire in 1291 caused it to be reconstructed in its present form. Six bays of the nave were destroyed in the Civil War, the stone being used to repair the castle and build a guard house (now demolished) near the old Guild Hall. The principal restoration was under Ewan Christian in 1856–7.

The first oddity can be seen immediately on entering the 19th c. S. transept doorway – tall 14th c. tower arches raised on shorter Norman piers with the earlier capitals left in place (or possibly moved to a lower position) half-way up. The S. transept itself is clearly Norman (though the wooden roof is 19th c.) and so are the arches to the nave aisles. The N. tower arch has Perpendicular tracery in its upper part, originally forming a window to light the crossing. Serious settlement of the tower foundations occurred about 1250 – as can be seen from the extraordinarily misshapen arch into the **S. nave aisle**.

Till 1870 what was left of the nave and aisles served as the parish church of St Mary and was cut off from the rest of the cathedral. Since 1948 it has formed the chapel of the Border Regiment, the centre part being enclosed by iron screens and hung with regimental colours. The S. aisle contains regimental memorials, collective and individual, and at its W. end is the tomb of Bishop Waldegrave (d. 1869), with effigy by John Adams-Acton. The **nave**, if it can still be called that, has short, very sturdy circular piers, blind triforium (big arched openings not subdivided at all) and quite simple clerestory with triple openings. The W. window is of 1870. Eastward are the great organ pipes above the quire entrance, and above them a 15th c. tierceron vault.

The **N. nave aisle** contains the font, of 1890, by Sir Arthur Blomfield in a kind of Decorated style with bronze figures at the

corners. Of the tablets on the W. wall the biggest is to Melchior
Beaume, 'late of Bengal' (d. 1795). In the N. wall are doorways to
vestries, dated 1957, and one window has fragments of old glass.

The **N. transept** is a mixture; at first Norman, much of it was
rebuilt early in the 15th c. with the tower. The big N. window which
appears 14th c. may in fact be post-Civil War; its glass is of 1858. In
the E. wall is the built-up archway to the N. quire aisle of the
Norman cathedral; it was blocked when the new quire was built
because that had been made wider than the Norman one and the
extra width was gained entirely on the N. side. In the 13th c. a start
was made on an enlarged N. transept by forming a new column and
arch for an E. aisle, but no further progress was made. The only
monument of importance in the transept is the simple early 16th c.
tomb-chest of Prior Senhouse.

Heavy black iron gates lead to the **N. quire aisle**. From this side
the one bay of Early English arcade with its dog-tooth ornament is
prominent, and the confused state of the top of the arch, caused by
settlement, is very curious; no doubt that is why the idea of the E.
aisle was abandoned The canted N. wall of the end bay dates from
the 15th c. when the transept was rebuilt in its present form. Now,
moving E., on the back of the stalls on the right are paintings of the
legend of St Anthony, *c*. 1500. Opposite are two late 18th c.
monuments. From the second bay onwards is basically Early English,
with shafted aisle windows and cinquefoil-headed wall-arcade with
dog-tooth. The vaults and the main arcades, as will be seen
presently, are rather later. The second and third bays of the quire
stalls have more paintings: the twelve Apostles and then the story of
St Cuthbert. In the fourth bay is a splendid screen of about 1540
with early Renaissance detail.

In the fifth bay the **quire** architecture can be examined: Decorated
clustered columns (probably earlier ones redressed) with carved
capitals, triforium of little openings in threes, and double clerestory
with passage. All this work was subsequent to the 1291 fire, though
the aisle vaults are unlikely to have been rebuilt. The easternmost
bay is wholly Decorated. The panelled wagon roof has a curious
history. Probably early 16th c., it at first had tie-beams and king-
posts but in 1720 these were cut out and a plaster ceiling put in. In
1856 Christian had that pulled down, exposing the wooden panels
again (they are unusual in being curved, not flat), and Owen Jones
provided the blue colouring with gold stars (re-done in 1970). What
look like hammer-beams are thus the sawn-off ends of tie-beams.

The pulpit was made in 1559 for the church of St Andrew,

Antwerp, but came to the cathedral in the 1960s from Cockayne
Hatley church in Bedfordshire. From within the quire the lop-sided
W. end should be noticed, with a blocked Norman arch and part of
the old transept triforium showing clearly how the present quire
absorbed the N. aisle of the Norman one. The baldacchino, now
richly coloured and gilded to match the roof, is by Sir Charles
Nicholson. Beyond, the E. window with its splendid flowing tracery
has glass mostly of 1861 by Hardman; but some at the top is 14th c.

Returning to the N. quire aisle, there are two tomb recesses, one
with the worn effigy of a 13th c. bishop. At the E. end is the tomb of
another bishop, with early 14th c. effigy; above it is a tablet to
Gustav Thompson (d. 1756). In the ambulatory behind the altar are
some minor tablets and a piscina; then, on the E. wall of the **S. quire
aisle**, a bronze tablet to Bishop Bardsley (d. 1904) by Andrea
Lucchesi, typically Italian of the Art Nouveau period. In the third
bay on the S. wall is a wordy pictorial brass to Bishop Robinson
(d. 1616); also another blank tomb recess. Various memorials to
recent deans and canons line this wall. Next, into the **quire** again to
look at the fittings in the W. part.

On the left, the bishop's throne is by G. E. Street (*c.* 1880). The
lower stalls are by Nicholson, extended in 1976 by Stephen Dykes
Bower; the upper ones are early 15th c., with tall canopies, carved
stall ends and fine misericords. Under the rug in the centre can be
found the big 15th c. brass of Bishop Bell. Before leaving the quire
look again at the carvings of the main pier capitals: each represents
a month, commencing with January above the S. end of the
communion rail.

In the **S. quire aisle** again, another set of paintings on the backs of
the stalls represents the story of St Augustine of Hippo. Notice the
two-faced devil at the bottom left (the extra face is on his rear
quarters) – meant to horrify but now quaintly amusing. Beyond is
an effigy of Dean Close (d. 1885) by H. H. Armstead in white
marble under a heavy wooden Gothic canopy, and one of Bishop
Goodwin (d. 1891) by Sir Hamo Thornycroft in bronze. The
wooden screen opposite is of *c.* 1500 and encloses **St Catherine's
chapel**; the rich tracery is of Flamboyant (i.e Scottish) type. The
chapel, reserved for private prayer, is approached from the S.
transept through a similar screen. Unlike the N. side, the arch is still
Norman, though the chapel itself was rebuilt in the 13th c. Its vault
springs from carved corbels. The alabaster Crucifix is medieval
Nottingham work; the S. window is by Christopher Whall (1916).

Architecturally the **S. transept** is like the nave. On the E. side, to

Double doorway to Cloister, Carlisle (13th c.)

the left of the chapel entrance, is a good marble bust of George
Moore (d. 1876). In the SE. corner is the medallion head of a
sculptor, Musgrave Watson (d. 1847); above is a bulbous cartouche
to Dorothy Dacre (d. 1761). Another tablet commemorates Bishop
Fleming, whose 'regretted Dissolution' took place in 1747, and
below is that of a child, Elizabeth Dunbar (d. 1821), daughter of
another sculptor. The tablet in the SW. corner is to Bishop
Fleming's wife (d. 1736). In the W. wall is a Runic stone, translated
as 'Tolfink wrote these Runes on this stone'.

   Outside, the S. transept front is largely by Christian. Ahead, the
path follows the E. range of monastic buildings: the double
doorway on the right led into the cloister, the single one on the left
probably to the night stair. The beginnings of the vault which
supported the dormitory above are visible. At the end on the right is
the 14th c. refectory which is virtually complete and restored for use
as a library (not normally open). Behind it is the Deanery or Prior's
Lodging which incorporates a pele or fortified tower of *c.* 1510. The

roadway runs between the Registry of 1699 on the left, and the 18th
century No. 2 Canonry on the right, to the Gatehouse of 1527.
Through this, a right turn leads into Paternoster Row and from
there can be seen the W. wall of the cathedral, also by Christian,
and the leaning Norman wall of the N. nave aisle with the 1957
vestries below. Castle Street provides a complete view of the N.
transept and 15th c. tower, and then of the 13th c. quire aisle and
14th c. upper part. The big iron gates back into the precinct (called
the Abbey) by the E. end are of 1930. Finally the interest of the S.
wall centres on the variations in window design, with examples
ranging from no tracery at all to full bar tracery in the Decorated E.
bay. The blocked openings in the third bay once led to a sacristy.

Chelmsford, St Mary, St Peter & St Cedd (Church of England,
Essex)

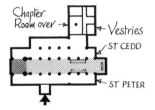

Though Chelmsford cathedral is only a slightly enlarged parish
church, its diocese, founded in 1914, is the second largest Anglican
one in England in terms of population. To all appearances 15th c., it
has in fact had several phases of alteration since. Following a
collapse, the nave was rebuilt in 1801–3 by John Johnson. The outer
N. aisle and transept were added in 1873, and the chancel was
extended a little and the chapter house and vestries added on the N.
in 1923–6 by Sir Charles Nicholson.

The **S. porch**, externally ornamented with flint flushwork in true
East Anglian style, has been embellished internally to commemorate
U.S.A. associations; the emblems used are all explained in a framed
description. The library on the upper floor is open on Tuesday
evenings only.

The interior of the **nave** and aisles is largely due to Johnson. The
tall arcades and clerestory are copies of the 15th c. work but on the
S. side he used Coade stone in the columns. His nave ceiling, with a

Cathedral from N., Chelmsford

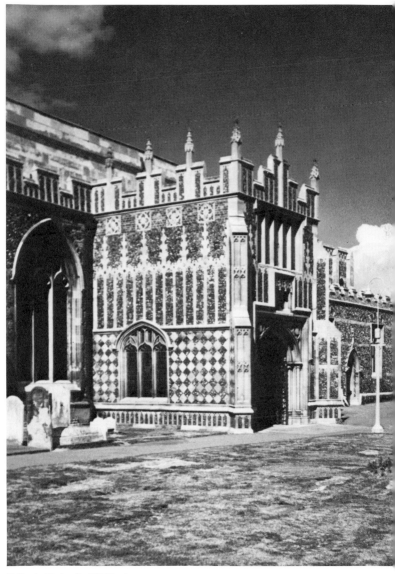

S. Porch, Chelmsford (15th c.)

sort of fan-vault panel pattern in plaster, and angel corbels supported on cherubs, was coloured and gilded in 1961. The low-pitched wooden S. aisle roof is no doubt a replica of the original. A gallery from the porch overhangs the aisle, and just W. of it is a window of 1905 in William Morris style. Memorials each side are to the Essex Yeomanry. The font is of 1869 and the incised window at the W. end of the S. wall is by John Hutton. The broken stone coffin lid by the tower pier is 13th c.

The **tower** ceiling is 15th c. and its Nativity W. window is by A. K. Nicholson (*c*. 1950). Below are two 17th c. chests, one plain and one arcaded, and some black marble ledger stones. In the **N. aisle** are preserved two inscribed pieces of 17th and 18th c. roof lead and the matrix of a brass with three figures. On the right are three 17th c. brass inscriptions. The aisle widens, with the extra arcade added in 1873. Over the N. doorway, close to the bookstall, hang four banners (three of them of the Essex Local Militia) and further along the aisle are a nice wall tablet to Robert Bownd (d. 1696) and a carved chair. The **N. transept**, also of 1873, is largely occupied by the organ, rebuilt in 1932–3, and beyond that is a passage to the vestries and chapter house. On the organ case hangs the cathedral banner by Beryl Dean (1960). Against the E. wall is the curious and uninspired Mildmay monument of 1571, newly coloured and gilded.

The **N. chapel**, St Cedd's, has a magnificent deeply carved late 17th c. communion rail with angels and grapes, said to have come from Holland. The carved chair is of 1614 and the big monument with giant urn and yellow columns is to a later Mildmay, Earl Fitzwalter (d. 1756). Two smaller early 18th c. memorials are on the E. wall.

The 15th c. arcade into the **quire** on this side is unusual, the W. bays being one round 'fan-arch' divided by a slender column into two pointed ones. The clerestory and low-pitched timber-roof, added above the old chancel by Sir Arthur Blomfield in 1878, were continued by Nicholson in two more bays of virtually the same design. He also re-used Blomfield's E. window, incorporating Clayton & Bell glass of 1858, and above his piscina and triple sedilia stands the wood figure of Bishop Watts-Ditchfield, first bishop of the diocese. The cathedral has a notable set of modern frontals and dossal curtains for its 'English' high altar. The pinnacled bishop's throne is by Sir Charles Nicholson, as well as the canons' stalls within the sanctuary. The stalls outside the sanctuary are 19th c., except that the provost's in the SW. corner is of 1936, by Wykeham Chancellor. The communion rail is a continuation of that in the N.

chapel, but formed in a gentle curve. The 'pelican in her piety' in the
left section is a specially fine piece of carving.

Delicate iron gates in a stone screen lead to the **S. chapel**
(St Peter's). Within the screen is the tomb of Archdeacon Mildmay
(d. 1878). The hanging lamp is Italian, and the plain low-pitched
roof was rebuilt in 1899. Of the many wall tablets on the S. wall the
best is that to Mary Marsh (d. 1787). The screen to the aisle was
designed by Chancellor; close to it is a brass-like incised tablet in an
alabaster frame showing the kneeling family of Mathew Rudd
(d. 1615).

In the **S. aisle** it is easy to see that the column bases are original
and that the stone changes at about waist height. The clear glass
window with emblems of the archdeaconries of the diocese is of
1971. Finally, in the nave, the marble pulpit is of 1873.

Outside the porch, turn left. After its flintwork, the aisle is plain
stone and the chapel and E. end are flint again. On the corner of the
chapel is a carving of St Peter in modern fisherman's dress by T. B.
Huxley-Jones. Nicholson's extensions, once pointed out, are clear
enough but blend well in design and materials. They comprise the
projecting sanctuary and the vestry block.

The big sweep of churchyard contains numerous old tombs
including four prominent ones in the E. part and another by the
path to the N. door. At the W. end, the colour of both aisles is
varied with a good deal of brickwork. The W. door has a boar in the
head of its arch; the de Vere star and de Bouchier knot can also be
seen. The tower is typically East Anglian of the 15th c., with flint
and stone ornament in its battlements; below these are more
carvings by Huxley-Jones. The lantern is of 1747 and the copper
spire with dragon weather-vane largely of 1932; it is best seen from
the SW. corner of the churchyard.

Chester, Christ & St Mary (Church of England, Cheshire)

This was one of the abbeys raised to cathedral rank by Henry VIII,
the last abbot becoming the first dean. A minster dedicated to
St Werburgh had been founded on the site in 907 to house his relics
and it was re-established in 1092 by St Anselm as a Benedictine
monastery. It is of interest that there was a cathedral elsewhere in
Chester, where the present church of St John the Baptist stands,
from 1075 to 1085.

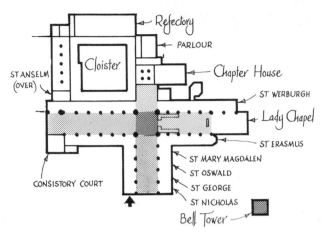

Original Norman work remains in the N. transept and incomplete W. tower, and in the W. parts of the cloister buildings. The Lady chapel is of *c.* 1270, the quire was rebuilt *c.* 1300, and the crossing slightly later, along with the much enlarged S. transept. Rebuilding of the nave was begun in the mid-14th c. but not completed (together with the S. porch and central tower) till the end of the 15th c. Successive restorations were done in the course of the 19th and early 20th cc. by Thomas Harrison, R. C. Hussey, Sir George Gilbert Scott and his grandson Sir Giles, and Sir Arthur Blomfield and his son Charles, and have confused the already complex interminglings of medieval work which had (and has) decayed badly through the use of soft red sandstone. The detached belfry was added by George Pace in 1973–5.

This tour begins at the **S. transept** entrance. The transept is aisled and as big as the quire. Its arcades and aisles are late Decorated, but the tall clerestory with quatrefoiled gallery is Perpendicular. The tierceron vaults, low as well as high, are almost wholly 19th c., that of the E. aisle being of wood. The big S. window's tracery is by Sir Arthur Blomfield and its glass by Heaton, Butler and Bayne (1887). The crossing arches are early 14th c., and beyond is the organ, with case by Scott.

Now the W. aisle of the transept in detail, starting in the entrance bay with two 18th c. tablets and a big, black, homely Gurney stove. Under the first two main arches are rolls of honour of the Cheshire Regiment. In the second bay stands a carillon mechanism of 1867;

Cathedral from SE., Chester

of the memorials nearby the most noteworthy is to John Buchanan, killed at Waterloo in 1815. The big bronze-railed tomb-chest under the third arch is of the first Duke of Westminster (d. 1899); it was designed by Charles Blomfield and the effigy is by F. W. Pomeroy. The three 18th c. wall tablets nearby are to members of the Booth family. Next on the left is a propeller R.A.F. memorial and on the right a chest of 1687. Another, 18th c., chest is at the nave aisle junction, and on the actual corner is a 14th c. niche.

Go past Francis Skidmore's brass lectern (1876) and into the **nave**. This was begun soon after the S. transept and is very similar in design except that the gallery is plainer and the vault is a wooden lierne one (by Scott, replacing an open timber roof). Also the easternmost arch on both sides is narrower, probably because these were built first as part of the crossing structure. The W. endings of the arcades, against intended towers, can be looked at presently. Perhaps the most interesting thing about the nave is that the S. side was built over a century later than the N., but differs from it only in minute details. In the E. corner of the window over the pulpit is the 'Chester Imp', a stone carving of a chained devil.

The **S. nave aisle** has a tierceron vault, also by Scott, and numerous minor tablets. A small brass in the second bay is to Mary Lloyd (d. 1684) and two 19th c. memorials in the fifth (porch) bay are of minor interest: to John Ford (d. 1807) and to Edward Jones (d. 1834). At the end seven steps and a pair of studded doors with 17th c. plaster strapwork over them lead to the **consistory court**. This room was the early 16th c. beginning of a SW. tower: the court furniture (chancellor's throne, table, box seating and benches) are of 1635 and there is a curious corner seat, high like an umpire's, said to have been for the apparitor who delivered the court's orders.

Back in the **nave**, the W. end should first be looked at. The brilliant W. window with figures is by W. T. Carter Shapland (1961). To the left amongst no fewer than ten wall memorials those to Bishop Stratford (d. 1708), Bishop Hall (d. 1668), and Edmund Entwhistle (d. 1707), are the most prominent. Pushed into the SW. corner is a black marble baluster font of 1697. On the W. wall the monument with naïve cherubs to John and Thomas Wainwright (*c.* 1720) was designed by William Kent; the rich tablet to the right with twisted columns and weeping cherub is to Sir William Mainwaring (d. 1644). On the N. side is the 12th c. arch to the former NW. tower, and on the blank wall to its right a tall early Gothic Revival monument to Roger Barnston (d. 1837).

Here is the best eastward view of the nave, with Scott's quire screen prominent, and at the end of the quire a window over the arch to the Lady chapel. The W. bay of the **N. aisle**, the former tower space, is the baptistry and has Norman arches on all sides including a blocked one in the W. wall and a window in the N. wall which opens into St Anselm's chapel. The big rectangular font on four groups of four shafts and with a tall pyramidal cover – all looking too heavy for the supports – came from Venice in 1885 and is probably not ancient. In the second bay is the **cloister** doorway. The cloister walls were rebuilt about 1525–37, and their vaults and worn but once fine corbels cut into the surrounding work without compunction. They were restored from near-ruin by Sir Giles Gilbert Scott in 1911–13. The W. walk has a kind of aisle on the right, each bay being a carrel or reading space; in them now are 13th and 14th c. coffin-lids. On the left is a late Norman window, also a doorway leading to a rib-vaulted undercroft used as a store.

Straight ahead another Norman doorway leads into a small vestibule to the right of which is the **refectory**. Basically Norman, this was altered about 1300. It was largely restored by Sir Giles Gilbert Scott, but the hammer-beam roof is of 1939, by F. H. Crossley; the line of the former lower roof can easily be seen. The big tapestry was made at Mortlake in 1515, the scene from the Acts of the Apostles being based on cartoons by Raphael for the Sistine Chapel. The twenty painted shields came from the former organ screen, removed in 1844. At the E. end is the dais for the 'high table' and to its right the well-preserved pulpit from which readings were made during meals, reached by a delightful open arcaded stair in the wall thickness. Refreshments are usually available to visitors in this dignified setting.

On the other side of the vestibule is the cathedral shop in another rib-vaulted undercroft; its iron screen and fittings are by George Pace. There is also an exit at this point into Abbey Square.

Now turn back into the cloister and left along the N. walk. On the left is the main Norman doorway into the refectory; into it a cusped Decorated arch has been inserted. Later vaulting and corbels are superimposed – as also upon the three bays of washplace beyond. The cinquefoil-headed doorway ahead leads to the parlour and dormitory stair. The big quatrefoil window round the corner lights this stair. Beyond is the slype or vaulted passage leading outside; then a restored 13th c. triple arcade to the **chapter house** lobby. The vaulting behind is unusual in being carried on columns without capitals. The chapter house itself, also 13th c., has double shafted windows all round, and a tierceron vault. It is used as a library and

has at the far end a cupboard with 13th c. ironwork and a great
disused wooden eagle lectern.

Continuing around the cloister (passing another door back into
the cathedral), the S. walk with its vaults is entirely reconstructed
but stands against the obviously Norman N. wall of the cathedral.
Some of the low arches, probably originally book cupboards, are
said to cover tombs of abbots. Beyond are a 13th and a 14th c.
tomb-slab and then the doorway back into the **N. aisle**. Its windows
are high because of the cloister; the mosaics under them, depicting
incidents from the lives of Abraham, Moses, David and Elijah, are
by J. R. Clayton, 1883. On the right the Gothic stone pulpit is by
Hussey (*c.* 1850), and the nave stalls are by Pace (1966); those facing
the altar incorporate panels from a pulpit of 1637. An iron mace rest
is of 1921, and on the back of the stalls is a little gilded oval
Ascension, a German carving of *c.* 1700.

The short **N. transept** exhibits the most impressive Norman work
in the cathedral, probably of *c.* 1100; the arch in the E. wall led into
an apsidal chapel. The top parts however are all Perpendicular,
including the roof with big gilded bosses. Being hemmed in by the
cloister and chapter house, this transept stayed in its original form
when the S. was so greatly enlarged. The central tomb-chest
commemorates the theologian Bishop Pearson (d. 1686), but is in
fact of 1863; the heads around it are of the Apostles. On the W. wall
is a processional cross stave, probably 17th c. Flemish and of
narwhal ivory. Amongst the wall tablets are three of particular
interest: to Colonel Egerton, who died at Sevastopol in 1855,
Edward Massy (d. 1836), a very similar composition, and Henry
Moor (d. 1837) with his bust ('skied'). The N. side is taken up with
the organ. On the E. is a screen of 1974 by Pace, closing off the
vaulted Early English chapel to form a vestry.

The iron gates into the **N. quire aisle** are of 1558 and came from
Guadalajara in Spain. On the right of the aisle the column bases of
the Norman quire have been exposed. The stone screenwork is from
the pulpitum that was dismembered by Scott.

In the fourth bay it is a good idea to turn aside into the **quire**
itself. This is of *c.* 1300 and thus Decorated in style, with well-
defined clustered columns, triforium of four small trefoil-headed
arches per bay, clerestory, and timber vault by Scott painted by
Clayton & Bell. The iron and wood communion rail is typical work
of Pace; the big candlesticks are early 17th c. Italian and the mosaic
reredos and floor are by Antonio Salviati and J. R. Clayton (1876).

Leaving the rest of the quire for the moment and continuing

along its aisle, there is a short junction-bay with a double piscina before the vaulted 15th c. St Werburgh's chapel. On its left is a ponderous wall tablet to William Bispham (d. 1685), with brass inscription. The canopied tomb to the right of the altar is of Bishop Graham (d. 1867).

Next the vaulted **Lady chapel** in the usual eastern position. Built *c*. 1270, it was last restored and re-coloured in 1960 by Bernard Miller. The copper-coned pendant lights are by Duncan Stewart, and the unusual and attractive glass with circular and vesica-shaped medallions is by William Wailes (1859). The sedilia and double piscina are probably reconstructions. At the W. end is the 14th c. shrine of St Werburgh, reassembled from fragments. Behind it is an Ascension painting, and a gap at the side of the high altar gives a good close-up view of the rich Decorated sedilia. These were originally in St John's church but not of course at the time it was a cathedral.

It is necessary to return to the N. quire aisle to enter the **quire** again. The wooden eagle lectern is early 17th c., and the bishop's throne is by Scott (1876). The stalls, the greatest glory of the cathedral, are late 14th c., rich with busy pinnacled canopies and poppyheads and with a marvellous series of misericords, and time should be allowed to study them. The screen at the W. end with its towering central canopy is however also by Scott (but added to by his grandson Sir Giles) and through it one passes to the **crossing** to see its W. face more closely. The gates are by Francis Skidmore and the rood figures by Ferdinand Stuflesser (1913). The marble-columned organ gallery and fretted case, filling the N. transept arch and topped by silvery angels, are by Scott too. The red and gold ceiling pattern of the crossing is by Pace.

On the right pier of the S. transept arch is a quaint memorial with standing figures of Thomas Greene (d. 1662) and his two wives. The entrance to **St Erasmus's chapel** in the S. quire aisle is marked by another Guadalajara gate. This part is reserved for private prayer. The vaults and the reconstruction of the apsed end are all Scott's. On the left are the backs of the sedilia and (in the sanctuary) tablets to Bishop Peploe (d. 1752) and Thomas Brassey (*c*. 1880, not *c*. 1770 as it seems). The 15th c. recess opposite it is a niche and the mosaic dado (1877) is again by Clayton and Salviati. The Resurrection window at the E. end of the S. wall was designed by Augustus Pugin. Along the S. wall (moving W.) come a Geometric double piscina and sedilia, two 14th c. tomb recesses, and the plain tomb-slab of the historian Ranulph Higden (d. 1364). Next are three good wall tablets of around 1700 and a black tomb-chest of unknown date. In the last bay, backing on to the transept, are several unsophisticated monuments, some of them repainted: a rustic inscription to William Case (d. 1644), a heraldic brass to Foulke Aldersey (d. 1577), painted heraldic boards to John Lecke (d. 1639) and Katherine Wynne (d. 1698), and a simple tablet to Robert Bennet (d. 1626).

Four banner-hung chapels occupy the E. aisle of the **S. transept**. St Mary Magdalen's has a red Gothic triptych by W. E. Tower (1922). In St Oswald's the reredos is by his partner Charles Kempe and was carved at Oberammergau. St George's, the Cheshire Regiment chapel, has an uncoloured triptych in Sir Giles Gilbert Scott's Spanish Gothic. Last is St Nicholas and St Leonard's, quite differently furnished by the same architect and containing the standards captured at Quebec by General Wolfe. Finally, on the end wall of the transept are a damaged piscina and sedilia, a classical tablet to Sir William Gerrarde (d. 1581), a South African War memorial, and two similar monuments with mourning women to George Ogden (d. 1788) and Anne Matthews (d. 1793).

Now the **exterior** taken clockwise, starting with the war memorial on the green between nave and transept. Genuine Decorated and Perpendicular design details are mingled with inventions of the restorers: the tower top and turrets by Scott, the aisle windows by Hussey, the S. transept turrets by Harrison, all the flying buttresses by Scott. The S. porch, along with what is now the consistory court to its left, is early 16th c., but the fan vault of the former is due to George Gilbert Scott junior.

The early 16th c. W. front is partly covered by a bank building which was once part of the abbot's house and then became King's School. The frieze of angel musicians over the main W. doorway into the cathedral is largely original. From here one has to go round the bank and through the 14th c. Abbey Gate into Abbey Square – mostly dignified Georgian but on its E. side a mixture culminating in the picturesque Lay Clerk's House on the site of the refectory kitchen. From here is a good NW. view of the cathedral. The railed-in area covers the cloister W. range undercroft and leads to St Anselm's chapel (originally the prior's private chapel) which can be seen on request. (It adjoins the NW. tower and though also essentially 12th c. it contains work of many different periods, including a 17th c. chancel with screen and communion rail and a pretty 19th c. plaster main vault).

Off the E. side of Abbey Square is Abbey Street. From its right a path edged with old roof bosses leads to the E. end of the refectory and one can then walk close beside the cloister buildings (parlour or warming room), the 13th c. chapter house (the E. wall is due to Blomfield) and the quire and Lady chapel. The detached bell-tower straight ahead across the Garden of Remembrance as one rounds the E. end is by Pace (1973) and has a concrete frame and slate facing. On its N. façade is a foundation stone and from there is a good SE. view of the cathedral including the tall stone spire which Scott put on the end of St Erasmus's chapel, claiming there had been evidence of a similar original feature. In the centre of the garden is the cenotaph of the Royal Cheshire Regiment.

Chichester, Holy Trinity (Church of England, Sussex)

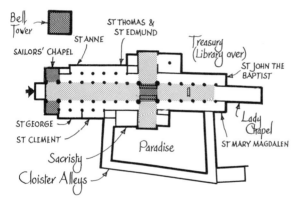

The see founded at Selsey in 711 was moved inland to Chichester in 1075. A new cathedral was begun there about twenty years later and consecrated in 1184. It comprises the greater part of the present building, moving forward in style very little from Norman. After a serious fire in 1187 the apsidal E. end was taken down and replaced by the straight-ended retro-quire and corner chapels. Similarly the round-ended transept chapels were enlarged to square. The clerestories were virtually rebuilt and vaults added. Late in the 13th c. the outer nave aisles were added and the Lady chapel lengthened. The transepts were remodelled early in the 14th c. The cloister and the detached bell-tower were built about 1400 and the central spire during the 15th c.

The spire collapsed inwards on itself in 1861 and was photographed doing so; Sir George Gilbert Scott rebuilt it. Pearson rebuilt the NW. tower from a ruin in 1901. 19th c. restoration work was otherwise modest in extent. Important structural repairs have, however, been in progress since the 1960s under Robert Potter.

The **bell-tower**, close to West Street, now contains the cathedral shop. The plain lower part is late 14th c., and the upper with octagonal lantern 15th c. It is the only surviving detached medieval cathedral bell-tower in England. The eight bells are variously of the 16th to 18th cc.

From the steps down to the W. front, note the 13th c. N. porch: rather cramped and now disused, it has a twin outer arch. The W. porch, with new plate glass doors, is larger and contains damaged tomb recesses on either side. It leads centrally into the **nave**, with the view beyond into the quire punctuated by the pulpitum or Arundel screen. The arcade system – walls pierced with openings, rather than arches on columns – is evidently late 11th c. in origin. But the clerestory, partially rebuilt after the 1187 fire, is largely Early English, also the nave and aisle vaults. There is much to study in the way Gothic work has been moulded on to Norman: the middle arch of the clerestory is round, not pointed, shafts have been carried down from the vault and visually tied in with rings, little Purbeck marble columns with foliage have been tucked in beside the older heavy ones, and so on. Moreover there are many subtle points of difference between bay and bay, and in addition the one next to the crossing was rebuilt following the collapse of the spire. The arcades continue across the towers with only a wider pier to mark the join; inside, however, the towers are hollow through four storeys. The **NW**. one, rebuilt by Pearson, contains the **Sailors' chapel** of St Michael and has memorials to seamen, late 18th and early 19th c., some flags, and the bell of H.M.S. *Sussex*.

The **N. aisle** soon widens out with a second arcade of *c.* 1270, quite richly moulded. This vaulted outer aisle was originally three separate chapels; various recesses and a part of one separating wall with shafts of its reredos remain. The glass all along portrays local worthies and is by Christopher Webb (1949). The prominent standing figure at the W. end is the Member of Parliament William Huskisson (d. 1830), said to have been the first man ever killed by a train. The centre memorial on the N. wall to Henry Frankland (d. 1823) is by John Flaxman. Moving E., the knight and lady under the arcade are an earl of Arundel who died in 1376 or 1397 and his wife; one gauntlet is off so that their hands may touch. On the outer

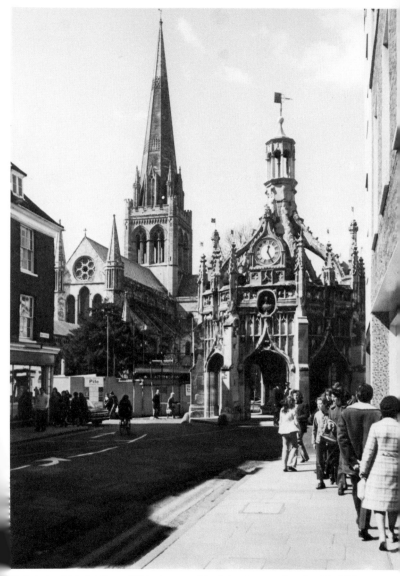

Cathedral and Market Cross, Chichester, a combined view temporarily enjoyed in 1973 during rebuilding of a shop

wall are more Flaxman female figures, to Thomas Ball (d. 1819).
The E. bay of the aisle, earlier than the rest, is still the chapel of
St. Thomas and St Edmund; its triple-arched reredos is original.

Back in the N. aisle, on the S. side is a memorial to Edmund
Woods (d. 1833): like Huskisson's it is by J. E. Carew. Then on the
left, against the chapel screen, a worn figure, possibly of another
countess of Arundel, *c.* 1275; this is amongst the earliest English
tombs with 'weepers', a feature imported from France. After this
comes a narrow bay alongside the pulpitum, with steps into the **N.
transept**.

Norman work outweighs the later additions again here, but as in
the nave the upper parts and the vault are Early English. The big N.
window is late 14th c. Starting from the N. aisle corner, there are
memorials to the composer Thomas Weelkes who d. 1623 (a modern
tablet); Bishop Grove (d. 1696), with weeping cherubs holding his
mitre; the composer Gustav Holst who d. 1934 (a plain floor-slab
nearby); Bishop King (d. 1669); and Bishop Carleton (d. 1685), with
flying cherubs. On the N. wall are wooden roundels with imaginary
portraits of early bishops, done by Lambert Bernard about 1520.
Towards the NE. corner is an old capstone from the spire dated
1814 and then a big arch into the Early English chapel of the Four
Virgins, now used as a treasury. Over it, a plate glass screen in the
triforium arch reveals the first floor library. Though of about 1300,
on graceful round columns with foliage caps, the treasury vault
mysteriously has zigzag ornament of Norman character, perhaps
re-used. Traces of wall-painting remain on the right jamb of the arch
from the transept. The entrance is from the N. quire aisle; in winter
it is open on Saturdays only.

Still in the N. transept: the E. wall has memorials to Eliza
Huskisson (d. 1856) and Rachel Harris (d. 1734). On the SE. pier is
a beautifully lettered slate tablet by John Skelton recording past
deans (similar tablets occur elsewhere in the cathedral) and on the
base of the organ an 18th c. map of Sussex.

On the left of the **N. quire aisle** are two disfigured 16th c. tomb
recesses of a type that recurs throughout the building and does not
justify further mention. Between these is the door to the treasury,
which has a fine display of Sussex church plate, an important 13th c.
chest, etc. On the right is a plain tomb, a scrolly iron screen to the
quire (one of many copied from the Lady chapel gates) and in the
third bay the tomb of Bishop Story (d. 1503), with alabaster effigy.
The inexplicably Jacobean-style monument on the left is to Bishop
Wilberforce (d. 1907). Then comes a bust of Bishop Otter (d. 1840)

and on the right the plain tomb of Bishop Barlow (d. 1570). On the
left amongst several wall tablets are two hands holding a heart, very
worn, said to commemorate Maud, Countess of Warenne and
Surrey (d. 1236). The predominantly red window above, on the
theme of Psalm 150, the Glorification of God, is by Marc Chagall
(1978).

St John the Baptist's chapel at the E. end of the aisle has a
Charles Kempe window and a large monument to Sir John Miller
(d. 1721) and his wife.

The **retro-quire** is unlike other parts of the cathedral because it
was built afresh in replacement of the Norman apse, at the time that
the quire itself and the nave were merely remodelled and provided
with new clerestory and vaulting. It marks an exact transition
between Norman and Gothic. The arch rhythm continues that of the
quire but there is an unusual yet seemingly natural mixture of round
and pointed arches; the middle pier each side, with one large and
four small Purbeck marble shafts, is particularly gracious. The
sculpture, confined in the triforium spandrels at the sides but
spreading around them on the E. wall, must have been added later
in the 12th c. The triforium can readily be compared with that of the
quire – but the clerestory is entirely of $c.$ 1200 and therefore runs
through unchanged. St Richard's shrine stood in the retro-quire.

Next the **Lady chapel**, where the first two bays are basically 12th
c. but the remainder of $c.$ 1300 – long, low, vaulted, undistinguished.
The green foliage on one vault bay is by Bernard (like the transept
bishops) and the 19th c. glass by Clayton and Bell. The gates at the
entrance are the only real medieval ironwork of this type in the
cathedral, though some has gone to the Victoria and Albert
Museum; they were made for the pulpitum. On the left is a kneeling
effigy of Thomas Bickly (d. 1596), and on the floor the simple tomb
of Bishop Luffa (d. 1123), with a crozier. The reredos and other
furniture are 19th c.; the double piscina and triple sedilia original
but restored. On the way out, on the left, is a beautiful chamber
organ of $c.$ 1800, also two more reputed tombs of bishops.

The **S. quire aisle** has the chapel of St Mary Magdalen at its E.
end, with Graham Sutherland's arresting *Noli Me Tangere* as
reredos and candlesticks and rail by Geoffrey Clarke. Then on the S.
side a wordy marble monument to Mrs Frances Waddington
(d. 1728), a 15th c. doorway cut into the 13th c. wall, and a great
gargoyle adapted to receive money. The railed-in area discloses a
relic of 2nd c. Roman mosaic pavement, *in situ*. Then on the wall a
large and justly celebrated 12th c. carving of Christ arriving in

Bethany. Beneath the second bay of the arcade is the plain tomb of Bishop Day (d. 1557) and, still on the right, a small wooden tablet to Henry King (d. 1668), and the fine marble tomb of Dean Hook (d. 1875) by Scott. Bishop Sherborne's tomb (d. 1536) on the opposite wall is substantially restored. Then comes the second of the splendid 12th c. carvings – the Raising of Lazarus. These two, and fragments of a third now in the library, are amongst the finest and most expressive of their date in existence.

Here the **quire** can be reached through its iron screen. All-powerful is John Piper's reredos tapestry (1966) explained by a note on the altar rail. The altar too is recent, the reredos itself 16th c. To its left is Bishop Story's tomb. The building details are like the nave and need no further general description. Again the bay nearest the tower is Scott's reconstruction. Looking W., the bishop's throne is also of the 1860s, the cast aluminium lectern of the 1960s, the stalls 14th c. in their rear parts but otherwise 19th c., the pulpitum 15th c. and the brass candelabra of 1752. The stalls have a fine variety of original miserere carvings, well worth detailed examination.

At the end of the S. quire aisle are some minor wall tablets. The **S. transept** is like the N. transept, and the big S. window has notoriously poor French glass of 1870. On the E. side a late Perpendicular screen leads to a display area of robes and tapestries in the 13th c. former chapel of St Pantaleon. A 16th c. Spanish antiphoner displayed beside it is said to be the largest in the world. Then the canopied tomb of Bishop Langton (d. 1337) and a mock-medieval one to John Abel Smith (d. 1843). From here is a good view back to the organ.

To the right of the door to the canons' vestry and chapter room is a list of benefactors dated 1686. Above are two imaginary historical paintings by Bernard, and more roundels, this time of kings and queens and continued by an 18th c. restorer on to the N. side. Most of this side is taken up by a 14th c. stone screen, probably the precursor of the present pulpitum. It houses a beautiful little heraldic tablet to the glass artist Charles Kempe (d. 1907), a brass to Dean Burgon (d. 1888), and in the middle the tomb of Bishop Stratford (d. 1362). On its right is a 15th c. oak cupboard.

In the **S. aisle** on the right is a tablet to Bishop Bell (d. 1958); then the aluminium-faced pulpit by Robert Potter and Geoffrey Clarke (1966). Here is the opportunity for a closer look at the pulpitum, 15th c. and not over-elaborate. It was removed in 1859 and reinstated in 1960. Though it is a fresh view of the quire, and, behind, the nave and W. window of 1848.

Back in the S. aisle, Bishop Arundel's plain tomb (d. 1478) is on the right, followed by a delicate but damaged little niche (mid-16th c. with mixed Gothic and Renaissance detail, the latter being the only trace of that style in the cathedral). Opposite, by the cloister doorway, is the fascinating Bradbridge brass of 1592 with a family scene. Now the **outer S. aisle**, which is like the N. but does not balance it. It is still two separate chapels with reredoses. The first bay of the arcade contains Bodley and Garner's full-blooded Gothic memorial to Bishop Durnford (d. 1896), the second an iron screen to St Clement's chapel (for private prayer) which contains three monuments of 1797 to 1811 by Flaxman. The second chapel, St George's, is the banner-hung war memorial shrine of the Royal Sussex Regiment: its 1914–18 roll of honour is revealed by opening the hinged wall-panelling.

The aisle leads into the baptistry beneath the **SW tower**. The font is of 1894, the orangey wall-painting by Hans Feibusch (1951). Amongst many wall tablets are two more by Flaxman, one to Sir Ernest Udny (d. 1806) by Sir Richard Westmacott's brother Henry, and one to the local poet William Collins (d. 1759).

Now the **exterior**, taken anti-clockwise. Opposite the W. doors is the Prebendal School garden and in the SW. angle of the churchyard the 13th c. chapel of the Bishop's Palace; both are private. From here is a good view of the sundial and Norman doorway of the S. tower, the Geometric tracery of the outer S. aisle, the 13th c. flying buttresses and 19th c. central tower and spire, and the vestry and chapter room building beside the transept. The path leads into the cloister, oddly shaped, non-monastic, no more really than three rather informal covered ways enclosing a space called Paradise with a reclining figure by Henry Moore. The cloister is of *c.* 1400 and has a simple open timber roof – no vault. The walls are lined with too many tablets to note here, mostly late 18th and early 19th c. Much the earliest is on the left of the W. alley, to Percival Smalpage (d. 1595). Ahead is the mid-13th c. St Richard's porch, double-arched, with a figure of 1894.

Turn back to the SW. corner. Opening from the right of the S. alley is St Richard's Walk. Then more wall tablets and a doorway to the Bishop Bell Rooms for refreshments (these are closed in winter and on Sundays). Next a doorway to the former Royal Chaplains' House, with arms of Henry VII above. In the SE. angle is another good viewpoint of the cathedral as a whole. Wooden panelling marks where the cloister stole the bottom end of what was St Faith's chapel. Alongside is an exit into Vicars' Close.

The E. alley is barred at the time of writing, so the rest of the tour is in the open. Starting with the Vicars' Hall on the right, it leads past the Lady chapel, with good views of the flying buttress system of the quire and retro-quire, and back into West Street. The various corner turrets are mostly 19th c. Note too the upper-level library on the E. side of the N. transept, and finally on the N. side of the nave the same kind of overlay of Early English work on fundamental Norman as has been seen inside.

Clifton, St Peter & St Paul (Roman Catholic, Avon)

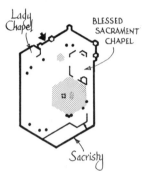

The first Catholic church at Clifton, that of the Holy Apostles on Honeypen Hill, was begun in 1834 and, after various vicissitudes, opened in 1848. It became the pro-cathedral in 1850 when the diocese was formed on the 'restoration of the hierarchy'. But it was never consecrated. An early scheme for building a permanent cathedral was abandoned and in the 1870s a remodelling was commenced, changing its style from Greek Revival to Italian Romanesque! Eventually, in the 1960s, it proved possible to replace it with an entirely new building on a different site. This was designed by the Percy Thomas Partnership and opened in 1973.

As at Liverpool, the whole concept of the building is based on congregational seating around a spacious sanctuary. Here, however, the difficulties inseparable from a completely circular plan do not arise, and whilst the resulting over-all shape is less arresting, the carefully contrived asymmetry not only expresses the functions and interrelations of the parts but also provides a constant variety of

Cathedral from N., Clifton (c. 1970)

vistas and spatial interest as one walks around, inside or out.

If one enters St Paul's door, on the upper (Clifton Park) side, one comes into a wide concourse, right and left, paved with hexagonal concrete tiles with embedded heating cables. The theme of hexagons and equilateral triangles pervades the whole building – though not to an obsessive degree – from the over-all shape, which is an extended hexagon, to such details as candle-holders and litter bins. The other all-important feature is the use of reinforced concrete with a near-white surface texture bearing the clear imprints of grained shutter-boards and their circular connectors. This technique has been used many times elsewhere but perhaps never with such attention to detail. So there is no plaster, no paint, no added colour except that provided by the simple furnishings and by the stained glass and vestments and congregation. Moreover, the natural lighting is funnelled and filtered, mostly from above, to avoid glare and to emphasize the focal points.

Half left inside the doors is the **baptistry**. The big font, carved by Simon Verity with intertwined fishes in the bowl and doves around it, stands by a chevron-shaped pool under a star-shaped canopy. This canopy, which has a hexagonal opening, forms the underside of the gallery. Beside the font is a great candlestick of gilded blocks threaded on a stem.

Half right is the main congregational space, on the axis of the ceremonial W. doorway. Now one can consider the construction which (without going into too much detail) is of three 'ring' walls like hollow boxes, one on top of another but of different shapes. First is the low outer wall of the ambulatory: second the tall wall on short columns that mostly follows the line of the rear of the seating. Third, there is the high ring wall forming the hexagonal lantern above the sanctuary. Two of the sides of this are continuations of sides of the second 'box' and the others are supported on beams that span the nave to its rear corners. The upper hexagon has a 'blind' clerestory of hexagonal openings in its three W. sides and goes on upwards to carry the more complex structure of the lantern and flèche.

The high altar is a great square of Portland stone; the grey ambo at its side is movable. The high-backed bishop's throne, flanked by stalls, stands against the E. wall. To its right, placed so as to play into the big reverberant space of the sanctuary, is the organ by the Austrian firm of Rieger. Hanging above the congregational chairs are great inverted wooden pyramids designed to adjust the acoustics in such a way that the spoken word is clear although music is still full-toned. Behind, around the ambulatory in twos and threes, are the Stations of the Cross moulded into concrete panels by William Mitchell.

In the **Lady chapel**, which occupies the widened and partially screened corner of the ambulatory close to St Paul's door, the bronze Madonna is by Terry Jones. The votive-candle stand takes up the 'equilateral triangle' theme, being a framework in the form of an icosahedron.

Now it is a good idea to walk along the back of the nave to see the sanctuary from different viewpoints, to appreciate Henry Haig's stained glass behind the baptistry and to see the gallery above it. The ambulatory then leads right round the sanctuary, passing the sacristy door on the right, behind the choir seats and in front of the organ. Then on the left is a little hexagonal stair leading up to the gallery (normally closed) and down to the undercroft. Near the bottom are the foundation stone (1970) and two architectural award plaques. The big social room at this level is called the Apostle room.

It now remains to continue along the ambulatory (passing various historical plaques transferred from the old cathedral) to the Blessed Sacrament chapel with its screen of vertical bars. This has its own view of the high altar and conversely its stainless steel tabernacle by John Alder is visible from the nave. The second main entrance, close to the chapel, is St Peter's door. The widened ambulatory or narthex then leads between the baptistry and the bookstall back to St Paul's door.

Turning left **outside**, there is more hexagonal paving leading round to the W. entrance. The bold rainwater troughs are provided with chains hanging from the spouts above, to reduce splashing. The big W. doors with glass fibre coats-of-arms of Bristol and the diocese are by Mitchell. The upper parts of the cathedral are of bush-hammered white concrete and the lowest of black concrete. In between, however, the facing panels covering all the main areas of walling are of concrete with pinkish Aberdeen granite 'exposed aggregate', and in Cathedral House just to the S. these are combined with plain white blocks.

On this side the way round the cathedral forms a balcony, with the low sacristy wall on the left. Steps presently lead to the car park below. Beyond that is a much grander flight from Pembroke Road to a great platform or atrium and thence to the NE. door which is St Peter's.

Coventry, St Michael (Church of England, West Midlands)

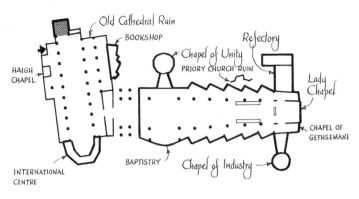

St Mary's Priory church was the cathedral of a separate Coventry diocese during the 12th c. It was destroyed at the Reformation, leaving the big nearby churches of St Michael and the Holy Trinity to continue serving their own parishes. For three centuries afterwards Coventry remained linked with Lichfield in the name of a joint see. During the 19th c. it was transferred to Worcester, but in 1918 the diocese was revived and the church of St Michael became its cathedral. Its S. porch was 13th c., the rest mostly Perpendicular in style. In November 1940 it was completely gutted by fire bombs, and when the new cathedral was built alongside in 1956–62 it was left as an open ruin.

The architect for the new building was Sir Basil Spence. His competition-winning design involved creating an open portico to link the new with the shell of the old and retaining as a landmark the tall 15th c. tower and spire that had survived the fire.

Visitors who make for the tower will first enter the **ruin**, in its SW. corner from Bayley Lane. Its size – it was one of the biggest English parish churches – seems accentuated by the column stumps that are left, and by the height of the steeple, 295 feet. The upward view into the high lierne vault of the tower is not enhanced by the shop now built into its base. Ascent of the stair is usually possible.

Several of the former guild chapels are traceable, relics of once-powerful trade brotherhoods, and the upper room of the S. porch is still used by the Cappers' Guild. Its ground floor is enclosed as a memorial chapel to Bishop Haigh. Past this on the right is Sir Jacob Epstein's '*Ecce Homo*' statue, violently controversial in its time

Two views of Cathedral from top of Tower, Coventry: under construction (1959) and after completion

(1935), and at the end of the S. aisle the simple tomb of Bishop Gorton (d. 1955). Close to it are steps down to a small coffee-room.

The old E. end is unusual in being (like Lichfield) a polygonal apse. Within it stands the 'Charred Cross' made of burned roof-beams and with the poignant inscription FATHER FORGIVE on the wall behind. The Cross is a replica of the original now inside. In the former NE. chapel lies the bronze effigy of the first bishop of the revived diocese, Bishop Yeatman-Biggs (d. 1922), holding a model of his cathedral as it then was.

Apart from one or two scarred memorials there is little else of interest in the old building, so at this point it is appropriate to go down the so-called Queen's Steps which lead under Spence's tall-columned portico to the new cathedral. To the left, up St Michael's Avenue, is the church of the Holy Trinity, and ahead the huge glass screen that forms the entire new W. wall of the nave: its engraved pattern of saints and angels, a modern equivalent of the W. front of Wells or Exeter, is by John Hutton.

Entry by the furthest doors at the right at once reveals the **interior**. The thin concrete columns and net vault are merely a veil to the true structure. The real roof is above the slatted ceiling and rests on the fin-like walls which direct light towards the altar. Prominent on these walls are Biblical passages carved in mannered lettering by Ralph Beyer. He also designed the huge inlaid brass letters in the floor under the W. window: 'To the Glory of God This Cathedral Burnt'. It is the green tapestry at the E. end, however, which dominates. 75 feet high, it is the largest in the world, made in France to a design by Graham Sutherland. The serene seated Christ is surrounded by four Evangelists' emblems, spiky and thorny like so much of the cathedral's symbolism. At the foot, serving also as a reredos for the Lady chapel, is a Crucifixion.

At the very start of the **S. aisle** is the baptistry, lit by John Piper's vast multi-coloured window with its gleaming white centre. The font is an unhewn boulder from Bethlehem. Just beyond it in the aisle is a Crucifix by the Czech Jindřich Severa, one of many sculptures added to the cathedral since the consecration. Just before the way narrows behind the quire stalls is the lectern, with a stocky bronze eagle by Elizabeth Frink. The massed thorn-like formations above the stalls, Spence's equivalent of Gothic canopies, have been likened to flocks of birds; their distracting openwork pattern (symbolizing the path through suffering to the Resurrection) intensifies above the provost's stall, and even more above the bishop's throne. At the end of the aisle is another sculpture, 'The Plumb Line and the City' by

Clarke Fitzgerald (1971). Behind, the procession of aisle windows
has now come into view – giant abstract patterns by Geoffrey
Clarke, Lawrence Lee and Keith New. They will be prominent again
on the way out.

Straight ahead, after passing beneath one half of the organ, is the
grotto-like **chapel of Gethsemane**, with its screen representing the
Crown of Thorns. The guardian angel behind the altar and the bas-
relief mosaic on the right-hand wall are by Steven Sykes.

To the right, linked by a curious tapered passage with shallow
steps, is the brilliantly lit circular **chapel of Christ the Servant** or
chapel of Industry. The hanging Cross and Crown of Thorns are by
Geoffrey Clarke.

Now along the ambulatory behind the high altar. On the right,
behind the heavy screen and at the foot of the great tapestry, is the
Lady chapel. On the left is the high altar itself. Its Cross, silver-gilt,
is by Geoffrey Clarke and holds in the centre the Cross of Nails
which became symbolic of reconciliation and all that that means to
Coventry. The three very large pottery candlesticks each side of the
altar are by Hans Coper.

Next is a lobby with some typically Swedish glass by Einar
Forseth, and stairs leading down to the concourse called
St Michael's Hall where the original Charred Cross may be seen. At
this point occasional guided tours begin, which enable the hall and
the **treasury and museum** to be seen. These contain a fascinating
collection of old engravings, photographs and documents, plate and
vestments, as well as many original sketches for the embellishment
of the building: Hutton's for the W. window, Piper's for the
baptistry window and Sutherland's for the tapestry. The remainder
of the extensive suite of undercroft rooms is not normally open to
the public, except for the refectory which is reached from the
outside.

On the way back up the stairs is more sculpture: a replica of a
carved head from Trondheim Cathedral, a Mother and Child by van
Vranken (1976) and a metal head of Christ by Helen Huntington
Jennings (1967). Above the top landing hang the colours of the 1st
Battalion Coldstream Guards.

Straight ahead is the **N. aisle**. As one walks back, the glass
mosaics of the aisle windows now show their best but are strongly
outshone by the clear W. window and it is never easy to appreciate
their message as a whole, which starts with 'Beginnings' and
'Creation' at the W. end, then 'Conflict', 'Struggle' and 'Maturity'
and finally 'Realization' with its golds and whites, intended to light

the altar and sanctuary. The specific message of each of the ten individual windows is left to the imagination; as with life you can only look back and see them fully.

On the left is the pulpit, and embedded in the aisle floor can be seen some of the pennies placed to guide the choir in procession.

Towards the W. end of the aisle are steps which can be used as a concert platform or stage. Ordinarily they lead into the **chapel of Unity**, star-shaped in plan and with very tall thin windows both within and beside the buttresses. The coloured glass here is by Margaret Traherne and the marble floor pattern by Einar Forseth. As one leaves the chapel, the brilliance of John Piper's baptistry is splendid, but ought not to blind one to the side views from the clear glazed lobby: the steeple to the right, and to the left a fine Georgian house used as the cathedral study centre. A final look at the W. glass screen, and out beneath the portico again: straight ahead are the Wyley chapel and the chapel of the Cross in the old crypt (not always open). To the right beneath the old N. wall is the bookshop.

Around the N. side of the cathedral a path leads between the Georgian house and the chapel of Unity and then down to the refectory or public restaurant. Beside the steps are clear remains of polygonal chapels of the E. end of the priory church, the one-time cathedral. Considerable other fragments have been identified to the N. of Priory Row, but little or nothing can be seen that dates with certainty from as early as the 12th c. when it was a cathedral. It may also be of interest to see the base of the W. front, with the start of late 13th c. clustered piers, lying practically N. of St Michael's tower.

Finally the S. side, reached by passing back through the portico and down the steps to Priory Street. On the left, beside the baptistry window, is Epstein's bronze of St Michael defeating the Devil, in a naturalistic style utterly different from his earlier '*Ecce Homo*' and indeed perplexingly different from most of the cathedral's individual works of art. Down the street the circular chapel of Industry is prominent; under it is a chapter room. Beyond lies a paved garden with the E. wall, marked by a huge Cross, towering above it.

It only remains now to return uphill to the outside of the ruins and the end of Bayley Lane. The E. apse was built around in 1885 with a suite of vestries and meeting rooms and in 1961–2 these were restored as an International Centre by a team of young Germans. Like the Cross on the new high altar, they are a symbol of reconciliation.

Epstein's sculpture of St Michael and the Devil, Coventry

Derby, All Saints (Church of England, Derbyshire)

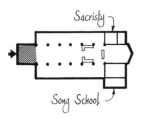

All Saints' is one of the six original parish churches of Derby. From
Saxon times it seems to have had a college of priests and to have
belonged to the King. Henry I gave it to the Dean of Lincoln and in
consequence it became independent of any diocese – a privilege that
was jealously guarded for centuries. Very little is known about the
medieval building except that its tower, which still stands, was
rebuilt during the years 1511 to 1530. The college was dissolved in
1549.

The body of the church was rebuilt in 1723–5, leaving the Gothic
tower standing. The architect was James Gibbs, designer of
St Martin-in-the-Fields and St Mary-le-Strand in London, and the
whole project became notorious because of the high-handed actions
of the then vicar, Dr Hutchinson. It was constituted a cathedral in
1927, but the E. extensions, comprising retro-quire and a suite of
rooms at lower level, were not built until 1965–72; the architect was
Sebastian Comper.

The **tower**, 178 ft high, is a stately example of late Perpendicular.
It was intended to carry either a spire or a lantern and has ten bells
and a carillon; eight of the bells are 17th c. and one 15th c. Along a
string-course on the S. side, not too high above the pavement,
appear the words 'young men and maidens', which may mean that
young people paid for the tower up to that stage. The main entrance
is beneath the tower, through two new sets of glass doors and past a
generous 18th c. double stair which sweeps up to a balcony and
thence to the gallery.

Inside, the clear rectangle of **nave** and quire with their aisles is the
James Gibbs building. The classical baldacchino straight ahead is an
addition of 1972 by Sebastian Comper. Beyond it is his retro-quire.
The Doric columns, each with its separate piece of entablature,
support simple plaster vaulting, all painted in a warm new colour
scheme since the extensions were completed. It is all much less

ornate than Gibbs's other churches. Across the whole church stretches the splendid wrought-iron screen, originally by Robert Bakewell.

Turning now to the **N. aisle**, the first big wall tablet is a design by James Gibbs himself, to Sarah Ballidon (d. 1736). Amongst many memorials along this wall those particularly worth noting are to Sir William Wheler (d. 1666) with busts of himself and his wife, William Alestrey (d. 1655) and his wife, with a miniature coffin, and Mary Chichester (d. 1830) by Sir Richard Westmacott. The Robert Bakewell (d. 1765) commemorated by the much simpler tablet just inside the screen was not the ironsmith.

Still on the left, the raised 17th c. wooden seat against the wall is a part of the former consistory court, a relic of the church's exemption from diocesan authority. Beyond are some more monuments including: Richard Croshawe (d. 1631) with kneeling figure, Sub-Dean John Lawe, a 15th c. incised alabaster slab, and Thomas Chambers (d. 1726) and his wife by Lewis Roubiliac (with an iron railing). A door in the E. wall leads to the vestries and undercroft and to its right is a quaint little tablet to Hannah Cotchett (d. 1698). The abstract glass in the window above is by Ceri Richards (1965) and symbolizes All Souls.

Now the iron screens, which not only divide the entire E. end from the congregational area, but also run lengthwise behind both sides of the quire. Designed from the start as part of the Gibbs building, they have been ill-treated and altered on so many occasions that only the centre portion across the nave can be regarded as wholly Robert Bakewell's work. The gate 'piers' and the royal arms on the overthrow are marvellous examples of craftsmanship in metal.

The pulpit is by Temple Moore (1873); its canopy is later. Close below it is the County Council pew, facing the Corporation pew on the S. side. The latter has ornamental ironwork by Bakewell or a pupil, the former a modern equivalent incorporating emblems of county civic heraldry. The brass eagle lectern is 19th c. The offertory table in the centre of the nave (1625) came from St Michael's church.

The **quire** and **retro-quire** are not normally accessible but can be seen well through the screen. The quire stalls are largely by Temple Moore (1894). The bishop's throne came from Constantinople at the time of the formation of the diocese and is 18th c. The baldacchino is by Sebastian Comper but incorporates a tester by his father Sir Ninian. The communion rail, similar in character to the screens, is probably by Bakewell too. Beyond it lies the retro-quire, entirely of 1965–72, plaster-vaulted and with a new small organ on the E. wall and choir seats below it.

Further along the screen is the curious 16th c. wooden monument of an unknown priest, and then the gates into the S. or Cavendish chapel, now used as the **baptistry**. The white marble font was made in 1974 from a design by James Gibbs; behind it is a door to the song school, and above that a companion window ('All Saints') to that in the N. aisle, by Ceri Richards. The great monument to Elizabeth, Countess of Shrewsbury ('Bess of Hardwick'), d. 1607, was made in her lifetime. Beside it are Michael Rysbrack's much more human memorial to Caroline, Countess of Bessborough (d. 1760), and the more modest tablet and bust of her husband (d. 1793) by Joseph Nollekens.

At the E. end of the **S. aisle** a stone stair to the crypt has recently been opened up, leading to a small chapel for private devotion, formed in what was one of the Cavendish family vaults. The balustrade round the head of the stair belonged originally to the consistory court. Of the memorials on the aisle wall two by the stair should be noted: one by Sir Francis Chantrey to Richard Bateman (d. 1821) and one put up in 1945 on the bicentenary of the Young Pretender's arrival in Derby. From this point there is a good view of the W. end with the organ case by Sebastian Comper and the gallery, which was originally erected in 1733 and later extended for a time over the aisles. Near the gallery is a tablet to the Rev. Michael Hutchinson (d. 1730), the vicar whose efforts resulted in the rebuilding.

Immediately outside the W. entrance is another pair of gates by Robert Bakewell. These came from a neighbouring house and replaced another pair that stood further S. and were sold about 1870. Along the N. side of the cathedral, College Place divides it from a group of diocesan buildings and leads down to Full Street where a proper appreciation of the two-storeyed E. additions can be gained. Where a power station stood, a green park has been opened up right to the river. From Amen Alley, which leads back to Iron Gate and the W. end, there is an excellent view of Gibbs's S. aisle, with its slow rhythm of round-headed windows and the 'intermittent' rustication of which he was so fond.

Dornoch, St Barr (Church of Scotland, Highland)

A see of Caithness was mentioned in the 12th c., with its centre at
Halkirk. In 1222 it was transferred to Dornoch where there had long
been a Culdee monastery (possibly even as early as 600 under
St Barr or Finbar whose precise identity seems uncertain). The
cathedral was thus built in the second quarter of the 13th c., and it
was little altered throughout the Middle Ages. In 1570 it was burnt
out in clan fighting and in 1614–16 all but the nave and aisles was
re-roofed. In the 18th c. what was by then a parish church was fitted
with galleries and the nave ruin was walled off.

In 1835–7 ruthless alterations were done under William Burn, the
nave being rebuilt without aisles and the remainder plastered over to
achieve a seemly uniformity. This coating remained until 1924 when
a proper restoration revealed the 13th c. stonework.

Inside the **S. transept** entrance, it is at once evident that the E.
wall, with its shafted windows and simple wall-arcade above, is 13th
c., whereas the one opposite is of 1835. The very wide arches of the
crossing-tower, strangely irregular in both shape and detail, are also
13th c., but not of course the plaster ceilings here and in the nave
and quire. The octagonal font on five columns is early 20th c.
Within the nearby blocked doorway is a little 'skull and crossbones'
tablet, one of five so-called 'mortality slabs' in the cathedral. The
glass of the three lancets in the S. gable is an inept assortment, the
centre one being by Morris & Co., 1930.

The **nave** is entirely of 1835, though just inside on the left a half
column of the S. arcade has been uncovered. The first window on
the S. is by Francis Spear (1952) and the second by Charles Kempe
(1905). Over the W. doorway is a tablet recording the work of 1835,
and in the SW. corner a damaged effigy ascribed to Richard de
Moravia, *c*. 1240.

The **N. transept**, like the S., shows 13th c. work in the E. wall and
there is a piscina. The **quire** too is essentially 13th c., with windows
once all shafted. The E. lancets, three with two more above, are
specially dignified and have glass by Christopher Whall (1913). The

Cathedral from NW., Dornoch

hexagonal pulpit (1911), though of wood, is designed as if of stone, with thick carving and heavy columns. On the S. wall is a monument to the Earl and Countess of Sutherland (d. 1766), an effective composition with a vesica-shaped glass panel in the base; below it is a piscina and there are traces of sedilia. In the floor behind the communion table is a big marble inscription to a Countess of Sutherland which formerly blocked the E. window. The centre S. window is by William Wilson, 1958.

Externally, the unifying plinth obscures the distinction between medieval work and that of 1835, though the latter can be picked out by the stonework pattern. The transept ends are both re-faced and the porches are similar. The tower, largely 13th c., is perhaps best viewed from the NE., where the stair turret is: its machicolated parapet is of interest for its three-quarters-round corner projections.

The tower of the Castle Hotel, just S. of the cathedral, is thought to have been part of the bishop's palace; it was restored in 1881 as a 'quaint dwelling place for English sportsmen'.

Dunblane, St Blane & St Laurence (Church of Scotland, Central)

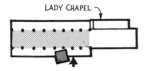

St Blane is said to have set up a church here in the 7th c. The
bishopric was re-founded about 1150; the existing tower may be a
little earlier than that but the cathedral itself was rebuilt in 1237–60.
The nave and aisles, which became ruinous after the Reformation,
were fully restored in 1892–5 under Sir Robert Rowand Anderson,
and the quire (which had continued in use as a parish church) by
Thomas Brown in 1861, Sir George Gilbert Scott in 1872–3 and Sir
Robert Lorimer in 1914.

The **tower**, bearing no particular relationship to the present
building, nor any obvious one to a predecessor, was probably
originally detached and may have been defensive. The main part is
12th c., the two top storeys 13th c. and the parapet c. 1500. Inside
the main entrance, to the right of the tower, it is best to go to the
centre of the **nave**. The arcades on clustered columns and the double
clerestory (outer windows and uninterrupted inner arcade with a
passage between) are well-proportioned 13th c. work. The barrel
roof is of 1893.

Now a clockwise tour commencing at the **tower** door in the S.
aisle. Wooden steps lead to the interior which has a 13th c. stone
vault on pointed arches; the round-headed arch in its E. wall is
evidently earlier. In the **S. aisle** are a case of books illustrated by
Dorothea Nimmo Smith, a brass to the Rev. John Kinross (d. 1883)
and, W. of the tower, two windows by Louis Davis (1917): *Nunc
Dimittis* and Arrival. The circular font on a clustered stem is by
Anderson, and behind it is a baptismal window by Douglas
Strachan, (1926); the sanctuary lamp above came from a Greek
Orthodox church at Edhessa. Steps in the SW. corner lead to the
tiny vaulted Clement chapel long known as Katie Ogle's Hole
(possibly after a witch who awaited trial there). It has a beautiful
little modern bronze Majestas by Maxwell Allan.

The six quire stalls now at the W. end of the **nave** are late 15th c.
Above, the double tracery of the W. window is remarkable; its Jesse
Tree glass is by Clayton and Bell (1906). Looking E., the big
unglazed windows over the chancel arch are also unusual;

inconspicuous above them are royal arms. Other special features are
the series of wrought-iron electric pendants by John Matthew, made
by Thomas Hadden (1935), every one with different floral panels,
and the holm-oak pews with foliage carving on their top edges and
an animal on each front one.

At the W. end of the **N. aisle** (the Keir aisle) is a Celtic standing
cross with animal carvings, possibly 9th c. Close to the stair
doorway is a tablet to William Coldstream (d. 1787). The arched
recess in the N. wall is a memorial to members of the Strathallan
family. Two bells on the floor nearby were re-cast in 1723 and 1809.
Further E. are two more fragments of Celtic crosses and very
mutilated effigies of Malise, fifth Earl of Strathearn (d. 1271) and his
Countess. There follow a number of 19th and 20th c. memorials to
the Stirling family and others and at the end of the N. wall a 20th c.
window by Gordon Webster depicting the Compassion of Christ.
On the E. wall the big Stirling memorial is by Anderson; so is the
canopied pulpit nearby with its seven figures representing the
cathedral's history.

The richly carved **quire** screen is by Anderson. Within the quire
the stalls and organ case and the coved screen at the E. end are by
Lorimer (1914). This was the last part of the cathedral to be built
but is still mostly 13th c. Only the N. side has a triforium and
clerestory, because it abuts the former Lady chapel which was built
first; the triforium, now largely occupied by the organ mechanism,
actually extends as an upper room over the chapel. The trefoil-
shaped panelled and boarded quire roof is largely due to Scott. The
E. window is by Charles Kempe (1901) and those along the S. side,
representing the Works of God in the *Benedicite*, are by Davis *c.*
1914; the fourth from the E. contains references to the men of
Captain Scott's Antarctic expedition.

In the centre of the quire floor are brasses to the Drummond
sisters (d. 1501) – actually replacements of 1897 with an explanatory
plaque. To the right of the stalls on the N. side the bronze tablet to
Lt Napier (d. 1918) is by Lorimer; then comes the doorway to the
Lady chapel, a long rib-vaulted room of five bays, now partly used
as a vestry and formerly as chapter house. It is of about 1240; in
1924 it was panelled throughout as a war memorial. The glass by
Strachan and the rolls of honour (written and illuminated, like a
number of other works in the cathedral, by Helen Lamb) form part
of the memorial.

Reverting to the N. wall of the **quire**: a wall tablet commemorates
Janet Wallace, benefactress of the 1893 restoration. The tomb recess

Cathedral interior, Dunblane

to its right has a worn effigy of an unidentified bishop, possibly Bishop Clement, the builder. The stalls each side of the communion table, three on the N. and seven on the S., with misericords, are 15th c. The big brass lectern with eight lions around its foot and Evangelists' emblems in niches around the step is by Anderson; on it lies a Bible of 1613.

Back in the S. aisle, behind the heavy curtain, can be found the 15th c. effigy of Bishop Ochiltree; the window above it is another memorial to Janet Wallace, and her husband David. **Outside** (turning right) the S. aisle tracery is all renewed, but at the W. end a good deal of old work remains. The many-shafted 13th c. W. doorway must indeed have been of special magnificence; above are the three double-traceried W. windows, and over them the so-called Ruskin window, highly praised by him for its leaf carving. The first windows in the N. wall have unusual, almost flat heads; most of the aisle tracery has, however, been renewed and the gables in the E. bays of both aisles are 19th c. additions. The N. doorway is 13th c., even more worn than the W. Back round the E. end to the S. doorway, traces of a former porch can be seen, including vault springers. Finally, moving back towards the road, notice the parapet added to the 13th c. quire walls about 1500.

Across from the main gate and slightly left is the Dean's House, which contains the cathedral museum; it is not open every day but entry is free. Also close by is the Cathedral Manse. In its grounds is the Leighton Library, built by the 17th c. Bishop Leighton for the benefit of the clergy of Dunblane; it may be seen on request to the minister in writing.

Dundee, St Paul (Scottish Episcopal Church, Tayside)

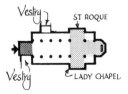

St Paul's church, erected on the site of the castle in 1853–5, was the successor of a number of chapels serving the not always united Episcopalians from 1689. Bishops (styled 'of Brechin') were first appointed in 1724. It was designated a cathedral in 1904.

The architect was Sir George Gilbert Scott and his style Geometric Decorated. Virtually a 'hall-church', without clerestory, it has a greater emphasis on verticality than much of his work, and this is evident at the start in the soaring 210-foot spire, so prominent in the city centre. The **tower** is unusual in having a band of machicolations below as well as above the belfry stage. The main entrance with steep steps through its vaulted ground stage anticipates the lofty **interior**, with arcades on very slender columns of quatrefoil section supporting high-pitched open timber roofs. All the windows are coloured except one in the N. aisle.

At the W. end of the **N. aisle** is the Lindores cabinet, the panels of which are thought to have come from the quire stalls of Lindores Abbey. After numerous vicissitudes they were assembled in this setting in 1923. They are probably early 16th c. The bust over the vestry doorway is of Bishop Forbes, builder of the cathedral (d. 1875). The N. transept, **St Roque's chapel**, contains the altar, reredos and war memorial from the early 20th c. church of St Roque which was closed in 1956; the restless pattern of the enclosing railing has nothing in common with Scott's work. The transepts have a clerestory but are not as high as the nave. The **quire** has a stone vault, and a clerestory over the bay containing the stalls. Not over-elaborate, these have an interesting alternation of plain and canopied seats in the back rows. The brass in the centre of the floor marks Bishop Forbes's tomb. The reredos is a typical Scott design, a giant trefoil-headed Italian mosaic panel framed in marble and alabaster (the mosaic artist was Antonio Salviati). The aumbry and piscina on its right were added in 1887. The fine triple sedilia, with marble canopies on free-standing columns, should also be noted.

The marble-lined **Lady chapel** is reached through the screen at the side of the stalls. Its altar and reredos were transferred from the previous chapel of St Paul in Castle Street. Amongst the 19th c. memorials in the **S. transept** the best is the brass in the SE. corner to James Guthrie (d. 1885). Finally the **S. aisle**. On the right is the stone and marble pulpit with wooden canopy; on the left a memorial to James Chalmers (b. 1819), the (disputed) inventor of the postage stamp. Only the bowl of the font is by Scott; the pedestal came from Lindores Abbey and is medieval.

Outside, the cathedral is hemmed in by other buildings to the S. and E. The best general view is from the NW. across the street intersection, but a glimpse of the polygonal E. apse can be had from an alley a little way down Commercial Street.

Dundee, St Andrew (Roman Catholic, Tayside)

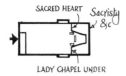

Built in 1836 to the design of George Mathewson, this has been little altered since, apart from a slight extension of the sanctuary by C. G. Menart in 1920–21. It serves the diocese of Dunkeld which was revived in 1878, and became a cathedral in 1923. Its early Gothic Revival embellishments are merely a veneer to a skilled treatment of space and levels which gave it internally an almost Italian air.

Behind the battlemented street façade is the usual lobby with gallery stair to the right, and baptistry (through glazed doors and a fairly new wrought-iron screen) to the left. The impression of great space in the **nave** is enhanced by a slightly sloping floor and by the view of it being framed in five Tudor arches on slender posts (of cast iron, one assumes) beneath the gallery. The sanctuary is high, distant and majestic. The main roof, a span of over 50 feet, rests on plaster imitation arches of vigorous Tudor form which spring from great foliage corbels and a wall-arcade high on the side walls. What may be called the chancel arch is similar, with angel corbels, but the further one to the sanctuary is a poor shapeless affair. All the windows have coloured glass, 19th c. except in the E. part.

The W. end of the nave is dominated by a war memorial with mosaic panel. On the right is the baptistry with Decorated-style font and traceried screen. The canopied marble Pietà at the W. end of the N. wall is a memorial to Bishop Macfarlane (d. 1912). Further along is a double confessional, and in the NE. corner the Sacred Heart altar.

Enlargement of the ritual **quire** has entailed bringing new marble steps forward to the rather flimsy Gothic rail. The E. end is a curiously effective amalgam of marble, light oak and gilding, with walls largely in pale green. The bishop's throne is an ornate chair with curtained canopy over, and the quire stalls are perched behind ambones. The reredos dominates by its gilding rather than its shape.

On the **S. side**, the marble Lady altar has a wooden Gothic reredos and at the W. end there is a wall tablet to Monseigneur Clapperton (d. 1906).

From Nethergate stepped side passages lead to the domestic

building behind, and it can be seen that there are a Lady chapel and parish hall in the basement. The confessionals actually overhang these passages, one side on a bridge and the other on a cantilever! Another odd but hardly attractive view can be had from the railway yard at the rear: the slope is so steep that the domestic buildings, though four floors high, extend only to the base of the sanctuary windows – also a kind of arrangement that could occur in Italy.

Dunkeld, St Columba (part Church of Scotland, part Scottish Development Department; Tayside)

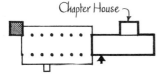

A Culdee settlement (Celtic monastery) is said to have existed here in the 6th c. and to have been rebuilt about 848. The see was set up or re-established about 1110 and lasted until 1571. The existing quire is of the 13th c., with 14th c. additions. The nave was begun in 1406 and consecrated in 1464. The chapter house, S. porch and NW. tower were added during the 15th c. The whole building was desecrated in 1560, but in 1600 the quire roof was repaired. It suffered severely both in the Civil War and in the 1689 Rebellion. Sporadic repairs to the quire kept it in use as a parish church and eventually it was thoroughly restored in 1908. The ruined W. parts were repaired in 1922–6 by the Office of Works and are maintained (with the usual opening hours but no charge is made) by the Scottish Development Department. Outside those hours the whole churchyard, one of the most beautiful in the country, is kept locked. Carpeted with mown grass and full of splendid trees, it slopes gently down to the bank of the Tay.

It is the **quire** that faces the gates, so that will be examined first. Inside, the prominent trefoil-headed arcade along the N. wall shows its 13th c. origin. The E. window, both tracery and glass (by Burmeister and Fulks), is of 1908, and so is the barrel roof with its small bosses. The archway to the nave, visible above and at the sides of the organ, is 15th c. Also at the W. end are a Bible of 1611 in a showcase and the square font, which is not ancient. On the N. wall the rough cartouche with 'JSMM' relates to the repairs of 1600. The

Nave and Tower from SE., Dunkeld (15th c.)

fine coat-of-arms over the doorway to the 15th c. **chapter house** is
that of the dukes of Atholl, who made it into a mausoleum. Its
quadripartite vaults support an upper room. On the left is a bell of
1688; the cross-slab by it is perhaps of the 10th c. and the big
canopied Atholl tomb is of about 1600. The contents of the
showcase are changed from time to time. The standing white marble
figure of the Duke of Atholl (d. 1830) is by John Ternouth (who did
one of the reliefs on Nelson's column) and the wall tablet is to Lord
Charles Murray (d. 1824). The encyclopaedic monument on the S.
wall with a Latin inscription flanked by 32 heraldic shields is to the
Duke of Atholl (d. 1703), whose ridiculously small portrait
medallion sits on top. Last and most important, is another Celtic
slab whose busy carving has been variously interpreted; commonly
known as the Apostles' stone, it is a fine example of Pictish art.

Continuing now along the N. wall of the quire: there are two 20th
c. tablets (with colours of the 42nd Royal Highlanders above) and
two quaint 17th c. ones. Beyond them the wall-arcade resumes. The
oak communion table, stalls and screens are rich 20th c. Gothic

W. doorway, Dunkeld (15th c.)

work by Sir Robert Lorimer. Behind the screen are the mutilated
14th c. effigy of Bishop Sinclair; the tomb of Alexander Stewart
(called the Wolf of Badenoch, d. 1394), with mailed effigy and
mailed figures in niches around the sides; the white marble
monument of Major-General Dick (d. 1846); and, centred on the E.
wall, the giant Black Watch memorial of 1872 in white marble by Sir
John Steel. Beyond that is a case of Highland Brigade relics.

Back in front of the screen, there are 14th c. stone sedilia on the S.
side, and two more heraldic stones.

At the time of writing the interior of the **ruin** (except the tower)
was closed to visitors indefinitely. Most of it can, however, be seen
through the doorways, particularly the W. First the S. porch (an
addition of the later 15th c.) should be examined; the heraldic stone
above must have been placed there after it had lost its roof.

Were it not for their moulded octagonal caps and bases, the
stumpy round piers would suggest a re-use of Norman work. The
triforium, though also 15th c., has round arches with giant tracery
of early character. The lack of uniformity in the clerestory shows
that completion was a gradual process. The S. aisle was evidently
vaulted. The great W. window, a quite late insertion, is now almost
devoid of tracery, but it must once have been a grand example of the
Flamboyant style. Its gable, with little wheel window, is curiously
lop-sided.

Of the many monuments and headstones inside, the principal one
can be seen near the E. end of the S. aisle wall: the ogee-arched
tomb of Bishop Cardeny (d. 1420). Just beyond it are the remains of
a piscina. In the NE. corner are the badly weathered remnants of a
memorial of about 1600. A stone by the stair doorway in the SW.
corner commemorates Colonel Cleland, Cameronian commander in
the 1689 battle.

The ground stage of the **tower** was used as a consistory court and
is of special interest for its early 16th c. wall-paintings, amongst the
very few medieval ones left in Scotland. They seem all to have been
judgement scenes: those above the windows on the N. and W. walls
are the Judgement of Solomon and the Woman taken in Adultery.
The others are fragmentary. Of several memorial stones preserved
here one is Celtic and another bears the effigy of Canon Douglas
(early 16th c.).

The **exterior** of the N. side largely repeats the S., but the
buttresses are shallower because the aisle was not vaulted. The
window tracery should be noted. In the ruins its decay has been
discreetly arrested by fitting bronze bars inside the randomly

weatherworn contours of the stones. In the quire is some well preserved 13th c. tracery of the period when Geometric forms were being tried in conjunction with the 'Y' patterns of intersecting lancets, and cusping was beginning to be used.

To the NE. is the custodian's hut, where official guides and postcards can be bought. The wrought-iron churchyard gates were made about 1730 for Dunkeld House and transferred here in 1832.

Durham, Christ & St Mary (Church of England, Durham)

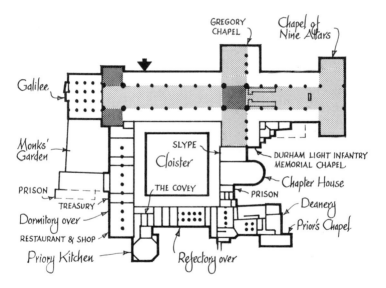

The founding of the monastery is credited to monks driven by the Danes from Lindisfarne and looking for a safer shelter for St Cuthbert's shrine. Their church was dedicated in 998 and the bones of the Venerable Bede were also brought to it before the Conquest. The first Norman bishop began to rebuild it on the grandest possible scale in 1093. Though he died three years later the quire and crossing were complete by 1099, the transepts by 1104 and the remainder by 1133. The chapter house followed, and before the end of the century the W. 'Galilee' chapel – attempts to build an E. Lady chapel having at that time failed. Instead the remarkable chapel of Nine Altars was built at the E. end early in the 13th c. The central tower was rebuilt or extended about 1465 and heightened again before 1500.

The interior suffered like all others at the Reformation. In the Civil War it was again desecrated, chiefly through being used as a prison for Scots taken by Cromwell at the battle of Dunbar. After the Restoration, Bishop Cosin, probably with James Clement as architect, renewed many of the fittings. Much destructive 'improvement' was done with the approval of the Dean and Chapter, first under John Wooler *c.* 1780 and then under James Wyatt *c.* 1795.

The bishops throughout the 11th to 16th cc. wielded civil and even military power as well as ecclesiastical. This is not only expressed in the awe-inspiring and well-nigh impregnable site of the cathedral but also reinforced by the adjoining castle, which until the establishment of the university there in the 1830s was the bishop's palace and personal fortress.

Alterations and repairs continued during much of the 19th c., becoming less destructive as time went on and passing ultimately (1870–6) to the control of Sir George Gilbert Scott. His quire screen, like too many other expensive additions at different periods, shows an arrogant disrespect for Durham's particular kind of grandeur. But for centuries the building has been great enough, powerful

Cathedral and Castle from NE., Durham

SW. Tower as seen from central Tower, Durham (early 12th c.)

enough, to hold its own against friend and foe alike.

The natural approach is from Palace Green to the N. doorway with a replica of its famous 12th c. bronze sanctuary knocker, one of the greatest treasures of early medieval metalwork; the original is in the treasury. The eyes, now blank, were once of coloured enamel. The doorway itself has 12th c. stonework, though the outer part is 15th c., and the porch (which had an upper room) has gone.

The Romanesque **nave** is overwhelming in its sheer majesty. The great solemn cylindrical piers, many of them with quite primitive helical and other incised patterns, alternate with even bigger, composite ones, so that the rhythm can be interpreted as either single bays or double, a reposeful arrangement that occurs in many great churches of this period. The quadripartite vault is arranged in pairs of bays too, with big pointed arches spanning only between the clustered piers; its ribs have zigzag enrichment. The clerestory is pushed perhaps a little uncomfortably into the vault; the triforium has twin round-headed openings beneath a dignified single arch with more zigzag. The aisle vaults also are quadripartite and ribbed and have additional transverse ribs. All this is of *c.* 1110–30. The crossing and transepts and the quire, which actually came first, will be seen later.

Turning W., it will be seen that the W. bays of the arcades are different. They look into the towers, so their triforium and clerestory are blank. The big W. window is of course a 14th c. alteration, Decorated in style; its fine glass is a Jesse Tree by Clayton & Bell (1867). The white marble font is of 1663 (i.e. Bishop Cosin's), a beautiful little classical 'baluster' dwarfed by its magnificent cover of the same date which starts off with Composite classical columns and entablature but then bursts forth with Gothic canopies and pinnacles, almost – but not quite – as though it were medieval. A line across the floor in Frosterley marble marks the limit to which women could go towards the altar.

Now into the N. aisle again and through its W. doorway into the **Galilee Lady Chapel**, added *c.* 1170–75. Though still Norman, its grace and lightness are the very antithesis of the nave. Indeed, the original two-shafted Purbeck marble columns were found to be too slender and in the 15th c. were each strengthened with two more shafts of sandstone; their unaltered form can be seen at the ends. The richly zigzagged arches and 'waterleaf' capitals help to date it. The five-aisled arrangement is unique. The windows are of course later and bigger than the original.

Along the E. wall the second bay has an altar with a modern

Sanctuary knocker, Durham, now in Treasury (12th c.)

Cross and a late 12th c. wall-painting with curtain ornament. Above, and on the walls above the adjoining arcades, are more wall-paintings. The centre bay, containing the original great W. doorway of the cathedral, was blocked to receive the tomb-chest of Cardinal Langley (d. 1437), which stands on a projecting platform bearing his arms; behind is a splendid triptych of *c*. 1500, and on the floor in front a deeply carved ledger stone of 1662. The ornamental texts in the fourth bay, designed by George Pace, are a memorial to Dean Alington (d. 1970). In front of them is the tomb of Bede, put up in 1542. Continuing clockwise, passing the S. aisle doorway, most of the windows contain ancient fragments set in patterned leadwork also by Pace. There is also a hog-back chest with a great padlock. The projecting bay on the W. side was probably a vestry; there is also a small doorway which gave access to a well.

Back now into the **N. aisle** beneath the W. tower, where the N. and W. windows are of a character entirely foreign to Durham. The wall-arcading, giant in itself, is yet outdone by the enormous scale of the main piers and arches. It is worth pausing again at the N. doorway to look at its inside arch with two shafts each side, one encrusted with surface ornament. More windows with boldly patterned cames and plain glass follow, then the reclining figure on a tomb-chest of James Britton (d. 1836).

In the **N. transept** the system of design is like the nave's but more compressed because the column spacing is closer. The W. side, having no aisle, has its triforium reduced to a mere walkway. The date is *c*. 1093–1104, i.e. immediately earlier than the nave. As in the nave, the great end window is of *c*. 1360; it is pushed off centre by the stair turret and has a passage across its centre with very thick mullions beneath. Dean Alington's resting place in the centre of the floor is marked with an octagonal piece of slate and incised heraldry. The E. aisle, reserved for private prayer, is the Gregory chapel (though actually St Benedict's), and has a simple classical gilt and black altar and communion kneeler. At its S. end and best seen from the **N. quire aisle** by going through the 17th c. doorless wooden screen is the curious sarcophagus of Matthew Woodifield (d. 1826), supported on stumpy Greek Doric columns.

This is the earliest part of the cathedral and the aisle vaults are considered to be the earliest rib-vaults anywhere (a development from earlier 'groin' vaults which are without ribs). The wall-arcading continues – as it does round the transept – and is an early instance of intersecting arches. To the right is the back of the organ, to the left a little blocked doorway containing a tablet to William

Galilee Chapel, Durham (late 12th c.)

Hartwel (d. 1725). The bright coat-of-arms on the next column on
the right is that of Bishop Crewe and is recent. Beyond under
another 17th c. Gothic wood screen is the tomb-chest of Bishop
Lightfoot (d. 1891), with effigy by Sir Edgar Boehm. The matrix of a
brass in front and the plinth opposite are relics of the chantry of
Bishop Skirlaw (d. 1405).

The last bay, at the bottom of the steps, took the place of an apse
when the Nine Altars chapel was added and is thus Early English,
with a pointed arch to the quire, vault ribs enriched with flowers,
and wall-arcade with Frosterley marble shafts and springing foliage
capitals. On the right is an Art Nouveau bronze plaque to the
Marquess of Londonderry (d. 1915) by John Tweed.

Steps lead up to the tomb of St Cuthbert in the **feretory** behind
the high altar. At the Reformation a plain slab (now surrounded by
rough stones and four aluminium candlesticks) took the place of his
shrine. The white outline on the floor marks the original central
apse. The painted and gilded Majestas tester above is by Sir Ninian
Comper and most of the Elizabethan-style screenwork is a
reconstruction. On the far side is a huge ironbound chest, and at the
N. end the 15th c. figure of St Cuthbert carrying the head of
St Oswald.

On now into the E. transept, the **chapel of Nine Altars**, begun in
1242 and therefore Early English. The nine altars were along the E.
wall, in an arrangement hardly paralleled except at Fountains
Abbey in Yorkshire. Each has its own giant lancet window, and the
N. end has a marvellous Geometric window with a second, internal,
set of mullions. The E. rose is Wyatt's conjectural restoration of the
original which (like the S. windows) has been replaced by
Perpendicular. Instead of a conventional triforium there are
passages at sill level (above the slightly clumsy wall-arcading) and
below the clerestory. The principal attractions of the chapel, or
rather chapels, are the alternating shafts of limestone and Frosterley
marble and the vault patterns they support – the outer ones
quadripartite, the next an ingenious kind of sexpartite with the
central rib missing the boss, and in the centre a four-pointed star
with a central ring bearing superb carvings of the Evangelists.

Within a blocked doorway in the NW. corner is a nice tablet to
Dean Cowper (d. 1774); this is the best of many in the chapel. The
thoughtful seated marble figure on a white circular plinth is of
Bishop van Mildert (d. 1836) by John Gibson. The six stone coffin-
lids ranged opposite the pier bases are probably 13th c. and, at the
S. end, the marble floor-slab of 1903 is in memory of Bishop

Dangerfield (d. 1845). By this is a 13th c. standing cross-head from
Neasham Priory at Hurworth-on-Tees.

In the S. quire aisle a second stair leads to St Cuthbert's tomb.
Then in bay 2 the **quire** itself can be entered. Its architecture differs
little from that of the nave; it is about 20–30 years earlier. The vault,
however, is 13th c. and has enriched ribs and bosses. It is thus
contemporary with the completion of the chapel of Nine Altars, and
so of course is the easternmost, junction bay of the main arcades, as
well as the canopy work and arcading applied to the blank walling
before it. The canopied and pinnacled reredos of Caen stone that
links these Early English arches, and the four sedilia within each of
them, form the Neville screen, given by Lord Neville in 1380. Like
some of the cathedral's window tracery, it havers between the
Decorated and Perpendicular styles though its general massing is
strongly vertical. It once contained 107 alabaster statues. The
communion rail is by W. Hollis (1940), in a bold effective 17th c.
style. The big altar stands over a small Jacobean marble one which
is revealed and used during Holy Week.

The patterned marble paving is all by Scott; under the centre
carpet, close to the communion rail, is a big (renewed) 16th c. brass
to Bishop Beamont (d. 1333). The bishop's throne, in a unique
arrangement, stands on top and forms part of the chantry of Bishop
Hatfield (d. 1381). His alabaster effigy lies in a deep 'tunnel' all re-
coloured in red, blue and gold. The throne above, canopied and
pinnacled to a great height, also has 17th c. work in its stair and
balustrade. Next is a heavily carved triple desk probably made from
a Spanish altar; then the rich stalls put in by Bishop Cosin in a 17th
c. version of Gothic. Their misericords may be looked at on request.
Scott's quire screen with its Frosterley marble columns has lost its
railing and gates but is still totally out of keeping. The two brass
candelabra are of 1751. Continuing clockwise: past the N. side stalls
is the modest hexagonal wooden quire pulpit (another Cosin piece)
and finally the Lightfoot tomb already seen from the aisle.

Back next into the **S. quire aisle**, in the second bay from the E.,
which has a jumble of old glass in its window. On the right is the
back of the Hatfield chantry, and then the aisle leads into the **S.
transept** through another 17th c. Cosin screen matching the N. side.
Architecturally the transepts are similar, though there are many
small differences in the upper parts. The S. transept is dominated by
the clock, which is partly of *c.* 1510 but largely of 1630; it was the
only wooden fitting spared by the Scottish prisoners in 1650. The
great *Te Deum* window above is by Clayton & Bell. On the E. side

the first two bays form the Durham Light Infantry chapel and contain banners and a war memorial cross and panelling. The base of the clock is worth a closer look, for on the doors is a delightful miniature painting of a church interior in Dutch style.

A spiral stair in the SW. corner of the transept is often open (for a small charge) and leads to the **tower** via a walkway along the interior of the transept roof and a long second stair to the top. Needless to say, there are excellent views: W. to the other towers and the river, N. to Palace Green and the castle, E. to the chapel of Nine Altars with its four prominent turrets, and S. to the cloister and monastic buildings, including the chapter house on the left and the Deanery beyond, the refectory and the kitchen with its complex roof, and on the right the dormitory.

Back in the S. transept, the kneeling marble figure on the W. wall is Bishop Barrington (d. 1826) by Sir Francis Chantrey. In the **crossing** the view up into the lantern tower is an impressive one. Above the four massive Norman arches the original ceiling was flat. But in the 15th c. that was taken out, so that now one sees a corbelled gallery and lantern windows and a lierne vault 155 ft above the floor. The classical lectern below is by D. McIntyre (1934), and the outrageously inappropriate Italianate marble pulpit either by Scott or by Anthony Salvin.

In the **S. nave aisle** is a painted wood inscription to Dean Hunt (d. 1638). The badly damaged tombs under the arcade in bays 2 and 3 are of Ralph, Lord Neville (d. 1367) and John, Lord Neville (d. 1388), each with two effigies. The wall-arcade has traces of original colour in bay 3, with a small portion restored to show what it was like. In bay 5 is the Miners' memorial, made up of cherubs from a discarded Cosin fitting and from the same (possibly Spanish) altar as the quire desk already seen. In bay 6 is the Monks' door to the cloister. This must be returned to, but the rest of the aisle should not be missed for it contains part of the front of Father Smith's organ case of 1683, looking rather strange at this level. Under the tower are two 18th c. wall tablets.

Back then to the 12th c. Monks' doorway, which has enriched shafts (the outer are double) and beautiful original ironwork. The cloister is essentially Norman too, though the arcades were rebuilt in 1390–1418; the curious simplified window tracery is of *c.* 1773 and the flat timber ceilings are largely of 1828. There are few memorials. Moving clockwise, i.e. taking the N. walk first, the rich Norman Prior's doorway at its end should be admired. Then there is a blocked opening against the transept; and along the E. walk a big doorway to the slype (later the parlour and now a vestibule leading to the song school) and one even bigger to the chapter house, flanked by windows. These are not normally open. These parts are early 12th c. except that the apsed E. part of the chapter house, destroyed by Wyatt, was reconstructed in 1895. There is wall-arcading of intersecting pattern and vaulting, the ribs of which in the apse rest on caryatid figures. The glass is by Hugh Easton. The next little doorway led to a small prison, now the sacristy.

At the corner, beginning the S. range which is even earlier than the cathedral itself, perhaps c. 1080–90, is a passage to the open space called The College with very low, primitive, almost Saxon-looking arches each side. It leads to a rebuilt porch. Returning to the S. walk, one has an excellent view of the Norman W. towers with their 13th c. upper stages and battlements of 1801 and of the three tiers of Norman windows of the nave: aisle, triforium gallery and (set back) clerestory. Here there are a few wall tablets, chief being a good cartouche to Dean Graham of Wells (d. 1705). A Classical doorway leads to the first-floor library, converted from the refectory in 1684 (not open to the public).

Ahead is the 13th c. dormitory undercroft with a passage leading outside and to lavatories. To the left are a restaurant and shop, with glazed screens by Pace; to the right the **treasury**, an exhibition area for which an entrance fee is charged. It contains an incredible wealth of very early embroidery, documents and books, rings, seals and plate, and, most precious of all, St Cuthbert's wooden coffin of 698 and his even older pectoral cross. A detailed catalogue is available.

From the W. walk one can look across to the chapter house and to the central tower with its very obviously added upper stages of c. 1465 and c. 1490. On the left, past various vestry doors, a stair leads to the **dormitory** of c. 1400 (small admission fee), one of the noblest rooms in England – spacious and well-lit and with a magnificent low-pitched timber roof, two trusses to every window. The first third or so is open as an exhibition area of Anglo-Saxon stone fragments (reputedly the best in England and dominated by two giant crosses which are in fact cast replicas) and of documents, etc., in glass cases; the remainder is occupied by bookcases.

Now back to the cloister, across the nave and out again through the N. door for a **circuit** anti-clockwise. Look left first at the N. side of the Galilee with its renewed doorway and window tracery. Then follow the path past the old grammar school (now University Music School) and turn along its N. side through Windy Gap. Pace's

addition to the University Library of 1970 is on the right. Reaching
the river bank, one turns left, with dramatic oblique views of the W.
front through trees and a close sight of the W. wall of the Galilee.
Next is the flank wall of the monks' garden. Shortly afterwards a
very sharp left turn and a steep slope lead into The College through
a sunless tunnel beneath one of the houses. Round to the left is the
dormitory undercroft (with the present-day kitchen). On the right of
that is the octagonal Prior's kitchen of 1366–70; then the Durham
Light Infantry memorial garden with the refectory windows above,
and close to it the porch leading to the SE. of the cloister.

   Just E. of the porch, iron gates by Pace lead to the Deanery, a
complex building on the site of the prior's lodging. The road skirts
its garden on the S. and goes through the main Gatehouse (c. 1500)
into North Bailey. Here one should turn left: presently an
opening on the left reveals the chapel of Nine Altars, with a war
memorial column in the foreground. Then the cobbled Dun Cow
Lane leads back to Palace Green. The legendary Dun Cow,
associated with St Cuthbert's coming to Durham, can be seen
carved in a niche on the NW. corner turret of the Nine Altars chapel
– but it only dates from c. 1800.

   From Palace Green the whole N. side of the cathedral opens out.
No one, however, should visit Durham without seeing it from the
other side of the river, or without enjoying one at least of the more
distant views, in which cathedral and castle complement one another
on their rocky peninsula.

Edinburgh, St Giles (Church of Scotland, Lothian)

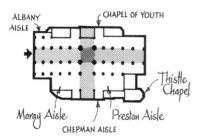

Having in the Middle Ages never been more than a collegiate
church, and having only contained a bishop's throne from 1633 to
1639 and from 1662 to 1690, St Giles' has only a slight claim to be

included amongst cathedrals; yet it retains its courtesy title and is popularly regarded as one. The earliest recorded date of a church here is 854. It was re-founded in the 12th c., burnt down in an English invasion in 1385, and almost at once rebuilt. Collegiate status, granted in 1466, coincided with the extending of the quire and transepts and prompted the adding of more chapels. The steeple was completed in 1495.

It was at the centre of the religious storms of the 16th and 17th cc. and became divided into three and then four separate churches. A destructive 'restoration' was done in 1829–33 under William Burn and a more responsible one in 1872–83 under the guidance of William Chambers. The Thistle chapel was built in 1909–11 under Sir Robert Lorimer.

The W. entrance is the best starting point. The **nave** arcades in their present form with octagonal columns and moulded capitals are by Chambers but the clerestory and plaster vault are Burn's; earlier roof levels can be traced on the E. face of the tower. In the 16th c. parts of the W. end were walled off to form an annexe to the Tolbooth or court building, and subsequently what was called the Tolbooth Kirk. The tattered banners are of Scots regiments, 18th and 19th c. The outer arcades with their clustered columns, and the aisle vaults, are 15th c. The elaborate W. door lobby with seats and canopies and a royal arms in the centre is of *c.* 1880 and the main W. window (Prophets) is by Daniel Cottier.

War memorials cover the W. wall of the **N. aisle** and its W. window is by Sir Edward Burne-Jones, made by William Morris & Co. (1881). A low iron screen separates off the **Albany aisle**, founded *c.* 1400 and now reserved for private prayer. Its walls, too, are lined with war memorials but its chief interest lies in the modern furniture and decoration – the Cross with four texts in stone, the big sanctuary lamp ornamented with thistles, the patterned marble floor with heraldic roundels, and the plain low chairs around the table.

Continuing along the aisle, there are yet more war memorials, the first (to the Royal Scots Fusiliers) being in a recess which led to Haddo's Hole, a small chamber where Sir John Gordon was imprisoned in 1644. Not only this but also the magnificent Romanesque 'Marriage porch' were removed in 1797, their place being taken by the former Session Room to which there is a small doorway. Next on the left is the former St Eloi's chapel, containing an ornate 19th c. memorial in 17th c. style to the first Marquis of Argyll, executed in 1661. The window behind, by the Glass Stainers' Company of Glasgow, shows the arms of the leaders of the

St Giles' Cathedral from W., Edinburgh

Covenanters. The banner on the W. wall is of the Edinburgh Auxiliary Air Force Squadron. The scrolly iron screen, the Irish marble and mosaic floor, two big upholstered chairs and the holy table frontal chest with fine ironwork are all worth noting.

The outer end of the **N. transept** was completely rebuilt by Burn to make a ceremonial entrance; its grey Gothic screen of Aberfeldy stone was added by Chambers. The figures represent patron saints of the craft guilds which had altars in the church. Of the memorials in the stair lobby, the bronze bas-relief head of Chambers's architect, William Hay (d. 1888) should be noted. Burn gave the transept a plaster vault like the nave. The **crossing** vault is medieval, however, and the big octagonal piers – no higher than those of the arcades – probably encase Romanesque ones.

Now up into the **N. quire aisle**, with first a look at the 14th c. quire design which (except in the two E. bays) is similar to the nave but lower and with a later, tierceron, vault. The aisles again have quadripartite vaults. The chapel of Youth on the left is virtually all 19th c.; its oak screen and Nativity reredos form a memorial to Dr William Chambers, benefactor of the 1870s restoration. The banners include one of Field-Marshal Earl Haig, and the Victorian carved seat with Flamboyant tracery is of interest. The glass here and in all the ensuing windows round to the SE. corner is by Ballantine.

On the left of the aisle is a door to St Margaret's room (an office). The recess beyond is of an unknown person's tomb; the many 19th and 20th c. memorials here are of only minor artistic interest, but include those of the two women medical pioneers, Sophie Jex Blake and Elsie Inglis; on the E. wall the royal arms and arms of the Company of Merchants commemorate the Queen's visit in 1953. Crossing the E. end (where a marble platform marks where the communion table stood till recent years), note the different treatment of the two E. bays where the columns are clustered and have heraldic capitals: these, with the whole quire clerestory and vault, are 15th c. The stalls by the last columns on the N. and S. sides are those of the Moderator and of the Dean of the Thistle and of H.M. Chapel Royal.

On the E. wall of the **S. quire aisle** is a war memorial to ministers, on the S. a Jacobean style one to Lord Justice Inglis (d. 1891), and a bas-relief bronze bust by Pilkington Jackson to the Rev. J. Cameron Lees (d. 1913). A similar memorial to Andrew Williamson (d. 1926) is just past the sumptuous wrought iron-screen to the ante-chapel of the Thistle chapel, made by Thomas Hadden. The chapel's designer,

Sir Robert Lorimer (d. 1929), is remembered on a tablet round the corner on the E. wall of the Preston aisle, and above it is another bronze bust, of Dean Stanley of Westminster (d. 1881). An older carved stone set in the wall bears the civic arms of Edinburgh, a castle. Another rich screen guards the ante-chapel which has giant bosses on its vault and a roll of knights on the left wall. A fee is charged for entering the **Thistle chapel** itself, built in 1909–11. In it an irrepressible flow of magnificent craftsmanship seems somehow to have overwhelmed other considerations, so that the high windws and over-bossed vault, and the rich stalls and their canopies with delicate twisted columns are quite alien to the sombre dignity of St Giles' itself. (It is only fair to add that the intention of the donors, the Earl of Leven and his brothers, was to restore the Chapel Royal of Holyroodhouse for the same purpose, to be the chapel of the Order of the Thistle.) There are more details to admire in the splendid royal arms on the sovereign's stall at the back, the stall plates on the panels and the crests over them, and the heraldic windows. Another royal arms set into the plain grey floor is a memorial to King George VI.

The **Preston aisle**, tierceron-vaulted, is furnished chapel-wise and contains the sovereign's stall on the S. side with seats for the royal suite and below for the Lyon Court. It was founded in 1454. From 1643 till 1829 it was used as a separate church. The little chapel opening off it through a low iron screen is the Chepman aisle (St John the Evangelist's), founded in 1513. It houses the big canopied monument (of 1888) to the Marquis of Montrose, executed 1650. A small but intricate brass by Francis Skidmore on the W. wall commemorates Walter Chepman (d. 1532). The heraldic window is by Ballantine. The framed parchment is the original portion of the National Covenant (1638) sent to Linlithgow for signatures. A portion of the **S. transept**, once St Anthony's chapel, is taken up with the organ.

Turn now to the **crossing**, passing on the left the wooden screen to the Moray aisle. The N. transept window, well seen from here, is by Douglas Strachan, and the main E. one by Ballantine (1877). The big Gothic oak communion table which stood beneath it is now placed further W. The ornate octagonal Caen stone pulpit is by Sir George Gilbert Scott, the Acts of Mercy scenes being by John Rhind; the rather similar lectern opposite has a curtailed appearance.

The outer S. or **Moray aisle** is temporarily devoted to sales space and there is no altar, though a brass eagle lectern and canopied

pulpit of 1884 by Sir Robert Rowand Anderson survive. The little
chapel at its SE. corner, originally the Holy Blood aisle but halved
in width in 1829, retains a 14th c. foliated tomb recess and a brass to
the Earl of Murray (d. 1570) set into a more modern memorial.
Outside this bay it is worth exploring along the S. wall amongst the
book stands for the memorials to Margaret Oliphant (d. 1897) and
Robert Fergusson, both in bronze by Pittendrigh MacGillivray;
John Blackie (d. 1895); and Thomas Chalmers and Dr John Brown
(both d. 1882), both portrayed by Jackson. The giant Art Nouveau
bronze plaque on the W. wall to Robert Louis Stevenson (d. 1894) is
by Augustus Saint Gaudens (1902).

On the outside of the iron screen are ranged several items of
interest – a 'music bell' of 1698 on a stand; a square grave-marker
stone (formerly outside) with the inscription IK 1572, and a stone
inscribed JOHN KNOX 1559 (these are the dates of Knox's last and
first sermons here); on the floor just E. of the gate, a bronze tablet
to Jenny Geddes who (so the story goes) hurled her stool at the
Dean; a bell from H.M.S. *Howe* (1942); and a vesper bell of 1452.

The outer S. arcade ends with two very shallow bays (till 1829 the
Moray aisle continued to the W. end). Both contain memorials
(mostly military) and in the second is the Angel with Shell font
carved in Caen stone by John Rhind in imitation of Thorvaldsen's
at Copenhagen. The white marble bust at the W. end of the main S.
aisle is of General Lockhart (d. 1900), by Sir George Frampton.
Close to it is a 16th c. English chest.

Apart from the tower, the **exterior** has been so much straightened
out and refaced as to have lost practically all interest. The big
monument outside the W. doorway is to the Duke of Buccleuch
(d. 1884), by Clark Stanton. On the S. side, past an oriel window
that formed part of the vanished S. porch, is a statue of John Knox
by MacGillivray, formerly inside the N. aisle. Further on is the
unsightly blocked window behind the organ, and then in the S. part
of Parliament Square an equestrian statue of Charles II. The Thistle
chapel in the SE. corner of the cathedral has an external entrance
which incorporates a 15th c. round-headed arch from the old S.
porch. The octagonal structure near the NE. is an 1885
reproduction of the 16th c. Old Mercat Cross.

Finally the tower, the most distinctive feature of St Giles', late
15th c. in its upper parts. The 'crown' is by no means unique,
though more elaborate than most in having eight flying buttresses.

Edinburgh, St Mary (Scottish Episcopal Church, Lothian)

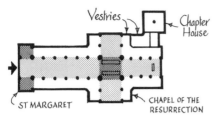

The history of St Mary's goes back to the foundation of a diocese of
Edinburgh in 1633 with St Giles' as cathedral. After the religious
split the Episcopalians moved to a chapel on the site of St Paul's off
the High Street. St Paul's itself later served as pro-cathedral.
St Mary's was substantially the gift of the sisters Barbara and Mary
Walker, built on their land after a competition won by Sir George
Gilbert Scott – whose masterpiece it is. It was consecrated in 1879, a
year after his death. The chapter house was not built till 1890 and
the W. towers (under J. Oldrid Scott) as late as 1917.

The dominating feature is the 275 ft central tower and spire,
supported by conventional crossing-piers but strengthened by great
diagonal buttresses across the transept/aisle junctions. The general
style is 13th c., with features borrowed from, for example, Jedburgh
abbey and Dunblane. The **nave** has alternate round and octagonal
columns with foliage capitals, triforium with two pairs of windows
per bay, and clerestory with prominent and varied mouldings. The
rather dark wooden 'vault' is really a slightly pointed wagon roof
with applied ribs.

The vaulted NW. tower space forms the verger's vestry. In the **N.
aisle** the Madonna painting in bay 3 is by Matteo Cerezo (17th c.).
To its right is Francesco Maria Mazzola's Christ Healing the Dumb
(16th c.). Back in the nave, the Rood at the crossing was designed by
Sir Robert Lorimer and carved by Pilkington Jackson, and the
Italianate pulpit by J. Oldrid Scott. The 'septum' (low pulpitum) is
Italian in style too.

The aisled **N. transept** design, much obscured by the organ, is like
the nave. The diagonal buttress-arches of the tower should be noted.
On the left the wooden font is by Mary Syme Boyd (1959). This is
the King Charles chapel and the brilliant altar frontal bears his
arms; the paintings of him and Bishop Forbes (1633) are modern
copies.

Now past the organ, and the office in the NE. corner, across the
N. quire aisle, and into the **quire**. This, with its clustered piers, blind
triforium and trios of lancets in the clerestory is quite different.
Moreover the vault is real stone and skilfully contrived to make the
square E. end look like an apse. The sumptuous reredos is by J.
Oldrid Scott, the iron screens by Francis Skidmore, later gaily
coloured. The altar rail is somewhat similar, neither Gothic nor
classical; inside it are brasses to Bishop Reid (d. 1943) and, further
E., Bishop Walpole (d. 1929). The quire proper is beneath the
crossing, further W. than Scott intended, with the bishop's throne
against the SE. crossing pier. Opposite, under the first arch of the N.
quire aisle, is the tomb of James Montgomery (d. 1897), with white
marble effigy. Brasses are to Bishop Dowden, d. 1910 (nearest the
organ console on the N. side), Bishop Cotterill, d. 1886 (inscription
in centre of floor), and Bishop Walker, d. 1841 (nearest throne). The
stalls, unusual in being of walnut, are of superb workmanship with
elaborately arcaded front desks and traditional but uncanopied rear
seats.

Go back to the altar rail and left into the aisle again. Here hangs
the painting 'The Presence' by A. E. Borthwick, with a plaque
describing its chequered history; also another copy of one of
Charles 1. The square **chapter house** may usually be seen on request.
It has a splendid vault on a central granite column, a display of the
architects' competition designs and a painting, 'The Incarnation', by
Brian Slack (1976).

The ambulatory behind the altar is used as a vestry, so the **S.
quire aisle** is reached across the quire again. The Lady altar here is
also rather Italian in style, with a narrow tapestry each side; on the
S. wall is an unusual brass with recumbent figure of Sub-dean
Cazenove (d. 1896). Another Skidmore screen leads to the **S.
transept** which has much of interest: a museum case of old books,
etc.; a 'rope' sculpture, 'The Crown of Thorns', by Edith Simon; an
attractive mahogany chamber organ; the Resurrection chapel and a
granite memorial cross of 1878 to the Royal Scots; an array of
banners (with explanatory notes to the left of the S. doorway) and a
painting, 'The Assumption of Elijah', by Ernst Degasperi (1976).
Here too are some good pieces of furniture: a long seat with 16th c.
carved panels, two richly carved 17th c. tables and a large 18th c.
cabinet. The little Madonna carving on the SW. crossing pier is by
Lesley Crowe (1971).

In the **S. aisle** are many 19th and 20th c. brass memorials and, on
the right, the splendid brass pelican lectern with enamel inlay.

Further on stands a second font, plain smooth octagonal with an openwork iron cover. An iron screen leads into St Margaret's chapel beneath the SW. tower, with a discarded Gothic reredos on its side wall. Finally, to the left of the main doorway, there is another modern picture, 'Altar I' by Robin Philipson (1971).

The triple-spired exterior, set down on green lawns, has a grandeur unapproached by any surviving Scottish cathedral. This description, taken clockwise, can only indicate its main features: the very elaborate W. front, particularly the main doorway and its ironwork, the grand towers and especially the central one which so subtly becomes octagonal as it rises, the N. doorway with more superb ironwork, the great diagonal tower buttress at the aisle/transept junction, the medieval Old Coates House to the N. (now St Mary's Music School), and the chapter house which also becomes octagonal in its upper part. Out then into Manor Place and past the stately E. end and back along the S. side. The most impressive view of all is from the SE. across the widest stretch of grass: it includes the wheel window of the S. transept and the richly detailed doorway below – all of it, for Scott, the expression of a more glorious renaissance of Gothic architecture than there ever was of the Classical.

Edinburgh, St Mary (Roman Catholic, Lothian)

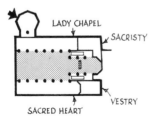

James Gillespie Graham's original chapel of 1813 was a plain rectangular building with an apse. Its W. front, in the Gothic style as then being revived, suggests an aisled nave but it seems that from the start the ceiling was a single wide span. A long 'cloister' chapel, added on the N. side in 1838 where the aisle and Lady chapel now are, was burnt down in 1865 and rebuilt. The building became a cathedral in 1878 and was given a W. porch. In 1891 another fire prompted the replacement of the cloister chapel with a proper arcaded aisle and a NW. baptistry and at the same time the S. aisle was added and a new aisled quire built. The nave roof was rebuilt in 1932. In 1974–6 the baptistry and W. porch were demolished and an octagonal porch built in a new position by T. Harley Haddow & Partners.

This concrete-framed brick-lined porch has its own altar with a painting of the Deposition by an unknown artist. The nave as reformed in 1932 in a daring style reminiscent of Arts and Crafts Gothic is of astonishing width, with great wooden arches on giant corbel angels wearing crowns and bearing shields. Graham's modest W. front (with low side extensions) being still retained as a screen, the arcades are very low with an extraordinary double clerestory, the upper windows being circular and having ornamental wall-plates both above and below. The painting over the chancel arch, also of 1932, is by Louis Beyaert.

The broad, low N. aisle has a Pietà in the second bay and the remainder of the side wall is take up with bas-relief Stations of the Cross by Mayer of Munich, a 1919 war memorial. The oak-panelled Lady chapel at the E. end has a white marble altar and reredos; the font, under the last bay of the arcade, is 19th c., round and undistinguished.

The quire (1891) has much taller arcades and windows of Perpendicular type. These (with the exception of some scattered thistles, etc. at the W. end) have the only pictorial glass in the cathedral. The hammer-beam roof continues awkwardly round the apse, the stalls discreetly occupy the aisles, and the organ stands at the NE., right behind the bishop's throne. The new Italianate altar should be noted, also the brass eagle lectern, the dark marble communion rail and the rather ungainly canopied octagonal pulpit. The SE chapel (Sacred Heart) has an oak-panelled sanctuary.

The partly re-faced W. and N. fronts, the latter with new entrance on a piazza, are attractive. A stepped way leads around the dingy E. end and down the S. side but there is nothing of interest there.

Elgin, Holy Trinity [Scottish Development Department] (Grampian)

After a period of uncertainty during which the bishop's throne of Moray was at Birnie, Kinnedar and Spynie, it was set up in Holy Trinity church in Elgin in 1224. However, the bishops continued to live at Spynie, 2 miles to the N., where the palace-castle still stands in ruin. The first cathedral was late 12th c. and had twin W. towers,

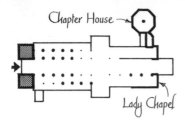

nave and aisles, crossing and transept with central tower, and quire, a short outer S. nave aisle being soon added. After a fire in 1270 it was extensively rebuilt with full outer aisles, S. porch, a much longer, aisled quire, and an octagonal chapter house. Even greater destruction resulted from a raid in 1390 by Alexander Stewart, the 'Wolf of Badenoch', in revenge for his excommunication by the bishop. Consequent repairs and renewals included the W. front and part of the nave arcades, the chapter house, and a complete new central tower.

In design and craftsmanship Elgin probably exceeded all other cathedrals in Scotland. It owed something to Lincoln but much also to the existence of a well-established body of skilled masons in Moray.

The roof was stripped of lead at the time of the Reformation, the interior was later wrecked by Cromwell's troops, and in 1711 the central tower collapsed, bringing much of the remainder with it. The ruins were tidied and repaired in the 19th c. and they passed in due course to the care of the Secretary of State for Scotland. Visiting hours are standard and the entrance fee allows ascent of the SW. tower.

The two 13th c. W. towers flank a splendid double doorway and window which were reconstructed c. 1395. The surround of this portal, of no fewer than eight orders, each with attached shafts at the jambs, is 13th c. and ornamented with dog-tooth. The vesica-shaped panel, now blank, and the twin trefoil-headed openings (all added later) enhance the somewhat French character. Each tower originally carried a leaded spire.

Now the **inside**: and firstly the bases of the clustered columns of both inner and outer nave arcades, which stand a foot or so high towards the W. end. Looking behind to the W. gable, it is easy to see how high the roof was. Also, high on the S. face of the NW. tower (as well as in the interior of both) areas of stone burnt in the 1390 fire can be detected.

Cathedral from E., Elgin (13th and 14th cc.)

Ahead, much of the quire still stands; of its E. gable only the tip
is missing, the side chapels have stone vaulting and, over to the left,
the chapter house has its walls and vault entire. As for the transepts
and the nave aisle walls, a great deal remains, particularly on the S.

The ticket office is on the immediate left, beneath the NW. tower.
A number of interesting heraldic slabs are displayed there. Just
outside it in the **outer N. aisle** the vault springer stones can be seen
on the tower wall. The **N. transept**, part of the original late 12th c.
building and formerly St Thomas à Becket's chapel, has the start of
a spiral stair in the NW. corner which led to a clerestory passage
and thence to the central tower. The tablet of 1590 on the W. wall
and the two earlier damaged figures under recesses in the N. wall
commemorate members of the Dunbar family. A piscina is in the
NE. corner.

In the **N. quire aisle** a big ancient standing cross-slab with a
spirited figure of a huntsman has been set up. Unconnected with the
cathedral, this was found buried near St Giles' church. The E. bay
of the aisle still has its tierceron vault; however, the opposite aisle is
more complete and the design will be better appreciated there. Here
on the left is the trefoil-headed doorway to the chapter house
vestibule, leading first to a little stone-roofed sacristy with a stone
basin. Then a fine 13th c. doorway with dog-tooth ornament leads
to the chapter house itself. This doorway belongs to the room as it
was first, with a timber roof. After 1390 the upper parts of the walls
were thickened and the splendid stone vault built, supported on an
added central column. A profusion of first-rate carving is to be seen
in the roof bosses and corbels, column capital and frieze below the
window sills, and in the arcading that runs round the walls forming
canopies to the low stone seats; five taller seats for dignitaries adorn
the N. wall. An unusual feature is the stone reading desk attached to
the central column. The sadly decayed window tracery has recently
been partially renewed. The memorials to bishops' families were
brought from St Giles' church when it was demolished in 1826. They
are of the period 1670–1720; the double one on the E. wall is
perhaps the most interesting, though it has lost a Corinthian
column.

Now back into the N. quire aisle (noting a piscina in the NE.
corner) and through a large or a small arch into the **quire**. These
arches are thought to have formed the tomb canopy of Bishop
Pilmuir (d. 1362). The quire is beautiful work of the late 13th c. (i.e.,
Elgin's second building phase) with a distinguished E. gable
containing two rows of five lancets and a rose window. The lower

W. doorway, Elgin (13th c., altered c. 1395)

part of the W. half of the N. wall is, however, part of the original chancel. The upper range of lancets continues along the N. and S. walls as a clerestory (there is no triforium, nor was there in the nave). In the N. wall, to the right of the Pilmuir tomb, is another big canopy, cinquefoil-headed, attributed to Bishop Archibald (d. 1298); on the S. side are a piscina and four sedilia. Amongst many floor-slabs the most interesting is a big one near the S. chapel arcade which evidently contained the fine Flemish brass of a bishop.

The S. chapel was the **Lady chapel**. Its three E. bays are still vaulted and the second one has its window tracery. The two free-standing tombs are of the first Earl of Huntly, d. 1470 (centre) and William de la Hay, d. 1422 (W). To the left of the remains of the altar is the well-preserved tomb of Bishop Winchester (d. 1460), with his effigy: on the soffit of the arch above some original line drawings of angels can be made out. Opposite is another piscina, then a monument to Henrietta, Duchess of Gordon (d. 1760). Many of the floor-slabs, of considerable antiquity and interest, commemorate church dignitaries. Lastly, the squashed-looking effigy under a canopy at the W. end of the N. wall is said to be the same Bishop Pilmuir whose tomb is on the N. side of the quire.

The **S. transept** too is comparatively well preserved, with more lancet windows and, over the S. doorway, a vesica-shaped one with stone seats beside it suggesting some kind of upper room. The clerestory and its wall passage should be noticed, also wall-arcading on the W. wall and another piscina. The two tombs in the S. wall are of Bishop Stewart, d. 1462 (but with the mailed effigy of one Robert Innes) and of an unknown knight. In the centre of the floor is one of many memorials to local glovers: HERE LYES ANE HONEST MAN . . .

Against the E. wall of the outer **S. aisle** the centre (headless) figure is virtually all that remains of the tomb of Bishop Innes (d. 1414). The other two were once in niches on the central tower: Bishop Innes again and the torso of a knight. In the second bay of the aisle is a stone coffin; in the third a piscina and another window with tracery; in the fourth another piscina; and, at the end, doorways into the S. porch and to the **SW. tower** stair.

The treads of the steep spiral have at some time been re-made out of ledger stones. The first stage still leads to a walkway that overlooks the nave and connects with the other tower where a collection of carved stones can be glimpsed through the doorway. The stair goes on up to a small railed enclosure at the top of the

Chapter House doorway, Elgin (13th c.)

tower, with a rewarding view. The 16th c. L-shaped building close to the NW. was the precentor's house.

Now return through the W. portal, turn left and go along the S. side. Little is left of the late 13th c. S. porch but it has its inner doorway complete and some signs of a vault. Under the middle window of the aisle is a quaint 17th c. tablet with a trumpeting cherub. The churchyard contains an inexhaustible series of such memorials and bigger tombs, and two with moralising verses which are particularly pointed out are on the churchyard wall: to John Geddes, d. 1687 (due S. of the SW. tower) and James Yong, d. 1679 (S. of the E. corner of the S. transept), both glovers.

The S. transept is remarkable not only for its vesica and lancet windows but also for the giant dog-tooth ornament on its narrow doorway. The quire and its aisles are better appreciated by walking far enough away to see their clerestory with its irregularly arranged lancets. Then, avoiding the walled-in mausoleum space near the E. end, one can walk round the chapter house (looking at the renewed window tracery) and back along the N. side of the cathedral.

Ely, Holy Trinity (Church of England, Cambridgeshire)

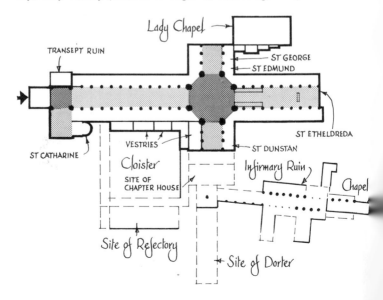

St Etheldreda's monastery, of which she became abbess in 673,
suffered at the hands of the Danes. After being re-founded in 970 it
quickly rose to more than local importance. Under the first Norman
abbot the present cathedral was begun *c*. 1083, starting with the E.
end which was later replaced. A shrine of St Etheldreda was set up
in 1106 and the see was established in 1109. The transepts and
crossing, nave and aisles, and big W. tower with its own transepts
were built during the 12th c. In 1234–52 the original E. end was
replaced by a much bigger, straight-ended quire; the W. porch was
also added.

The Lady chapel was begun, in an unusual detached position on
the N. side, in 1321. The following year the central tower collapsed.
In its place the unique 'Octagon' was built, and the remaining
Norman bays of the quire (no doubt also severely damaged)
reconstructed. This work being complete about 1335, the Lady
chapel was resumed and itself finished by 1353. The NW. transept
fell down in the 14th or 15th c. and was not rebuilt. The monastic
buildings were very largely converted to other uses after the
Reformation. James Essex did some alterations about 1770 and Sir
George Gilbert Scott some more extensive rebuilding with many
new fittings in the 1850s.

The main entrance is by the rich **W. porch**, lined inside with two
tiers of rich wall-arcading of which the lower is double and 'out of
step' like the quire aisle of Lincoln. Dog-tooth ornament abounds,
even in the vaulting (but one bay only of the two). The outer
doorway however was redesigned by Francis Bernasconi early in the
19th c. and the inner by Scott later.

Inside, the porch leads to the **tower** space. Its ceiling decoration
was done in 1855. To the right is one arm of the tower transept,
mid-12th c. in design like the tower itself. To the left was the similar
arm which fell down before the Dissolution. Ahead is the
marvellous vista of the Norman **nave** and the quire, punctuated by
the Octagon at the crossing. The system of arcades and triforium
and clerestory, immensely powerful and robust, is at first seemingly
quite repetitive in its arch rhythms, but in fact alternates in both the
lowest storeys between big columns and clusters of smaller ones. It
is thought to have been begun about 1110. The boarded ceiling was
painted in 1858–65. The main W. window is of 1800–7 and typically
pictorial for the date.

In the **N. arcade** the W. arch is blocked and the smaller opening
within it now leads to the shop. The aisles have groined vaults and
wall-arcading, both typical of Norman work before it entered the

N. side, with Lady Chapel and Octagon, Ely

phase of rich decoration exemplified by the outside of the tower. In
the fourth bay of the N. aisle is a mosaic-faced tomb with the
bronze-plated effigy of William Hodge Mill (d. 1853), and in the
fifth the effigy of Bishop Woodford (d. 1885), on a canopied tomb
by G. F. Bodley. The bell on the floor is late 15th c. and dedicated
to St Etheldreda; it came from the destroyed tower of St Nicholas's
church at Feltwell. In the last bays are a miscellany of minor
features: a big black Gurney stove of the type which still lends
atmosphere – and warmth – to many cathedrals; traces of medieval
painting on one of the pier capitals; on the next pier a delicate
canopied niche; near it a wooden model of the cathedral; and lastly
a display of the different types of stone in the building.

The Octagon is best appreciated by sitting for a while. The
Norman transepts, quire and nave, all fully aisled, met here at a
square crossing tower. When it collapsed in 1322 its great piers were
cleared away altogether and the crossing space opened out to take in
one whole bay of each of the four arms. The idea is more classical
than Gothic, and yet its realization is one of the masterpieces of
Gothic ingenuity, with its eight arches (four opening to the arms and
four reaching to clerestories), eight groups of vaulting coves and
eight-sided lantern poised above – itself delicately vaulted at the very
top. Nearly all the upper part is wood, and was much restored by
Scott; a model of the framework can be seen later. The glass, like
most in the cathedral, is Victorian, and so is the sculpture in the
triplets of niches. However, the niche corbels at the angles (one is
immediately over the pulpit) have original scenes from
St Etheldreda's life. The central altar and stalls are of course
modern but it is interesting to reflect that the quire occupied this
area till Essex moved it to the E. end.

Next the **N. transept** should be looked at. This is very like the
nave but a little older. Two Perpendicular windows have been added
in the end gable; the coloured hammer-beam roof with angels is of
the same period. The glass, all Victorian, is an odd mixture,
especially on the N. side. In the W. aisle are some minor wall
tablets. On the N., free-standing columns support a narrow gallery,
evidently an afterthought. Beneath it at the far right a prettily lobed
doorway leads by a spiral stair to the Stained Glass Museum
recently set up in the N. triforium. This is open from 11.0 a.m. to
4.0 p.m. each day (Sundays 12 noon to 3.30 p.m.). The entrance fee
gives one the additional pleasure of walking round the transept
gallery with its magnificent view of the crossing, and of seeing the
great and otherwise unused spaces in both nave triforia. For the

most part the exhibits are from redundant churches; they are
changed from time to time and will eventually extend to the far end.

Returning to the corner of the transept turn now sharp left into a
lobby with on the left an exit and on the right a group of nine wall
tablets. Ahead is a second lobby; the nice cartouche over the
doorway is to William Marsh (d. 1708). This leads into the **Lady
chapel**.

Begun before the Octagon and finished after it, this is virtually a
separate building and indeed served as a parish church for nearly
four centuries till 1938. Its lightness and breadth are breathtaking –
and so, after those have been assimilated, is the richness of the white
stonework: the Decorated window tracery, the sumptuous niches
between them, the equally rich wall-arcading and wall seats below,
and the comfortably spreading lierne vaulting with knobbly bosses –
surprisingly, the widest-spanned medieval vault in England. Once, of
course, the windows were full of colour and the carvings, before
they fell victim to iconoclasts, told stories of the Virgin Mary and
were coloured too. The little recess on the S. side was the original,
more direct, approach, through a double doorway from the N. quire

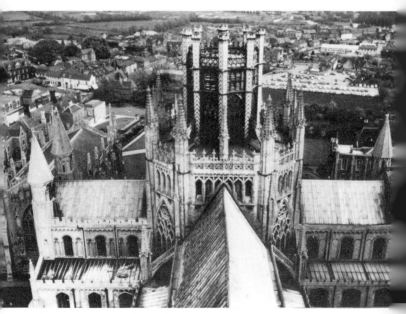

Octagon as seen from Tower, Ely

aisle. In it is a good wall tablet to Robert Lightfoot (d. 1730).

Over the doorway leading back into the **N. transept** are two 18th
c. gold-lettered benefaction boards. The first chapel on the left,
St George's, has folding wall-panels with war memorial rolls of
honour and a screen to match them, all designed by Sir Guy
Dawber (1922). St Edmund's, the second, has a screen of *c.* 1400
and faded wall-paintings of *c.* 1200. At this corner of the crossing is
the pulpit, by Scott (1866), and in the triangular bay leading to the
N. quire aisle the canopied monument of Dean Caesar (d. 1636),
with kneeling effigy.

This is the start of the Gothic E. end – and first the three bays
rebuilt around 1330 after the fall of the tower. Except to note the
(rebuilt) lierne vault and the absence of any wall-arcade, it is best to
defer looking at their design till it can be seen from inside the quire.
In the first bay on the right is the monument to Bishop Fleetwood
(d. 1723); Ely is unusual in that her bishops at that time did not
favour effigies. In the next bay is a rather similar monument to
Canon Fleetwood (d. 1737), by Peter Scheemakers: also a bas-relief
tomb-slab attributed to Bishop Nigel (d. 1174) and an unnamed,
headless one. Opposite are the remains of a black-letter inscription
and, up the steps, the elaborate Decorated doorway that led to the
Lady chapel. The open spiral stair on the right leading to the organ
loft is by Scott.

Past that, the elaborate but restored canopied tomb is that of
Bishop Redman (d. 1506), and on the other side of the aisle are
R.A.F. rolls of honour and banners: this is the first bay of the six
built in 1234–52 to replace the Norman E. end. The next contains,
on the left, a floor-brass to George Basevi (d. 1845) and another
medieval coffin-lid, and on the right a much more elaborate Purbeck
marble slab with the effigy of Bishop Kilkenny (d. 1257). The
monument to Bishop Patrick (d. 1707) on the left is heraldic, again
with no effigy. The six-columned structure on the right probably
covered the tomb-slab of Bishop Hotham (d. 1337), which is now in
the S. quire aisle; the carved fragments beneath may have formed
part of St Etheldreda's shrine. The seventh bay has a memorial to
Bishop Mawson (d. 1770) and, at the side of the high altar, the
Purbeck 'marble' effigy of Bishop Northwold, builder of this part of
the cathedral (d. 1254) – artistically a memorial of very high rank.
On the wall in bay 8 is another unostentatious tablet, to Bishop
Laney (d. 1675). Ahead, occupying the whole end bay, is the Alcock
chantry with its sumptuous screen. Begun long before Bishop
Alcock's death in 1501, it is fan-vaulted and of exceptionally

crowded detail inside; his figure lies high on one side, inconspicuously under the window.

The **retro-quire** occupies two bays. Architecturally it is part of the quire, the earlier or Early English part. Like the Angel Quire at Lincoln, but a little earlier, it has clustered piers of the utmost delicacy, each with eight Purbeck marble shafts and springing foliage capitals, the epitome of Early English. The shafts of the tierceron vault descend to big carved corbels; the traceried triforium and the clerestory of lancets are liberally enriched too. The three big E. lancets and the five stepped ones above form a very satisfying tie between the two sides and are also filled with 19th c. glass, by William Wailes and considered to be his masterpiece. The E. chapel with simple classical panelling is St Etheldreda's; to its right is the much restored tomb of the Cardinal de Luxembourg (d. 1443).

The E. bay of the **S. quire aisle** is Bishop West's chapel, made (like Bishop Alcock's) some years before his death in 1534. Being so late, it begins to show Renaissance detail – particularly in the panels of the delicate miniature vault. The E. window and curious reredos are by Sir Ninian Comper, and the floor-brass is in memory of Bishop Sparke (d. 1836). In the third bay from the E. the white marble recumbent effigy is of Canon Selwyn (d. 1879) and opposite is the tomb of Bishop Hotham (d. 1337), with alabaster effigy. Bay 4 has on the left Bishop Gunning (d. 1684), a reclining figure in white marble, and on the right the canopied tomb of John Tiptoft Earl of Worcester (beheaded 1470), with effigies of his two Countesses and himself. Beyond is the plain tomb of Bishop Barnet (d. 1374). In the centre of the sixth bay is a fine floor-brass to Bishop Goodrich (d. 1554); all along this aisle are many other stones which once contained brasses. Against the wall is the sombre columned memorial of Bishop Heton (d. 1609), with recumbent effigy.

Now a diversion into the **quire**, passing beneath the canopy of the once splendid monument of Bishop de Luda (d. 1299): the actual tomb-chest has disappeared. The design of the Early English bays to the right has already been examined from the retro-quire and it can now be compared with the three subsequent bays towards the Octagon. The differences are mostly in detail and concern intricacies of mouldings, provision or not of individual shaft capitals, and so on: the most obvious is the addition of lierne ribs in the later vaulting.

The stalls were originally within the Octagon and were constructed as soon as it was ready for them. Essex moved them further E. than their present position, which is due to Scott. It was

Scott, too, who filled their upper canopies with 19th c. Belgian carvings sadly out of character with their delicacy and, along with his coloured floor, rood screen and organ case, tending to give an impression that the whole interior is merely Victorian. Yet detailed examination is very rewarding, especially of the many carved misericords. The bishop still occupies the return stall on the S., used by the abbots of the monastery who were his predecessors. In the centre of the floor are brasses to Bishop Hotham and Prior Crauden (d. 1341), but only the stone of the latter is original.

Looking E.: the reredos is Scott's design, too. The prominent monuments, already seen from the aisles, are (taken clockwise, starting on the N.) of Bishops Redman and Hotham, the Earl of Worcester, and Bishop de Luda – through the last of which one returns to the **S. quire aisle.**

In the centre is a floor-brass to Dean Tyndall (d. 1614) and on the wall the reclining coloured effigy in armour of Sir Robert Steward (d. 1570). Opposite is a monument, with urn but again no effigy, to Bishop Greene (d. 1738); the Art Nouveau tablet alongside is to Bishop Harvey Goodwin of Carlisle. The ostentatious canopied tomb in the next bay is of Sir Mark Steward (d. 1603) and on the right is a large tablet to Bishop Butts (d. 1748), breaking convention both by being horizontal in format and by having his bust on top. In the last bay before the iron gateway is the effigy of Bishop Allen (d. 1845): a classical type of reclining marble figure by John Ternouth on an incongruously Gothic tomb. Opposite him are two cherubs flanking a 'drapery' inscription to Bishop Moore (d. 1714), and just beyond the gate are several minor tablets including a cartouche to Peter Gunning (d. 1735).

The **S. transept** and its roof are similar to the N. but the end wall and its gallery are different; possibly through a mistake, the alternation of the plain and clustered main piers is the reverse of that on the N. Some of the capitals have been timidly re-coloured. In the first bay on the left are a medieval chest and a well-annotated painting showing knights and their monk hosts; the picture of St Peter above is 18th c. Italian. The splendid cope in a glass case is 15th c. The last bay is St Dunstan's chapel, reserved for private prayer; it contains two panels of tapestry and a medley of old glass.

Close to the gallery is a bronze figure of St Mary Magdalen by David Wynne (1964) and in the SW. corner is a wooden model of the Octagon construction. The W. aisle is walled off as a vestry and just left of its door is a quaint tablet to John Thompson (d. 1615); the medallion to the right is to Dean Merivale (d. 1906).

Just inside the **S. nave aisle** is a coin box for lighting the roofs which can be useful on a dark day. The second doorway, the Monks', leads to one of the small remaining sections of **cloister**. On the outside it is richly ornamented, mid 12th c. Beside it is a curious memorial of 1845 to two men killed in a railway-building accident, with a poem, 'The Spiritual Railway'. Turning S. again: on the left is a second doorway (both are spoilt by later buttresses strengthening the Octagon area), also a fragment of 14th c. wooden net tracery from Prior Crauden's study and, at the end, a large tablet to Humphry Smith (d. 1743), with bust and weeping cherub.

Back in the **aisle**, most of the memorials are 19th and 20th c. In the fifth bay is a curious 'folk art' grotto-like Second World War memorial to choristers, and in the ninth the 7th c. shaft and base of a Cross, a memorial to Ovin, steward to St Etheldreda, who entered her religious community. The Prior's door in the next bay must also be seen from the outer (cloister) side. Like the Monks' but even richer, it is typically late Norman in its mixture of religious and grotesque themes.

The **SW. transept** is late Norman, richly arcaded and ornamented with zigzag. The apsed chapel of St Catherine on the E. side was entirely rebuilt in 1848. The SW. corner stair is opened to limited parties at 11.0 a.m. and 2.30 p.m. (except Fridays and Sundays) and gives access first to a gallery along the S. side of the transept and then to the main stair to the top of the tower, from which splendid views of the Octagon and the precinct can be obtained. In the transept is the font by Scott (1853).

The following external tour runs clockwise, starting to the right outside the W. porch with the big buttress where the N. transept was, and the beginning of its E. arch. The churchyard alongside the N. aisle provides a good diagonal view of the Octagon. Half-way along the aisle the date 1662 indicates a post-Civil War repair. Rather more surprising is the classical doorway on the N. transept which is of 1699 and shows the hand of Sir Christopher Wren; there had been a minor collapse here. Close by, in the end niches of the Lady chapel, are two 18th c. cartouches. Next, the enclosed area of churchyard, with at first the Lady chapel on the right, and on the left various formerly monastic buildings now part of the High Street: Steeple Gate alongside the W. end of the Lady chapel, Goldsmith's tower, the Sacrist's Gate, and the Almonry (much of which is of *c.* 1200). A sweeping path leads round the E. end to the S. side of the quire, the irregularity of which at upper level is explained by the provision of windows to light St Etheldreda's shrine within the area of the present sanctuary.

To the left and left again is the infirmary, approached by a passage with Early English wall-arcading. The lane through the middle, flanked by Norman arcades, is where the nave was; the aisles have been absorbed into domestic buildings. Beyond the Norman doorway at the end was the infirmary chapel, now occupied by the Deanery. From this direction there is a good view of the tower and SW. transept, with what is left of the cloister in the foreground. Now turn S. On the right successively are the Bishop's House which was originally the great hall, the Queen's Hall, now the Headmaster's house, the Prior's House (now a King's School boarding house) and Prior Crauden's chapel. This beautiful little chapel at first-floor level (also used by King's School) can be reached by turning right and right again and up a spiral stair; it is early 14th c. and specially remarkable for its window tracery and tiled floor.

The circuit can be completed by turning back S. The very long building in front is the monastic barn, now the school dining hall. Turning right through the great gatehouse called Ely Porta (c. 1400), another right turn leads towards the W. porch again down the street called The Gallery. The building with a tower at the left corner where it opens into Palace Green is the former Bishop's Palace, once connected by a bridge or 'gallery' to the SW. transept.

Exeter, St Peter (Church of England, Devon)

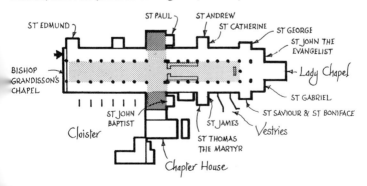

'n 1050 when the see of Devon was moved from Crediton to this more easily defended city there was already a Benedictine monastery. Nothing remains of its church. The Norman towers which are so distinctive a part of the present building represent its successor, 1112–*c*. 1150. That the aisle walls, at least to sill level, are also Norman is rather less obvious. The chapter house was added in the 13th c. and the now almost vanished cloister early in the 14th c., but both were altered later. The remainder was entirely rebuilt in a continuous building programme from 1270 to 1370, and it was probably nearly the end of the 14th c. before the W. front was complete. About 1480 the top of the N. tower was rebuilt so as to house a bell-frame.

Sir George Gilbert Scott restored the cathedral in 1870–7 and J. L. Pearson reconstructed part of the cloister in 1887. St James's chapel and parts of the S. side of the quire adjoining were destroyed by a bomb in 1942 and rebuilt.

Whichever way the **W. front** is approached it is clear how the 'Image Screen' winds round the slightly older W. wall. In the principal view from the W. it distracts the eye from the great nine-light wheel window and from the sloping aisle ends, themselves designed to hide the flying buttresses over the aisle roofs. The statue

Intersection of Transept and main roofs, Exeter, showing inaccuracies of construction

of St Peter, high in the apex, is said to be a portrait of 14th c.
Bishop Grandisson. In the screen there appear to be two and a half
rows of statues, the upper being largely devoted to the Apostles and
the next to kings and prophets seated on pedestals enriched with
half-angel figures. Two kings, to the left of the main right buttress,
are omitted so as to allow light into the tiny Grandisson chapel
behind. Though now so weatherworn, much of this is extremely
valuable sculpture of its date (*c.* 1350 onwards).

The little SW. porch of the W. front (the right-hand one) has
fragmentary Nativity and Adoration scenes of the same period. The
NW. one has a restored fan vault; this is the usual entrance for
visitors.

The exuberance of the interior is overwhelming compared with
that of almost any other building of its size. The vaulting is the
longest unbroken line in the Gothic style anywhere, although there
is a clear punctuation at the crossing of the transept, where the main
arches extend right into the crown of the vault and become part of
it. The quire was begun about 1275 and completed *c.* 1325, the nave
not till about 1369. The expert can detect stylistic differences in
detail along the way – subtle changes in the manner of carving
foliage and a slight increase in the complexity of window tracery –
but fundamentally the same design was used throughout. The busily
clustered piers and arches are entirely typical of the Decorated style.
The triforium was at first intended to be omitted, and perhaps this
accounts for the comparative lowness of the vault – 13 feet lower
than Salisbury's, which was already complete when building at
Exeter began. The vault itself is as good an example as can be found
of the tierceron type, that is with palm-like branches radiating from
the main corbels, but without liernes or linking ribs between the
branches. The corbels and bosses throughout the cathedral form a
study in themselves: they include superb naturalistic carving and
delicate figure-work, pure labours of love by their carvers long
before the time when strong field-glasses and the telephoto lens
could reveal them. Much of this sculpture in the nave has recently
been re-coloured and gilded.

The organ and pulpitum break the vista to just the right degree,
concealing the quire and yet revealing it, and suggesting in a way
approached by few other cathedrals the mystery and glory of what
lies beyond. The pulpitum is of *c.* 1320, but the paintings in its
upper part are 17th c. The organ case is of 1665 and still bears the
maker's name John Loosemore on its E. side; the organ itself has
been reconstructed again and again.

From the fifth bay, opposite the N. porch, one can look up to the minstrels' gallery inserted into one bay of the triforium. Fourteen angels stand in its niches; those facing the nave are playing the citole or zither, bagpipe, recorder, viol, an unidentified wind instrument, trumpet, hand organ, gittern (early guitar), shawm, timbrel and cymbals.

Now the **N. aisle**, where the outer wall is still Norman in its lower part and there are hanging banners. The aisle vaults are similar in date and character to the higher ones, but with fewer ribs. Amongst innumerable monuments here the principal are to the 9th Lancers (1860, after the Indian campaign) and (in bay 6) to Matthew Godwin, a cathedral organist who died at the age of 17 in 1586; the latter is specially attractive after cleaning and re-colouring.

At Exeter the quire is wholly E. of the main transept, for the late medieval plan provided plenty of eastern space, avoiding the constrictions generally so evident where Norman plans still effectively survived. So from the N. aisle one can pass into the **crossing**, remembering that there is no tower over it but instead two at the ends of the transept. From here the pulpitum and organ can be inspected more closely, and the two altars beneath. At the end of the transept hang elaborate candelabra.

The **N. transept** merges into the space beneath the tower, the 13th c. builders having daringly removed the Norman tower wall facing S. Above the transept is a 14th c. gallery level with the triforium but corbelled out on little half-vaults like the covings of Devon wooden chancel screens. On the N. wall is the famous late 15th c. clock. Its square dial indicates the hours on a 24-hour circle by a moving fleur-de-lys, and the state of the moon by the 30-day inner circle. The separate minute-hand dial above was added in 1760 when the whole was redecorated. On the floor below is the original mechanism, accompanied by an ample description. To its right is the little stone-screened chantry chapel of Precentor Sylke (d. 1508); its wooden door belonged to another screen. Other memorials include on the E. wall the portrait bust of Benjamin Dollen (d. 1700), with a naval scene, on the W. side Sir Francis Chantrey's seated statue of James Northcote (d. 1831), and to the left of the clock a memorial to Bishop Wolton (d. 1593).

From the E. side of the N. transept projects St Paul's chapel, three-quarters of its length being contained in the thickness of the Norman tower wall. It has a stone screen and its own little vault, 14th c.

Next the **N. quire aisle**, architecturally very similar to the nave

aisles but with a less complex vault. On the right at first are the
backs of the quire stalls and a chest with its intricate locking
mechanism on view; on the left a tablet to Robert Hall (d. 1667) and
the columned memorial to Bishop Carey (d. 1626), with recumbent
effigy. Half-way along is a projecting bay divided into the twin
chapels of St Andrew and St Catherine. Each altar has its little
piscina, and on the N. wall is a triple canopy, perhaps part of a
former chantry. A somewhat damaged screen separates these
chapels from the aisle.

Back in the N. quire and continuing E.: a cadaver
monument of about 1500 is on the left, and the tombs of Bishop
Marshall (d. 1206) and Bishop Lacy (d. 1455) on the right. On the
left again is an unidentified, probably 16th c. memorial, followed by
the sadly mutilated early 14th c. cross-legged figure of Sir Richard
de Stapledon. Facing him is his brother Bishop Stapledon, beneath a
once splendid canopy with still some original painting in its roof.

At the end of the aisle on the left is the tiny but richly ornate
chapel of St George, which is the chantry of Sir John Speke
(d. 1518) and contains his tomb; its stone screen, panelled and
niched walls and pendant vaults are all clean and white. There are
also fragments of old heraldic glass. Next, and separated from the
Lady chapel by the splendid tomb of Bishop Stafford, is St John the
Evangelist's chapel. Here are another stone screen, more medieval
glass (14th and 15th cc.) in the E. window, a brass in the floor to
Canon Langton (d. 1413) of the somewhat uncommon type with a
scroll issuing from the figure's praying hands, and the double-decker
Carew tomb (1589).

Just outside the Lady chapel two late 17th c. wall monuments,
one each side of the early 15th c. stone screen, are worth a glance.
Here in the ambulatory stands a little chamber organ. The **Lady
chapel** itself is thought to be on the site of the Saxon monastery
church. Though this is the earliest part of the present main structure
(excepting of course the towers), it is obviously Decorated, and
indeed post-Geometric Decorated. The glass in the E. window is
20th c. work by Marion Grant. To its right are a double piscina
and three stepped sedilia, and next in the S. wall in 14th c. recesses
the worn effigies of two bishops, Bartholomeus Iscanus (d. 1184)
and Simon of Apulia (d. 1223). Opposite are the separate tombs of
Sir John Dodderidge (d. 1623) and his wife (d. 1614).

The marvellously ornate tombs each side of the W. part of the
chapel are of Bishop Stafford (d. 1419) on the N. and Bishop
Branscombe (d. 1280) on the S. It was Branscombe who initiated the

rebuilding of the cathedral; his tomb's canopy and other
embellishments were added in the 15th c. in order to match the
Stafford tomb and to make a unified group with the stone screen
that links them.

Catching the eye as one leaves the Lady chapel is an exquisite
copy of a 16th c. Flemish wooden group of St Anne, the Virgin and
Child (against the S. end of the screen).

The chapels on the S. repeat the pattern of the N., with similar
stone screens. The next after the Lady chapel is St Gabriel's,
reserved for private prayer. Both its windows have medieval glass.
The chapel of St Saviour and St Boniface, the next to the S., matches
St George's on the N. and has the sumptuous tomb of Bishop
Oldham (d. 1519). The wooden door in the screen is original and the
reredos is notable for its panels of the Annunciation, the Vision of
St Gregory, and the Nativity.

On the left, following the **S. quire aisle** westwards, is the brass of
Sir Peter Courtenay (d. 1409), with Gothic 'frame' around the effigy.
Near it is the doorway to a private passage leading across towards
the old Bishop's Palace and now serving vestries. On the right, i.e.
the presbytery side of the aisle, are the plain Purbeck marble tomb-
slab (the brass demi-effigy has disappeared) of Bishop Berkeley
(d. 1327), and two cross-legged knights in stone, said to be Sir
Henry de Ralegh (d. 1303) and Sir Humphrey de Bohun (d. 1322).
This is the part of the cathedral that was severely damaged by a
high-explosive bomb in 1942. The double chapel of St James and
St Thomas the Martyr had to be completely rebuilt and so lacks the
elaboration and the patina of age of its counterpart on the N. side.
Very severe damage was done to the old centre of the city in the
same air raid.

This is the point to enter the **quire**. Little more need be said about
its structure, except to remark on the marvellous foliage-carved
corbels between the main arches, and on the low two-bay E. arcade
to the ambulatory. The clumsiness of the junctions between high
and low arcades is more than atoned for by the size and splendour
of the E. window. The stained glass is known to have been put into
it in 1389, panels of 1303 being re-used in the six side lights. It has
been pointed out that yellow stain must have become available
between those two dates, and of course the style of tracery had
changed from Decorated to Perpendicular.

Approached from the S., it is the stalls that impress first. But they
were renewed by Scott with the exception of the celebrated
misericords. Believed to be the earliest series in England (late 13th

c.), these include an elephant and a mermaid amongst their many carvings. The lofty canopied and pinnacled bishop's throne is of 1312–18, one of the finest pieces of woodwork of its age. The modern figure of St Peter in its topmost niche is a likeness and memorial of Bishop Lord William Cecil (d. 1936). Towering almost as high, the organ case is nearly as impressive as from the W.

Still looking clockwise round the quire: on the N. side are the comparatively modern quire pulpit and the Marshall and Lacy tombs, then within the sanctuary the 'domestic' throne and the other face of the Stapledon tomb. On the S. side of the sanctuary (unfortunately somewhat tucked away) are the very elaborately carved canopied sedilia (early 14th c.) and then, close to the great throne again, the brass eagle lectern of 16th c. East Anglian origin.

Resuming inspection of the **S. quire aisle**: the monument ahead with bust is of Canon Cotton (d. 1675); the next big arched one on the left is to his father, Bishop Cotton (d. 1621). After that is a doorway to the verger's office. On the right are two 17th c. chests and a modern stone spiral stair to the organ. The big monument on the left just before the screen is to Bishop Weston (d. 1741).

In the **S. transept** (half of which is within the Norman S. tower) the most prominent objects are the enormous bass organ pipes, too big to be accommodated on the pulpitum. In the centre of the transept stands the tomb of the 2nd Earl of Devon (d. 1377) and his countess, with recumbent effigies; this originally stood in its own chantry in the nave. The canopied tomb on the S. side is of Sir John Gilbert (d. 1596) and his wife (recumbent figures); the memorial above is to Sir Peter Carew, who d. 1589 (kneeling figure).

On the E. side of the transept, mostly within the tower wall thickness, is St John the Baptist's chapel with another stone screen and fairly recent stained glass. In the SW. corner of the transept a small doorway and a flight of steps lead to the **chapter house**, Norman in plan and therefore rectangular. However, in its lower parts it is almost all Early English and in its upper, Perpendicular. The sculpture within (in some cases springing out of) the niches formed by the wall-arcading, somewhat astonishing at first encounter, is by Kenneth Carter and dates from 1975. The subjects – starting at the SE and moving clockwise – are all based on the theme of the Creation, beginning with Genesis and ending opposite with the Resurrection. Above, the vault prepared for by the shafts was never built, and instead the timber roof was constructed in the 15th c. The external (W.) doors to the cloister have little sliding shutters associated with a ritual whereby a procession will not emerge until the verger has pronounced that all is well. These doors are usually locked, so it is necessary to go back into the transept and thence into the **S. nave aisle**.

There is another door to the cloister, and numerous wall monuments. At the W. end of the aisle is the handsome white marble font of 1692.

Two chapels remain, though the first, the tiny Grandisson chantry within the very thickness of the W. front and approached by way of the central W. doorway, is not normally open to visitors; it was made *c*. 1335 for the Bishop, and he was buried in it in 1369. Last is St Edmund's chapel, beside the NW. doorway. This has the only lierne vault in the cathedral and is thus regarded as the last addition. It serves now as the chapel of the Devon Regiment and contains banners and a bronze memorial.

The **outside** has to be seen in two parts, for there is no public way through the Bishop's Palace grounds around the E. end. On leaving the NW. door turn right, and ahead is the marvellously assorted row of buildings on the N. side of the Close. To the right again is the N. porch, a very solid 14th c. building, though with little now that is

Replacement gargoyles in masons' shop awaiting erection, Exeter (1975)

ancient on the outside; it is unusually far E. From here there is a
good view of the N. tower, the top stage of which is the cathedral
belfry with the 'Great Peter' bell. Once the fact that the two tower
tops are different is pointed out, the differences seem obvious, but it
is remarkable how unobtrusively the 15th c. top on the N. tower
merges with the Norman work below. Both originally had low
spires.

The aisle walls, for all their complex tracery and buttresses, are
nevertheless Norman at least up to their window sills, but only as
far as the second bay beyond the tower. After that came originally
an apsidal E. end. Past the N. side of the quire there is no way out,
and to see the S. side of the cathedral it is necessary to re-pass the
W. front.

After the SW. corner, the Deanery can be seen on the right and
then the cloister on the left, now a garden enclosed on three sides.
Straight across it the chapter house can be seen, and on the right
Georgian houses-turned-offices, with in between a few bays of actual
cloister walk rebuilt by J. L. Pearson in 1887. These were enclosed
by an oak screen c. 1958 and part of the cathedral library housed
there. Tucked into the SE. corner of the cloister is a passage with
steps which lead down past the masons' yard to the gateway of the
Bishop's Palace, the nearer part of which is now devoted to the
library and diocesan use. Looking back from here, there is an
imposing view of the S. tower, the chapter house and the S. side of
the quire. The roadway, Deanery Place, can then be followed past
the front of the Georgian building back to the W. front again.

Fortrose, St Peter & St Boniface [Scottish Development Department]
(Highland)

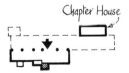

A monastery at Rosemarkie is said by some to have been founded
by Moluog, Bishop of Lismore (his spelling varies) who d. 592, and
by others to be associated with an obscure St Curitan, or Boniface,
c. 700. The bishopric of Ross was founded or re-founded there c.
1125, and its seat moved to Fortrose, only a mile away, some time in

the 13th c. Though some earlier work survives, the cathedral was mostly rebuilt in the 14th and 15th cc. and was never of any great size. Its roof lead was stripped after the Reformation, but in the 17th c. it was repaired and brought back into use. Then Cromwell demolished the nave and quire to help build his fort at Inverness, leaving standing only the S. aisle and the so-called chapter house. The upper part of the latter was rebuilt in the 18th c. as a council chamber. The entire ruin, in its big churchyard in the centre of the town and still overlooked by houses with traces of former cathedral associations, is now in the care of the Secretary of State for Scotland. No entrance fee is charged and no guide book is available.

The aisle that stands is of bright red sandstone, soft to the chisel yet hardened by exposure. It can be entered through the enclosing railing that now follows the arcade of clustered columns. Of its two well-defined parts the right (W.) end is probably the older, though the tierceron vaulting (datable *c.* 1430 by a bishop's arms on a boss) is uniform right through. Immediately to the left, the half effigy under a slender arch is probably of Bishop Cairncross (d. 1545); the further tomb, a plain chest with moulded canopy, is supposed to be that of Eufamia Countess of Ross (d. 1398), wife of the notorious 'Wolf of Badenoch' who destroyed Elgin cathedral. At the end of the aisle are an aumbry and piscina: this may have been the Lady chapel. The plain octagonal font is probably pre-Reformation.

On the S. side a huge monumental erection to Sir Alexander Mackenzie (d. 1706) frames a little vaulted recess containing some 17th c. memorials on the floor and walls; the tablets in the railed-off end bay, mostly of *c.* 1800, are only of minor interest, but in the blank bay opposite the Mackenzie monument stands the tomb of Bishop Fraser (d. 1507), with his very worn effigy and an enriched canopy.

The undercroft of the early 13th c. 'chapter house', which adjoined the N. side of the quire and probably served also as a sacristy, may be seen on application to the custodian, who has a hut near the W. end of the aisle ruin. It is vaulted and contains a small collection of carved stones. A stone stair at the W. end was blocked at the top when the upper room was rebuilt with outside access in the 18th c.

Lastly, back to the outside of the aisle, across the stretch of gravel which roughly marks the extent of the quire. The five-light E. window has lost its tracery. On the S. side the little tower which becomes octagonal in its upper part contains the burgh clock and a bell of *c.* 1460 dedicated to St Mary and St Boniface. Continuing

W., one comes to the foundation of the evidently two-storeyed porch, and the former main doorway (in a greyer sandstone) which is the earliest part of the existing building and probably late 12th c. On the W. wall is a monument to Thomas Forbes (d. 1622).

Glasgow, St Kentigern (Church of Scotland, Strathclyde)

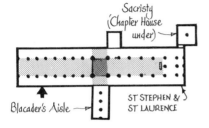

It is said that a burial ground was dedicated here by St Ninian in the 4th or 5th c. and that a church was built by St Kentigern (also called Mungo) in the 6th c. Nothing is known of any of the early buildings. A stone cathedral consecrated in 1136 was burnt down. A new E. end with a crypt was finished in 1197 and a new nave within the next thirty years. Within a very short time, probably *c.* 1240–55, the quire with crypt or Lower Church was again rebuilt, in its present form; the non-projecting transepts followed very soon afterwards. The nave was again rebuilt (though using the older wall-base up to about sill level) in the 14th c.: this may have been necessitated by war damage.

The NE. sacristy and chapter house (the one over the other), as well as the central spire, were added in the first half of the 15th c., and the S. transept crypt, called Blacader's aisle, about 1500; the upper part of this extended transept, which may have been intended to provide a permanent place for St Kentigern's shrine, was never built. An archbishopric was created in 1492.

Like all Scottish churches it suffered badly in the 16th c., but it narrowly escaped complete destruction and unlike most it has never been roofless. Till 1689 there was an intermittent succession of Protestant archbishops. A second congregation (the Barony parish) was established in the Lower Church in 1595, and a third (the Outer High Church) in a divided-off part of the main church in 1647–9. These moved out to new churches in 1798 and 1836 respectively, though Barony continued to use the Lower Church for burials. It is now a single parish church and Crown property, an extensive – and at first destructive – restoration having been carried out in 1840–56, with Glasgow Corporation and the Commissioners of Woods and Forests both contributing.

In the latter part of the 19th c. the cathedral was almost completely re-glazed with stained glass made in Munich. However, this deteriorated and in 1938 an ambitious programme of replacement was inaugurated, largely sponsored by descendants of the donors of the Munich windows. The work of eleven artists is represented. During the same period and up to 1967 extensive improvements and additions were also made to the furnishings and fittings under the guidance of Sir Albert Richardson, and to the structure under the Ministry of Public Building and Works.

In the main building only the little rose window over the S. doorway retains its Munich glass. Enter by this doorway and look first at the fairly austere **nave** bay design: 14th c., but rather earlier in style with heavy clustered main columns, and triforium and clerestory united under a single tall arcade, two bays to one main

St Mungo's Cathedral from SE., Glasgow

bay. The plain high-pitched wooden roof has many original timbers.
The aisles, however, have eight-part vaults, with a wall-shaft at each
bay.

At the W. end of the **S. aisle** are colours of the Cameronian
Regiment in a glass case, with memorials and roll of honour and
three commemorative windows (two by Harry Stammers and one by
William Wilson). Prominent too is the memorial to Andrew
Cochrane (d. 1777), with winged Fame and urn. The square font
under the arcade is 19th c. In a glass case by the first N. arcade pier
a voussoir from the 12th c. cathedral is preserved: this is remarkable
for the amount of original painted decoration surviving on it.

Francis Spear's splendid W. window (The Creation) and the fine
clock beneath are both of 1958. To the right of the W. doorway is a
war memorial cross of 1900, and along the nave hang regimental
colours, one over every column.

In the **N. aisle** most of the memorials are arranged with a soldier
in the centre of each bay and a doctor or politician on either side.
The principal ones are: on the W. wall to John Stirling (d. 1829); in
the first bay to Henry Cadogan, fell at Vittoria 1813; in the
fourth bay to Robert Anderson, d. 1860 (in bronze and marble); in
the fifth bay to William Middleton, d. 1859 (white marble); and in
the seventh to the 71st Highland Light Infantry, a sentimental group
with standing soldiers and a boy. The bell on the floor near the W.
end of the aisle is dated 1594, and the coloured window half-way
along (Moses) is by Douglas Strachan. On the right, just before the
crossing, the octagonal nave pulpit is 19th c., and on the left is the
stair to the former rood loft, with the upper opening still visible.

In the **crossing** the tower vault is 19th c. The pulpitum, the only
one left in a non-monastic church in Scotland, is early 15th c. and of
very solid design. Altars flanking the steps up to the archway still
remain, with saints in niches along their sides. More steps in each
transept lead to the Lower Church; they formed a one-way
processional route for pilgrims to St Kentigern's shrine.

The transepts, which do not project beyond the aisles, are late
13th c. and quite different from the nave. Here the triforium and
clerestory are separated, the former three-arched under a bigger
semicircular arch and the latter a triplet of lancets. The big N.
window by Wilson (1960) commemorates twelve Scottish regiments
in its upper lights and the other Services in the lower. The S.
window opposite, by Gordon Webster (1954), is a memorial to both
world wars.

Next the mid-13th c. **quire**, accessible through the pulpitum and different again from the nave. In this case the triforium has two two-light openings with plate tracery and the clerestory is triple – having three distinct storeys like the transepts, and splendid clustered columns with foliage caps. The four great E. lancets contain glass by Spear depicting the Evangelists, and beyond them is the lower, square-ended retro-quire. The main boarded barrel roof, including the bosses, is restored. The aisles again have eight-part vaults but (especially in the N. aisle) were extensively reconstructed in the 15th c. The pulpitum has a 19th c. wooden addition on this side; beneath it are two framed colours of the Scots Guards, with description.

Moving E.: the pulpit on the left, with semicircular-headed panelling and an hour-glass, was made about 1600 for the Lower Church. The wooden communion table, carved with the Last Supper, stands on a rich scarlet carpet (by Macdonald Scott) where St Kentigern's shrine once was. The seating is 19th c. but was reconstructed in 1957; on the S. side is a Royal pew, the Queen's chair being marked with her arms.

Move now to the W. end of the **N. quire aisle**. The first window (1939) is by Herbert Hendrie, the second (grisaille) by Carl Edwards (1944), the third by Hendrie again (1946), and the fourth another grisaille, by Robert Armitage (1953). All are clearly labelled. The next is by Sadie Pritchard (1938), and the last (St Andrew and St James) is another Hendrie. Through the doorway beyond is the sacristy. Lead bullets are embedded in its oak doors, the only original ones in the cathedral. The room itself is of about 1440 and has a central column and vault; it contains a fireplace, more banners and a beautifully carved royal arms of George III. In the 15th c. it was one of the first meeting rooms of the university. It still retains its Munich glass of 1862.

In the ambulatory or **retro-quire**, where the vaulting has particularly fine carved bosses, there were four chapels. Of their eight lancet windows the first two have glass by Marion Grant; the next four are by Spear. A museum case contains various relics of interest, and nearby is a disused brass eagle lectern of 1890. The SE. chapel of St Stephen and St Laurence has a piscina; the big tomb there, not unlike a fireplace of the period, is that of Archbishop Law (d. 1632).

Now the windows of the **S. quire aisle**, commencing at the E. end. The first (at the side of the SE. chapel) is by Christopher Webb and depicts Queen Margaret and King David I; the second, a Masonic window, is by Armitage. The third by Sadie Pritchard and the fourth and fifth by Wilson show scenes from St Kentigern's life, and the sixth (St Nicholas) is by Marion Grant.

Next, return to the quire; go back through the pulpitum to the crossing and, turning right, down the N. stair to the crypt; this will be taken clockwise. The pierced stone balustrades in the transepts are 19th c. On the first landing the giant horizontal wall tablet with medallion and figure of Fame is to the Rev. George Burns (d. 1896). At the bottom two heraldic carved stones from the former bishop's palace are displayed. The crypt, always known as the **Lower Church**, was built *c.* 1240, i.e. as part of the same building programme as the quire above. Structurally it has two bays to every one above, each with quadripartite vault and central boss, though the system was changed around the shrine and the altar of Our Lady. The piers are sturdier versions of those above, and again have foliage capitals. Nearly all the windows are now clear glass, with attractive patterns in their lead cames. The E. end is at a lower level still and had four more chapels. Opening off its N. side, and beneath the sacristy above, is the vaulted chapter house, completed in the 15th c. but probably begun earlier. Its 13th c. doorway has fine leaf capitals and a band of carving and it still has the 15th c. stone seat for the dean. It is not open to the public.

The first two E. chapels are those of St Nicholas and SS Peter and Paul. The effigy beneath the enlarged arch between the second and third is ascribed to Bishop Wishart (d. 1316). The third and fourth, St Andrew's and St John the Evangelist's, share a piscina on their dividing wall – an unusual arrangement. The latter contains the holy well of St Kentigern on its window sill; above is a window by Clayton and Bell. On the way back up the S. side, the bulky tomb is of Lady Colquhoun (d. 1595). Further up the aisle are a few supposed fragments of St Kentigern's shrine.

At the upper level the piers vary in size from the massive type supporting those above to a more graceful clustered version around the altar which marks the place of St Kentigern's tomb. The changes from two to three bays across the centre must have presented a considerable challenge to the designer, but he solved it calmly and ingeniously with his vault shapes. Another centre bay further E. is specially distinguished by a lierne vault: here stood the altar of Our Lady, immediately beneath the shrine in the E. bay of the quire to which St Kentigern's relics were transferred from his tomb. The four portrait-head bosses in this vault are said to represent Bishop de Bondington the builder, Isabella de Valoniis a benefactress, King Alexander II, and King Alexander III as a boy.

Near the W. end of the centre aisle are two very worn coffin-lids,

probably 13th c.; another near the way out at the SW. corner has
interlaced ornament around the edge and is of about 1200. In the
left corner immediately at the top of the four steps are one stone
shaft and a piece of walling which formed part of the E. wall of the
crypt transept of the 1197 church.

Half-way up the longer flight to the S. transept are doors on the
left into **Blacader's aisle** or Fergus's crypt which is really the crypt of
a greatly enlarged transept that was never built. It was begun at the
same time as the Lower Church or quire crypt (which explains why
its windows are of early 13th c. type) but not continued and
completed until the very end of the 15th c. The rich tierceron vault
with its grand collection of recently coloured bosses is encountered
at unexpectedly close quarters before one descends the steep steps.
In a spandrel between the vault ribs springing from the column
nearest the entrance is a carving relating to the legend of Glasgow's
founding by Kentigern: two oxen drawing a car with the body of a
man called Fergus, with the words 'this is the ile of car Fergus'.
Some microscopically small painted scenes at the S. end are 17th c.
Bavarian or Swiss, but the remainder of the windows are by
Stammers: along the E. side Archbishop Blacader, followed by
scenes of the Birth and Childhood of Christ, and on the W. side
scenes of His healing, preaching and prayer.

Now back to the **S. transept** where there are a number of 19th c.
brass memorials and the big war memorial window already seen, and
then into the **S. aisle** with numerous monuments arranged similarly
to those in the N. aisle. In the third bay is a strange-looking and
oddly worded 17th c. wall tablet to the Lords Minto; it contains one
of the few surviving Scottish brasses. Two bays further W. a sphinx
and a battle scene at Tel-el-Kebir embellish the 74th Highlanders'
1882 memorial.

Outside, the S. doorway is flanked by big 19th c. tablets – two
only of the hundreds in the entire churchyard, many much older and
most of them on (or embedded in) its outer wall. Some are of vast
size and some are entrances to vaults. It would be impossible to deal
with them here but even in their often deeply weatherworn state they
are a rich field of study for the sociologist and the art historian. Even
richer is the Necropolis which covers the hill to the E. The
dominating figure up there is of the reformer John Knox; his
monument (1825) was designed by Thomas Hamilton.

The S. view of the cathedral shows at once the stepped levels
which are so marked internally. The steeply sloping site was used to
great advantage, so that virtually no part of the lower building is

below ground. The tower is late 13th c. but its 225 ft spire was not completed till about 1420; it, too, is best seen from the S. Blacader's aisle should be examined outside for the sake of the sculptured heraldic and other panels.

The Lower Church has a separate entrance on this side: a weatherworn but once fine portal with foliage caps and a little vault over. Against the NE. corner of the cathedral stands the sacristy-chapter house building. Finally, continuing up the N. side with an unending array of monuments on the churchyard wall and passing the barrel-vaulted 13th c. former treasury (not open to the public), once topped by the W. sacristy, one comes to the W. front. This was the subject of an architectural scandal in the 1840s when the authorities removed two 13th c. W. towers, one 120 ft high with a short spire and the other unfinished and used as a consistory court – with the apparent object of tidying up the appearance. Countless valuable documents were destroyed in the process. The W. doorway is 14th c.; the window above is probably 15th c. but much renewed.

Glasgow, St Mary (Scottish Episcopal Church, Strathclyde)

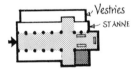

Designed as a parish church by Sir George Gilbert Scott and standing in Great Western Road not far north of his more celebrated and contemporary University buildings, it was built in 1870–1 and completed in 1892–3 (tower and spire) under J. Oldrid Scott, but did not become a cathedral until 1907. The vestries and hall along the N. side are of 1913.

The general style is a version of Decorated. The W. doorway, still with empty niches, leads into the tall **nave** with alternate octagonal and clustered columns, clerestory of sexfoils and plain high-pitched timber roof with white ceiling. The whole church has white plaster internally and the coloured windows are by Clayton & Bell to a unified scheme of the 1870s; only the clerestory is of clear glass. Quire and transept arches are like the main arcades but the tower, behind the organ to the right of the quire, is not noticeable internally.

Scott's font at the W. end of the **N. aisle** is octagonal on nine
columns, Gothic but of white marble, with a Perpendicular-style
pinnacled cover of 1903. The 1920 war memorial on the N. wall of
the aisle is formed from the central panel of the former reredos.
Beyond the transept a wrought-iron screen leads to **St Anne's chapel**
and then a wooden one by Scott to the **quire** where the present
reredos is by Sir Robert Lorimer, with five painted panels by Phoebe
Traquair and a frame with saints and foliage in subdued colours. To
the left of it stands the bishop's throne of simple design and to the
right a chest obviously older than the building. In the floor is a brass
to Bishop Campbell (d. 1921).

Next through the very slender iron screen with intricate tracery
and cresting (probably also by Lorimer) into the **crossing**, with a
wooden platform to bring it up to chancel level. The ungainly stone
pulpit on marble columns is typical of Scott's less attractive work.
In the **S. transept**, beside the striking Majestas against a red curtain,
stands another old chest, probably 16th c.; a third one, at the W.
end of the S. aisle, is 17th c.

Outside, it is a good idea to cross the main road so as to
appreciate the imposing massing and proportions, particularly the
tower and 205 ft spire. The single series of very tall lucarnes and the
statues in niches in place of corner pinnacles, as well as the 'trellis'
texture of the stage below, make it a distinctive landmark.

Glasgow, St Andrew (Roman Catholic, Strathclyde)

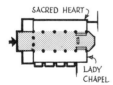

Facing across the river from Great Clyde Street, this church was
built in 1814–16 on a very restricted site, superseding one of 1797 in
Gallowgate. It later became a cathedral and the seat of an
archbishop. The architect was James Gillespie Graham, and
structurally his work has been very little altered.

The style is late Perpendicular, somewhat foreign to Scotland, but
important as an early example of Gothic Revival; the W. front is
not unlike a miniature version of King's College Chapel,

Cambridge, but with added aisles. The central doorway with five
orders of shafts and cabbagey capitals bears the architect's name
and date boldly on its soffit. Inside, there is first a quite low space
beneath the organ gallery, with a pretty tierceron plaster vault and
central rosette; a screened-off 'crying room' separates it from the
nave, and at each end is an enriched doorway: on the left to the stair
and on the right to the former baptistry.

The wide nave has clustered columns of mechanical precision –
not stone but plaster – with a clerestory and plaster vault with white
ribs on a pale blue ground. The aisles, too, have imitation vaults,
quadripartite in form. Though the sanctuary arch and vault ribs are
perhaps over-heavily painted and gilded, in contrast with the
restraint of the remainder, the E. end with its wall-panelling raised
in the centre and a gently curved tester over the altar is little altered.
Only the sanctuary has coloured glass; wooden screens separate it
from the twin side chapels, each with a grey canopied and pinnacled
altarpiece. The Decorated-style font of 1867 stands near the NE. or
Sacred Heart altar. From this end of the cathedral the extent of the
organ gallery can be seen, and the organ itself flanking the big clear
W. window.

Though it has no outstanding features, this is a specially attractive
little building.

Gloucester, Holy Trinity (Church of England, Gloucestershire)

This is one of the cathedrals Henry VIII's 'New Foundation',
established in a monastery founded *c.* 681 which had become
Benedictine in 1022. Of the church rebuilt in 1058 nothing survives;
of that begun in 1089 the greater part does. The central tower was
rebuilt *c.* 1220 (and again later) and the nave vault completed by
1242. The S. aisle was rebuilt and many windows elsewhere altered
early in the 14th c.

In 1331, as a result of pilgrims' offerings at the tomb of Edward II
(murdered at Berkeley in 1327) there began the phase of
Perpendicular building and encasing for which Gloucester is famous
– starting with the S. transept, and continuing with the quire and
(by *c.* 1370) the N. transept. During that time the cloister was also
built, with the earliest surviving fan vaults in England. A complete
rebuilding of the nave began *c.* 1430, but only two bays and the S.
porch were finished before attention turned to further rebuilding of
the tower and the Lady chapel. William Kent did a typical 18th c.

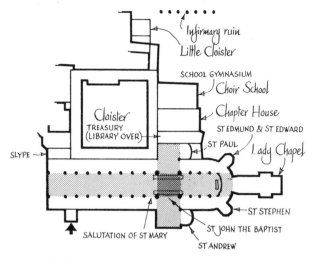

'restoration' and Sir George Gilbert Scott a typical 19th c. one. Large restoration schemes have continued in the 20th c. and continue today.

The two-storeyed **S. porch** of *c.* 1430 reinforces one's false first impression that the whole cathedral is mostly Perpendicular. The figures over the outer door are 19th c., by Frank Redfern. Inside are typical 15th c. wall-panelling and a lierne vault; the inner doors and ironwork, however, are 12th c., transferred from a predecessor and adapted.

Inside, the two Perpendicular W. bays represent the **nave** reconstruction that started in the 15th c.: clustered columns, with flat sides and single shafts facing into the nave, no triforium, quite small clerestory, and lierne vault with big bosses. The end bay is wider and its upper levels jump up. The rest of the nave is essentially Norman, its giant round piers so closely spaced that they nearly hide the aisles; moreover, their arches are small, much less significant than those of, say, Durham or Peterborough. The octopartite vault is 13th c., and the low clerestory arches too (though provided later with Perpendicular windows for external uniformity). The dwarf triforium of two twin arches per bay is Norman. Beyond the pulpitum and organ can be seen the quire with its immensely complicated lierne vault, and it is clear even from here how the quire space has overflowed beyond the confines of the Norman E. end, through the crossing and into the nave – a typical Benedictine plan, like that of Westminster Abbey.

Back now into the W. part of the **S. nave aisle** (also lierne-vaulted). Amongst numerous wall tablets these are worth noting: to Bishop Nicholson (d. 1671), Bishop Ellys of St David's (d. 1761), John Jones *c.* 1630 (with frontal bust and symbols of his post as bishop's registrar), and Sir Hubert Parry the composer (d. 1918). The cathedral bookstall is here; its screens recall the proportions and colours of East Anglian medieval screens. At the end of the nave the standing figure is of Dr Jenner, by R. W. Sievier (1825). The wall behind is wholly panelled in true Perpendicular style; the glass of the great W. window is by William Wailes (1859).

The **N. aisle** is dominated at the W. end by the monument to Charles Tyre (d. 1811), with medallion likeness and two angels. Various smaller tablets include several to the Rudhall family of bellfounders; Elizabeth's of 1699 has a bell at the base. In the second bay is the cloister doorway; the monastic building all lay to the N. Then a Gothic tablet to Col. Edward Webb (d. 1839), with Hope kneeling, and in bay 4 a nice group of three of 1784–1822. Next, a big monument by John Flaxman to Sarah Morley (d. 1784), with mother, child and angels. To the right under the arcade is the hexagonal pulpit – 17th c., but the canopy is of 1950. In the next bay are two somewhat unusual early 19th c. double oval tablets. Then a big coloured monument to Thomas Machen (d. 1614), with kneeling figures, and beyond that an excellent example of Art Nouveau design by Henry Wilson: the kneeling bronze figure of Canon Tinling (d. 1897), facing the wall and into the arms of a receiving angel. On the left is another doorway to the cloister and on the right one into the pulpitum.

Next the **N. transept** – out of sequence in that it was finished in its present form after the S. transept and the quire (i.e., *c.* 1370) but usefully seen first as a perfected example of the clothing of Norman work with Perpendicular which is such an outstanding feature of the cathedral. That it is superficial and not a reshaping like Winchester is obvious, especially on the E. side where the Norman main and triforium arches are at once visible behind the 'veneer' of stone panelling. The upper part with its lierne vault is all of *c.* 1370. So is the big N. window (with glass by Hardman, 1876). The Art Nouveau clock on the W. wall is by Wilson, 1903; below it is a small tablet also by him to Canon Price (d. 1898). The big monument is to John Bower, (d. 1613); instead of being carved, the family effigies (with sixteen children) are painted on the back wall. The three projecting bays of Early English work beneath it, with Purbeck 'marble' shafts and stiff-leaf capitals and looking oddly out of place, are believed to have been moved here from the former Lady chapel; they are called the Reliquary. The **treasury**, reached through this, and through an entrance made in the Norman wall, occupies the monks' parlour. It has a display of church plate of the diocese, and was given in 1977 by the Goldsmiths' Company of London. It is open at advertised times.

The E. chapel of the transept, irregularly apsidal, is St Paul's. It retains its 12th c. radiating groin vault, but the windows are Perpendicular insertions and the elaborate niched stone reredos is late 19th c. An interesting 17th c. chest is inscribed YE HOLIE LADIES CHAPEL GLOCESTERE.

Back in the transept itself and looking S., a stone screen encloses a vestry at the back of the stalls. Beyond and above hangs one of the marvels of Gloucester: the incredibly complex lierne vault of the tower (really a continuation of the quire vault) seeming to be carried on the slenderest of flying arches within the transept arches – themselves built off the tops of the Norman piers. Beside the steps at the 14th c. screen to the **N. quire aisle** is a stone desk, possibly a control point for monks coming in for services or for recording pilgrims. The aisle, the start of the Norman ambulatory, is groin-vaulted and thus late 11th c. The windows here are Perpendicular insertions too. By the side arch into St Paul's chapel is a processional cross of 1922 – facing the entrance to the **quire**, which should be seen next.

Here again the Norman arches and triforium are veiled by slender screens of open stone panelling. From the start they were of quite different design from the nave, of more normal porportions with lower main arcades and much bigger triforium. The clerestory and the superb vault with its magnificent bosses were completed c. 1360. The designer's ingenuity in making the crossing space a part of the quire can now be fully appreciated – a scheme of internal planning completely belied by the exterior. But perhaps his finest achievement was the great E. window, likened in size to a tennis court and in its time the biggest in the world. Its side panels are canted to add strength. Completed c. 1350, it is sometimes called the Crécy window, and contains in its largely original glass many heraldic references to those who fought there in 1346. The main subject is the Coronation of the Virgin and the figures include Apostles, martyrs, abbots and bishops; during more than six centuries, however, much of it has been altered and even repaired with glass from other windows.

The quire furnishings owe much to Scott. The bishop's throne is
his. The stalls are excellent work of *c.* 1370, with a rich array of
canopies, and 44 original misericords to which Scott added fourteen
more. The organ case is of 1665; one should stand beneath it to
enjoy the westward view of the nave and another look at Wailes's
beautifully coloured W. window. Around the E. end the tombs (to
be seen from the ambulatory) are of Abbot Parker, Edward II and
Osric. The sumptuous reredos, recently coloured and gilded, is
Scott's, with figures by Redfern. The 16th c. piscina and quadruple
sedilia are so much restored as to be virtually 19th c.; some of the
sanctuary paving is 15th c., but in the presbytery it is Scott's, with a
series of square black and white sgraffito scenes. On the S. side, on a
ledge in the third bay from the E., is a 13th c. effigy thought to
represent Serlo, the first abbot, holding a model of his church. The
14th c. central tomb-chest, of wood marvellously preserved and
coloured, is of Robert Duke of Normandy, the Conqueror's eldest
son (d. 1134). His figure, also of wood, is 13th c.

Finally a look at the lively 19th c. brass eagle lectern, and back
into the **N. quire aisle**. Up the steps and on the right is the chantry
of William Parker, the last abbot (d. 1539), with tomb-chest and
alabaster effigy within stone screens; but he was not buried in it.
Then the tomb of King Edward II (d. 1327) – an alabaster effigy
under a sumptuously pinnacled two-tiered triple canopy. The
Norman arch soffit above has medieval red colouring and the
column capitals a late 14th c. decoration of running harts. Beyond
this is an early 16th c. monument to Osric, reputed 7th c. founder of
the monastery.

On the left is another early Norman apsidal chapel, St Edmund's
and St Edward's, with stone screen, reredos (only the smallest of the
figures which adorned it still survive) and floor tiles all 15th c. Used
as a war memorial chapel, it contains regimental colours and rolls of
honour.

Following the ambulatory, one now leaves the Norman fabric to
enter the wholly Perpendicular E. part, behind the high altar
reredos, with the musician angels of the vault far above. Here is the
base of the great E. window, the centre part of it left as an unglazed
screen forming a way through into the **Lady chapel** beneath a
bridge, with a small chapel or 'whispering gallery' above and
medieval floor tiles under. Though not finished till *c.* 1500, the Lady
chapel and its lierne vault are remarkably similar to the quire.
Throughout the floor, good heraldic ledger stones are set amongst
old tiles.

Along the N. side are, first, the classical marble monument of the judge John Powell (d. 1713), with standing figure by Thomas Green; then the canopied memorial of Elizabeth Williams (d. 1622), with her child's effigy beside her own, and two little painted 17th c. tablets. Next is a doorway to a stair to a minstrels' gallery over a fan-vaulted chantry chapel with tomb and effigy of Bishop Goldsborough who d. 1604 (the chapel itself is a century older). The reredos, piscina and triple sedilia are original but much hacked about; the early 17th c. communion rail was formerly at the high altar. The E. window has a large proportion of 14th and 15th c. glass in a somewhat confused state. On the S. side are a balancing chantry and gallery; then a small early 17th c. tablet (a painted interior view with a man praying), a plain tomb-chest of *c.* 1520, a tablet to Margery Clent (d. 1623), and under the bridge a 12th c. lead font from the ruined church of Lancaut, by the river Wye.

Back in the **ambulatory**, the chapel on the left is St Stephen's, with restored 15th c. screen and reredos, more medieval floor tiles, and revived wall-paintings on the apse vault and arches. On the right of the **S. quire aisle** is the tomb of Bishop Ellicott (d. 1905), with effigy by W. S. Frith. Opposite are a cast of a Nativity sculpture by Josephena de Vasconcellos, and a 15th c. cope chest. On the platform opposite the S. entrance to the quire is the medieval-style canopied memorial to the Rev. John Kempthorne (d. 1838), with big brass inscription behind.

The **S. transept** is very similar to the N. though some 30 years earlier and with a less accomplished lierne vault. Its S. window of *c.* 1335 is considered to be the first ever built in the Perpendicular style. On the right, under the S. crossing arch, is the chapel of St John the Baptist which also has old floor tiles; its 15th c. wooden screen and stone reredos have been restored and repainted, the former with crowned initials. In the E. wall to the right of the quire stair is the doorway to the **crypt**, opened daily in the summer to guided parties at 10.30 a.m. and 3.30 p.m.

The extent of the crypt corresponds with the Norman quire with its ambulatory and three apsidal chapels (i.e. including the one where the Lady chapel bridge now is), as well as the two chapels E. of the transepts – but not the transepts themselves nor the crossing. It is substantially of *c.* 1090, with various minor additions and strengthenings. Turning left (N.) at the bottom of the steps, one comes to the central area, groin-vaulted on three rows of three-centred (not semicircular) arches. The floor is higher than it was originally. Returning to the S. side, one can then walk right round the ambulatory, visiting the SE. chapel (with a stone altar and double piscina), the centre chapel (where Scott's giant pink granite font is relegated), the NE. chapel (with the remains of an external stair), and at the end the crypt of the N. transept chapel; the last was reconstructed in the 15th c. A similar one lies on the S. side, just beyond the steps leading back to the **transept.**

Turn left at the top and go clockwise, starting with the curious L-shaped bracket carved with the likeness of an apprentice falling from scaffolding while the master mason looks on helpless: there is no certain explanation of its purpose. Then the arch to St Andrew's chapel (used by the Scouts and Guides) with a great buttress diagonally across it, part of the system strengthening the tower. The chapel has dark wall and ceiling paintings by Thomas Gambier-Parry, 1866–8, tiles of the same period, and another restored 15th c. reredos. Either side of the arch are similar tablets to Dean Tucker (d. 1799) and Dean Plumptre (d. 1825). The splendid canopied tomb is of Richard Pates (d. 1588); its effigies are lost. Next, with a tablet behind and two fine alabaster effigies, is the tomb-chest of Abraham Blackleech (d. 1639). The W. wall has many tablets, of which the most interesting is Wilson's to Canon Evans (d. 1891), in bronze repoussé with marble surround, and the biggest is Frith's medallioned bust of Thomas Lloyd-Baker (d. 1886).

The **S. nave aisle** and its vault were reconstructed *c.* 1320, in advance of the invention of 'Perpendicular'; there is ballflower ornament in the three E. bays. On the S. side are 15th c. figures possibly of Sir John Brydges and his wife, under an earlier, ogee-arched tomb. To the N. is the chapel of the Salutation of Mary (Abbot Seabroke's chantry), enclosed by a stone screen and with his effigy under a canopy (d. 1457); the rich tablet on its W. wall is to Francis Baber (d. 1669). On the left of the aisle are three more wall tablets, and on the right a big early 18th c. bishop's throne formerly in the quire. Cross into the nave to look at this and the accompanying stalls now used with the nave altar, and at the stone pulpitum which is of 1820 – and look through that into the quire again.

Back in the aisle, the many memorials include in bay 3 a big tablet to the Rev. William Adams (d. 1789), in bay 4 a strange one in coloured marbles to Mary Singleton (d. 1761), in bay 5 the tomb-chest of Sir George Paul (d. 1820) with bust by Sievier, and a good monument to Mary Strachan, (d. 1770) with medallion head, in bay 6 a big Gothic memorial to Richard Raikes of Sunday school fame (d. 1823), and in bay 7 a locally made tablet to Eli Dupree (d. 1707).

Cross the nave again to the **cloister**, rebuilt in 1373–1412. The fan vaults (apart perhaps from those of the former chapter house at Hereford) are the earliest known; the traceried wall panelling and glazed windows preserve an unusual uniformity and feeling of enclosed security. Much of the floor is composed of well-lettered black ledger stones. Go straight ahead along the W. walk and pause to look through the doorway to the garth, across to the chapter house and N. transept with the upper-level library between them. In the centre of the garth is the 'convent well': the buried arches in the NW. corner are a water tank and drain and just round the corner in the N. walk are eight half-bays of washplace, with miniature fan vaulting. The recess opposite housed towels and to its left (now a window) was the 13th c. refectory doorway.

At the far end of the N. walk the vaulted 13th c. Dark Cloister led to the infirmary. Continue however into the E. walk: on the left is the doorway to the Norman **chapter house**, which is partly pre-1100 but mostly later, with a tunnel vault. Its side walls have zigzag-ornamented arcading. The E. bay is a late 14th c. alteration, with lierne vault. In the N. wall, close to the dais, is a fragment of a 10th c. sculpture of Christ. Back in the cloister, two small doorways on

W. walk of Cloister, Gloucester (late 14th c.)

the left lead to the library stair and to what is now the treasury
(these are private). Finally the S. walk, the most impressive of the
four because of the twenty half-bay carrels or monks' study cubicles
all along the right-hand wall. There are also some panels of 16th c.
glass. The left-hand wall is a Norman one encased, and contains a
few memorials.

Back now to the S. porch for an **external** circuit, starting with the
straightforward early 15th c. W. front. Though having at the base
only an insignificant doorway, it blossoms above into an openwork
parapet like the tower. Against it is the slype, followed by the
Norman and 13th and 15th c. Church House which was once the
Deanery and before that the prior's house, and which now presents a
mostly Victorian façade. The path leads past bollards to the 13th c.
St Mary's Gate which has some 18th c. iron gates from Nuremberg.
Turning aside just before this, one passes through the Inner Gate
into Miller's Green where the principal house on the left is now the
Deanery. From its gateway is a splendid view of the 225 ft 15th c.
tower, with the 15th c. timber-framed Parliament Room, once part
of the abbot's house, in the foreground. The way continues out of
the NE. corner, past a shafted 13th c. doorway to Little Cloister
House, and a gateway to the remains of the 15th c. Little Cloister
itself. The 15th c. wood-framed house partly on the refectory site is
used by King's School. Next to it is the end of the Dark Cloister. To
the N. of the playground are the six remaining arches of the 13th c.
infirmary; at the end of these a gate leads to the churchyard.

The chapter house is now seen, and the school gymnasium beside
it on the site of the dorter; then the N. transept and the N. quire
aisle with their Norman walls overlaid with Perpendicular detail,
and the 'bridge' joining the N. quire aisle and the Lady chapel
which, with the chapel itself, is wholly Perpendicular. Round the E.
end more gates lead into College Green. On the right is the S.
transept with the 12th c. zigzag-enriched but pointed 'Pilgrims' '
doorway and the big 'pioneer' Perpendicular window above it,
reminders again of Gloucester's fusion of styles; in fact a number of
Norman chevron-moulded stones have been incorporated into later
work. Finally comes the Decorated S. nave aisle with ballflower
ornament round the windows.

Guildford, Holy Spirit (Church of England, Surrey)

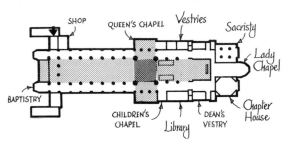

When the diocese was formed in 1927 the parish church of Holy Trinity was at first used as a cathedral. The design of a new building was the subject of an open architectural competition in 1932, won by Sir Edward Maufe. Building work was badly interrupted by World War II when the E. parts were still incomplete and the nave hardly begun, and it was not resumed until 1952. With minor exceptions it was complete for its consecration in 1961.

The cruciform plan, traditional in its essentials, has several special features: reduction of the aisles to narrow passages allowing for a relatively very wide nave; omission of any pulpitum or similar break in the main internal vista; inclusion of vestries and other ancillaries in the over-all design instead of accepting them as untidy additions; and provision for the arrival and parking of cars. The walls are mostly of brick, the vaults reinforced concrete, and the roof covering copper. Stone is used extensively for the finer detail, Clipsham externally and Doulting internally.

The main approach is centred on the 156 ft tower with its 15 ft gilded copper angel and on the three giant windows of the W. front. On each side is an arcaded loggia. The usual entrance is on the left (N.) side, through the glazed porch, past the cathedral shop and into a low W. aisle. Opening off this to the right is the main W. porch with three pairs of doors, each door engraved by John Hutton with an angel musician on its glass.

To the left is the **nave**, light stone and plaster, with tall arcades, no triforium and little more than a hint of a clerestory. The great arches across the nave span 41 feet. A special feature is the collection of kneeling cushions, each worked with an individual pattern. On the first column on the left is a Madonna and Child by John Cobbett.

The **N. aisle**, devoid of seats and used solely for circulation, is remarkable for the perspective effect of its very narrow tall arches

S. Aisle of Nave, Guildford (c. 1955)

leading the eye eastwards. Little coloured glass is intended, but the aisle windows contain discreet panels honouring various trades and organizations. Through an iron screen on the left, embellished with badges and mottoes, is the chapel of the Queen's Royal Surrey Regiment, dedicated to King Charles the Martyr. The prow-shaped light fittings are reminders of the regiment's naval associations. Its historic banners hang from the N. wall and the Lamb and Flag altar frontal is by Miss Malcolm Wood.

Most of the Queen's chapel is within the N. transept. At its W. end is a stair leading to the organ gallery above. The **crossing**, particularly spacious because of the great size of the tower, has at its exact centre a brass stag, marking what was the highest point on Stag Hill on which the cathedral was built. From here the **quire** can be appreciated, with its fittings in a kind of watered-down classical style: on the left are the sub-dean's stall and the positive organ; on the right the dean's stall and at the far end the bishop's throne; on the E. wall the great dorsal curtain and above that Moira Forsyth's blue rose window symbolizing the attributes of the Holy Spirit. The quire clerestory, in contrast with the nave, is tall and slender. Visible also from the crossing are the S. transept gallery with the richly coloured banner of General Sir George Giffard, and the three great W. windows given by Freemasons.

The **N. quire aisle** passes vestry doors on the left, and gives a closer glimpse of the sanctuary on the right, with its great heraldic carpet and simple sedilia with angels between the arches. Straight ahead is the sacristy doorway crowned with the arms of Bishop Greig, the first bishop (by Vernon Hill). The eastern **ambulatory** contains the foundation stone, and memorials to bishops on its right-hand wall; on the left is a screen to the **Lady chapel**, reserved for private prayer. The Madonna and Child over its altar are by Douglas Stephen, and lilies and stars decorate its roof. It has its own bell-cote, with the rope hanging near the altar rail on the right.

The next doors on the left lead into the chapter house and allow a good view inside without entering. The clergy entrance doorway beside it has another coat-of-arms, that of Bishop Macmillan. A stair leads to the song school in the crypt. The **S. quire aisle** has a memorial to the Surrey Yeomanry, with book of remembrance, and to the right views of the quire clerestory windows by Rosemary Rutherford and Moira Forsyth. Just before the crossing is the Children's chapel on the left, which has iron gates given by Scouts and Guides, and big limewood angel corbels at the corners.

From the **S. transept** three more pairs of glazed doors with

A S. window of Nave, Guildford (c. 1955)

engraved angels by John Hutton on their fanlights lead into a secondary entrance lobby, lit on its W. side by a children's window in red and blue. The **S. aisle**, like the N., has a striking vista, leading this side to the baptistry. The aisle windows were the gifts of various professions and contain their emblems. The travertine font is seven-sided, carved with a fish and anchor; its cover has flights of gold doves coming down from a gold star and a blue vault.

Across the cathedral, balancing the baptistry at the N. end of the W. arcade, is the stair to the W. gallery. At its base stands another Cobbett figure, St Francis of Assisi, and at the top (not normally open to the public) a railing given by stamp-collectors and incorporating a representation of the 'Penny Black'.

On the **exterior** is sculpture by several artists but none of it of outstanding quality. Typical are the Hands and the Dove of the Holy Spirit over the E. doorway of the N. porch, and the Seven Gifts of the Spirit at the base of the mullions of the N. aisle windows. The tower brickwork still shows clearly where work was re-started after the war. A similar point of interest is the series of dates on rain-water heads: 1939, 1961, etc. Continuing clockwise – opposite the Lady chapel at the E. end is a great teak Cross, put up to mark the cathedral site before it was built. On the S. side notice the Lady chapel bellcote, the SE. clergy doorway with croziers on the doors and the diocesan arms by Eric Gill above, the impressive view of the tower from this angle, the tablet recording the gift of land to the cathedral, and the S. transept entrance dominated by Gill's St John the Baptist. Vernon Hill's bronze doors here symbolize ordinary men and women by means of their 'elemental' occupations. Tucked into the corner just to the right of this transept is the architect's 'signature' stone: 'MAUFE'.

The way continues past the nave (the window carvings this side represent Seven Virtues) and the SW. loggia, back to the W. front where the stone above the doors is 'boasted out' for carvings of the Risen Christ and the Evangelists not yet begun.

It is interesting that the architects of both Guildford and Coventry cathedrals have said that Albi Cathedral in France provided inspiration. This is perhaps easier to believe of Guildford, where the great expanses of sheer brickwork are not only in a special bond but also built to a slight 'batter' or slope to give an additional impression of stability and grandeur. Most of the facing bricks were made from the clay of Stag Hill itself.

ebus of the architect Sir Edward Maufe, Guildford

Hereford, St Mary & St Ethelbert (Church of England, Hereford & Worcester)

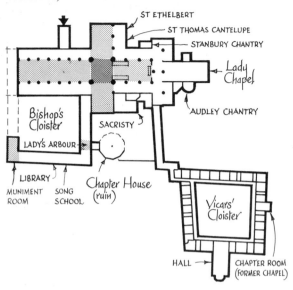

The bishopric was formed in 676. The nave and quire arcades of the present cathedral were begun *c.* 1110 and completed *c.* 1145. Around 1190 to 1230 the three-apsed E. end began to be replaced by the present transepted retro-quire with Lady chapel – though these transepts were not proceeded with till at least 1300. Next in date are the quire clerestory and vault and the rebuilding of the N. transept. Early in the 14th c. the central tower was completed and a W. one built; the inner N. porch was also added and the aisle windows altered. Changes in the 15th c. were comparatively minor. Following the collapse of the W. tower in 1786, however, James Wyatt rebuilt the whole upper part of the nave and reduced it by one bay. Around 1845 Lewis Cottingham made many alterations, especially to the E. part of the quire. Sir George Gilbert Scott did restoration at the E. end *c.* 1860, and last but not least John Oldrid Scott completely rebuilt the W. front in 1902–8.

The two-storeyed 14th c. **N. porch** was extended outwards in 1519. The lierne-vaulted outer bay is open, and what was the outer doorway is now in the middle, enriched with foliage and quaint

N. Porch, Hereford (14th and early 16th cc.)

figures. Though the inner bay is altogether plainer, its cinquefoil-headed inner doorway is remarkable; the ironwork on the doors themselves is 19th c.

In the **nave** the ungainly appearance of the Norman arcades is not helped by the curiously small attached shafts which no longer support anything, thanks to Wyatt's redesigning of everything above. The arches themselves, zigzag-enriched, sit uneasily on capitals of this shape and the pier surfaces have been retooled to a mechanical smoothness. Wyatt's triforium and clerestory are Gothic, not Norman; his vault is wood and plaster with pretty painted patterns. The fussy responds which now terminate the vault shafts were added by Cottingham. Wyatt also shortened the W. end by one bay but his W. wall was subsequently replaced by John Oldrid Scott; the W. window is a memorial to Queen Victoria (by Clayton & Bell, 1902).

The big black 'Gurney stoves (there is one in the N. aisle) are a welcome survival. The aisle windows and the quadripartite vault are early 14th c. and the tomb with gilded effigy under a cinquefoil canopy in the N. wall is of Bishop Booth (d. 1535).

The arch into the N. transept, and the one ahead into the N. quire aisle, are of Norman form, but also re-worked. The transept itself however is a remarkable example of Geometric Decorated of *c.* 1255–70, closely modelled on Westminster Abbey. The Purbeck 'marble' shafting, foliage capitals and dog-tooth ornament are normal for their period: the almost triangular arches, both in the main E. arcade and in the twin three-light triforium openings, decidedly less so. The triforium is blank because the library lies behind at that level. In the clerestory the 'spherical triangle' windows are also derived from Westminster. The grand N. window has Hardman glass dated 1863. Of the two very tall Geometric ones in the W. wall, one has some 15th c. glass. On the N. side are, first, the tombless effigy of Bishop Westphaling (d. 1601), then the free-standing tomb of Bishop Atlay (d. 1894), with white marble effigy by James Forsyth, and the canopied tomb of Bishop Charlton (d. 1343).

The E. aisle has two chapels. The left one, St Ethelbert's, has the bust of Bishop Field (d. 1636) in the left corner, and under the mat in the opposite (SW.) corner a big brass to Richard Delamare (d. 1435) and his wife. The right-hand chapel is dedicated to Bishop St Thomas Cantelupe (d. 1282), and his shrine is between the two, in the form of a tomb-chest with arched upper structure; the carvings of knights around the base are excellent sculpture of their period.

Font, Hereford (12th c.)

On the right of his chapel is the damaged 14th c. figure of a priest,
possibly Dean Aquablanca (d. 1320), and then – separating the
chapel from the quire aisle – the tall canopied tomb of Bishop
Aquablanca (d. 1268) with a marvellous and airy display of
Geometric design. Under a mat nearby is the brass of Dean
Frowsetoure (d. 1529).

Next, round the Aquablanca tomb into the **N. quire aisle**, with
Norman arcade and outer wall but Decorated windows and vault.
On the left is the first of a series of 14th c. effigies of earlier bishops
under canopies, uniform and characterless. This one is labelled
Bishop Mapenor (d. 1219): the others, as they come, will merely be
noted 'standard'. Opposite it is the famous *Mappa Mundi*, drawn on
vellum about 1283 and showing Jerusalem as centre of the known
world. Beyond are, first, the tombless effigy of Bishop Bennett
(d. 1617) and then one labelled Bishop Braose (d. 1215), standard.

On the left is the stair to the **chained library**, open (for a small fee)
from Easter to September, 10.30 a.m. to 12.30 p.m. and 2 p.m. to
4 p.m.; also for a short time on weekdays in winter at 11 a.m. and
3 p.m. This was originally in the cloister, then in the Lady chapel.
After being partially dismantled for almost a century, the 17th c.
bookcases with their desks and seats and most of the 1,440 chained
books (the largest such collection in the country) were reinstalled in
1930 in what had been the muniment room.

Next on the left in the aisle is the standard tomb of Bishop de
Clive (d. 1119). Opposite is a showcase of books printed in Oxford,
and above that two Latin inscriptions and a brass to Bishop
Stanbury (d. 1474). His chantry on the outer side of the aisle is
richly panelled and fan-vaulted and has a 19th c. reredos. But the
effigy on the right of its altar is probably of Bishop de Capella
(d. 1127), and Stanbury's own is in alabaster on a tomb-chest in the
last bay, beneath the main arcade. On the left of the aisle is Bishop
Reynelm's (d. 1115), standard. The last bay, it has been deduced,
had a Norman tower over it, and the arch, now to the transept,
opened into an apse.

The **NE. transept** is early 14th c. though it seems to have been
started nearly a century earlier. The modern screen with frosted
glass heraldic panels encloses a vestry and hides the tombs of Bishop
Swinefield (d. 1317) and Bishop Parfew (d. 1557). On the W. wall
are several heraldic cartouches. The free-standing tomb-chest in the
SE. corner is of Dean Dawes (d. 1867), and there are various relics
of earlier monuments: several coffin-lids on the E. wall, probably
13th c., an effigy of *c*. 1300 in the S. wall under a ballflower

encrusted canopy, and, to its right, parts of three 17th c. brasses to
the Harford family.

The **ambulatory** or retro-quire was much rebuilt by Cottingham,
but the rather strange combination of round columns, scalloped
capitals, springing foliage, zigzag vaulting ribs and pointed arches is
thought to be exactly like the original. He did however reopen the
big Norman arch behind the altar and had the spandrel wall above
the central column, thus exposed to the quire, filled with carving;
this will be seen later. The reredos is by his son N. J. Cottingham
and its diapered back is visible from here; on its right is a curious
Gothic tablet to Bishop Butler (d. 1804).

Under the **Lady chapel** is a crypt which can be visited for a
nominal charge. It is early 13th c., i.e. Early English, and has thick-
ribbed vaulting on quite tall octagonal columns. Some
unrecognizable effigies have been relegated here, two each side of the
altar, and at the W. end is a big flat tomb-slab with incised effigies
and inscription to Andrew Jones (d. 1497). The crypt altar
(St Anne's) and reredos are by Sir William Goscombe John (1920).

The chapel itself is broad and well proportioned, with
quadripartite vaulting and specially rich lancet windows with dog-
tooth in their arches and vesica shapes over. On the N. wall are a
panel of 17th c. Italian embroidery, the rich canopied tomb of Peter
de Grandison (d. 1358), and the much less sumptuous one of Lady
Joan de Bohun (d. 1327). The reredos is by Randoll Blacking, *c.*
1950. The glass in the chapel is mostly by C. A. Gibbs, *c.* 1860, but
includes some 13th c. pieces in the W. window on the S. side. On the
S. is the tiny octagonal vaulted chantry of Bishop Audley (d. 1502);
its door has linen-fold panels and flowers and good ironwork and a
stair leads to an upper chantry (not open to the public). A 15th c.
Italian Madonna forms the reredos. Back in the Lady chapel are a
hagioscope and a blocked doorway, and the amusing, re-coloured
tomb of John Swinfield (d. 1311), with swine in a field running all
round the arch. The brass beneath is to Canon de la Barre (d. 1386);
then on the wall to the left of the back of the high altar are several
other brasses and fragments.

The **SE. transept** is similar to the NE., though the craftsmanship
of the bosses is later and noticeably inferior, and has quite a number
of memorials. Starting on the N. wall, i.e. left on entering, they are:
Bishop de Charlton (d. 1369), damaged effigy on tomb-chest; Bishop
Coke (d. 1646), recumbent effigy (but canopy of 1875); James
Thomas (d. 1759), lively bust formerly attributed to Lewis
Roubiliac; after the choir vestry doorway, brass of a knight, *c.* 1480;

brass of William Porter (d. 1524); along the S. wall many minor
brasses; Bishop Lindsell of Peterborough (d. 1634), another effigy
bereft of its tomb; Dean Hervey (d. 1500), tomb-chest; on the W.
wall another small brass and the good brass figure of Archdeacon
Rudhale (d. 1476); on the floor a brass to Sir Richard de la Bere
(d. 1514).

First in the **S. quire aisle** is a 15th c. figure of St John the Baptist.
In this bay is some 14th c. glass and, as on the N. side, there was a
Norman tower above. Then on the left are no fewer than four of the
standard bishops' tombs, all adequately labelled. On the right,
beside the high altar sanctuary, is the elaborate but restored tomb of
Bishop Meyew or Mayo (d. 1516). After the first group of organ
pipes is yet another standard tomb purporting to be of Bishop de
Losinga (d. 1095), and at the end are iron and brass gates made by
Francis Skidmore to Scott's design (1874).

The most recent, most hotly debated, of Hereford's many
misfortunes was the removal of the rather similar, highly ornate,
High Victorian quire screen, also by Scott and Skidmore. Tell-tale
patches in the paving, as one enters the **quire** past the eagle lectern,
show where it stood. The quire was treated in the 13th c. much as
the nave was treated later by Wyatt, though here the rebuilding
proceeded downwards only to a little below the clerestory. The big
Norman E. arch was filled in but, it will be remembered, was later
reopened by Cottingham to expose the view into the Lady chapel.
The spandrel carving is due to him, the reredos to his son.

The stalls are early 14th c., i.e. Decorated, distinguished by their
forward-leaning ogee canopies. Rearrangements have taken place
but the two main banks as they stand are largely original; the front
desks and the third bank in the W. part are 19th c. The misericords
are original too, with a variety of carved scenes and figures. Note
also the animals on the arm rests. Continuing to the E.: on the left
below the Braose tomb is the big restored brass of Bishop Trilleck
(d. 1360). The chair made up of turned shafts of wood is called King
Stephen's and may be as old, i.e. 12th c. The communion rail is by
John Seely, Lord Mottistone (1958), and the mosaic floor by
Scott. The high triple E. window is by Hardman (1870). To the
right, already seen, is the Meyew tomb, and further along the S. side
the splendid bishop's throne with flanking seats for chaplains, *en
suite* with the stalls.

Moving back into the **crossing**, one can enjoy the view down the
nave, and look upwards into the tower. Its piers and arches are
Norman (but much rebuilt by Cottingham) and the upper part 14th

c. The pulpit is 17th c., with 18th c. Gothick canopy.

The **S. transept** is quite unlike the N., for it retains a Norman E. wall which looks earlier than either the nave or quire. The rest, with very large S. window and tierceron vault, is mostly 15th c., and the glass in the big window is by Charles Kempe (1895). The chapel reredos contains 16th c. German paintings. In the SE. corner the tomb-chest with alabaster effigies is of Alexander Denton (d. 1576); on the S. side is the canopied tomb of Bishop Trevenant (d. 1404). The five stalls against the W. wall were reconstructed in 1934 around surplus pieces from the quire.

In the S. aisle on the left is a long brass inscription to Richard Philipps (d. 1522) and then the doorway to the so-called **Bishop's cloister** which should be seen at this point. Only the E. walk is open, the S. being occupied by the song school and the library of unchained books. The W. side has largely disappeared (the library was extended partly along it in 1897 by Sir Arthur Blomfield) and there was no N. walk. What is old is mostly 15th c., though the E. outer wall (on the left) is mostly Norman. The wall-arcade is filled with too many monuments to enumerate, but that in bay 1 to Col. Matthews (d. 1826) should be noted, as well as several good ones in bay 5. Bay 5 gives access to a garden containing the 14th c. **chapter house** ruin. This was ten-sided and probably unique in being fan-vaulted. Its double entrance doorway comes in bay 7 of the walk. At the far end are many more memorials and, straight ahead, a private doorway to the Bishop's Palace garden. The library in the S. walk not being open to the public (except for enquiries and research on Tuesdays, Wednesdays and Thursdays from 10.0 a.m. to 12.30 p.m., or by appointment), one must then return to the **S. aisle**.

Next in the outer wall are two 14th c. tombs of uncertain identity. The knight on a tomb-chest under the arcade is Sir Richard Pembridge (d. 1375), and the curious and rather primitive square pulpit in the next bay, no longer used, is probably 16th c. Then the font, Norman and dignified, with lions around the base and defaced figures of Apostles round the bowl.

The entire W. end is John Oldrid Scott's work. This should now be looked at **outside**. Originally it was rather like Rochester's. A tower was added in the 14th c. and it was that which collapsed and prompted Wyatt's rebuilding (with the loss of one bay). Scott's style is Decorated, with rich doorways and windows that bear little relationship to the austerity of the nave. To the right (thanks to the gap in the W. walk) much of the Bishop's cloister can be seen too, including, near the S. end of its E. walk, the upper room called the

Lady's Arbour. The newer building forming the SW. part of the cloister is Blomfield's library of 1897. To the right of that are the wall and 15th c. gatehouse of the Bishop's Palace.

Now back up Palace Yard and along the N. side of the cathedral, looking at the Decorated central tower (lavishly ornamented with ball-flower), at the nave and quire aisle windows, also Decorated, and at the tall Early English N. transept. The Perpendicular Stanbury chantry is tucked in beside the Decorated NE. transept; the scanty evidence of a Norman tower formerly over the adjoining bay of the aisle is hardly visible from ground level. Beyond the transept, the Lady chapel is Early English, though the crypt entrance on the N. side contains re-used Norman zigzag-moulded voussoirs; its E. wall is a curiously bitty composition.

Leading off the SE. transept is the entrance to the late 15th c. Vicars' cloister (or one can go straight through into the chapter house garden again). Left, however, is a corridor with Tudor windows one side and an attractive timber roof with an unusual amount of carving. A few minor monuments are on the wall, and at the end a great pile of carved stones, many of them superb early 12th c. capitals from the former E. parts of the cathedral. Then a fan-vaulted porch leads to the cloister proper, surrounded by dwellings. It is permissible to walk round the whole court, provided one respects its privacy. In the centre of the E. side is the former chapel, now used as a chapter room; if the door is locked the inside with its canopied seat can still be seen through the 17th c. balustered screen. Similarly placed in the centre of the S. side is the Vicars' College hall, mostly now 18th c.

Hexham, St Andrew (Church of England Parish Church, Northumberland)

By far the greater number of Saxon cathedrals in England have disappeared without trace. Hexham's is the only one no longer a cathedral but still the nucleus of a church in use, of which undoubted walling of the Saxon period survives. It was the seat of a bishopric from 681 to 821. After that it was overrun by the Danes but an Augustinian priory was founded in 1113 and it is the church of this (now parochial), together with various monastic remains, which is seen today. Mostly it is late 12th to early 13th c., but substantial rebuilding was done in 1858 and in 1907–9.

At the time of writing, detailed archaeological re-examination of the Saxon crypt was about to begin, precipitated by problems with the E. part of the nave floor under which it lies, and it is premature to attempt a proper description. There is, however, little doubt that it is a part of the church reputed to have been founded by Wilfrid just before 681.

Under the chancel floor, only to be seen (with permission) beneath a trapdoor, are the foundations of an apse which is considered to be of the same period. There is some stonework in the W. wall of the nave which has been thought to be 7th c. too; this, however, seems fairly unlikely.

The other, important, cathedral relic here is the stone chair in the chancel, called Wilfrid's throne and probably of the 7th or 8th c. It is believed to have stood in the apse, as in the restored arrangement at Norwich.

Inverness, St Andrew (Scottish Episcopal Church, Highland)

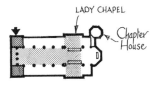

Begun in 1866 under the Inverness architect Alexander Ross, it was finished almost in its present form in 1869, though the W. towers were intended to have 200 ft spires and the flèche formerly over the crossing was taken down *c.* 1960. The original plans also showed a more ambitious E. end.

The general style is Decorated and on a first impression from the W. end the **nave** is tall, wide and rather dark. The impressive crossing arches rise almost to the ridge of the boarded Gothic-arched roof. The arcades have polished pink granite columns with foliage capitals, and triplets of shafted windows form the clerestory. Across the first crossing arch is a high open Rood screen; at the W. end heavier, stone arches separate the entrance lobby.

At the W. end of the **N. aisle** a bust and white marble tablet commemorate Bishop Eden, the founder (d. 1886). Further along is a group of Russian ikons, three of which are said to have been given to him in Russia by the Tsar; also a 15th c. painting by Sano di Pietro. The pulpit, typically Victorian, has figure sculpture and

stands on four robust pink granite shafts. In the N. transept, which
is the **Lady chapel**, is a cartouche to Bishop Hay (d. 1707). Next,
back into the nave close to the oak screen, which is by Sir Robert
Lorimer (1923). Then the canopied and richly carved **quire** stalls
beneath the crossing, which are a memorial to Bishop Kelly
(d. 1904), and the bishop's throne at the far right. Against the pier
opposite is a processional cross, thought to be 16th or 17th c.
Dutch or German. The communion rail and panelling in the
sanctuary apse are by Alistair Ross *c.* 1945. The Caen stone altar
and the reredos with three carved panels are, however, original. Here
and over the crossing the boarded ceilings have original but faded
stencilled patterns.

The S. transept, largely occupied by the organ, is not open, so one
must return to the nave, past the brass desk lectern of 1869, and
then into the **S. aisle**. The White Ensign there was formerly on the
Cenotaph in Whitehall. The main W. window, possibly the best in
the cathedral, is well seen from this angle. The SW. tower space
forms the baptistry, where the Angel and Shell font by Frank
Redfern (1871) is a copy of Thorvaldsen's in Copenhagen
Cathedral.

The W. front with its twin towers is dignified and slightly French.
The elaborate tympanum depicting Christ blessing the Apostles was
added in 1876. A walk right round the outside is well worth while,
for at the E. end is the diminutive chapter house (now used as a
vestry and so not open to the public), and along the N. side a
pleasant riverside walk from which the copper cross in place of the
former crossing-flèche may be noticed.

Iona, St Mary (Church of Scotland, Strathclyde)

There is little doubt that St Columba founded the first monastery on
Iona in 563, on what may well have been already holy ground.
Continual Viking and Danish raids failed to cause its complete
abandonment, and it is possible that Queen Margaret may have
assisted its re-founding after one of these in the latter part of the
11th c. In 1098 it passed under Norwegian rule (along with its
diocese of Man and the Isles, based on Peel) and into the archdiocese
of Trondheim, a position which subsisted until 1266. By then it had
again been re-established as a Benedictine abbey. Some of the
present church is of that period; most of it, however, probably dates
from a 15th c. rebuilding.

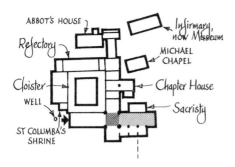

Though the abbot was from 1499 Bishop of the Isles, it is by no means certain that the church was regarded as his cathedral (which had hitherto been at Skeabost in Skye). If so, it was only from about 1507 until the Dissolution in 1561. The E. parts were repaired in 1635–8 when for a short period the diocese was a more definite entity. After further long neglect the ruins, by then the property of the Dukes of Argyll, were given to Trustees for the use of the Church of Scotland in 1899. The church was restored in 1902–10

Cathedral from SW., Iona

under John Honeyman, Thomas Ross and P. Macgregor Chalmers, and the remaining buildings from 1938 onwards under Ian Lindsay for the Iona Community who now use them.

The W. entrance leads straight into the aisleless **nave** of bare multi-coloured masonry with a plain stone floor and simple flat 20th c. roof. The N. and W. walls are largely 12th c., but the W. was re-faced and the S. side extended outwards in the 15th c., when the tower was also built. A stair in the NW. corner leads to a tiny watching chamber. The font, lifelessly carved with Celtic emblems, is of 1908. More in keeping are the simple seven-fold standard iron candlesticks, and the octagonal pulpit with linenfold panels standing against one of the very weatherworn tower piers.

The **N. transept**, set aside for private devotion, is separated by a screen given by the Queen in 1956. The doorway in its W. wall goes to the cloister, and the stair at the N. end to the rebuilt dormitory of 1954. The rose window is of 1905. The thick E. wall with its two deep window recesses is considered to be of *c.* 1200 and contains a wall passage above the windows; the Crucifixion painting over the altar between them is by Roy le Maistre. The carved capitals of the 15th c. E. arch of the crossing should be looked at before moving into the **quire**. One of them bears a damaged inscription formerly recording the 15th c. master mason's name, Donald O'Brolchan.

The whole floor of the E. part was originally at the level of the piano loft with its two 13th c. arches, and there was a crypt beneath. The loft was meant as the start of a N. quire aisle. By the time the sacristy was formed on that N. side in the 15th c. (the aisle above it being removed and the arches blocked) the quire floor had been lowered; but its rather fine trefoil-headed doorway is probably 15th c. too, though copied from 13th c. types. The glass of the N. clerestory is by Douglas Strachan (1939). On the other side, the arcade and aisle are 15th c. though (as will be seen outside) a big transept of quite different form seems to have been begun in the late 13th c. The pillars have a fascinating set of capitals, some Biblical and some showing everyday happenings such as the scene with a cow. The two banks of stalls are 20th c. and in the centre of the floor is a fragmentary grave slab. The big communion table is 20th c., of Iona marble. The effigy resting on four lions (one is medieval) to the left is of John MacFingon, the last abbot (d. 1499). Opposite is the earlier figure of Abbot Dominic, behind are a piscina and triple sedilia, and in the floor is the matrix of a big Flemish brass, said to have been of a Maclean. The Flamboyant tracery of the E. and S. windows is a special feature.

The **S. chapel** also retains its piscina. The internal flying buttresses are a device to arrest movement of the arcade, the capitals of which are worth examining again from this angle. The **S. transept** is dominated by the tomb-chests of the 8th Duke of Argyll (d. 1900) and his wife (d. 1925), with effigies by Sir George Frampton. Only the Duchess is buried here. In front of the rail is a showcase with a facsimile of the Book of Kells.

Now across the nave, past the pulpit and into the **cloister**. The monastic buildings were, unusually, on the N. side because running water was there. The sculpture in the centre of the garth is the Descent of the Spirit by Jacob Lipschitz. Almost all the cloister arcading has been rebuilt since 1960 on its original base and the capitals are still in the process of being carved by different sculptors with their own naturalistic designs. Those of the E. walk are leaves and flowers. Off to its right is the chapter house, restored in 1940. The further half with seat recesses. separated by two 13th c. arches with dog-tooth ornament, is the chapter house proper and now has a library above; the upper floor of this E. range was the dormitory, and as now rebuilt it has 15 little bedrooms within the roof space.

Go on up the E. walk and turn left along the N. walk where some of the capitals are still uncarved. The doorway near the W. end led to the refectory on the upper floor. This range was rebuilt in 1948–9. In the corner the trefoil-headed opening leads to the bookshop, and across the garth the unusual tracery of the tower belfry can be seen. The W. range, rebuilt in 1965, contains kitchens; towards the end of its arcade are a bay and a half of original stonework, incorporated in the modern rebuilding. The first bay of the S. walk also contains 13th c. stones but built into heavier work of later date; the new part has birds carved on the capitals. Two restored doorways lead back into the nave: take the second and go back out of the W. doorway, which is 15th c. Of the three big stone **crosses**, thought to be of about 850, that immediately beyond the well is St Matthew's – part of a shaft only. To its left is St Martin's, a single piece of epidiarite with superb jewel-like carving facing the cathedral and a Virgin and Child and Old Testament scenes on the W. face. The third and biggest cross, to the right, is St John's: what is seen now is a replica, the original having been too often broken in gales since its restoration in 1927.

Now a circuit anti-clockwise round the **outside**, starting at the S. wall of the nave with its great pink blocks of stone and the S. transept with its fine main window tracery flanked by modern head stops of a girl and a boy. The clock-face on this side of the tower

St John's Cross, Iona (probably 9th c.), now replaced by a replica

replaces a medieval one. S. of the S. chapel a depression and a piece
of foundation wall indicate the transept that was begun in the 13th
c. and never built. Here the 15th c. quire clerestory and corbel table
are visible, and next the fine tracery of the S. and E. windows.
Round on the N. side are the sacristy and the other transept, the E.
wall of which, like the adjoining N. wall of the quire, is of *c.* 1200.
Then comes the chapter house. The nearer, separate building, which
can be entered, is the infirmary chapel, probably 13th c. and now
called the Michael chapel. Its roof and simple dark furniture of W.
African hardwood are all modern. The other detached building is
the infirmary itself, also restored in recent years and now used as a
museum. It contains a great number of local carved stones of the 7th
to 16th cc., a rich field for study. The small part of the main block
projecting over the drainage channel was the reredorter, and that
round the corner the abbot's house; in their rebuilt form these are
staff quarters. Then the restored N. and modern W. wings lead back
to the W. front and just to the left of this is a tiny chapel (with
seating for four) revered as St Columba's shrine and restored in
1954.

The rocky hillock called Tor Abb just to the W. has been
identified as the site of St Columba's cell. It provides an excellent
view of the buildings, of the ancient cobbled way which led from the
village, and of Reilig Odhrain, the burial ground reputed to contain
the bones of 48 Scottish, 4 Irish and 8 Norwegian kings close to the
walls of its little Romanesque chapel of St Oran. In the area S. and
E. of Tor Abb, excavation has revealed traces of timber buildings of
the Columban monastery; this was surrounded by an earthwork
whose impressive remains are visible W. of the road $\frac{1}{4}$ mile or so to
the N.

Kirkwall, St Magnus (Church of Scotland, Orkney)

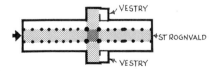

Magnus and his cousin Haakon quarrelled over the succession to
the earldom of Orkney. Magnus was slain and his nephew Rognvald
founded Kirkwall cathedral in his honour in 1137, the bishop's seat

being moved from Birsay. At that time Orkney and Shetland and much of northern Scotland were ruled by Norway, and indeed Kirkwall was only transferred from Trondheim archdiocese to that of St Andrew's in 1472. So although essentially Romanesque, the building wears a definite Scandinavian air, especially in the narrowness of its nave in relation to the height and length. Initially it was shorter at both ends; the extra bays were begun in the 13th c. but the W. end, at least, was not finished till the 15th c. The crossing arches were rebuilt *c*. 1190 and the tower made higher in the 14th c. For such an apparently straightforward design the sequence of building is far from easy to understand.

The cathedral was much less of a victim to religious quarrels than most Scottish mainland churches. Services did, however, become confined to the quire, the nave being insufficiently maintained. In 1671 the spire was burnt and was replaced by a low stone pyramid. Ownership was granted to the town by James III and has now passed to the Orkney Islands Council. In the 1840s, however, the Crown assumed possession for a brief period and promoted a necessary if somewhat ill-judged restoration, immediately followed by a more destructive 'tidying up' by the town council. In 1913–30 more scholarly repairs were done under George Mackie Watson, though these did include the adding of the incongruous copper spire and a renewal of vaulting in the nave which subsequently again became insecure.

The narrowness, if unguessed at from outside, is at once evident on entering the W. doorway and is accentuated by the massive round columns, which are attributed to Durham masons. Their arches have the simplest of chamfer mouldings. The triforium is equally plain – the added ornamented bronze guard-rails seem to emphasize its severity – and the small clerestory of uncertain shape is 13th c. and wholly within the height of the vault. Actually these upper windows are single small lancets, evidently later than those of the quire which are round-headed in true Romanesque style. The ribbed quadripartite vault is not quite what it seems for towards the W. end the panels have in recent years been renewed in glass-reinforced plastic. A long-standing structural weakness, evident also in the dramatic lean of one or two piers, is believed to be due to an ill-advised sequence of operations when the W. end was completed and vaulted.

A special feature of Kirkwall is the decorative alternation of red and white stone, seen for instance at the W. end of the N. arcade. Another is the splendid array of boldly lettered grave-slabs, mostly

S. doorway, Kirkwall (13th c.)

17th c., set up all round the aisle walls, and too numerous to
describe individually.

Near the W. end of the **N. aisle** is a big monument to John
Cuthbert (d. 1650), flanked by Corinthian columns. The doorcase in
bay 3, one of many by Watson, partly hides a 13th c. arch enriched
with ball moulding (two of the W. doorways are similar). In the
fourth bay interlaced wall-arcading begins and the aisle windows
become shafted – another reminder that the W. bays are of later
date though the general design was so little altered. Their vault,
carried on a foliage-carved respond, is believed to be 15th c. In the
fifth bay one panel of the vault retains its original red and black
painted decoration; similar traces may be found elsewhere. Close to
it, on the nave column, hangs the so-called Mort Brod or Death
Board, a double-sized wooden memorial to Robert Nicolsone
(*c.* 1685). In the aisle are memorials of both World Wars, including
one to men of the *Royal Oak*, sunk in Scapa Flow, 1939.

Next the **N. transept**, entered beneath an arch rebuilt *c.* 1200 with
the crossing arches. It is astonishingly tall and narrow, with four
storeys of openings in its gable wall, including the topmost 'rose'.
The base wall-arcading continues around, and the triforium
walkway too but within the wall thickness. The roof here however is
timber, of wagon type. A screen by Watson encloses the vaulted
13th c. former chapel on the E. side, now a vestry; whether there
was originally an apsidal chapel here is not known. Beside this
stands the Town Cross of 1621 from Broad Street, brought inside in
1954 and replaced there by a replica.

Through another screen is the **N. quire aisle**, where the stone floor
gives way to tiles. There is no wall-arcade but the windows have
zigzag ornament and the wall pilasters are capped by what are
probably portrait heads. The vault ribs are wider than before and
therefore earlier. In the first bay is a big 18th c. monument to the
Traill family and in the third a particularly large stone to David
Monroe (d. 1684). Here the Romanesque work ends and early
Gothic begins, with pointed windows, and foliage caps both to their
shafts and to the vault shafts. In bay 4 is a 13th c. coffin-lid; the
statue of St Olaf opposite was copied from an old one in Trondheim
cathedral (1937). At the end is the cenotaph of William Baikie
(d. 1864), translator of the Bible into African languages.

The central **E. chapel** is dedicated to St Rognvald and contains
beneath its arcade wooden sculptures of him, his father Kol, and
William, the first bishop. These with the desk and lectern and the
table incorporating 16th c. carved panels were designed by Stanley

Cursiter (1965) and carved by Reynold Eunson. The model of a
Viking longboat on the table was made by Stanley Cursiter.

At this point the design of these three E. bays should be
examined; they replaced the original apsidal end in the 13th c.
Though the main arches are still round-headed they are richly
moulded and their clustered piers have some foliage capitals. The
triforium arcade is still semicircular too, but the clerestory is pointed.
The quadripartite vault now has ridge ribs and its shafts come right
down through the triforium.

In the E. bay of the **S. quire aisle** is the free-standing tomb of the
explorer John Rae (d. 1893), with his exhausted figure lying on a
rock (sculptor Joseph Whitehead). Nearby are six admirable brass
tablets of 1944–76 to famous local people. Moving W.: many more
16th and 17th c. slabs line the walls and in the sixth bay an
opening into a void called Marwick's Hole, once used as a prison.

The **quire** itself, which should now be entered, is much like the
nave, but the clerestory is more definite in form. The third bay is
narrower than the others and followed by blank walls – between
which stands the organ – and beyond that was the apse. The vault is
a continuation of the eastern one and also 13th c., but here the
shafts stop above the triforium, on corbels with groups of heads
which are undoubtedly portraits. Metal plaques on the large
rectangular piers each side indicate loose stones where the bones of
St Magnus and St Rognvald were found and still rest, the former
including a cleft skull, just as described in the ancient Orkneyinga
Saga. The seating, two banks of traditional stalls with kneeling-angel
ends, leave a severely cramped way between. The lace-like screen
behind the table conceals the organ. All this belongs to Watson's
restoration, as does the commanding octagonal wooden pulpit with
high canopy against the NE. pier of the **crossing**. The E. window
glass is a memorial to Sheriff Thoms, whose munificence made the
restoration possible.

The font, by the SE. crossing pier, is an admirable design of 1883,
with angels forming corners to a round bowl. It is unusual in being
of wood. The pointed crossing arches, rebuilt *c.* 1190, should be
noticed.

Now into the **S. transept**, passing an aisle screen like that on the
N. The transept design also repeats the N., except for the later
(renewed) rose window in place of two round-headed ones. Here too
the little E. chapel is now a vestry. The **S. aisle**, lined again with
mostly 17th c. inscribed slabs, has a piscina in its first bay, and in
the second a 14th c. tomb recess attributed to the Paplay family. In

Tower and S. Transept, Kirkwall (12th and 14th cc.)

the next three bays wall-arcading reappears. Bay 4 has an attractive tablet to Captain Peter Winchester (d. 1674) with Ionic columns garlanded with vine. Further on is an unbelievably rustic monument to Mary Young (d. 1750), with angel-like floating effigy and emblems of mortality and bamboo-thin travesties of Ionic columns. Past the big Romanesque S. doorway is an almost identical memorial to Elizabeth Cuthbert (d. 1685). At the W. end of the aisle, as on the N., foliage capitals indicate a later date.

The **W. front** expresses the internal form with no more elaboration than the three shafted doorways and the four somewhat odd chimney-like pinnacles; yet the intention was to have twin towers. The lower parts were built in the 13th c. and seem to have stood for generations as an isolated screen; the upper are 15th c. The banded masonry was clearly meant to be continued, but restorations have in fact somewhat reduced its extent.

On the S. side the difference in character of the W. bays is obvious at both levels, though the irregularity of the line of change confirms that the extension was not a clear-cut operation but a gradual and delayed process during which changes of style were only partially resisted. The curious truncated triangular head of the doorway in the third bay results from a 16th c. alteration. It led to a cloister. Further on the Romanesque window stonework is renewed but the corbel-table is original; next to the transept are traces of a second cloister doorway.

In the S. transept the spectacularly weathered doorway is mostly early 13th c. but the rose window is renewed and so is the main E. window of the quire which at one time had tracery of Perpendicular type. On the other side of the road stand the ruins of the Earl's palace and Bishop's palace.

From the upper end of the churchyard the copper spire added by Watson to the 14th c. tower top is all too prominent. Finally one can walk back along the N. side, passing the proud N. aisle doorway of *c.* 1190 with its unusual pointed gable.

Lancaster, St Peter (Roman Catholic, Lancashire)

The first purpose-built Roman Catholic chapel in Lancaster was founded in 1767. Its eventual successor was built in 1857–9 under the local architect E. G. Paley and is a prominent landmark on the E. side of the town. The spire is 240 ft high and the style of the whole building Geometric Decorated. It was created a cathedral in 1924.

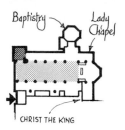

Baptistry   Lady Chapel

CHRIST THE KING

   Tall nave arcades on slender round columns, two-light clerestory windows with detached shafts, and a plain dark trussed roof produce an impressive interior. Under the tower (at the W. end of the N. aisle) is the original reredos, a coloured and gilded triptych; also a statue of St Peter. The N. aisle, where the glass is late 19th c. and of good design, leads into the **N. transept**. Iron gates screen the vaulted octagonal baptistry, planned like a small chapter house but with a small altar on its E. side. The font is of black and grey marble with a simple pinnacled cover, and the floor marble; all appears to be in its original form. Next the Lady chapel; then the **quire**, with more elaborate arcades, clerestory with round windows, and wood and plaster lierne vault, painted and gilded. Additional richness is provided by the dark wall-paintings and the pinnacled stalls. The recent altar, long and low and brought forward on an extended wooden floor, is of white marble with a Last Supper carving. From here the W. end is best appreciated: the superb five-light Geometric W. window full of angels and prophets and flanked by the halves of the organ is by Dunstan Powell of Hardman & Co. The E. apse has earlier Hardman windows. The separate chapel of Christ the King facing into the quire from the S. is only approachable from the domestic buildings adjoining. The altar next to it, nearer the high altar, is dedicated to St Charles Borromeo. The former bishop's throne now stands in the **S. transept**. Close to it is an early 19th c. tablet to the Rev. John Rigby. Off the **S. aisle** are two vaulted chantries, with low two-bay arcades, first the Whiteside and second the Coulston.
   Outside, the SW. porch adjoins the domestic block by the same architect, facing St Peter's Road. Turning right, however, it is worth going up East Road a little way to see the outside of the copper-roofed baptistry, and for another view of the tower with the town below.

Leeds, St Anne (Roman Catholic, West Yorkshire)

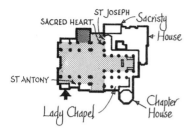

In these days of compulsory road schemes it is strange to reflect that the rebuilding of Leeds cathedral in 1902–4 resulted from just such an improvement. The original building had been founded by the Dominicans in 1793. Their chapel gave way in 1839 to a bigger church of St Anne in a Gothic design by John Child which became a cathedral in 1878 when Yorkshire was divided into two dioceses.

The architect of the present building on its new site was J. H. Eastwood, though the actual design work was by his assistant S. K. Greenlands. His style was late Gothic Revival, of the so-called Arts and Crafts period when the slavish copying of medieval forms and details was being abandoned in favour of more practical planning and a much freer use of mouldings and embellishment.

Immediately on entering the S. door one is conscious of this freshness of interpretation – the wide span of the **nave** with clustered piers, and niches at the tops of the shafts, the lateral roofs to the aisles as though every bay were a little transept, and the attractive woodwork in the doors, etc. (unfortunately not improved by layers of paint). The air of spaciousness is enhanced by the new light grey travertine floor and the clean lines of the main barrel roof, which is steel-framed.

Straight ahead is the baptistry, with attractive recent gates of brass and iron; the font is a very ordinary 14th c. reproduction. In the second chapel off the **N. aisle** is a Pietà, a memorial to two 19th c. priests. The next bay is the base of the tower – followed by the shallow main transept with glass of the period at its N. and S. ends. Two more chapels face E.; then the **chancel**, which is distinguished by a very wide arch (its shafts again capped by niches) and an arched passage along both sides and behind the altar.

Re-ordering of the chancel has left it, as usual, an amalgam of old and new. Here they merge happily, and it does not matter that

the canopied reredos is Eastwood's and the green and white marble
finishes (even the communion rail is marble) are modern. The
Gaudi-like light over the altar is in keeping, the alabaster pulpit with
coloured inlay less so. The **Lady chapel** is very similar but smaller;
its (Augustus) Pugin reredos of 1842 was transferred from the old
cathedral.

The exterior is of great interest too as a late version of Gothic
Revival and particularly in its contrasts of plain wall surfaces with
lavish decoration. Turn left up St Ann Street outside the S. porch to
see the octagonal chapter house, then back past the W. front in
Cookridge Street to the tower in Great George Street. Beyond that
is a domestic block that also contains sacristy and offices.

Leicester, St Martin (Church of England, Leicestershire)

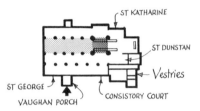

Leicester was a diocese from 680 to 870 and then not till 1927. The
whereabouts of the original cathedral are unknown: the present one
was chosen from the five remaining ancient parish churches of the
city and apart from the vestry block by William Keay (1938–9) no
enlargement has been attempted. The nave and aisles are basically
Early English; there is also an outer S. aisle, which is slightly later,
i.e. early Decorated. The W. end of the nave is 15th c., and the
chancel chapels and N. porch were added about 1500. The central
tower and spire, transepts, clerestory and chancel chapels were
rebuilt by Raphael Brandon in 1847–67. The S. aisle was restored
and the present porch added in 1896–8 by J. L. Pearson. Sir Charles
Nicholson re-ordered the quire in 1927.

Brandon's Early English-style steeple is 220 ft high, a landmark
that at close quarters seems to overpower the rest of the church. It
has 13 bells. Pearson's dignified vaulted two-storeyed porch (known
as the Vaughan porch) is more in scale. It leads into the wide **outer
S. aisle** which with its tall arcade is late 13th c. Its roof (like all the
others in the building) is 19th c. but retains a series of curious full-

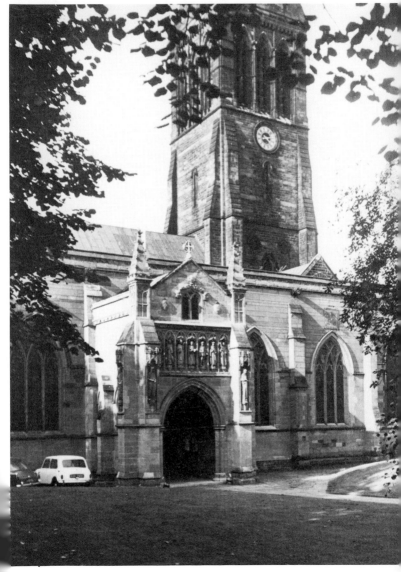

Cathedral from S., Leicester

length corbel figures which have never been satisfactorily explained.
Just inside on the left is a large medieval chest. The W. end of the
aisle is St George's chapel, the chapel of the Royal Leicestershire
Regiment. Amongst the densely hung banners is one of 1799
showing the Union Jack before St Patrick's cross was added. On the
S. wall is a Crimean War memorial and there are books of
remembrance and many brass plaques.

The **inner S. aisle** has a slightly earlier and lower arcade, mid-13th
c. The W. window depicting St Martin is by Christopher Whall. Of
the many tablets here the one to Thomas Cobley (d. 1797) is the
most prominent. On the organ case to the right is a 16th c.
Resurrection painting by Vanni, originally given as an altar-piece.
Beneath the organ gallery in the **nave** stands the font with eight
portrait heads, 14th c. in style but dating from 1849. The main W.
doors behind it are 15th c. The N. aisle arcade matches the S. The
clerestory and roof are 15th c. in style but rebuilt by Brandon.
Looking eastwards: the rood screen is of 1927. At the W. end of the
N. aisle is a further section of organ, moved from the N. transept in
the course of Nicholson's re-ordering of the interior.

Around the N. doorway is another group of wall tablets, and then
the sombre monument to John Whatton (d. 1656) with busts of
himself and two wives. On the right, just before the 19th c. transept
arch, is a huge floor-slab (placed upright) from which the original
brasses have gone and which was used five times in the course of
three centuries: a description hangs beside it. Above is a short piece
of billet moulding, the only evidence of the preceding Norman
church.

The **N. transept** has some good slate tombstones fixed
decoratively to the N. wall. Their colouring is thought to be original.
The chest beside them is 17th c. On the E. wall is a 16th or 17th c.
Spanish or Italian painting of the Scourging of Christ. Another
19th c. arch leads to the Herrick or **St Katharine's chapel** which is set
aside for private prayer. The arch to the chancel, with embattled
capitals, is of about 1500. Here too the N. wall is lined with slate
and stone slabs, embellished with coats of arms and first-rate
lettering; more can be seen in the floor, and two particularly early
ones on the S. wall are dated 1589 and 1609.

Now pass through the screen into the **chancel**. Here and in
St Katharine's chapel the flat timber roofs with bosses are copies of
the late Perpendicular originals. On the left of the sanctuary is the
pinnacled bishop's throne by Nicholson (1927). The marble
monument beside it is to the Rev. Edward Vaughan (d. 1829) and

his family. The E. window by Christopher Whall and the altar and
reredos by Temple Moore form a 1919 war memorial. The big
monument on the right with three busts is to Gabriel Newton
(d. 1746). The three 15th c. stalls below are used as honorary
canon's stalls. The **quire** extends back to the space beneath the
tower; the arches and capitals, and ceiling with big gilded bosses,
are all 19th c. The stalls, like the screen, are entirely of 1927.

St Dunstan's chapel, S. of the chancel, is reached through a similar
arch and screen to St Katharine's. The saints in the coloured and
gilded reredos are the four Evangelists, St Martin and St Dunstan.
Of the great number of memorials the best is by John Bacon to John
Johnson (d. 1780), with a standing allegory of Hope.

The **S. transept** is virtually a continuation of the inner S. aisle.
Just beyond it, facing the nave, is the canopied pulpit, late 17th c.
The desks in front of the pulpit and lectern incorporate 15th c.
traceried panels. Now back into the **outer S. aisle** through the E. bay
of the arcade. The balustered enclosure against the E. wall, with
three carved chairs and a table, is the 18th c. archdeacon's court. On
each side are more slate slabs, and to its right a piscina and sedilia
used when this was the Lady chapel. Here again are many wall
tablets, especially around the S. doorway; between the first and
second windows is a curious memorial to Nicholas Throsby
(d. 1782), with a Shepherd and Lamb painted on the background
obelisk. Nearer the doorway is a shelf mounted on three figure
corbels discarded from the roof above.

The exterior can be seen at close quarters on all sides. St Martin's
West, the alley on the W., leads round to the N. porch, essentially
15th c. but wholly rebuilt in 1880. The traceried doors are original
but the unusual oak vault is a reconstruction. St Martin's East leads
back down the E. side past the song school and from this SE.
direction it is worth looking back at the cathedral as a whole. The
churchyard has a rich assembly of slate headstones, uprooted and
arranged around the perimeter.

Lichfield, St Mary (Church of England, Staffordshire)

Lichfield Cathedral owes its foundation to the devotees of St Chad.
He had set up a Midland bishopric at Repton in 656; thirteen years
later it was moved to Lichfield and in 700 a new cathedral was built
here to enshrine his remains. The importance of the see waxed and
waned for over a thousand years: for a short period it was even an

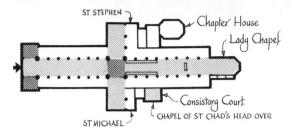

archbishopric, for centuries it was linked with Coventry, and only in 1836 did it finally become separate and distinct.

Virtually no trace remains of the Norman or earlier buildings above ground, though their position and extent beneath the present floor have been partly discovered. They were all taken down and rebuilt during the period 1195 to 1336, starting with the W. part of the quire and its aisles, including the chapel of St Chad's Head on the S., and continuing with the transepts and chapter house (around 1240), the nave and W. front (around 1270), the central tower (*c.* 1300), and finally the W. towers and the entire E. end with Lady chapel and E. part of quire (early 14th c.).

The cathedral was very badly damaged in the Civil War and the central spire collapsed. Much of the quire is consequently of the 1660s. Sydney Smirke did further work in the 1840s, and further restoration under Sir George Gilbert Scott and his son John Oldrid Scott continued for the whole latter half of the century. As a result much of the surface of the building, particularly outside, is not medieval but Victorian, and so much detail is altered that it is no longer possible to be sure what is authentic copy and what was invention.

Approached from the W., the early Decorated main front is overwhelming in its intricacy, but its faults soon become apparent: the indefinite form of the towers and their loss of symmetry and identity as the eye moves down from the rather undersized spires, the meaninglessness of much of the applied decoration (e.g. in the main gable), the 'stuck-on' appearance of the statues and niches, and above all the harsh mechanical quality of the figure-carving. St Chad is in the niche immediately above the central doorway, and the line of kings on each side of him stretches right round the corner turret of each tower. Yet there is a moving quality in the 19th c. figure of Our Lady on the slender central column of the W. doorway, and some of the ironwork of the doors is original. The usual entrance is either here or by the NW. door.

The **nave** is only a little earlier than the W. front. The 'spherical triangle' pattern on the clerestory windows is similar to Westminster Abbey's, and the whole design of arcade, triforium and clerestory is of 'classic' Gothic proportions not yet influenced by the later excesses of the Decorated style; the bisected cinquefoils in the arcade spandrels are unusual. The entire rhythm continues across the inside faces of the towers, obliterating them in the way that the rows of statues do on the outside. Five bays of the vaulting are of 18th c. wood and plaster. Ahead is the Victorian screen, transparently embellishing the quire entrance with its newly restored lustre. The lumpish square marble font is of about 1862, and the brass eagle lectern Victorian too.

From the W. end of the nave the following route is a figure-of-eight, at first clockwise. It starts at the N. tower space with its 18th c. monuments to the Walmesley family (W. wall) and Seward family (N.). The **N. aisle** has a quadripartite vault largely by Scott, as well as wall-arcading which continues with little interruption along the whole length of the building both sides. This provides a framework for numerous memorials. The glass here is largely 19th c.; the sixth window from the W., a Staffordshire Yeomanry memorial, is of 1951.

Close to the N. arcade is the pulpit by Francis Skidmore: iron and brass encrusted with enamels and coloured marbles and with two iron staircases in the manner of fire escapes. It is still not always easy to appreciate this particular aspect of High Victorian craftsmanship.

The **N. transept** is slightly older than the nave: its five-lancet main window proves that. The glass is by Clayton & Bell (1893). But the clerestory is Perpendicular like that of the quire and so, it seems, is the tierceron vault. The large number of white marble memorials, newly cleaned and gilded, are mostly to clerics of the cathedral. The cadaver effigy in the NW. corner beside the steps is the only surviving part of a large monument to Dean Heywode (d. 1492). From the top of the steps is an impressive view of the main S. transept window, Perpendicular with glass of 1895 by Charles Kempe. The two tomb-chests beneath the E. arcade are of Canon Iles (d. 1888) with stone figure, and Canon Lonsdale (d. 1907) with marble figure. To reach **St Stephen's chapel** beyond this arcade it is necessary to go round by the N. quire aisle; it is reserved for private prayer and will be seen later. Its vault is probably original 13th c., but the wall-arcade is a 19th c. restoration.

Now move into the **crossing** for a closer look at the quire screen, also by Skidmore, and of the same type as those removed from Hereford and Salisbury, i.e. designed by Scott and made in iron and brass and copper. Unlike many a cathedral pulpitum it could never be accused of breaking the cathedral in two: rather its superb craftsmanship unites the quire and the nave.

Entry into the E. end is subject to payment at the **S. quire aisle** gate, so the route now becomes anti-clockwise. The first three aisle bays are 13th c. The vaults, however, though again quadripartite, are 14th c., the E. bays having ridge ribs. On the left are the backs of the quire stalls, with draught-preventing glass behind, and the tomb of Major William Hodson, killed 1858 at Lucknow, said to be by G. E. Street: a strange chocolate-coloured cross-slab and various carved scenes. Opposite are a 19th c. medallion in memory of Erasmus Darwin and the richly carved double-arched tomb of Archdeacon Hodson (d. 1855), also by Street; then the damaged tomb of John Stanley (d. 1515). After the doorway is a fine brass cross with marginal inscription to the Rev. James Sarjeantson (d. 1886). The Purbeck marble effigies on the left are of 13th c. bishops, their identities doubtful.

Next is a two-storeyed projection towards the S., which is the consistory court at ground floor level and the **chapel of St Chad's Head** above. The court room is vaulted and fitted out partly with old quire stalls but with a canopied 17th c. principal seat. Steps lead from the aisle up to the chapel. On the way is a 14th c. gallery which served originally for displaying the Head relic and now provides an interesting vantage point for seeing the quire with its newly embroidered stall-backs. The chapel itself with its shafted windows is much restored in appearance though only the vault is wholly 19th c.; it is reserved for private prayer.

On descending the steps again it is best to go straight across the aisle into the **quire**. Architecturally this part of the cathedral is made complex by the fact that the three W. bays belong to the early 13th c., whereas the remainder was built in a westward sequence following completion of the Lady chapel, and joined up in the middle of the 14th c.; but confusion has been increased, first by conversion of part of the clerestory tracery to Perpendicular after the ravages of the Civil War, and subsequently by Scott's work. In the nave the shafts of the tierceron vault are carried down to the floor, but in the quire Scott stopped them on canopied niches which many suspect to have been his own invention. The other unusual feature is the bands of quatrefoils around the upper windows, and certainly they were part of the 14th c. design even if the stonework now seen is much renewed. The gallery beneath these windows is quite different from the full triforium of the nave.

The furnishings of the quire can be taken clockwise, starting with the bishop's throne. This is a Scott design and has some fascinating carving, particularly good being the openwork sides with birds; the carver, George Evans, was an uncle of George Eliot. The stalls are by the same hands except that Skidmore is believed to have been responsible for the very unusual and intricate iron front desk in the centre of each side. Turning now to the E.: the reredos (by Scott) is 19th c.; the pinnacled sedilia on both sides of the sanctuary were made out of its dismantled 15th c. predecessor. The stone and tile floor throughout the quire and presbytery deserves special attention; it too was designed by Scott.

Now back into the **S. quire aisle** at the point where the chapel gallery projects on coving. The wall-arcade now becomes more elaborate; this marks the change from 13th to 14th c. work. The angels in the spandrels are all either mutilated or renewed. The tomb of Archdeacon Moore (d. 1876) on the right was designed by Scott; so was that on the left to Dean Howard (d. 1868). The tall tomb-chest in the window recess, with recumbent effigy, is of Bishop Hackett (d. 1670) and beyond it is a tablet to Col. Richard Bagot, killed 1645 at the battle of Naseby.

Within the wall-arcade there are too many monuments for many to be singled out individually, but through the gates and near the E. end is one of several memorials of the very odd type in which most of the effigy is made out to be incarcerated in the wall; in this case only feet seem to remain, draped and coloured and partly behind a shaft of the arcade. Close to the E. wall is Sir Francis Chantrey's monument to the children (d. 1812) of Prebendary Robinson – two exquisite sleeping white marble figures. To its right is a piscina recess with a medieval Crucifixion painting on the back. The glass in the E. window and in the three adjoining on the S., as well as more which will follow, came from Herckenrode Abbey near Liège and is 16th c.; it was bought by the Dean and Chapter in 1803.

To the left is a little chamber organ assembled from parts of different dates and different woods. In the **Lady chapel** ambulatory the Lichfield Theological College altar (designed by George Pace) is kept when not in use at the crossing. The height of the chapel vault, equal to that of the nave and quire vaults, is unusual. The tall half-octagonal E. end, more usual in Continental churches than English, seems a specially appropriate setting for the principal Herckenrode windows. There are seven here, mostly with Scriptural subjects. The altarpiece is foreign too, a richly carved triptych from Oberammergau (1895). The wall-arcading is at its richest, with 'nodding', i.e. forward-leaning, ogee arches. In unfortunate contrast, the sumptuous carving of the comparatively modern communion rail seems wasted on such heavily veined marble. Along the S. side are three chantries designed to be seen through the arcade, and one of these houses the tomb of Bishop Selwyn (d. 1878). He had been the first Bishop of New Zealand and so the gay wall-tiling depicts 19th c. South Seas scenes as well as heraldry.

Looking back towards the W. from the Lady chapel, the twist in the line of the high vaults is noticeable. The slight misalignment of the chapel (caused, it is said, by the contours of its rock foundation) presented difficulties when the 14th c. work had proceeded far enough W. to be joined to the earlier: this is the junction already seen within the quire.

In the **N. quire aisle** is more Herckenrode glass (including the E. window with the purchase date 1803) and some 19th c. The solitary kneeling figure in the end bay is of Bishop Ryder (d. 1841), by Chantrey. Moving now W.: on the right is the bronze bust of Bishop Woods (d. 1953) by Sir Jacob Epstein, and on the left past the gates Scott's canopied tomb of Bishop Lonsdale (d. 1867), with alabaster figure by G. F. Watts. Opposite is a rich late 17th c. cartouche to Theophanie Coningsby, and on the left again a book of benefactors.

In the sixth bay is a return to the simpler 13th c. work (though the vault is still 14th c.) and on the right an opening of that date leads to the chapter house through an access corridor and waiting space lined with wall-arcading, each bay with a red seat-mat. The chapter house itself is a compressed decagon (or an extended octagon): this unusual plan shape was due to the existence of the two chapters of Lichfield and Coventry, each of which had equal status in the election of a bishop. The foliage capital of the central column is supposed to have been the work of four different carvers. It supports an upper floor which was the treasury and is now the library. That too is vaulted.

From the end bay of the aisle St Stephen's chapel can be entered; its numerous monuments are only of minor interest. Go out again now into the transept area and past the quire screen again to the S. side.

The **S. transept** is rich with glass, banners of the North and South Staffordshire Regiments, and memorials. The main S. window

Statue of Charles II by S. Transept, Lichfield

already seen from the N. transept is the only significant point of difference between the two. The E. aisle is the Staffordshire Regimental chapel and dedicated to St Michael. The large free-standing Egyptian-style monument in the N. bay is to the fallen at Sutlej, 1846. On the N. wall is a group of three rather ordinary tablets; these are followed on the E. wall by a tablet and bust of Dr Samuel Johnson (d. 1784) and in the same bay a similar tablet and bust of David Garrick (d. 1779). Out of many others a large cartouche to John Rawlins (d. 1685) is worth noting. At the S. end of the chapel, behind the altar, is another Herckenrode window; to the right is a regimental memorial book.

The **S. aisle** is like the N. In the first bay of the wall-arcade is an attractive angel brass to Helen Spode (1870) – highly polished like all the others – and in the third and fifth bays two more 'boxed-in' effigies, showing heads and feet only. Beneath the nave arcade is the splendid enamelled brass effigy of the 1st Earl of Lichfield (1854). Then under the SW. tower is the cathedral bookshop.

The **Close** has a pronounced cross-slope from N. to S. So a good general vantage point is just N. of the W. front, by the refreshment kiosk. This gives a view of the central tower and spire, of which the latter is 17th c. Also the 'spherical triangle' clerestory windows are prominent. On the N. side of the Close the beautiful seven-bay brick house of about 1700 is the Deanery. It looks down on to the N. transept, which has a rich 13th c. twin doorway encrusted with foliage, and on to the chapter house beyond. The even grander stone house past the Deanery, dated 1687 and now St Chad's Cathedral School, was the Bishop's Palace. From the E. end of the Close is a view of quite open country, with Minster Pool and Stowe Pool.

Back along the S. side, the cathedral is a good deal more interesting than the houses. On the S. face of the tall Lady chapel are three tomb recesses, corresponding with the three little chantries inside. Then on the end of the E. aisle of the S. transept is another recess with an effigy, and beyond that a double doorway like that on the N. Lurking round the SW. corner of the transept is a very weatherworn stone figure of Charles II that started its life on top of the main W. gable. Then comes an attractive sundial on a tall column, and after that the more open W. part of the Close again; on its W. side are many pleasant minor houses, and in the NW. corner a little passage leads to the secluded half-timbered Vicars' Close.

Lincoln, St Mary (Church of England, Lincolnshire)

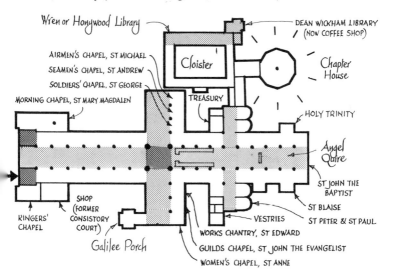

A minster crowned the hill at Lincoln by the middle of the 10th c.,
but it was subject to the enormous diocese of Dorchester, over 100
miles away on the Thames. The transfer of the Norman Bishop
Remigius about 1072 was part of a general policy of moving sees
from villages into fortified towns. His new cathedral was
consecrated in 1092 and part of it (which can be called phase A) still
stands as the core of the W. front. A second phase (B) of Norman
work is thought to have been prompted by a fire in 1141; this is
represented by much of the ornament of the three central bays of the
W. front, and by the W. towers (excluding their tall top stages).

An earthquake in 1185 forced a complete rebuilding in Early
English style which began with the E. end under Bishop Hugh. It
had a complex series of apses forming a chevet – all of which has
gone – and an E. transept with two more apses on each side, which
remains. He, or his immediate successor, built the quire, still known
as St Hugh's, with its aisles, and in addition the crossing and the
innermost bay of each main transept. St Hugh's work can be called
phase C.

After a break came a readily distinguishable later Early English
phase D (about 1220–50), comprising the completion of the main

transepts, the whole of the nave, an upward and outward extension of the W. front including chapels beyond its wings, and the chapter house. The central tower collapsed at this time and was also rebuilt.

The last important work was the replacement of the chevet by a rectangular retro-quire, now always called the Angel Choir, in 1256–80. This phase, Geometric Decorated, can conveniently be labelled E. The cloisters are mostly of about 1300. The central tower was heightened in 1307–11 and the W. ones in the 15th c. The N. range of the cloister was rebuilt by Wren about 1680, with a library above. James Gibbs about 1730 and James Essex about 1760 carried out strengthening work within the W. end, and the latter made several other additions.

Of the many outstanding viewpoints of the cathedral none surpasses that from the castle, especially from the romantic little 19th c. turret overlooking the square called Castle Hill. If the castle steps are too daunting, however, go straight through the 14th c. Exchequer Gate into Minster Yard.

The raising of the biggest of the three Norman arches (A) into pointed form when the spreading Early English screen wall (D) was built around them is very evident. So is the Norman work (B) in the twin W. towers, reaching above (and considerably behind) the top of the screen. The upper parts of the towers are 15th c.; they once had thin spires, which were removed in 1807. The central tower, in the view from the castle hidden behind the SW. one, is rich 14th c. work in its top stage and 13th c. below; its own spire blew down in 1548.

Now a closer look from Minster Yard. There are in fact five early Norman arches of graduated height. Later Norman (B) are the three rich doorways of which the centre one, especially, rewards careful examination with its wealth of carving; the figures and animals on the shafts are remarkable. Its outer moulding is cruelly cut into at the top by the row of eleven kings added with the new W. window late in the 14th c. Another late Norman addition is the frieze of sculptured scenes just above the doorways. Very highly regarded artistically, they are believed to have been inspired by similar work at Modena in Italy. They represent Biblical events – on the N. side the Harrowing of Hell, the death of Lazarus and other New Testament subjects, and on the S. Old Testament stories including the easily identifiable Noah and the Ark with animals, and Daniel with the lions. They continued around the ends where the Early English screen wall was later joined on, so that at the S. end the last one, the Flood, is now inside the building in damaged condition.

The rest of the W. front is of the second Early English phase (D):

Chapter House buttresses, Lincoln (early 13th c.)

the pointed top to the middle arch, row on row of blank arcading, and at the ends spired turrets topped by figures of St Hugh and of the legendary Swineherd of Stow.

Inside the SW. doorway the 14th c. lierne vault of the tower is visible; but the walls of the lobby ahead and to the left are part of the strengthening work done by James Gibbs (c. 1730). To the right is the Ringers' chapel, not normally open.

Turn left into the **nave**. At its W. end is a low arch apparently medieval but actually a further strengthener inserted by James Essex (1761); by that date the Gothic style was just beginning to be understood again. The bay between the towers is essentially Norman, but Early English (phase D) in its upper parts and vault.

The nave and aisles are wholly of phase D, and are not unlike the quire, which was built before them. Dark Purbeck marble shafts to the main piers and the upper arches. Stiff-leaf capitals. The piers are much more varied in form than at first appears. The gallery arcade is equally rich, with two triple arches to each bay, and plate tracery; the main vault is of tierceron type, i.e. quite complex for Early English work. The **N. aisle** has a similar but simpler set of vaults and an introduction to the wall-arcades which are a specially memorable feature of Lincoln. Here they are trefoil-headed arches on Purbeck shafts, the insistence of their rhythm being interrupted by the main shafts from the vaults. W. of the aisle is the NW. tower-base, treated like the SW. by Gibbs; on the W. wall proper is a good convex wall tablet to Elizabeth Scrope (d. 1719).

An arcaded stone screen separates the **Morning chapel**, St Mary Magdalen's (also phase D) from the aisle. An elegant space with its central column and high vault, it is reserved for private prayer. The space to the W. has been reunited with it.

Back in the N. aisle is a little chamber organ on the left, and then beneath the nave arcade the tomb of Bishop Kaye (d. 1853) with effigy by the younger Westmacott. All along the N. wall the glass is by Ward and Hughes, and of excellent quality like most of the 19th c. glass in the cathedral. Under the last bay of the arcade is the reconstructed 12th c. black marble tomb-slab attributed to Remigius, the first bishop, but more likely to be that of Bishop Alexander. The design is a Jesse Tree.

In the N. transept phase C (i.e. the first Early English, and the same as the quire) is entered for the first time. But its N. half is phase D again and there are plenty of differences in the mouldings and other details between the two. The obvious one is the change in the wall-arcading which occurs quite suddenly in the middle chapel.

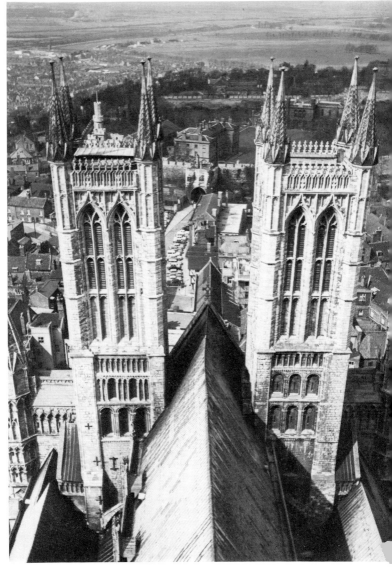

W. Towers as seen from central Tower, Lincoln (12th c. with 15th c. tops)

The 'C' kind is a fascinating design with two separate arcades superimposed, the one out of step with the other, and it occurs elsewhere only in the triforia at Worcester Cathedral and Beverley. The transept is dominated by the great 'Dean's Eye' circular medallion window, with its original 13th c. glass, a rare treasure. The variety of figures and scenes is too complex to describe here, but in any case its aesthetic value lies more in its contribution of colour and pattern. At the other end of the great transept is the 'Bishop's Eye', a 14th c. insertion, its own glass a collected miscellany of medieval bits. The names refer to the former directions of the bishop's and dean's residences; in course of time these have become interchanged.

Back to details of the N. transept. In the N. wall (at low level) are more angels in 14th c. glass; the other N. lancets mostly have 13th c. grisaille glass. Near the NW. corner, the little wall tablet to Dean Garnier (d. 1863) is belatedly classical. The E. aisle contains three interconnected chapels all associated with the services and hung with their colours and standards. St Michael's on the left is the Airmen's and has memorial glass by Harry Stammers. St Andrew's in the centre is the Sailors' and has Christopher Webb glass. The third, St George's, is the Soldiers' and contains numerous military memorials and rolls of honour and has glass by A. K. Nicholson. Its screen is a painted one, probably of 1911, but the other screenwork seems to be 15th c.

Move now into the **crossing** and look up into the tower lantern with its diaper work and 14th c. lierne vault. Beneath is the marvellous Decorated pulpitum. The carving is as fine and as detailed as anything of its period. Within its thickness are a staircase and a little vaulted room.

At the entrance to the **N. quire aisle** is one of the most beautiful doorways in any English cathedral, standing proudly on its own as though waiting for a wall to be built over it. Its openwork carving is almost beyond belief. It belongs to phase E, i.e. three-quarters of a century later than the aisle itself. On the left is more of the double wall-arcading: on the right a plainer arcade which is the back of the stone screen to the quire. The floor has a central line of empty stones which evidently once contained a wonderfully rich series of brasses. They were torn out in the Civil War and the stones were rearranged around the aisles in the 18th c. A doorway on the left with modern metalwork leads to the treasury, formed and furnished by Louis Osman in 1960 for a changing display of church plate. The glass is by Geoffrey Clarke. The treasury is not always open.

The aisle now widens into the **NE. transept**, again part of phase C. As with so much at Lincoln, this is an instance of unity in variety. All is rich Early English, with the Purbeck shafts so typical of important work of the period, a good deal of dog-tooth ornament (as elsewhere in the building) and some fine sculptured detail. The oddest feature is the so-called Trondheim pillar in the angle between aisle and transept where the main shaft, enclosed by eight lesser ones, sprouts enormous crockets. There is a similar one in Trondheim Cathedral. To the right of that is a doorway with 13th c. ironwork; above are four paintings of bishops done in 1728 and an Annunciation of 1799 which belonged to a reredos. At the N. end of the transept is another strange feature: a tall room at gallery level, probably a garderobe. Beneath that is the door to the **cloister**.

It leads to a vaulted corridor of about 1300, very small in scale. The cloister itself, non-monastic, is also of modest size. The S. walk, left on entering, and the W. are also of about 1300 and have wooden vaults. There are some medieval incised slabs turned upright. The prominent stone of Richard of Gainsborough on the floor is a 19th c. replica of the original on the wall. In the W. walk is a stone coffin with interlaced ornament. From there one can look across the chapter house, and diagonally to Wren's Honywood Library. The N. walk beneath it has Tuscan columns and a plain flat ceiling, and offers a very impressive view of the N. side of the cathedral; it leads to an open stair where there is a discarded classical reredos. At the top, the Medieval library of c. 1420 is opened during the summer (a charge is made). In it can be seen original 'presses' in the form of wide lecterns, one of the four originals of Magna Carta, and other priceless documents. Also one can look through into the Wren library, a splendid gallery 104 ft long; this is not open to the public.

The E. walk has a wooden vault too, though here the outer wall is Early English (phase D) with rich arcading and dog-tooth ornament, much restored, and a double doorway which leads to the beautiful vaulted **chapter house** of the same period. It is ten-sided, the earliest in England to be polygonal. The glass, not ancient, portrays historical scenes. A canopied chair is original 13th c., but much restored.

Back in the N. transept, the two little chapels on the left are now used as vestries; the left one was longer before Essex reduced it to its original apsidal form; it may once have been the Lady chapel; both have 15th c. screens. The N. quire aisle continues past the back of the stalls on the right. After them is the canopied cenotaph of Bishop Wordsworth (d. 1885), by Bodley and Garner. This is really

part of the retro-quire or Angel Choir (phase E) but it is best to go
on to the E. end of the aisle before becoming concerned with
architectural details. On the left is the chantry chapel of Bishop
Fleming (d. 1431). Like two similar chantries on the S. side, it is
normally locked, but the stone effigy and cadaver are readily seen.
Beyond, in the last bay, the very ornate canopied and vaulted tomb
is of Lord Burghersh (d. 1355). The aisle E. window contains 13th c.
glass; that of most of the remainder of the aisle is again 19th c. The
floor here has many good black and white marble ledger stones.

Now the **Angel Choir**, which extends back W. of the reredos into
the quire proper, so that only three bays are fully visible at first.
This is Geometric Decorated at its most lavish. The resemblance to
the nave is obvious, but in the triforium bar tracery takes the place
of plate tracery, and in the clerestory plain lancets are superseded by
complex four-light windows, again in two layers with a passage
between. The vault is actually simpler than that of the nave, but the
main supporting shafts end in big knobbly foliage corbels; in the
first of these from the E. end on the N. side can be found the famous
Lincoln Imp. But the finest carvings are those in the spandrels of the
triforium which give the Angel Choir its name and, less easy to see,
in the many roof bosses. The outline of the previous many-apsed E.
end is marked out on the floor.

The middle chapel is St John the Baptist's. Of the three tombs to
its left the nearest is the only remaining part of the 14th c. shrine of
St Hugh's Head and the others are of Robert Burghersh and Bishop
Burghersh (d. 1340), with an effigy. The rich blue main E. window is
of 1855, by Ward and Hughes. To the right the bronze figure of
Queen Eleanor is a replica of that in Westminster Abbey; further
right, under the arcade, is the double-canopied Cantilupe chantry
(1355) with tombs of Baron Cantilupe and, under the W. arch of
Nicholas Wymbyssh (d. 1461). The S. aisle E. window is 13th c. like
the N.

Against the easternmost bay of the S. wall is a Gothic cenotaph of
the painters William Hilton and Peter de Wint. Off the second bay is
the Russell chantry (chapel of St Blaise, not open to the public); the
tomb is of Bishop Russell (d. 1494), and inside are paintings by
Duncan Grant (1958) on the theme of sheep. Finally in the retro-
quire at the W. end are the alabaster tomb of Dean Butler (d. 1894),
four table-tombs (one of them set up in the 17th c. to mark the site
of the shrine of St Hugh's Body) and another chamber organ.

Next the **S. quire aisle** proper, starting on the left with the
Longland chantry fronted by the tomb of Bishop Longland

(d. 1548) – at that late date more Flamboyant than Perpendicular in detail. On the right are the 15th c. tombs of Catherine Swynford and her daughter, incomplete and with a later, Renaissance, cornice.

As on the N. side, the E. transept forms a break and has two apsidal E. chapels; their attractive glass is mid-19th c. The left one, now a vestry, has a 15th c. wooden screen and contains two Baroque cupboards. The other, St Peter and St Paul's, was furnished by Randoll Blacking as a memorial to the 13th c. Bishop Grosseteste; the tomb-slab is by John Skelton. This is phase C again, so the double wall-arcading recurs. On the W. side there is, first, a doorway to the Song School, not open to the public (a phase D addition); then what was possibly another chapel but is now another vestry. This is separated from the transept by a 15th c. wooden screen and from the aisle by a remarkable 14th c. stone one covered with diaper pattern and incorporating a washplace; there is also a fireplace.

Cross the aisle and go through the scrolly 13th c. wrought-iron screen into the **quire**. To the right is Angel Choir, phase E, and to the left St Hugh's Choir, phase C. The differences are inescapable. In all its essentials St Hugh's is like the nave which it preceded, but the insertion of the stalls, as well as various repairs done during phase D after the fall of the tower, have marred its purity. The vault, however, is like no other, for its pattern is regular yet not symmetrical. It has been likened to a series of scissors set diagonally. Moreover it is considered to be the earliest rib vault to have tierceron ribs.

Fundamentally the stalls are of about 1370 but much is 19th c., especially in the lower parts of the figures. A booklet is available, describing in detail the wealth of miniature medieval carving, especially in the misericords and on the arms between the seats. The organ case over the W. side is of 1826 and 1898, the brass eagle lectern of 1667, and the two-tier candelabrum of 1698. The pulpit is of 1863, by Sir George Gilbert Scott. Turning E, the Gothic altar screenwork, surprisingly, is partly by Essex (1769), though the actual canopy is 19th c. Left of the sanctuary the beautiful six-gabled monument (*c.* 1300) is partly Easter Sepulchre (with Roman guards in the plinth) and partly the supposed tomb of Bishop Remigius. On the right is the Swynford chantry.

Before returning to the S. quire aisle, notice the wooden beams left across the transept arches as ties. In the aisles on the right are parts of a 15th c. reredos, probably Rhenish, then the quite plain 14th c. shrine of Little St Hugh. On the left, two more 19th c.

windows and a group of four wall tablets. The **S. transept** is entered
through another marvellous 14th c. doorway matching the one
opposite; these walls and doorways probably originated from a
desire to give the tower extra buttressing after its collapse.

The Bishop's Eye has already been noted but deserves a closer
look, particularly for the delicate 14th c. surround. The lancet
windows below contain more 13th c. glass, but in the three
interconnected E. chapels it is 19th c. The first, the Works chantry
(St Edward's) has a fine late 14th c. stone screen with restored
figures; the other two have 15th c. wooden ones. The centre chapel
is St John the Evangelist's; the furthest, St Anne's, contains the
tomb of Sir George Tailboys (d. 1538). At the S. end of the transept
stands the splendid bronze figure of Bishop King (d. 1910), by W. B.
Richmond; close to it is a movable early Gothic Revival pulpit
probably by Thomas Chippendale. The door in the SW. corner leads
into the Galilee porch, to be seen from outside. On the W. side is
more 19th c. glass; also the memorial of Dean Fuller (d. 1699), with
pouting bust, and two embattled pillars, remains of the shrine of
Bishop St John Dalderby. This transept, like the N., is of slightly
later date (D) in its outer bay.

The **S. nave aisle** has more good 19th c. glass throughout. The
large wall tablet on the left is to Dean Honywood (d. 1681). By the
second arcade column stands the pulpit, originally in St Mary's
English Church, Rotterdam. Then, towards the W. end, the font;
this is big, black and square, of Tournai marble, 12th c., carved with
strange beasts and leaves. The cathedral shop is the former
consistory court, similar to but by no means identical with the
chapel opposite, for its vault has no central column. Outside on the
W. wall of the aisle is a good tablet to Elizabeth Hatton (d. 1724).

Outside again in Minster Yard, turn left and follow the S. side of
the cathedral. High in the topmost tracery of the consistory court
gable is another famous carving, the Lincoln Pilgrim. On the side of
the S. transept is the Galilee porch, a seemingly unnecessary
appendage but built as one with its completion during phase D.
From the W. it seems like no fewer than seven doorways stacked
against one another, with a double opening at the end. But it should
be examined from the inside too for its beautiful carving. Next are
the main S. transept itself, St Hugh's Choir and the SE. transept (C)
with the Song School (D) added to its SW. corner. Immediately past
the transept apses are the late Perpendicular Longland and Russell
chantries, flanking the very rich but over-restored Judgement portal,
said to be based on earlier work at Westminster Abbey; the

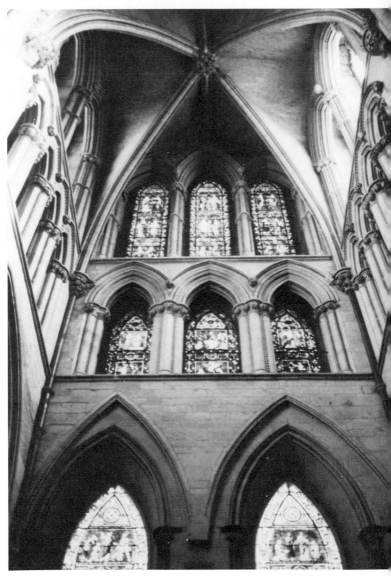

S. Transept interior, Lincoln

Madonna on the trumeau is of *c.* 1930. The buildings at a lower level include the Bishop's Palace and Vicar's Court.

Then the E. end, with the great Geometrical E. window of the Angel Choir, the design of which has earned high praise: Pevsner says it 'combines breadth and generosity with logic' while an earlier writer called it 'one of the loveliest of human works'. By the NE. angle is a well-head, probably not medieval but by Essex, and further round on the N. side is the Fleming chantry. Priory Gate, spanning Minster Yard East, is of 1816.

The giant flying buttresses make Lincoln's chapter house the most spectacular of all from the outside. The little Tudor-style building to its right was built as the Dean Wickham Library of *c.* 1910 by C. Hodgson Fowler and is now the cathedral coffee shop. Towards Eastgate, the big statue of Tennyson is by G. F. Watts. Following Eastgate is unrewarding as far as the cathedral is concerned but Minster Yard, leading off to the left, offers views of the W. wall of the cloister and the double N. doorway of the N. transept. Finally it leads past the side of the NW. tower, where the Norman arcading can be seen on all but the topmost (15th c.) stage, and back to the W. front.

Pulpit in S. Transept, Lincoln (c. 1800)

Lismore, St Moluog (Church of Scotland, Strathclyde)

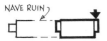

The bishopric of Argyll seems to have been founded *c.* 1185 though a monastery founded by St Moluog had existed here for centuries. Its church was rebuilt in the 13th and 14th cc., but the cathedral establishment gradually lapsed and before the Reformation it was already merely parochial. By 1679 it was roofless, and in 1749 the quire was reduced in height and repaired. Its orientation was abandoned in favour of a centralized arrangement but in 1900 the altar was again moved to the W. end, a small vestry built within the one-time nave and the main entrance switched to the E. end.

The present **entrance**, through a cramped porch formed *c.* 1900 from an annexe of 1749, brings one in at the site of the original altar, beneath a gallery on iron columns. On the left are a 13th c. piscina, triple sedilia with sloped-back jambs, and a 14th c. priest's doorway: on the right a doorway that led to a sacristy. The original floor was of course about two feet lower. The heavy hammer-beam

Cathedral from SE., Lismore

roof and the communion table and pulpit are of 1900. The end wall, including the rough semicircular arch, is basically the medieval pulpitum.

Under the gallery stair three medieval slabs with interlaced ornament are preserved. The W. window glass, best seen from gallery level, is of 1926 and depicts St Moluog and St Columba.

Outside, the building appears merely as a humble wayside church with harled walls, slated roof, little bellcote and embattled porch. Turning right (i.e. true S.) outside the porch: the first gate leads only to a burial area, with a wall tablet to James Macgregor (d. 1759). The second takes one round to the W. end where the nave foundation can be seen over the field wall outside the vestry (the more clearly defined square ruin is a burial enclosure and much later). On the N. side there is no way out, but two more medieval slabs may be found embedded in the grass.

The tumbled and overgrown nave and W. tower **ruins** are accessible from the lane through the glebe field on the N. and are fairly readily traceable.

Liverpool, Christ (Church of England, Merseyside)

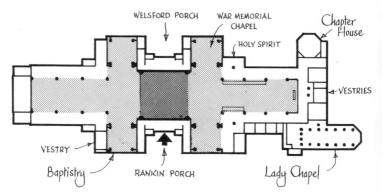

The diocese was formed in 1880, and after one abortive competition a design by the 22-year-old Giles Gilbert Scott was selected as winner of a second (with a different and dramatically placed site). Building work began in 1904. The Lady chapel was complete by 1910 and used as a cathedral until the quire and E. transept were finished in 1924. The central tower was completed in 1942 and the nave begun in 1948. Scott died in 1960 with the nave unfinished. Like Wren with St Paul's, he drastically revised his original design in the course of the work – to the extent of replacing two transeptal towers with a single central one. The W. front is a simplified scheme by F. G. Thomas.

What amazes at Liverpool, and will never cease to amaze as one walks round, is the sheer scale of the building. Conversely, the quality of detailed craftsmanship in stone and wood in the Gothic style – long outmoded though that may be – often verges on the unbelievable, the kind of work one might think could not still have been possible in the 20th century.

There is a good deal of Spanish Gothic in many details: for example in the S. or **Rankin porch** flanked by the two great transepts and forming a main entrance to the cathedral. Imposing steps, intricately traceried outer doors, and an inner vaulted porch with three pairs of ceremonial doors ahead prepare one for the grand entry into the tower space. Everyday visitors, however, enter on the left into the **SW. transept** near the buff marble font, carved with figures of the Apostles by E. Carter Preston: Spanish influence is evident again in its lavishly crested baldacchino 39 ft high. The windows in the main building are mostly by Powell & Sons; detailed descriptions are impracticable here, but the progression in style from E. to W. is quite marked.

Moving into the central space one can begin to comprehend the internal layout – to the left the nave separated yet linked by the great bridge, to the right the stupendous space beneath the tower, and beyond that the E. transept and the quire dwarfing the human figures in them. Left and left again, i.e. off the S. nave aisle, is a lift lobby from which the ascent of the **tower** is sometimes possible. One lift goes as far as the transept vault, and above that is a series of concrete steps to a second lift. Finally there is a zigzag stair within the vast hollow space of the belfry – which has diagonal concrete beams supporting its centre, curiously like those of the Roman Catholic cathedral. That can of course be seen, along with much of the city, from the flat boarded copper roof. The height of the tower is 330 feet, and the thirteen bells are both the highest and the heaviest peal in the world.

From the lift lobby the way to the W. end of the **nave** passes the entrance to the Radcliffe Library (only open to the public by special arrangement). Go next along the S. aisle, through its arches piercing the great buttresses, and then down the eight steps into the two W. bays of the nave. Above is the splendid W. window, unusual in

Cathedral from NE., Liverpool

having its top spandrel entirely glazed instead of having a circular top light as originally planned. The glass predominantly blue, on the theme of the *Benedicite*, is by Carl Edwards. Looking E. from beneath it, the view of the quire is impressively framed by the nave bridge.

Long stairs each side lead to the **bridge** which if open is a marvellous vantage point for seeing the nave arcades and clerestory (there is no triforium), the very high quadripartite vaults, the W. transepts with their own arches and vaults, the great tower arches (102 ft high and 72 ft wide and probably the biggest Gothic arches ever built), and beyond them the E. transept and the organ cases on each side of the quire. Offshoots from the bridge lead to little balconies overlooking the W. transepts. On the wall of the S. stair, facing into the nave, is a stone unveiled by the Queen at the completion of the cathedral (1978).

Back at floor level again, the **NW. transept** is used as an exhibition area. The Nativity sculpture by the NW. pier of the tower is by Josephena de Vasconcellos, a cast of the original in St Martin-in-the-Fields, London. In the very centre of the floor beneath the **tower** is a big memorial roundel to Sir Giles Gilbert Scott, and on the N. wall of the tower space are modest commemorative inscriptions to members of the Vestey family who enabled it to be built. The **NE. transept** is the War Memorial chapel, with roll of honour on the central cenotaph. On the left is an aircraft propeller, on the right the cenotaph of the King's Regiment and the bell of H.M.S. *Liverpool.*

Next pass to the left of the pulpit and beneath the organ into the **N. quire aisle**. The small chapel on the left is reserved for private prayer and dedicated to the Holy Spirit; its gilt framed reredos depicts Christ in prayer. Further along the aisle, past some more small memorials and the frontal cupboards and with glimpses of the sanctuary, is the chapter house lobby, containing a case of old books, etc. The octagonal chapter house itself is not normally open to the public.

An ambulatory leads across the E. end, past the vestries and with steps on its right up to the high altar sanctuary. Ahead is the W. gallery of the **Lady chapel**, the main floor of which is unexpectedly at a much lower level. With its rich lierne vault, gallery with intricate cresting, gilded chandeliers and high clerestory, this is even more elaborate than the remainder of the building and it shows the influence not only of Spanish Gothic (for example in the curved vault-ribs and the fanciful reredos) but also of G.F. Bodley who assisted Scott while he was so young. The kneeling figure of the

Virgin Mary in the sanctuary is by della Robbia (15th c.). The glass,
all replaced after the Second World War, has Womanhood as its
over-all theme. From the gallery a stair leads down, passing on the
left a tablet to Helen Swift Neilson (d. 1945) by Preston and a
women's war memorial. The reduction of the aisles to mere passages
is typical of the period. On the string course above the arcade is a
decoratively treated text from St John's Gospel, and over the song
school doorway in the N. wall the single word ALLELUIA. At the W.
end the oak organ case is particularly splendid.

Now back up the stair to the S. quire and through bronze gates
into the huge **quire**, with on the right the gilded stone reredos and
bronze communion rail, on the left the stalls and organ cases and (in
the centre of the S. side) the bishop's throne. Though the seats and
fronts are of oak, the canopies and panelling behind are designed as
part of the red stone wall. A special feature is the central coat-of-
arms in the marble floor.

In the **S. quire aisle** (reached by returning through the bronze
gates) are most of the comparatively few memorials in the cathedral.
The canopied bas-relief to Bishop Chavasse (d. 1933) is by David
Evans. Round the corner to the left, the tablet to Sir Robert Jones
(d. 1933) is by Preston. On the right, against the back of the quire
stalls, are the effigy of Bishop Ryle, first bishop (d. 1900), and Dean
Dwelly, first dean (d. 1957), both also by Preston. To the left of the
arch into the **SE. transept** is the foundation stone of 1904, and under
the main W. arch of the transept the bronze effigy of the Earl of
Derby (d. 1908). Behind that, on the wall to its E., is another
memorial by Preston to Admiral Horton (*c.* 1950) while on the
opposite side of the transept the monument at gallery level is to the
55th Division, whose motto refers to the rose of Lancaster.

Finally, with a look at both E. transept windows, back through
the tower space (which though so overwhelming has the undeniable
effect of dividing rather than uniting the two ends of the cathedral)
to the SW. transept again, where the bookstall is, and **out** again by
the N. porch with its great arch and dolphin-crested bronze gates.
To the right is the entrance to the Western Rooms, a suite of social
rooms under the W. transepts. Further along, the car park entrance
provides an impressive view of the W. front with its three great
lancet windows. A way leads on to the Welsford porch. Also
starting close to the road, a dramatic path leads through a rock
cutting and tunnel down into the ravine below the S. side of the
cathedral. The open space at the bottom is St James's Cemetery, the
Greek Doric building of *c.* 1830 at the corner of the street (by John

Foster) being its mortuary chapel; it gradually comes into better view if one climbs Upper Duke Street and turns along Hope Street. Far below, the Corinthian 'temple', also by Foster, is a monument to William Huskisson who d. 1830 (see Chichester). From this side the siting and size of the cathedral are really awe-inspiring. Between the transepts is the Welsford porch, balancing the Rankin porch on the other side. To the left is the copper pyramid of the chapter house. Then the Lady chapel comes into view, and Upper Parliament Street down the W. side of the cemetery (called also Cathedral Gardens). At the bottom corner is a public entrance to it. Then the road runs level, past a private drive and the Lady chapel and back to the Rankin porch.

Liverpool, Christ the King (Roman Catholic, Merseyside)

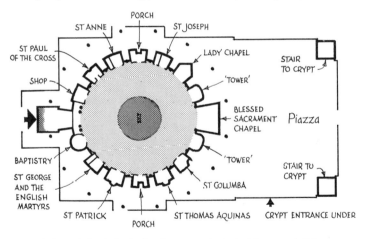

One of the original Catholic dioceses of 1850, Liverpool did not possess a completed cathedral till 1967. Edward Pugin designed one in the suburb of Everton in 1856 but building was abandoned when only the Lady chapel was complete; it still stands, pathetically neglected. In 1933 Sir Edwin Lutyens began a great classical building which would have had a dome even bigger than St Peter's in Rome. Of this only the crypt was built. Finally, as the result of a competition, Sir Frederick Gibberd capped off the crypt at main floor level to form a vast platform for open-air services and built his cathedral alongside.

In its circular form it carries to the logical limit the liturgical conception of worship 'in the round', of participation from all sides in ritual at a central altar. The main **entrance** is marked by an acutely pointed bellcote and a giant recessed pattern by William Mitchell intended to represent Our Lord's Cross and those of the thieves. Like the great sliding bronze glass-fibre doors with monster emblems of the Evangelists, also by Mitchell, the primeval, almost Aztec design provides an awesome welcome into the porch – which is high-ceilinged at first and connected to the main building by a low concourse.

The first, immense, impression of the **interior** is of blue space with a glowing lantern crown high above. All around are chapels (sixteen if one includes the three porch bays and the so-called towers either side of the organ), each framed in blue glass spattered with crimson and each of distinctive form. The great concrete buttresses supporting the lantern pass between these blue frames and are lost to sight outside. The central white altar is further emphasized by the open-framed hanging metal baldacchino. The candlesticks are by Robert Goodden, the high bronze Crucifix by Elizabeth Frink, and the archbishop's throne by R. D. Russell.

The **chapels** will be taken in clockwise order and are described as at the time of writing: obviously there will be changes. The first, St Thomas à Becket's, is taken up by a temporary shop approached from the porch. The second, the chapel of St Paul of the Cross, has a very tall window with glass by Margaret Traherne. St Anne's, no. 3, is empty except for some school appliqué work, and the next is the 'west' porch with a gallery above.

Chapel 5, St Joseph's, is a very tall pyramid with square 'eye' on top, dark tiles and plain panelled walls. Then comes the Lady chapel, with tall slit windows (this glass again by Margaret Traherne), diagonally squared concrete roof, marble floor and dado, and ceramic Madonna by Robert Brumby. Bay 7 is the W. 'tower', and no. 8, the biggest and the one diametrically opposite the entrance contains the organ and, below it, the Blessed Sacrament chapel, reserved for private prayer. The tabernacle and the yellow and blue painting and windows are by Ceri Richards and the upward canted roof continues beyond as a canopy over the piazza altar outside.

Continuing round the second half of the circle, the E. 'tower' contains a bronze holy water stoup presented by Pope Paul VI

(1967): the carvings round the bowl representing events in Christ's life connected with water are by Virginio Ciminaghi. Close to this bay is the head of the processional ramp leading up from the sacristies and other rooms beneath. Bay 10, St Columba's chapel, is very tall and unfurnished; its small round-headed arch alludes to early Celtic forms. St Thomas Aquinas's, with ascending and diminishing windows each side of the altar, is also bare. The twelfth bay is the 'east' porch with gallery, and the thirteenth St Patrick's, with a slit window each side and temporary altar. No. 14, of St George and the English Martyrs, is complete, with plain white marble altar, deep green walls and a column of horizontal windows by John Piper and Patrick Reyntiens. Lastly before the porch, the circular baptistry with simple white font, inverted hemispherical ceiling, and wheel-like floor; the bronze gates are by David Atkins.

At this point – or any other – one can break off and go closer to the central sanctuary. On the edge of it, in front of the choir, is the simple throne. The low choir enclosure behind also contains the organ console. The lantern glass, wholly visible only from the centre, is by Piper and Reyntiens.

Now back through the main entrance, which provides access to the shop, as well as a stair down to lavatories, tea-room, car-park etc., and an undisguised cylindrical lift enclosure. On the **outside** platform the sheer stone walls of the variously shaped chapels (starting, to the left, with the round baptistry) alternate with recesses containing the buttresses and double windows. In addition to the prominent diagonal supports there are thin vertical columns between the windows, making thirty-two main supports in all. At the end the platform opens out into a paved piazza with open-air sanctuary and wooden Cross. At the far corners of this vast area little pyramids cover two staircases from the Lutyens crypt; from there the central lantern can be seen as well, a crown of pinnacles which in more distant views carefully answers the Anglican's cathedral's tower. To the right and at a lower level the spike on the Lady chapel roof is conspicuous.

Complete the outer circuit, follow the ramp with chevron-shaped drainage channels back to the road, and turn left. On the left is the sacristy approach, then Cathedral House, the Convent of Christ the King, and the University Chaplaincy, all by Gibberd. Between the last two is the way to the Lutyens **crypt**. Though normally closed to visitors, it is regularly used for services and can be discreetly seen during the quarter-hour or so before they start. A dramatic stepped approach, past tumbled granite blocks, leads to the monumentally grand façade. Inside, the massive, dark and seemingly unending brick-vaulted spaces verge on the frightening, and a small taste will probably suffice. The chapel just inside is that of Our Lady of Sorrows. On its left an aisle opens out into a Lady chapel transeptal to the chancel of the first. Further left still and running parallel is the long barrel-vaulted Pontifical chapel with six typical Lutyens columns at its entrance end. Half-way along is the famous 'rolling gate' to the Archbishop's chapel – a 6-ton circular stone as a door; inside are the tombs of Archbishops Whiteside, Downey and Beck. On the right of the central chapel the planning is similar except that the outer space is a multi-purpose hall with arches to the road. This façade can be seen by returning to the road and going to the paved area alongside Brownlow Hill, from which steps lead to the piazza above.

Further down the hill, however, is the back of the crypt cut into the rock. Beyond is a dead-end driveway, and then a side road from which more steps lead back to the podium and so to the main entrance once more. A wide axial approach to Hope Street is planned here, to supplement the present ramp.

Llandaff, St Peter & St Paul (Church in Wales, South Glamorgan)

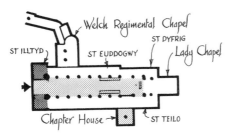

Tradition says that the first church at Llandaff was founded by St Teilo in the middle of the 6th c., and that Dyfrig and Euddogwy were bishops. Building of the present cathedral began about 1120 with the presbytery (sanctuary) and quire. The outer walls of the nave aisles were built later in the 12th c., still in a rich Norman style followed by the three W. bays of the nave arcades in early Gothic and then their continuation eastwards, as well as the W. front and the nave clerestory. The chapter house was added about 1250, and the Lady chapel slightly later.

In the 14th c. the main arcades were continued by piercing the presbytery walls, though on the S. side this work came to a halt; many of the windows throughout the cathedral were enlarged. The NW. tower was rebuilt in the 15th c. After the Reformation poverty and decay set in and during the Commonwealth the building was desecrated. Finally, early in the 18th c. storms brought down the nave roof and much else with it.

Eventually John Wood of Bath was commissioned to take charge of repairs and converted the eastern part into a Classical building with lowered walls and plaster ornament. Funds failed again, the 'Italian Temple' scheme was abandoned, and the remainder stayed a ruin.

From 1835 to 1869 a proper restoration took place under John Prichard and J. P. Seddon, and the SW. tower was rebuilt to a new and grand design. In 1941 immense damage (amongst British cathedrals third only to that sustained by Coventry and the Catholic cathedral of Southwark) was done by a German land-mine, and this was repaired mainly under George Pace, who also added the pulpitum (the concrete arches and organ-case across the nave) and the Welch Regimental Chapel with processional way and vestries.

The approach to the cathedral is down one of the steep paths from Cathedral Green, which finish opposite the W. doorway. The centre part of the W. front is largely a reconstruction by Prichard, but the actual doorway is 13th c., a curious design with a central pendant containing an old carving thought to represent St Teilo. The NW. tower is called the Jasper tower after Henry VII's uncle, Jasper Tudor. Like that of St John the Baptist's church in Cardiff its openwork parapet resembles many across the Bristol Channel in Somerset. In it are a carillon and 10 bells, of which only the tenor is as old as the 18th c. The SW. or Prichard tower is also un-Welsh in design, being said to be modelled on the style of south Normandy; its spire is 195 ft high.

Immediately on stepping down through the W. doorway, one's attention is arrested by the pulpitum, the 20th c. equivalent of the organ screens which punctuate the length of more conventional cathedral interiors. At Llandaff the main part of the organ is housed in a great hollow cylinder, mounted on giant concrete parabolic arches straddling the nave, and providing a background for Sir Jacob Epstein's great statue of Christ in Majesty, cast in aluminium. Around the back and sides of the cylinder are little openings for the organ pipes interspersed with saints and angels taken from the 19th c. quire stalls after they were shattered by the land-mine.

Cathedral interior, Llandaff

Overhead is the new ceiling of traditional panelled form but made of tropical hardwoods. The clerestory, still Early English in character, is a reconstruction of what was already a reconstruction, and there is no triforium. The nave arcades are in the same style, the three W. bays being different in detail from the slightly later next three (for example the attached triple shafts which lead the eye in three stages from floor to roof are more prominent). The tall Gothic arch separating the quire from the presbytery is entirely 19th c. Beyond it is a splendid Norman arch to the Lady chapel, the most impressive remaining portion of the 1120 building, and above that is John Piper's window depicting the Supper at Emmaus.

Beneath the NW. tower is St Illtyd's chapel, with a triptych by Dante Gabriel Rossetti 'The Seed of David', originally in the high altar reredos. Between this chapel and the **N. aisle** is a dark wooden screen with heavy columns, typical of the work of Pace.

A Norman doorway in the N. aisle leads into the irregularly shaped **Welch Regimental Chapel** (St David's), wholly designed by George Pace and begun in 1953. A prominent feature is the series of lettered tablets recounting the Regiment's battle honours. The ceiling is of suspended plaster, in a form which defines the 'working area' of the chapel. The side aisle, with a 17th c. chest and the roll of honour, leads into the processional way, past vestries and out into the open again beside the Prebendal House. Many of the cathedral's old books are housed in this passage, as well as two rather splendid domestic carved cupboards of the 16th or 17th cc., four amusing medieval gargoyles rescued from the war-damaged ruins, an ancient Flemish statue of a bishop, and a beautiful majolica plaque.

The outside of the big Norman doorway, seen on returning through the chapel into the cathedral, is specially beautiful and impressive, and it is easy to believe that it once formed the W. entrance to the 1120 building and that it was moved here when the W. front was reconstructed.

Back in the **N. aisle** is another carved chest, also the canopied tomb of Henry Thomas (d. 1863) and further E. the tomb of Bishop William of Radnor (d. 1265). Under the arcade lie alabaster effigies of Sir William and Lady Mathew (d. 1526 and 1530) on a tomb-chest, now facing the six black and gilt columns which screen the stair to the simple panelled pulpit (1957). **St Euddogwy's chapel** at the E. end of the N. aisle has interesting ironwork by Pace – communion rail, flower stand, lectern, etc. – and beside the altar the canopied tomb of the famous Dean Vaughan (d. 1897), a one-time headmaster of Harrow School who also re-founded the cathedral

choir school. Behind this altar is part of the main organ. On the N.
wall, seen only by going right up to the altar rail, is a late 15th c.
painting on wood of The Assumption of Our Lady.

From the **quire** the whole lower organ-case is visible. Pace's very
individual interpretation of Gothic is carried on into the stalls,
though here a certain amount of 19th c. carved woodwork was
rescued and re-used, especially in the tall pinnacled bishop's throne,
the chapter stalls, and the canopies over the dean's and archdeacon's
seats. The spiky wooden light pendants in the aisles also have Pace's
unmistakable imprint.

The high altar communion rail is his work too; at its S. end is the
tomb of St Teilo – a worn 13th c. effigy (now within a 19th c. arch)
which in medieval times is said to have watched over transactions of
many kinds at this sacred spot. Above it are parts of Norman arches
with billet moulding – clear evidence of the age of this wall before
the Gothic arcade, still unfinished, began to be inserted.

Within the arch on the N. side of the **presbytery** is the tomb of
Bishop Marshall (d. 1496) and in the next arch that of Bishop
Ollivant (d. 1882). These lead to **St Dyfrig's chapel**, reserved for
private prayer. Here are six pretty porcelain panels of della Robbia
type depicting the Creation; they were designed by Burne-Jones,
though not for the cathedral. The tomb of Sir David Mathew
(d. 1461) on the S. side has his effigy. The stone panelling on the N.
wall is part of the 14th c. reredos which stood behind the high altar;
it still has traces of original colour. The tomb opposite, its canopy
forming a 'squint' through to the Lady chapel, has figures of Sir
Christopher and Lady Mathew.

Next the vaulted **Lady chapel**, in the normal eastern position. Its
founder, Bishop William de Braose (d. 1287) lies under a stone with
a low-relief effigy. On the E. wall the repaired 15th c. reredos
contains bronze carvings by Frank Roper of twelve flowers named
in Welsh after Our Lady: Gold Mair = Marigold, and so on. The
windows here are all by Christopher Webb, the eastern being a Jesse
window.

Looking back from the Lady chapel, the entire nave with the
pulpitum and roof is seen framed by the Norman arch, and in the
foreground the back of the high altar with its Italianate Cross and
six candlesticks – a breathtaking view that encompasses work of all
the main periods of the building in complete harmony.

S. of the Lady chapel and presbytery is **St Teilo's chapel**, with
altar furnishings of the utmost simplicity. In its N. wall is the
ancient tomb of Lady Audley. The panels of 19th c. carving in this

chapel were salvaged from the débris of bombing.

The S. arcade of the presbytery having been left incomplete, the aisle bay behind it is rather darker and cut off. It forms a pausing space and, unlike the rest, is vaulted. A 10th c. cross found in the precincts is mounted on a pedestal here. A rich 19th c. doorway leads back into the presbytery beside St Teilo's tomb, and opposite is the entry to the **chapter house**. This is a square vaulted 13th c. room with no old furnishings, but the octagonal upper storey is used as a museum.

From the **nave S. aisle**, there is another arresting view of the pulpitum; beside the SE. leg of its arch is the organ loft, and beneath that an early 15th c. carving of the death of Our Lady. Then there are two more ancient chests, one adorned with 16th c. tracery and the other with funny dancing figures, and lastly the font, and so back to the W. end. The font is of Norman shape but with curiously Art Nouveau figure-carving by Alan Durst (1952); it contrasts oddly but refreshingly with almost everything else of its date in the cathedral.

Turn right on coming out through the W. doorway: the

S. Aisle window, Llandaff (c. 1960)

Ironwork of S. door, Llandaff (c. 1960)

Prebendal House is straight ahead, containing vestries and
conference room and connected now to the cathedral by the
processional way. Outside are two urns, relics of John Wood's
'Italian Temple'. Through the open porch there is access to the N.
side of the churchyard. Beneath the aisle parapet begins the second
part of a series of sovereigns' heads which starts on the other side
with Richard III at the E. end of the S. aisle and finishes with
Edward VIII close to the Prichard Tower. Here on the N. side are
George VI and Elizabeth II.

The way leads round the Lady chapel at the E. end to the outside
of St Teilo's chapel; its ornate 19th c. entrance is called Prichard's
doorway. Close to it is Prichard's own tomb. Facing the chapter
house, which is topped by a gilded figure of St Gabriel, is a large
churchyard cross, the memorial to Dean Conybeare (d. 1857). The
two windows nearest the chapter house have interestingly carved
stops representing the four phases of the cathedral's building. Then
there is a small Gothic doorway into the S. aisle, with a vesica-
shaped panel above, and finally the main S. doorway, one of the most
magnificent Norman doorways anywhere. It has four orders of rich
ornament, and on its doors is splendid modern ironwork designed
by Pace and wrought by the local blacksmith.

Steep steps lead back to Cathedral Green from the W. front. The
19th c. bishop's house (*Llys Esgob*) here replaces a grander building
that has become part of the Cathedral School and is approached
through the even earlier ruined Bishop's Castle. The smaller ruin on
the Green was a Norman bell-tower; it fell to ruin in the 15th c. The
white house at the E. end of the Green (not the one so called) is the
Deanery.

Manchester, St Mary, St George & St Denys (Church of England,
Greater Manchester)

The bishopric was created in 1847, with the great Perpendicular
parish church as cathedral. This church had been re-founded with a
college of priests in 1421: its quire was rebuilt *c.* 1425–50 and the
nave *c.* 1470–80. The outer N. and S. chapels were added early in
the 16th c. to house extra chantries. The outer S. chapel and the
tower were rebuilt (the latter six feet higher) in 1862–8 by J. P.
Holden. The arcades were largely rebuilt, apparently to the old
design, by J. S. Crowther in 1881–91. At the same time the N. and S.
porches were rebuilt and the fretted parapets put on the outer walls.

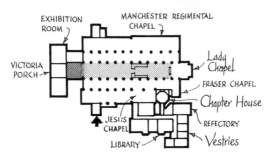

Basil Champneys built the W. porch and vestries in 1898 and the big
SE. group of vestries, library etc. in 1902–3 (these were extended in
1930). The war-damaged Lady chapel and the outer N. chapel were
rebuilt by Sir Hubert Worthington after 1945.

The two-storeyed **S. porch** by Crowther is dated 1891 and has two
separately vaulted bays. The inner doorway and that on the N. side
are unusually elaborate on the inside: each in effect a blank
Perpendicular window with the actual ogee-headed doorway
superimposed. The five aisles and the consequent great width of the
building in proportion to its height and length are at once apparent
– also their uniformity of style. Crowther's renewal of the arcades
and other internal stonework was made necessary by structural
weakness: so much of the surface had been cut away in 1815 for the
purpose of plastering the whole interior. At the W. end of the S.
aisle is a white marble tablet to Dauntsey Hulme (d. 1828) and in
the inner aisle a group of brasses with a St George window above by
Antony Hollaway (1973).

The tall **tower** arch and the stonework around are late 15th c.
though the rest of the tower is of 1867, including its fine fan-vault.
On its wall-panelling the names of lord mayors, bishops and other
dignitaries are recorded. The exhibition room beyond is used for the
occasional display of plate, etc. The **nave** is best seen from this end.
The panelled arcade spandrels capped by a continuous cresting, big
clerestory and rich panelled timber roof are all typical Perpendicular
work, but the treatment of the wide chancel arch and even the
clerestory with similar spandrels is exceptional. The roof has a
wealth of foliage bosses, and corbel angels each playing a different
instrument. The aisle roofs are similar but much plainer.

Continuing across the W. end, the inner N. aisle has another
Hollaway window of brilliant reds: its subject is St Denys. In the

outer N. aisle the memorial with seated figure is to the school
founder Humphrey Chetham (d. 1653): it is by William Theed
(1853). The heraldic tomb slab to the right is to James Chetham
(d. 1696). Over the N. doorway hang regimental colours, and among
a number of wall tablets in the aisle is one in the E. bay to Sir
Hubert Worthington (d. 1963). The outer N. chapel, St John's, is
now the Manchester Regimental chapel. A piscina in the right pier
of its arch indicates a former altar of St James nearby. Break off at
this point to the N. end of the quire screen, where a Saxon carving
of an angel has been inserted in the end pier of the nave arcade. This
is the only indication of any building earlier than the 14th c.

Now into the **Regimental chapel** through the side screen. This
corner of the cathedral (also called the Derby chapel) was rebuilt by
Worthington c. 1950, and has a timber roof of his design. The little
Ely chapel which projected from the fifth bay was not rebuilt. The
hanging colours all have descriptions below. The E. window, by
Margaret Traherne in memory of Worthington, gives the
unfortunate impression of being temporarily washed over with
vermilion colour of varying density. Along the N. wall, the
following are also worth noticing: a tablet to Charles Lawson
(d. 1807), rolls of honour, a set of well-designed brass tablets of 1971
recording the destruction of tattered colours, and in the last bay the
easily missed brass demi-figure of Bishop Stanley (d. 1515). The
wooden screens to the inner quire aisle incorporate a little
Perpendicular work and the font at the SW. corner is 18th c. with a
modern cover.

The **inner quire aisle** starts uninterestingly with the back of the
organ; then come three bays of splendid 15th c. wooden screens. But
the big ogee arches and the wrought ironwork between them,
capped with crocketed 'pinnacles', are of 1750. Through the centre
bay the **quire** can be entered; the three-sided wrought-iron
communion rail there is of the same date.

Architecturally the quire is very like the nave, differing mainly in
its roof. The stalls are the glory of the cathedral and few even of the
older cathedrals can match the luxuriance of their canopies or the
wealth and variety of the misericords, poppy-heads and other
carvings. The misericords can moreover be much more easily seen
than is often the case. They date from the early years of the 16th c.
The bishop's throne is of 1905, the brass candelabra of 1690 and
1715. The two brasses in the floor are (nearer the altar) to John
Huntington, first warden of the college and builder of the quire
(d. 1458) and to Dean Maclure (d. 1890). Huntington's double rebus

– a man hunting with dogs and a man with tuns of ale or wine – can be found on the middle roof beam looking eastwards, and at the sides of the arch to the Lady chapel.

Now back into the N. quire aisle, past a showcase of plate and behind the altar into the **Lady chapel**. Its mid-15th c. screen survives with even some original statuettes, but the chapel itself (already rebuilt in the 18th c.) is by Worthington. The tapestries on the side walls were designed by Austin Wright and executed by Theodora Moorman (1957). The engraved glass is by David Peace.

Off the **S. quire aisle** the little Fraser chapel lies straight ahead. Reserved for private prayer, it was built as a memorial to Bishop Fraser (d. 1885), whose effigy by James Forsyth lies in a plain recess. Next in the aisle is the tomb-chest of Hugh Birley (d. 1883); then the double doorway to the 15th c. **chapter house**, set like the main entrances within a blank-traceried window-like surround. The paintings in the tracery represent the Beatitudes and are by Carel Weight (1962). The chapter house has modern panelling on an intimate scale and a flat wooden ceiling with central star.

Continuing along the aisle: a group of wall-tablets on the left includes an unusual wood-framed brass to William Heyric (d. 1667). Then another 15th c. screen to the outer S. or **Jesus chapel** which has a Cross, frontal and candlesticks by Theodora Moorman and Bryant Fedden. On the S. wall are two 19th c. brasses and two 'kneeling family' scenes typical of their period to Antony Mosley (d. 1607) and Oswald Mosley (d. 1630). Another group of minor tablets is on the pier at the NW. corner.

Next the quire screen should be inspected, from the nave side. Though the entire intricate upper part is by Sir George Gilbert Scott (1872), the lower is of about 1500.

Three ancient royal charters are displayed in frames. The earliest, of 1421, hangs to the right of the arch to the inner S. quire aisle; the others, on the **outer S. wall** to the right of the piscina, are of 1635 and 1578. The tiny chapel off this outer aisle, with its own arcade, has two monuments of interest, to Elizabeth Trafford (d. 1813) and Thomas Fleming (d. 1848), by E. H. Baily (a full-sized white marble standing figure).

Now the outside, completely refaced with Derbyshire stone in place of the softer red stone which only remains inside. From the S. porch steps lead to the W. end. This entrance, added by Champneys with its flanking rooms in 1898, is the Victoria porch. More steps lead round to the N. porch (by Crowther, 1881). Crowther's too are all the openwork parapets of the aisles; it is doubtful whether their

Quire interior, Manchester

design was based on anything existing. The centre of the E. wall (the Lady chapel) is marked by a simple niche with a Madonna by Sir Charles Wheeler. Cathedral Street leads to Cathedral Yard and from there the Eric Gill carving over the W. entrance to the SE. building can be seen – the Christ Child with St Mary, St Denys and St George, patrons of the cathedral. S. of the library stands an attractively robust sundial, and from this direction there is a good view of Holden's tower.

To the N. of the cathedral and across the road stands Chetham's Hospital School, the original home of the warden and priests of the college. It survived through being bought in the 1590s by Chetham for his school.

Middlesbrough, St Mary (Roman Catholic, Cleveland)

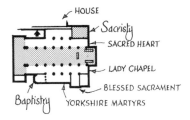

Yorkshire was divided in 1878 into the Catholic dioceses of Leeds and Middlesbrough. St Mary's at the latter was then newly built by George Goldie. Today it stands in a sadly run down part of the town, waiting for better plans to come to fruition around it.

The W. entrances have been modernised; however, the usual way in for visitors is via the house on the N. side, along a passage and into the outer N. aisle. This way the first view is across the five aisles and through the Decorated-style main arcades. A shallow arcaded marble dado runs round the walls.

Going anti-clockwise, i.e. first to the W. end: the new W. entrance has involved changes to the underside of the gallery and the hiding of two of its iron columns with plastic board to imitate the real marble. Over the new plate-glass main doors is a glass tympanum with etched Madonna. The **nave** has a high dark hammer-beam roof, and a clerestory mostly of twin lights. The E. wall (there is no intervening chancel arch) has a curiously patchwork treatment:

stone, mosaic, paintwork and gilding, and above it all a rose
window.

In the **S. aisle** a window looks into the vaulted baptistry, which is
sunken in level and reached from the outer aisle. At the other end of
the outer aisle is the chapel of Yorkshire Martyrs, and beyond that
in the transeptal position the distinctive Blessed Sacrament chapel
with scarlet iron screen, barrel roof, mosaic-lined walls and floor,
and large wooden reredos with a Last Supper painting.

The inner aisle ends at the daintily carved reredos of the Lady
chapel, with scrolly foliage on rather flat panels in a very unusual
style; above it is an ikon. Next, a closer look at the **quire**, first
passing the giant square wooden Gothic canopied pulpit. The high
altar, which matched the mosaic part of the reredos, is now forward
of it and replaced by the bishop's chair. The central painting above
stands out from those around; it is of the Virgin, St Peter and
St Gregory the Great, by Girolamo Cotignola (1528).

The Sacred Heart chapel at the E. end of the **N. aisle** is
overlooked by the windows of the upper sacristy. This brings one
back to the Pietà near the door to the house again.

Outside, hard brick, crumbling stone and the absence of a tower
are not entirely attractive. The best feature is the **W.** doorway with
its fancy brick arches and new glass tympanum. Nothing of interest
is to be seen from the school grounds on the **S.** and **E.** sides.

Millport, Holy Spirit (Community of Celebration, Strathclyde)

LADY CHAPEL

The status of the Cathedral of the Isles on Great Cumbrae is a little
confusing even by Scottish standards. The priests' college here was a
product of the Oxford Movement and founded in 1850 by the Hon.
George Boyle who became sixth Earl of Glasgow. Its church became
a cathedral in 1876 but in 1888 the college failed and subsequently
Millport and Oban shared co-cathedral status. Though Oban only
has had the bishop's official throne since 1920, there have continued
to be a throne and a provost at Millport and the courtesy title of
cathedral is staunchly retained. Since 1975 the buildings have been

'Cathedral of the Isles' interior, Millport

used and maintained by an American Fisherfolk community called
the Community of Celebration, still under the aegis of the
Episcopalian Church.

The architect of the whole little group of buildings was William
Butterfield and his work is hardly altered to this day. The cathedral,
open 2 p.m.–5 p.m. every day during the summer months, is
approached from the W. by a series of flights of steps beside
terraced lawns, or from the E. past the two-sided cloister of the
college. Either way it dominates in spite of its minuscule size: the
slender tower with square stone spire, refined by their proportions
rather than by any enrichment, is only 123 ft high. Its base forms a
porch to the aisleless **nave** which has a very plain high-pitched roof
and, at the quire arch, an open stone screen with marble columns
modelled on that of Great Bardfield church, Essex. Around the arch
is a pattern of green, red and black tiles.

Displayed on the plinth of the octagonal font (1881) are
fragments of ancient crosses found on the island, and behind it on
the W. wall is a brass to Provost Cazenove (d. 1896), in the form of
a Celtic cross. The painting on the N. wall is a copy of 'The
Visitation' by Albertinelli (16th c.); the smaller one behind the plain
wooden pulpit is an Italian Pietà of c. 1600. The little square nave
altar is of course a recent addition; otherwise most of the fittings are
Butterfield's. They include the brass gates in the screen, the brass
candelabrum in the **quire**, and the oak stalls, but probably not the
brass eagle lectern. His reredos has, however, at some time been
replaced by an 'English' altar with riddel posts, and his communion
rail by a poor wooden one of 1931. The quire roof is enhanced by
stencilled patterns, and polychrome tiles cover most of the wall
surfaces in true Butterfield manner.

Just inside the quire on the left is a brass to Canon Robertson
(d. 1859) with his figure in prayer, and just inside the sanctuary
stands the bishop's throne. Above it is a tablet to Alexander
Chinnery-Haldane, the first bishop (d. 1906). To the right of the
priest's doorway is a processional cross with bronze head thought to
be of c. 1000; it shows Christ and emblems of the Evangelists.

Through iron screens, the organ chamber and vestry lead rather
oddly into a separate Lady chapel adjoining the former seminary
wing. It was formerly the chapter house and has a roof similar to
that of the main church but altogether plainer.

Outside, a little graveyard stands below to the NW.: beyond is
private. In the other direction, the S. wing of the college forms
another arm of the cruciform group and terminates in the oriel

window of the provost's study. Round the corner in the SE. re-
entrant angle is the cloister: this again is private. Finally it is worth
going S. down the lawn away from the oriel for a good general view
of the cathedral.

Motherwell, Our Lady of Good Aid (Roman Catholic, Strathclyde)

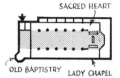

The first Catholic chapel in Motherwell was founded in 1873, to be
replaced by a larger in 1875, again in 1883, and finally by the
present red stone building in 1900 to the plans of Peter Paul Pugin,
who had in 1881 produced a much more ambitious design. It
became a cathedral on the creation of the diocese in 1948.

Cathedral interior, Motherwell (c. 1900)

The NW. porch leads into the W. lobby, made more spacious by
the removal of a dividing wall. At its S. end is the former baptistry,
now disused. The general style, with only slight mannerisms, is late
Gothic – arcades on round columns with octagonal tops, clerestory,
low-pitched dark timber main roof and lean-to aisle roofs – and the
present colour scheme mostly cream and pale green.

Follow the S. aisle to the Lady chapel. The plain stone font is now
there. A stone screen separates the sanctuary, brought forward with
a heavy green marble altar in the newly raised chancel. The
communion rail, the pulpit moved to behind it, and the two side
altars are all of red and green marbles. The pointed-arched
baldacchino against the E. wall is modern. Looking W., the
unattractive timber and glass framework of the gallery is prominent,
but above is the cathedral's finest feature, the superbly coloured
Jesse Tree W. window by Dunstan Powell of Hardman & Co.

Externally, in spite of plain detailing and a certain flatness, the
building is a distinguished one and can be seen from all sides – but
best from the SW. Vestries adjoin it on the E., and confessionals
along the N. side.

Newcastle, St Nicholas (Church of England, Tyne and Wear)

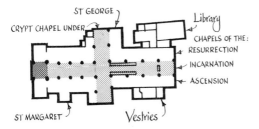

The biggest of the four parish churches of medieval foundation in
the city, St Nicholas' became a cathedral in 1882. Mere fragments
exist of 12th and 13th c. work; the majority is 14th c. The outer
walls were much altered in the 15th c. and in 1824 and 1834–6, so
the resulting general appearance is Perpendicular. The tower and
crown-spire are 15th c. too, the S. library and vestry of 1736, the
porches of 1832–4, and the NE. vestries of 1926.

The font of c. 1500, ahead under the tower as one enters, is the
first prominent feature – a simple octagonal bowl with shields, and a

splendid pinnacled cover. Inside the cover is a little vault with a boss representing the Coronation of the Virgin. High above, the tower vault has coloured bosses. The porches, forming NW. and SW. transepts and strengthening the base of the tower, are of 1832 (N.) and 1834 (S.). The **nave** arcades are 14th c., on octagonal columns with capitals – a consistent design feature which continues through the crossing and the quire. Some of the walling below the N. clerestory is considered to be 13th c. The timber roofs too are consistent in design and date, their plainness being enlivened by gilding on some of the bosses. Behind, the W. wall has war memorial panelling by R. J. Johnson which includes the W. doors.

In the **NW. transept** is a big white marble monument to Admiral Collingwood (d. 1810) by J.F. Rossi: a rather theatrical bust on a pedestal. The **N. aisle** has banners all along, colours of the Fifth Fusiliers. The monument on its W. wall, with figure sculpture by E. H. Baily under a semi-Gothic canopy, is to Calverley Bewicke (d. 1815). Numerous tablets along the aisle include one of *c.* 1690 on the W. wall, now illegible, and several military memorials, chief amongst which is a brass to Col. Philip Fitzroy (d. 1892). The painting of St George at the end is also a memorial; it is by Louis Raemakers, to General Riddell (d. 1915). Opposite, the slight remains of a Norman window arch in the NW. crossing pier and of a shaft of the 13th c. arcade are visible.

The **N. transept** has W. and E. arcades, all like the nave. On the W. wall are a big wall tablet with the bust of Joseph Bainbridge (d. 1823) by Baily, and another to William Peareth (d. 1775). The N. window of the W. aisle is by Stanley Murray Scott (1971). A doorway and steps lead down to the crypt chapel, reserved for private prayer. Also 14th c., this has a stone arch-ribbed roof, little windows on the N. between the ribs, and a small wheel window over the altar that looks into the chapel above. It was long used as a burial vault.

Back along the transept, the octagonal pulpit standing ahead by the NW. crossing pier is by Johnson, of Uttoxeter 'marble' and typical of its date (1887). A little brass inscription in the nave floor beneath is to Thomas Loraine (d. 1649). The organ case (in the transept) incorporates in its upper part one of 1676 by Renatus Harris that stood on the chancel screen; the trumpeting angel on top belongs to Johnson's 1891 reconstruction. Beside it on the E. wall are tablets to John Cuthbert (d. 1746) and Major-General Skerrett (d. 1814), also a good brass to Henry Watson (d. 1887).

The N. quire aisle is separated by a 19th c. wooden screen; by it

stands a richly carved credence table of 1604 embellished with texts
and with SAYNTE NYCHOLAS NEWCASTELL along the front. **St George's
chapel** is reached from the quire aisle through another screen against
which books of remembrance are displayed. Its left side is enclosed
by another face of the organ. The monument to William Hall
(d. 1631) with kneeling figures is much restored; below it is the
round window to the crypt. Several other monuments include a
cartouche to Robert Shafto (d. 1705) and a tablet to Thomas Curteis
(d. 1629). A number of famous men are commemorated in glass of
the 1930s by A. K. Nicholson.

The start of the **N. quire aisle** is behind the quire stalls. Some of
the many memorials are worth picking out: a cartouche to Robert
Buggin (d. 1688), the bust of Archibald Reed (d. 1843), an oval
cartouche to Patrick Crowe (d. 1694), with specially good lettering.
The very elaborate Gothic canopied tomb beneath the arcade on the
right is of Bishop Lloyd (d. 1908), with effigy by F. W. Pomeroy.
The first bishop, Ernest Wilberforce (d. 1907) is commemorated by a
big framed brass to the right of the steps. The doorway on the left at
the bottom leads to a library and small refectory.

Across the E. end at this lower level are three chapels. That of the
Resurrection has an 'English' altar and, on its right, a memorial to
Nicholas Ridley (d. 1805). Its N. window, based on a cross and
globe pattern in leads, is by L. C. Evetts. The chapel of the
Incarnation has an E. window by William Wailes typical of its date
(1860) and a rich Gothic altarpiece. The third, the chapel of the
Ascension, has another 'English' altar and a war memorial window
of 1962 by Evetts, an angular design with reds and blues and greys.

Now W. again along the **S. quire aisle**. The free-standing tomb is
of the historian John Collingwood Bruce (d. 1892). The giant double
brass, mounted high on the S. wall, is to Roger Thornton (d. 1429)
and his wife; it is one of the largest in England. Minor memorials
are again numerous: the more important on the S. wall are to John
Smith (*c.* 1830) with bust, Matthew Ridley (d. 1787) with seated
mourning woman by John Bacon, and Henry Askew (d. 1796), a
spirited group by Henry Webber. Opposite this is a glass case with
Bishop Wilberforce's staff (1883). The doorways in the S. wall lead
to vestries on the ground floor and song school above; the library
for which this addition was built in 1736 is now incorporated into
the City Library.

The **quire**, accessible at this point through the side screen, was
completely refurnished under Johnson *c.* 1882 with alabaster reredos
full of saints, stone flanking screens and sedilia, wooden screens

further W., bishop's throne, richly carved stalls with angels on their canopies and misericords beneath, organ case on the N. side, and screen across the W. end. The craftsmanship is first-rate. Bishop Lloyd's tomb at the N. end of the marble altar rail is prominent.

Back in the **aisle**, on the left is a tablet to Matthew Deane (d. 1785); then 18 plain old chancel stalls discarded by Johnson. The **S. transept**, the chapel in which is known as St Mary's porch, matches the N. but has a W. aisle only. On its E. wall is a memorial by John Flaxman to the Rev. Hugo Moises (d. 1806). The very worn knight's effigy in a recess by the piscina in the S. wall may be of Peter le Mareschal (d. 1322). The many wall tablets are not specially notable but on the W. wall is a big and excellent fully coloured monument to Henry Maddison (d. 1634), with a complete kneeling family; its unusual shape is explained by its former position on a crossing pier. High above it are the carved arms of Charles II. The chest under the arcade is of 1604 but restored. The brass eagle lectern by the SW. crossing pier is one of the cathedral's greatest treasures; the backward-leaning stance of the bird shows that it is medieval (*c.* 1500).

Now the **S. nave aisle**, which has curious arched recesses broken only by the projecting chapel of St Margaret with its low wooden screen. All along are minor wall tablets, including one of 1680 just before the chapel. In the chapel are two particularly good black heraldic ledger stones (there are many more in the cathedral), a roundel of ancient glass in the E. window, and two big and two small coffin-lids, one with head and feet strangely carved on. The worn upright slab with cresting on the W. wall of the aisle is probably 16th c.

In the **SW. transept**, which is of 1834, are several big monuments of the period: James Archbold (d. 1849), with bust; Robert Williamson (d. 1835), with standing figure by David Dunbar; and Sir Matthew Ridley (d. 1813), a standing figure in Roman costume by Flaxman. Finally, by the NE. tower pier is a small ancient iron chest used now as a collection box.

The exterior, though much refaced, repays making a complete circuit. This can start along the N. side, where the main transept is in fact much less restored. From this angle the 15th c. tower with its daring crown, comprising a miniature square tower held aloft by four flying buttresses and itself carrying a crocketed spire with flying buttresses, can be well seen. It was rebuilt late in the 19th c. by Sir George Gilbert Scott: the height is 193 ft. Past the E. end of the 1926 vestry building is a table tomb (of Joseph Barber, d. 1784) on six fat legs; this is typical of a number in the churchyard, the E. part of which is formed into a paved court. Further round, past the classical library building of 1736 with its Ionic pilasters, are three medieval stone coffins. The S. part of the churchyard, pleasant with trees and seats, then leads back to the W. tower and its porches.

Newcastle, St Mary (Roman Catholic, Tyne and Wear)

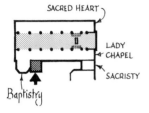

Built in 1844 by Augustus Pugin as a parish church to replace an 18th c. chapel, it became a cathedral shortly afterwards, the diocese being at first called Hexham. Joseph A. Hansom added the tower and spire to his own design in the 1860s, and the baptistry is of 1902.

Apart from the excellent, upward-thrusting tower with its 220 ft spire, it is a rather ordinary Gothic Revival building. **Internally**, plain arcades on clustered columns support a high-pitched 'scissor' roof with red painted boarding and striped trusses and rafters. Instead of a clerestory there are irregular dormers. To the left inside the tower-porch is the baptistry, housing not only the low octagonal font but also a Boer War memorial in the form of a great canopied tomb.

The **N. aisle** has an unusual, but unattractive, tiled dado displaying scrolls with martyrs' names; at its E. end is the Sacred Heart chapel, with a simple Gothic reredos and an open stone screen to the **quire**. At the quire the main arcades stop and start again with a foliage-capped bay and then finish with a curiously acute arch. Two saints each side are all that remains of an over-all decorative scheme.

Next across to the quire itself past the plain stone pulpit. It has a low white and gold screen and a white reredos, evidently Pugin's, richly carved and with red backgrounds to the figures; in the side panels are four tall fully-coloured saints. The Jesse Tree E. window

was designed by Pugin and made by William Wailes. The SE. is the
Lady chapel, with big standing Madonna and Gothic reredos with
panels repainted alternately light and dark blue. Another stone
screen separates it from the quire; through it can be seen the lightly
framed canopied bishop's throne and, in the floor, a brass to the
founder, the Rev. James Worswick (d. 1843).

At the time of writing the interior is to be reordered: the above
may thus be found not entirely accurate.

Outside, the Madonna over the S. doorway is of 1954. Further
from the road, the tomb-chest in the churchyard is of Bishop Robert
(d. 1847). A circuit of the surrounding streets is worth while, starting
at the ballflower enriched W. doorway. On the W. and N. sides the
buttresses die into the plinth, since the building directly abuts the
public pavement. The best view, with the three blackened E. gables
and the steeple behind, is from Neville Street by the bus station.

Newport, St Woolos (Church in Wales, Gwent)

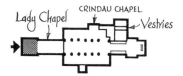

The diocese, called that of Monmouth, was formed in 1921 but the
cathedral status of the church of St Woolos was not confirmed till
1949, and the substantial eastward extension that this necessitated
was deferred until about 1960; the architect was Alban Caroe. The
old building is basically Norman, with arcades of that date and the
remarkable feature of a big W. galilee chapel which may in part be
older still. The aisle walls and the tower are 15th c. Extensive
restoration, especially of the now demolished E. end which had been
walled off as a charnel house, was done in 1854.

The main approach is to the prominent **W. tower**, which has the
only peal of twelve bells in Wales. The lower part is early 15th c.;
the upper was completed by Jasper Tudor (uncle of Henry VII) and
it may be his worn statue that stands in a niche near the top. Inside,
through the tower, the galilee or **St Mary's chapel** forms a kind of
grand inner porch or narthex with downward-sloping floor, Norman
walls (or possibly earlier) and a grand Norman arch into the
cathedral proper. The font too is partly Norman. The recesses in

Tower, Newport (15th c.)

both side walls contain various worn effigies and other carved stones, the six figures on the N. side being all that is left of a monument to Sir John Morgan (d. 1493). The octofoil window near the E. end of the S. wall is 13th c. and was moved from the upper room of the S. porch in 1913.

A closer look at the big Norman archway with its billet and zigzag mouldings confirms that its two free-standing shafts may be re-used Roman ones from Caerleon; certainly their mouldings are of pure Classical type. Though not on a grand scale, the Norman **nave** arcades are impressive too, with sturdy round columns and scalloped caps. The clerestory is Norman (except the fifth bay, altered to give extra light to the rood loft) but because the aisles were heightened in the 15th c. it now serves little purpose. The barrel roofs of nave and aisles are also 15th c., of the utmost plainness (till 1913 they were boarded), and contrast with the light and colour of the quire beyond – the swirling pinks and greys of the E. wall and the orange of the rose window, both by John Piper.

From the **N. aisle** it is odd to see the outside of the clerestory. The outer wall and its windows are Perpendicular and there are some minor wall tablets. In the E. bay it widens into the Crindau chapel, where a door leads through to the vestries added beyond. The E. window of the aisle, also Perpendicular but apparently not in its original position, now screens the organ; the altar is of 1963.

Back into the **nave**, which extends one bay past the end of the arcades. The wide arch to the organ (1966) is probably 13th c. Above it are two 15th c. clerestory windows and an upper doorway that led to the rood loft (the lower door is behind the organ console). Opposite, on the S., a new arch has been cut into 13th c. walling; the three windows above it are new, too. To the E., the big chancel arch of 1854 opens now into the Caroe **quire**. Here the windows are a modern version of Perpendicular and the ceilings are boarded. On the N. side, the doorway to the sacristy is an old one re-used. In the E. part the ceiling is white, fanning out into the projecting bays. Here one can look more closely at the Piper E. window and the unusual 'marbled' reredos. The oak stalls are all quite plain, the bishop's near the E. end of the S. side being marked by a higher back and a coat-of-arms.

Continuing back along the S. side of the quire, an oblique hagioscope cut through the S. wall (behind the choir seats) gave a view of the original altar from the S. aisle. Past this is the 19th c. Gothic traceried wooden pulpit. The little chapel in the new S. transept is reached through an arch cut in the E. wall of the aisle and has 19th c. glass re-set in its E. window.

The **S. aisle** is similar to the N., but with 19th c. windows and with further minor wall tablets. Towards the E. end, however, is a 15th c. piscina, and at the W. end a monument to Sir Walter Herbert (d. 1568), with an arched canopy on Ionic columns and only half of an effigy. Finally at the W. end of the nave is a series of war memorial panels.

The **exterior** has to be seen in two parts. Starting on the N. side, one passes first the wall of St Mary's chapel, the windows of which were altered in 1818. Nearby is the base of the medieval churchyard Cross, in very decayed condition. The ground slopes steeply past the aisle and chapel, which enabled Caroe to build an undercroft of vestries and meeting-rooms beneath his new E. end. The entrance to these is below the 'leper' window. There is no point in going much further since there is no way out at the bottom of the churchyard.

It is best to return to the W. end and to the lychgate, passing several pretentious tombs and obelisks. Turn left outside and go up the steps and along the high pavement on the S. of the Lady chapel. At the end of the chapel (actually on the SW. corner of the nave) is an amusing gargoyle. The projecting S. porch, now used as a store, is 15th c.; it had an upper floor and was the principal entrance. Further down, the new E. end can be seen again, and it is worth noting how carefully matched the new stonework is to the old.

Northampton, St Mary and St Thomas (Roman Catholic, Northamptonshire)

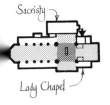

The present sacristy was the original chapel of St Felix, opened in 1825. A. W. N. Pugin built a church in 1844 on the site of the present tower and chancel; this became a cathedral in 1850. In 1863 a bigger aisled church was added by his son Edward, with reversed orientation: this is the present nave and aisles. Finally in 1954–60

E. end and Tower, Northampton (1954–60)

the orientation was corrected by Albert Herbert, with a new quire
and crossing-tower in place of Augustus Pugin's building.

It is this modern E. end which faces the main road and the brown
brick tower which dominates the view seen by passers-by. To the N.
stands the 18th c. Cathedral House, and next to it the sacristy, the
original chapel of 1825, in local Duston ironstone, with a re-used
14th c. quatrefoil and niche bracket. The entry, oddly tucked in
beside it, leads to an undistinguished porch and thence point-blank
to the side of the nave altar. The ungainly crossing-arches contrast
strangely with the elegant Pugin arcades beyond, but white paint
throughout gives a sense of unity. Pugin's roof is a strange two-stage
affair with a barn-like structure on top, all in dark wood and pastel
green.

From the N. aisle the varied floral capitals of the arcades can be
appreciated. Steps at its W. end lead to the modern gallery in the
1863 chancel, giving an impressive view of the interior as well as a
close-up of the Hardman windows of the apse, c. 1865. The two-
light window to the S. beneath the gallery opened into the former
baptistry at the SW. corner, with simple wrought-iron gates and a
Sebastian Comper pendant light.

In the nave floor is a brass to Bishop Amherst (d. 1883). Past the
crossing and to the right is the Lady chapel. Three old panels of
glass here came from Ashby St Ledgers, Sir William Catesby's house
near Rugby. The canopied bishop's throne by the SE. tower pier is
Italian and has intricate inlaid work, probably 17th c. The E.
window glass includes seven more saints like those in the Lady
chapel. The stalls are modern Gothic with some 'poppy-head' and
animal carvings.

In Marriott Street, just S. of the cathedral, a rear entrance to what
is now a university building offers a side view of the Pugin nave with
its odd clerestory gables, their apex crosses just piercing the roof.
Another drive just before Bishop's House leads right up to the
apsidal W. front; its strangely narrow, un-cathedral-like look is due
to its having originally been the 'East' end.

North Elmham [Department of the Environment] (Norfolk)

Though Elmham was always known to have been the seat of East
Anglian bishops before the see was moved to Thetford in 1075 (and
soon after that to Norwich), the existence of its actual cathedral had
been forgotten until 1903, and only in the last few decades has it

been disentangled from the later walls and vegetation which had obscured it.

The bishopric was originally set up not later than 800, went into eclipse and was re-founded about 955 with a secondary cathedral at Hoxne. At Elmham the E. end dates from about 1000 and the nave and W. tower are slightly later. The cathedral survived after 1075 because it formed part of the bishops' estate and became their manorial chapel. Late in the 14th c., however, Bishop Despenser irreverently converted it into a fortified house, a kind of hunting lodge, complete with moat; in due course it all went to ruin.

The whole site is now under the Department of the Environment, and subject to standard visiting hours, without charge. The first parts to be seen from the approach path are two half-round turrets, the left containing the W. tower stair, the right being part of the 14th c. additions. The entire 11th c. S. wall, complete to sill height and composed of brown conglomerate stone (originally plastered),

Saxon Cathedral from SW., North Elmham (early 11th c.)

runs off to the right. Beyond that are the SE. tower and transept.
Between the turrets more of the inserted domestic walls are visible.
External steps to the left lead to a vantage point above the W.
tower-stump and down again to the N. side, with the inner moat
(14th c.) on the left and the main N. wall on the right – 11th c. with
some interruptions by Despenser's work. The block of walling left
standing free was part of his kitchen chimney. The E. end (*c.* 1000)
commences with the clearly defined NE. tower; one can then step
over the footing into the E. transept. The apse, partially destroyed
by the moat, is marked in the grass. The chancel arch, partly
blocked by later walling, leads into the nave where a line of columns
supported Despenser's hall above; behind them are other domestic
remains. It is best then to return to the transept, to look at the SE.
tower and particularly at the unusual quarter-round pilaster bases at
the angles, and then to go back along the outside of the S. wall. The
inside of the W. tower can readily be seen by climbing over the low
wall.

Norwich, Holy Trinity (Church of England, Norfolk)

The bishop's see was transferred from North Elmham to Thetford in
1075, and in 1094 to Norwich, where a Saxon church already stood
probably on the site of the N. transept. Building work started in
1096. It had proceeded westwards as far as four bays of the nave by
1119 and to the W. front (including the cloister and other buildings
of the Benedictine priory) in another twenty-five years. The tower,
at first capped with a low spire, was finished about 1170.

The cloister was rebuilt in the 14th c. and the spire *c.* 1480 after
being struck by lightning in 1463. Replacement of the high roofs by
vaults began in the middle of the 15th c. but continued well into the
16th c. Anthony Salvin re-faced the S. front *c.* 1830 and Sir Charles
Nicholson built St Saviour's chapel in 1930–2. Apart from the
cloister, the priory buildings either went to ruin or were converted
into houses after the Reformation.

The Norman **W. front** is much altered, first by the big
Perpendicular window and doorway and latterly by alterations by
J. P. Seddon and others – Edward Blore, for example, added the
corner turrets in 1840 – but it can never have conveyed an adequate
suggestion of the grandeur within. The NW. doorway, one of the
usual entrances, leads into the **N. aisle**, one of the least altered
Norman parts of the cathedral. The vaults are groined, i.e. fairly

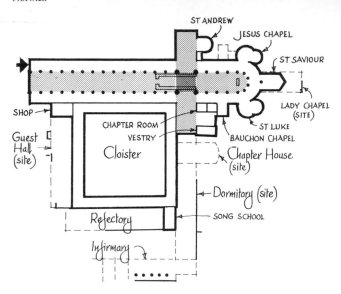

early, and there are wall-arcades, but the windows are later enlargements. The main arcades, as can next be seen by moving into the **nave**, gain interest from the variety of treatment of the shafts attached to their clustered piers. The gallery arcades are remarkably tall and treated very similarly, except that there begins to be some zigzag moulding instead of billet, a sign of a date after about 1120. Above them comes the much shorter clerestory, and then the marvellous 15th c. lierne vault with hundreds of carved bosses, a daring insertion on walls without flying buttresses.

At first it is not obvious that the pulpitum (with organ above) stands not E. of the crossing but three bays to its W. The quire thus occupies part of the structural nave as well as the crossing and the E. arm was not, as so often elsewhere, rebuilt on a bigger plan. That is probably because Norwich never possessed the shrine of any important saint to attract pilgrims. So from the extreme W. end the crossing, and the ceiling of the chancel, seem far distant.

Moving E. to about the fifth bay, one can look back at the pictorial W. window glass by G. Hedgeland – of 1854 but almost 18th c. in character. Returning to the **N. aisle**: there are attractive little heraldic panels in the first windows, and in the fifth bay under the arcade the tomb-chest of Sir Thomas Wyndham (d. 1521). The

tablet on the pier beyond is to Osbert Parsley (d. 1585). The seventh
bay has a blocked doorway of *c.* 1330 with monsters in the
spandrels, now containing the bronze bust of Bishop Herbert
(d. 1959) by Sir Martin Charteris.

Back in the **nave** again, the brass eagle lectern is of 1892, and the
stone pulpit of 1889. By the lectern is a mayoral pew with sword and
mace rests. This is the point to have a closer look at the stone
pulpitum, originally of *c.* 1470 but re-made by Salvin in 1833, and at
the organ-case by Stephen Dykes Bower (1939–50). Another look at
the nave bosses, preferably with field-glasses or the trolley-mirrors,
is even more rewarding.

At this point suddenly there is a cylindrical column in each arcade
with helically incised grooves – a complete change of pattern to
the Durham type, never fully explained. Close to it in the **N. aisle** is
a memorial window of 1849 by William Warrington, and in the next
bay under the arcade the tomb of Sir John Hobart (d. 1507). The
doorway in bay 11 led to the Bishop's palace; above it is a brass to
Dean Pellew (d. 1866). Then on the right is a screen to the ante-
quire within the pulpitum. On the right of that, part of another
helical column is visible under the glass panel; it was so badly burnt

iew from the Riverside, Norwich

in the 1463 fire that it had to be encased in stone work of the clustered type. Next come the backs of the stalls, and a stone screen to the **N. transept**.

Here the architecture is very like the nave, three-storeyed, with wall-arcading continuing around the base, and a lierne vault of 1509. In the W. wall the first window on the left is by Burne-Jones (1901). The prominent monuments are to Bishop Bathurst (d. 1841), a white marble seated figure by Sir Francis Chantrey in the NW. corner; Bishop Pelham (d. 1896), the tomb-chest with recumbent figure by James Forsyth in the centre of the N. side; and Violet Morgan (d. 1921), with kneeling girl by Derwent Wood in the NE. corner. The coloured screen to St Andrew's chapel on the E. side is of 1920; this chapel is kept for private prayer and it has various fragments of 16th to 18th c. glass and a Madonna by John Skelton.

Next the **crossing**, rather cluttered with stalls, for the overflow of quire into nave is seldom a happy arrangement. The four great tower arches, unusually, are plastered and whitened on their soffits. The work above is later (mid-12th c.) for it could not be safely supported till the nave was well advanced: gallery, wall-arcade, lantern storey and flat boarded ceiling. The stalls, not in their original position, are mostly 15th c., with misericords. They continue into the nave part of the quire which should be looked at next and is of course architecturally a continuation of the nave. Some of the miserere seats there are usually tipped up for viewing: permission should be sought before looking at the others. A specially attractive one is the owl, third from the E. on the N. side. The canopies, less uniform in style and date than at first appears, are also 15th c.

Now E. of the crossing into the **presbytery**, passing on the left the pulpit by J. P. Seddon (1889), on the right the bishop's throne by J. L. Pearson (1895) and, more important, the Flemish brass pelican lectern which with the exception of its little statues is late 14th c. In this part of the building the 15th c. remodelling proceeded much further than the mere provision of a rich lierne vault. Except in the apse and in a small piece of the E. arch on the N. side, four-centred arches totally replaced the round ones at the lowest level. The Norman triforium and gallery are unchanged but the clerestory is now wholly Perpendicular, wonderfully heightened and with extremely slender columns supporting the springers of the vault. But whereas the vault is late 15th c. the clerestory is at least a century earlier and at first had only a wooden roof. The tombs around the presbytery, and the bishop's throne within the apse, will be taken in sequence and for the moment it is sufficient to note the elaborate re and gold canopy on the S. side marking Bishop Goldwell's chantry.

The **N. quire aisle** can conveniently be entered under the first of the remodelled arches on the left; it has an 18th c. tablet within it on each side. In the second bay is the Erpingham window, a collection of 15th c. glass fragments. On the left of the arch opposite it is a medieval wall-painting of the Trinity, also fragmentary; beneath that is the tomb-slab of Sir Thomas Erpingham (d. 1428) and on the right a nice tablet to Thomas Moore (d. 1779) by Thomas Ivory.

The tomb-chest in the next bay (in a blocked arch to a former chapel) is of Elizabeth Calthorpe (d. 1582); under the arcade opposite is the base of a 15th c. monument, possibly of John de Berney, and to the right of that another 18th c. tablet. Here one can step back into the presbytery to see the bronze and marble communion rail, and the dean's chair on the N. side, a Continental X-framed one of 1512 with a painting of Emperor Maximilian. Back in the N. quire aisle a low vault supports an upper storey once the relic chapel but now used as a treasury, with access from the aisle (for a small charge) by a spiral stair. A visit is doubly justified, for the display of Norfolk parish plate and for the 13th and 14th c. paintings on the vault, Apostles on the arch and saints around a central Christ. One can also look down on the Victorian mosaic floor in front of the high altar and into the **Jesus chapel** with its (restored) decoration of arches and capitals in primary colours. From ground level the odd shape of the chapel, consisting virtually of two intersecting circles, is noticeable. The altar apparently had to face E. even though the chapel is in a diagonal position, and some ingenuity in vault design was called for. In the floor are some well-lettered ledger stones. The reredos Adoration painting is by Martin Schwartz (*c.* 1480) and the W. window by Sir Thomas Jackson. The carved angel-brackets added to the Norman wall-arcade caps each side were statue bases. On the left is a small brass to Ralph Pulvertoft (d. 1505).

Crossing the ambulatory, one can now have a closer look behind the altar at the bishop's throne in the **apse**; this is one of the few instances of a survival of the traditional position. The present steps and platform and the low-level flanking seats for the dean and chapter are of 1959. The stone throne incorporates arm-rests believed to have formed part of that used at North Elmham in the 8th c. and possibly at the even earlier cathedral in Suffolk.

The extreme E. chapel is not the Lady chapel but **St Saviour's**, now the chapel of the Royal Norfolk Regiment, with their banners, roll of honour and memorial panelling. The double entrance arch

with dog-tooth is 13th c. but the building itself is by Nicholson.
There had been Early English and Norman chapels on this site. Its
great treasure is the reredos made up of four panels from the church
of St Michael-at-Plea, four 14th c. and one 15th c. On the right as
one returns to the **ambulatory** is a Snetzler chamber organ.

Moving now round to the S. side: the bright window with figure
of St Brice is 16th c. but foreign. Beyond it, the wall effigy of *c.* 1100
flanked by helical columns has been brought inside from the N.
transept and may be a memorial to the cathedral's founder Bishop
de Losinga, or it may be earlier.

St Luke's chapel on the left, corresponding with the Jesus chapel
opposite, has a restored painted pattern on its apse arch. The superb
five-panelled reredos painting is said to have been given in 1381 by
Bishop Despenser. The sadly mutilated 15th c. Seven Sacraments
font from the former church of St Mary-in-the-Marsh is here
because this chapel serves as parish church for the Close. Three wall
tablets are worth noting: to the left of the altar John Harwood
(d. 1691), and on the S. wall Susanna Addey (d. 1765) and Susanna
Moore (d. 1790). The E. window has Hardman glass (1868) and the
W. some by Clayton & Bell (1881).

It is probably simplest to go straight to the next chapel, the
Bauchon chapel of Our Lady of Pity. Though its arch and walls are
Decorated, the rich vault and bosses are late 15th c. The iron screen
is of 1968 and the Madonna in the ancient niche is also modern.
Above the altar hangs a Byzantine crucifix, and to the right are a
piscina and a tablet to Thomas Batcheler (d. 1729). The S. window
glass is by Moira Forsyth (1964) and the tablet with cherub on the
W. wall is to William Rolfe (d. 1754). The painting of the
Presentation in the Temple is by John Opie (1791). There are also
several interesting black marble ledger stones.

Now the **S. quire aisle**, starting one bay back, i.e. opposite the
window between the chapels. The low early 16th c. recess under the
main arcade was the chantry of Prior Bozoun and has a Jacobean
chest in it. To its right, quite small, is an ogee-arched panel of *c.*
1500 in memory of Richard Brome. In the next bay the elaborate
plinth with shields and little figures covers the tomb of Bishop
Wakering (d. 1425), and the tablet on the right of the arch is to
Bishop Overall (d. 1669). Then the very tall canopied chantry-tomb
of Bishop Goldwell (d. 1499), already seen from the presbytery, and
in the last bay two more 18th c. tablets.

An early 16th c. screen leads into the **S. transept**. Here the
architecture virtually repeats the N. except for Salvin's quite

extensive remodelling of the S. wall. The clock jacks over the entrance lobby are 17th c., but the rather quaint clock is clearly much newer. A doorway in the E. wall leads to the dean's vestry, formerly St Catherine's chapel. This transept contains few fittings of any note to distract the eye from the building itself, but another sword and mace rest on the stalls under the crossing arch should be noticed before passing into the **S. nave aisle**.

On the left is the Prior's doorway to the cloister. Opposite is a Cingalese chest of 1690, followed by the way into the ante-quire under the pulpitum, and the sub-sacrists' office. It is well worth going into the ante-quire for another look at the quire – by far the most impressive view of the E. end. On the left in the fourth bay is a 16th c. memorial to Thomas Gooding with the often-used wording 'As I am so shal you be . . .' On the arcade pier is a painted inscription to Willyam Inglott, organist (d. 1621). The painting on the vault and arch, very faded, is late 12th c. Then in the main arcade two round piers with helical ornament (one cased) match the one on the N. side. The tombs in the sixth bay are of Dean Gardiner (d. 1589) by the wall, and Bishop Parkhurst (d. 1575) with a Purbeck top under the arcade. The two following bays were drastically altered by Bishop Nykke early in the 16th c. to house his own chantry: the Norman main arches were changed to four-centred and the groin-vaults replaced by panelled barrel-vaults leading transversely to enlarged windows. The tomb is under the large flat area beneath the E. arch; the other contains that of Chancellor Spencer and at its side a good wall tablet to Dean Fairfax (d. 1702), by William Stanton. The window in the ninth bay has flowers in its arch surround. The doorway in the tenth leads to the cloister, and will be returned to; over it is a late 17th c. tablet. Further on a modern opening in the wall-arcade leads to the cathedral shop, formerly the monks' locutory or outer parlour and later the song school. It is mostly Norman. From it an external door leads out by the W. front.

To the left, on leaving it, are steps to the 'visitors' centre' (refreshment and exhibition rooms) newly formed over the W. walk of the cloister. The ruin beyond is part of the guest hall.

On the other side of the W. front are the grounds of Norwich School, formerly Carnary College, and of the former Bishop's Palace. These are private, so the N. side of the cathedral cannot be seen at close quarters.

To see the **cloister** it is necessary to return to the S. aisle, to the doorway just beyond the shop. The Norman cloister was entirely

Tower as seen from Cloister, Norwich

rebuilt in the course of the 14th c. and not finished until *c.* 1430. It is
remarkable in being two-storeyed. Part of the upper storey of the W.
walk has already been seen in the visitors' centre. The tierceron
vault has hundreds of carved capitals of incredible variety and
quality, mostly illustrative of Biblical and other stories. The window
tracery changed from early Decorated to Perpendicular as the work
progressed; this is at once noticeable in the N. walk, which begins
with flowing patterns, continues with Perpendicular ones, and
finishes by joining on to the bays where work commmenced, which
are almost Geometric in character. The coats-of-arms on the N wall
(which is Norman, re-faced) are hardly ecclesiastical, for they
commemorate local nobility who dined there in 1578. At the far end
of the N. walk (to the left of the three niched bookshelves) is the
beautiful Decorated Prior's doorway back into the S. aisle; the
radial arrangement of the figures in niches (the centre one being
Christ) is most unusual.

   In the E. walk there is first a doorway which led to the slype, and
then the 14th c. triple entrance to the chapter house. That has gone
and the openings look into the lane outside. The doorway straight
ahead led to the Dark Entry, Norman and still barrel-vaulted, now
the song school. Turning right again along the S. walk, behind
which was the refectory, one can enter the garth by steps at the SW.
corner to view the S. side of the cathedral and the tower. The tower
is all Norman except for the 15th c. pinnacles and battlements and
the 315 ft spire, the second highest in England. For the rest it is
equally clear which is Norman and which Perpendicular. At the W.
end of the S. wall is the refectory doorway; then just round the
corner two elaborated bays of washplace, their niches containing
easily recognized but incongruous figures of 20th c. royalty.

   Go out by the refectory doorway (if this is locked, go out through
the S. transept). Outside to the left is the refectory ruin with its very
long line of Norman windows. The pillars on the other side of the
road were part of the infirmary. Turning left again, one comes
towards the S. transept, over the site of the dormitory and chapter
house; the inside of the E. wall of the dormitory is thus the outside
wall of the Deanery on the right. Salvin's mock-Norman work on
the transept is only too obvious. To the left is the inside of the
chapter house doorway to the cloister. Now the lane curves right,
past the SE. chapels. The grave of Nurse Cavell is just beyond the
curved end of St Luke's chapel, and there is a bronze tablet on its
wall. At the extreme end is Nicholson's St Saviour's chapel, and
beyond it the foundations of its 13th c. predecessor survive in the

grass. Then the lane leads away from the cathedral and eventually round to Palace Street on the N. Looking back, one has an impressive NE. view of the apse with its flying buttresses, and of the tower and spire.

The four priory gatehouses involve a longer walk. The 15th c. Bishop's Gate is in Palace Street. This leads back to Tombland where first the early 15th c. Erpingham Gate and then the early 14th c. St Ethelbert's Gate lead back into the Close. The road straight ahead through the last, if followed through the lower Close, leads to the 15th c. Water Gate, standing next to the famous and picturesque Pull's Ferry house.

Norwich, St John the Baptist (Roman Catholic, Norfolk)

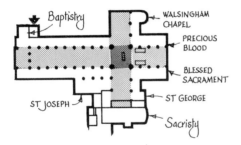

The diocese of East Anglia was formed in 1976 out of that of Northampton, having a ready-made cathedral in the great church of St John the Baptist which the 15th Duke of Norfolk built between 1882 and 1910 as 'an act of thanksgiving to God for a happy marriage and other favours'. Its predecessor in Maddermarket, opened in 1786, is now the Norwich Players' Theatre.

The architects were George Gilbert Scott junior and his brother John Oldrid Scott, and their style Early English. The nave (by G. G.) was built first, in Beer stone from Devon; the remainder also has Ancaster and Clipsham stone. The scale of the building and the quality of construction and craftsmanship throughout are astonishing. The N. porch, the usual entrance, is typical – a lavish door surround with little figures of saints in the arch, rich foliage capitals, and excellent scrolly ironwork on the doors themselves, both inner and outer.

The rather ponderous **nave** and aisles with stout round piers,

triforium, clerestory and vault were finished in 1894. The dark stone
used ornamentally in the manner of medieval Purbeck is Frosterley
marble from Durham; it occurs, for example, in the N. aisle wall-
arcade. The foliage and dragon carvings on the upper surfaces of the
pier bases should be noticed; the aisles are also vaulted.

The large **crossing** space beneath the lantern tower has a lierne
vault and now contains the main altar; the Rood above is by Peter
Rendl of Oberammergau. The windows almost throughout the
cathedral are from the firm of Hardman – by John Powell in the W.
parts and Dunstan Powell in the E. – and are superb. That of the **N.
transept** which centres on Our Lady with Child Jesus is however a
replacement of the original design following war damage. To its left
is a double doorway, to its right the apsidal Walsingham chapel with
free-standing coloured and gilded reredos. There too the glass is
post-war.

The E. aisle of the transept leads into the **presbytery**, passing the
disused NE. chapel of the Precious Blood, screened by the bronze
former gates of the Rectory. Here the architecture is like the nave
but more elaborate – tierceron vault, foliage carving on the responds
supporting it, richer triforium, etc. – and the six rich blue E. lancets
are specially fine. The view back along the nave is equally
impressive, culminating in the multi-coloured W. window featuring
St John the Baptist.

Now across to the SE. chapel of the Blessed Sacrament with
another mainly blue window and into the **S. transept** with a very
dark one symbolizing the Church. In the centre bay of the E. aisle is
a small organ, and beyond it the chapel of St George which has war
memorial panels. A gallery runs along the S. side of the transept
above confessionals and in the SW. corner is the entrance to the
sacristies.

Next the **S. aisle**, with a glance across to the curiously small pulpit
by A. P. Rossi, replacing the original canopied one. An outer arcade
separates St Joseph's chapel, also vaulted; its altar is in the
windowless bay next to the sacristy entrance. The four windows
represent the Christian names of the Duchess of Norfolk: Flora,
Pauline, Esther, Barbara. Further along the aisle the windows have
attractive patterns, almost monochrome, almost grisaille, quite
different from the others in the cathedral. Then a low aisle beneath
the W. gallery leads across to the baptistry, with an elaborate
wrought-iron screen. The nine-columned font is of Frosterley
marble and has a simple pinnacled wood cover.

The **outside** has to be looked at in two parts, for the S. aisle is abutted by the domestic and administrative buildings and cannot be seen properly. Taking a right turn first, one starts outside the N. porch with a good view of the commanding central tower. The double W. doorway of the N. transept has rich figure and foliage carving in the stonework, and more ironwork of first quality; even the little door on its right into the aisle has most delicately wrought hinges and straps. The E. end can then be seen by going into Earlham Road and then round into Unthank Road. The patterned ferramenta of the lancet windows contribute much to the liveliness of what might otherwise be merely rather grand imitation Early English façades. Along Unthank Road is the driveway in front of the ancillary buildings: beyond that the United Reformed Church.

The W. front, then, must be returned to by retracing the way past the N. porch into the car park. It is worth seeing, if only for another very rich doorway.

Nottingham, St Barnabas (Roman Catholic, Nottinghamshire)

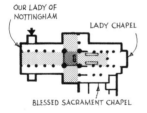

The first Roman Catholic chapel in Nottingham was founded about 1790. A larger one on a new site was opened in 1828, and finally the present cathedral was built, as a parish church, in 1842–4. It became a cathedral on the 'Restoration of the Hierarchy' in 1850. The architect (it was all built at one go) was A. W. N. Pugin.

The best general viewpoint is just off the main street, from the corner of the little piazza against the W. front. Pugin's flatness and cheapness of detail are evident, though less so than in some of his churches; it is hardly obvious that Salisbury was his model! In the W. front, only the three-order doorway provides some relief. The central tower and spire, with niched buttresses instead of broaches at the spire base and bands of surface ornament at upper levels, offer other interest. The rest is flat black millstone, made flatter and duller by the window grilles.

Just inside the N. porch on the right is a small chapel with a Pugin-designed Madonna. The **nave** is now tastefully painted in grey-green and white, with the W. wall and the extreme end of the presbytery deep red. The typical acutely pointed Pugin arcades have mouldings of Nottinghamshire type and a clerestory of double lancets. Apart from some obvious replacements, the coloured glass, mostly shields and geometrical rosettes, is of Pugin's design, and so is the hanging Rood. The light pendants are not; nor is the present colouring of his barn-like roof; nor of course the iron and brass communion rail around the sanctuary, now brought forward into the crossing-space. From the N. aisle and the **N. transept** this can be seen more closely.

Both transepts have great triple lancet windows with glass of about 1940 by Luttgens – nine Sacraments on the N. and fifteen Mysteries of the Rosary on the S.: the latter gains enormously from being carried down to a slightly lower sill level. In the **N. presbytery aisle** are stairs to the crypt chapel of St Peter beneath the presbytery (normally locked, it contains the tombs of several bishops), also a Gothic-style pulpit of 1948, already discarded.

The three **E. chapels**, as well as the presbytery, have a profusion of 19th c. patterned encaustic floor tiles. The centre one, the original Lady chapel, is used by the Polish community and has a reredos painting of the Black Madonna of Czestochowa. The SE. chapel, which has had a succession of different dedications, has Pugin glass of particularly hectic colouring in its E. window.

In the **S. presbytery aisle** is a rich brass to the Rev. John Mulligan (d. 1872). Next the **presbytery** itself: its architecture is similar to the nave's, but the roof has wind braces, and gilded chamfers on the rafters, and the columns are of quatrefoil section. Around the presbytery is a thin Gothic screen, and the bishop's throne on the right has a modern wooden surround to harmonize with it. Pugin's rood screen has gone, but the upper and lower doorway of the stairs to the loft can still be seen in the W. bay on both sides.

Now the **S. transept** – in order to see the Rosary window at close quarters and to look eastwards into the **Blessed Sacrament chapel** with its overwhelming colouring and gilding. This decoration originated from Pugin but was re-done in 1933 and is not wholly authentic. Its features include a rich panelled hammer-beam roof on angel corbels, twelve painted angels with sacramental emblems on the side walls, as well as eight bishops' shields of arms, a reredos painting of Christ with a Nottingham Cross, and more encaustic tiles with the lion emblem of the Earl of Shrewsbury, the great benefactor of the church. The additional tie-beam over the altar is part of the destroyed Pugin rood screen. The only jarring note is struck by the communion rail, in the same style as that now round the high altar.

Outside the N. porch turn right and walk round the E. end. SE. of the cathedral is the red brick Cathedral House, and beyond that the pyramidal roof of the new hall (1977). There is no point in going any further round the block.

Oban, St John the Divine (Scottish Episcopal Church, Strathclyde)

The diocese of Argyll and the Isles contains also the former cathedral at Millport on Great Cumbrae island, keeping its courtesy title of Cathedral of the Isles. Oban Cathedral, consecrated as such in 1920, was originally built as a parish church in 1864; the architects were Thomson & Turnbull. After an abortive scheme for a big enlargement (by Ross & Macbeth), with the object of coping with increased numbers of summer visitors, a modest S. aisle was added in 1882. In 1909 a complete rebuilding was commenced on the (true) N. side, which involved turning the axis through 90 degrees. The architect was James Chalmers: work only progressed for a year or so, leaving the building much as it exists today. Another completely new scheme prepared in 1928 by Harold Tarbolton was abandoned, and eventually various comparatively minor improvements were done in the 1950s and 1970s under Ian G. Lindsay & Partners.

This arrested stage of development is especially interesting to the historian – hard to understand from outside but clearer as soon as one enters the spacious **W. vestibule**. This with its arch-braced roof was the simple original S. aisle. It now contains the octagonal pink and white marble font. A glazed screen of 1972 with sliding doors leads into the 1864 nave, with the old E. window on the right. Further round, one jamb of the old sanctuary arch is still in position. Only parts of the 19th c. roof are visible here; the rest is temporary and flat.

The E. parts are in a state perhaps not unlike that of many of the older cathedrals as they were at an intermediate stage of their development, with new (neo-Romanesque) transept arches and one bay of the new **nave** with its clerestory, and then diagonal steel shores where the work stopped. The S. transept is complete with all its arches and its gable wall. On the left at the E. end of the nave is the pulpit of 1910, circular and ungainly. The brass eagle lectern is of 1881.

Now into the **quire**, occupying the crossing. The timber roof here was framed up in 1958 but left with temporary skylight glazing. The oak stalls have upstanding carved ends like Celtic crosses; the bishop's is an ordinary one with an added canopy, but over that, in the blocked N. transept arch, is a splendid metal eagle of St John the Evangelist. The Gothic reredos contains an Ascension painting flanked by niches. The organ gallery cantilevered over the stalls on the right is agreeably painted and grained in a light wood texture. Finally, the **S. chapel**, with a number of modern brass tablets on the wall and an altar of Iona 'marble'.

The intention is to complete the crossing-tower with a much lighter construction than in Chalmers' scheme (owing to foundation problems), to place the high altar beneath it, and to move the bishop's throne and stalls into what is now the sanctuary. When the nave is complete it will displace the original parish church, but a similar system of screens will be kept so as to allow for widely varying sizes of congregation, summer and winter.

Now the **outside** will seem less difficult to understand. From the porch it is best to cross George Street and look from the other side. First comes the 1882 gable, then the chancel of 1864 with its traceried window; then a clear change and the new aisle wall with two windows and a new roof that already sails over the old chancel; then the big new transept gable with the incomplete high roof of the nave and quire behind; and finally the vestry with doorway to the street. It is worth going down the lane on the left, past what was the (true) S. wall of the original aisle, and along the N. side where a similar pattern is repeated in reverse: the two 19th c. gables and then the N. wall of the new quire, exposed but with an arch ready to receive its transept. Beyond that the cathedral is hemmed in by other buildings; this is a very restricted site where every inch has to be used to best advantage.

Oban, St Columba (Roman Catholic, Strathclyde)

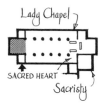

The Marquess of Bute founded a church here in 1886 which became known as the 'tin cathedral'. Its successor, begun in 1932, is by Sir Giles Gilbert Scott. Work was interrupted by the war and the big sturdy tower and the interior were not finished till after 1945. Its sea-front site, its rough-hewn granite surfaces (pink from Aberdeen outside and blue, more local, Kentallen inside) and its noble proportions combine to make it an unusually distinguished and inspiring building. Though Gothic in general form, but of no particular period, it seems to express even earlier virtues and ideals – and in a new building that is a rare quality.

Inside the S. aisle, the first impression is of tall rough arcades with octagonal bases and primitive round-to-square capitals. With no clerestory and a high nave roof, it is almost a hall-church, but the aisle roof trusses rest on stone brackets on the outer faces of the columns, and the outer walls, with windows of Tudor appearance, are not particularly tall. Beneath the **tower**, which has an unusually wide arch, is a spacious area used as a baptistry; the saucer-bowled font has a copper cover. In the **N. aisle** a painting of the Dead Christ hangs over the W. doorway; like others in the cathedral this doorway has a distinctive 'dropped ogee' head and the doors themselves have an adzed finish. At the opposite end of the aisle the Lady chapel has a fine modern Gothic reredos with Madonna and angels. Another Madonna on the N. wall is probably Italian. The taller compartment beyond is intended for a bigger organ than the building so far possesses.

The extension of the raised **quire** floor into what was the E. bay of the nave has been subtly done; the communion rail is a granite wall with wooden capping, and the adjoining pulpit is granite too. The stalls are traditional Gothic; the bishop's chair behind the altar is marked out by its triangular-headed back. The wooden reredos with scenes from St Columba's life was carved by Donald Gilbert. The

Sacred Heart chapel on the S. should also be noticed, with its simple dossal curtain and tester and dove.

Outside the 'Tudor' windows resolve into individual lancets more resistant to the elements, and the aisle ends have stepped gables. Up the hill are the domestic buildings and it is not possible to walk right round the cathedral.

Old Sarum, [Department of the Environment] (Wiltshire)

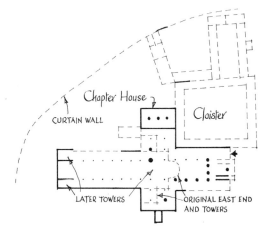

The conquering Normans' policy was to transfer bishoprics from unfortified places to stronger ones. Those of Ramsbury and Sherborne which had been united in 1058 were transferred in 1075 to Searisbyrig, the Iron Age fort which under Roman and Saxon rule had become an important town. Within its great dry moat and circular rampart they built a castle in its own circular inner bailey; a quarter of the space between these two rings was allocated to the cathedral, which was consecrated in 1092 but severely damaged in a storm only five days afterwards. It was much enlarged at the beginning of the 12th c. The exposed situation, coupled with bad feeling against the soldiery, led to the decision to move to the valley, where the present cathedral of Salisbury was begun in 1220. Then the old one was dismantled, much of its stone being reused in the new precinct wall. The Lady chapel, however, continued in use for a

century or more. The whole town was abandoned by the end of the
15th c.

After passing under numerous ownerships, including latterly the
Dean and Chapter of Salisbury, the whole fortification has since
1936 been in the care of the Department of the Environment, and
subject to an entrance charge and the usual visiting hours.

To visit the cathedral one should not cross the inner moat bridge
into the castle, but instead turn right and follow the outside of the
moat. The plan of the entire building is soon seen, clearly laid out
on the ground; this was done in 1909–14, before which virtually
nothing was known about the layout.

Looked at from the E. end, the positions of the crossing and nave
and W. towers are readily seen and the base of the pulpitum is clear,
along with a patch of paving nearby. First, however, one should
imagine the 11th c. cathedral, consisting of the same nave and aisles,
an apse-ended quire where the present crossing is, and transeptal
towers like Exeter's but smaller. The towers had E. apsidal chapels.
The much enlarged E. end and aisled transepts, as well as the W.
towers, represent the 12th c. work.

Go now to the W. end, to the tower bases, and look back up the
whole length, imagining the early Norman nave and beyond it the
later Norman and therefore less severe crossing and quire. Then go
back along the N. side towards the transept. From its NE. corner
dangerously worn steps lead to the crypt of the chapter house, the
only substantial masonry that survives in the cathedral. It includes
the remains of circular columns and pilasters. Back at transept level,
more steps lead to the cloister garth – carefully excavated to its
original shape and level. No walling is left here, though some
fragments can be seen to the N. where the original bishop's palace
adjoined the city wall.

A fascinating bird's eye view can be obtained by going into the
castle and crossing the inner bailey to the tower-base at the NW.
corner.

Oxford, Christ Church (Church of England, Oxfordshire)

The status of the cathedral of Oxford is unique: having in the
Middle Ages been the church of an Augustinian priory, it became in
1546 simultaneously both the chapel of the newly established college
of Christ Church and the seat of the bishop.

Hardly any authenticated dates exist for the building's previous

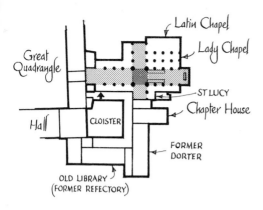

history, and it is not even known whether St Frideswide (who lived around 700) founded the original nunnery which was dedicated in her honour. It was raided by Danes in 1002 and rebuilt, re-established as a priory in 1122, and rebuilt again at or towards the end of the 12th c. That church is basically the present cathedral. The tower top and spire were added in the 13th c. and the outer chapels of the quire in the 13th and 14th cc. The quire clerestory and vault and the cloister were rebuilt *c.* 1500.

The creation of Christ Church was far from straightforward. When Wolsey had suppressed the priory he began in 1525 to build what was to be called Cardinal College and demolished three or four bays of the church to make way for the great quadrangle now known as Tom Quad. The present college hall and much else are of that date. After Wolsey's fall the king re-established it as King Henry VIII's College. He set up the bishopric of Oxford in 1542 with Osney abbey church as cathedral but quickly changed his mind and set up Christ Church in its dual role only four years later. The church of Osney was subsequently demolished, leaving virtually no trace.

The W. porch into Tom Quad was built by G. F. Bodley in 1872–3 and Sir George Gilbert Scott did an extensive general restoration in 1870–6, rebuilding one of the destroyed bays of the nave.

Visiting times are 9.30 a.m.–12.30 p.m. and 2 p.m.–4.30 p.m. Visitors are asked to enter through the War Memorial garden to the S. and to go into the college through Meadow Buildings, by a well signposted route. A charge is usually made for admission to the precincts, including the cathedral itself, entry being then via the cloister into the S. door.

The **cloister** should be looked at first, the route through the cathedral being a controlled one. It is quite clearly incomplete, the W. part having gone with the W. bays of the nave when Tom Quad was formed. It had only been rebuilt a few years before (begun in 1499) and has a flattish tierceron vault mostly rebuilt by Scott.

On entering, turn left first along the S. walk, with the former refectory on the left (long ago formed into a library and then into college rooms). From this can be seen one of the very limited external views of the cathedral   the upper parts of the Norman nave and S. transept, and the Early English top to the tower with its not very tall stone spire.

Where the S. walk stops short, turn aside into the garth to look at the enclosing buildings; the exposed foundations are unidentified.

Now return to the E. walk where the centre part of the vault is higher and of wood; this too is 19th c. On the right is the big Norman doorway to the **chapter house**, often open for exhibitions. Though both the E. end with its lancet windows and the quadripartite vault are obviously Early English (much restored 1881 by Bodley) it is basically Norman and has the recently discovered remains of wall-arcading of that date on the N. side. The masonry-patterned painting is based on parts which are original, notably in the vault of the E. bay with its medallion angels. There is 15th and 16th c. heraldic and other glass in the N. and S. windows. Further along the E. walk is a doorway to the slype, tunnel-vaulted and therefore quite early Norman; it is now used by the choir.

The N. walk, which has many minor wall tablets, leads to the main S. door into the cathedral. The S. aisle is seen first, with a view across the **nave**. The Norman bay design, with the triforium not above the main arches but tucked into them, is extremely unusual though not unique (Romsey and Jedburgh abbeys are similar). The sub-arches rest rather arbitrarily on the main piers, the capitals of which have quite early examples of foliage ornament. The clerestory has pointed arches and is 13th c., but the timber roof was put on c. 1500 and renewed in 1816.

Look next at the fine W. window of the **S. aisle** (Faith, Hope and Charity) by Sir Edward Burne-Jones and William Morris (1871) and the good monument to James Narborough (d. 1707) – then across the nave at the clerestory, and up at the panelled timber roof, which is mostly Scott's. The aisle itself has a ribbed quadripartite vault, 12th c., and one window of the same date. In the last bay is a cartouche to John Corbet (d. 1688); on the pier nearby is a white marble tablet with bust of Edward Pocock (d. 1691).

The **S. transept** has arcades like the nave, but its clerestory is round-headed, i.e. also Norman. On the W. side the triforium has one bay with earlier Norman shafts than elsewhere, probably of *c.* 1100 and thus the oldest visible part of the cathedral. The flat wooden roof, early 16th c., ignores the vaulting shafts. The S. wall is early 13th c. but Scott added the vestry in front, as well as the gallery. The 13th c. chapel of St Lucy on the E. side has a high-pitched 19th c. roof. As elsewhere in the cathedral there are many monuments. These will be taken anti-clockwise, starting on the right nearest the nave aisle: Edward Lord Mounslowe, d. 1683 (large white marble with urn); Viscount Brouncker, d. 1645 (little seated figures in a classical frame); over that the Garter banner of Prince Paul of Yugoslavia; Peter Wyche, d. 1643 (big cartouche with weeping cherubs on S. wall of St Lucy's chapel); John Banks, d. 1644 (another cartouche); Viscount Grandison, d. 1643 (big white marble with urn); Richard Gardiner, d. 1670 (cartouche at far right). The E. window of the chapel has Decorated tracery and original 14th c. glass with the murder of Becket portrayed in the centre light. The canopied tomb on the left, facing into the quire aisle, is of Bishop Kynge (d. 1557), last abbot of Osney and first bishop.

The **crossing** should be looked at next. Though the arches of nave and quire are round, those of the transepts are pointed. Above them is a gallery, above that the lantern windows, and then a flat ceiling.

The **S. quire aisle** is the regimental chapel of the Oxfordshire and Buckinghamshire Light Infantry, and has a 20th c. Jacobean-style screen. Just inside on the left are rolls of honour; opposite, the first window has a figure of Bishop Kynge and is early 17th c. The bust on the right is of Dr Pusey (d. 1882). At the end is a 14th c. piscina with thick ogee surround; also the small framed brass figure of Stephen Lence (d. 1587). The wooden balustered communion rail though apparently 18th c. is in fact 20th c., the E. window (St Catherine) by Burne-Jones (1877).

Now across into the **quire** in front of the communion step (there is no rail) for a closer look at its arcades and ingenious late Perpendicular vault – not a fan vault but a series of square and extremely complex lierne vaults held aloft by arches. Stone pendants hanging at the corners of each square disguise the fact that these are the points where the main support is provided. The quire clerestory is of *c.* 1500 too, but the arcades are Norman like the nave. The

Cathedral interior, Oxford (late 12th c. with vault of c. 1500 and E. end of 1870–6)

entire E. wall with its rose window is by Scott, with glass by Clayton & Bell, but the reredos is by G. F. Bodley (1881). The curiously unassuming bishop's throne was re-made under Sebastian Comper (1959). The marble floor is Scott's and is of 1871. Looking W., the stalls and ornate iron screens are also Scott's; the latter, made by Francis Skidmore, are elaborated into canopies in the bay E. of the crossing.

The **N. quire aisle** is rib-vaulted like the other aisles, but its outer arcade is 13th c., its clustered columns being tacked on to the Norman pilasters. The E. window (St Cecilia) is again by Burne-Jones. To its left, under the last bay of the arcade, stands the shrine of St Frideswide, later 13th c. and pieced together from fragments in 1889–90.

The second chapel is the **Lady chapel**, with a plain 13th c. vault not unlike the Norman aisles; its E. bay is reconstructed, its second has eight original painted angels. The E. window is another by Burne-Jones, made like the others by William Morris & Co. Below it is a piscina. The arcade to the outermost or Latin chapel is 14th c. in the two E. bays, and 13th c. in the third. The structure beneath its E. arch may be the watching loft and chantry for the shrine, the upper part of wood in two stages, richly pinnacled, and the base of stone, arcaded and vaulted rather like a big tomb; it is of c. 1500.

In the floor of the second bay – is a modern slate slab with the single word FRIDESWIDE – merely a commemoration and not marking her grave. The lady on the tomb-chest next to it is the priory benefactress Elizabeth Montague (d. 1354). The larger of the brasses on the column to its left shows the kneeling figure of John Bisshop (d. 1588), and under the next arch is the early 14th c. canopied tomb of Prior Sutton, rich with ball-flower ornament. There are also brasses in the floor to Edward Courtenay (c. 1450) and John Fitzalleyn (d. 1452). The fourth bay of the chapel is really part of the E. aisle of the N. transept, and therefore Norman again. The early 15th c. tomb-chest is thought to be that of Sir George Nowers but the knight's effigy is not his. On the pier to its right is the sad bearded jack-in-a-box bust of Robert Burton (d. 1639); below, a cartouche to George Croyden (d. 1678).

Turning back towards the quire for a moment: on the left of the pier at the end of the Lady chapel arcade is another bust – William Goodwin (d. 1620).

Now the outermost N. chapel, called the Latin chapel because services were held in it in Latin almost continuously till the 19th c. This again has a simple vault, though now octopartite, i.e. with ridge ribs. The windows along the N. side (except the last) contain much 14th c. glass, considerably restored. Also along the N. side, and around the W. end, are the stalls which Scott replaced in the quire, some probably 14th c., and some of Wolsey's time. Two of them have misericords. The brasses are all 19th c., the biggest being to Frederick Barnes (d. 1859). The E. window is one of the first works of Burne-Jones, before his association with Morris. Its subject – in many vivid scenes – is the life of St Frideswide. The richly carved and coloured triptych reredos is by C. E. Kempe. Under the arcade and already seen from the other side are the watching chamber and the Montague and Sutton tombs.

The **N. transept** is like the other Norman parts, though many differences of detail may be observed. The flat timber roof matches the S. transept. The N. window is of 1872, by Clayton & Bell. Under it is a tomb with brass matrices, probably of James Zouch (d. 1503). To its left are two 16th c. brasses, one a curious palimpsest (i.e. re-used) to Henry Dow (d. 1578), the other to Thomas Morrey (d. 1584); to its right are two nice cartouches with gilded backgrounds. Several other small tablets in the W. aisle of the transept hardly merit individual notice; near them stands the curious chocolate marble 19th c. font with a domed wooden cover.

On the wall of the **N. nave aisle** (starting at the transept end) these memorials are worth noting: Bishop Gastrell of Chester (d. 1725); Alexander Gerard (d. 1601) – a quaint miniature painted tablet; Philip Barton (d. 1765); John Wall (d. 1666) – a large cartouche; John Fanshawe – a flat 18th c. sarcophagus with ostentatious lettering but no date; William Levitt (d. 1694) – another cartouche; on the W. wall three nicely lettered 17th c. tablets, and above them a fascinating early 17th c. window by Abraham van Linge depicting Jacob and the city of Nineveh.

Back now under the organ gallery, which is largely of 1888, and through into the nave to look again at the marvellous quire vault, and back and up at the organ itself, the case of which is basically late 17th c., and at several memorials on the nave columns. The first on the left (i.e. N. side) bears a brass to John Walrond (d. 1602), and the second a well-designed memorial to Bishop Berkeley of Cloyne (d. 1753). This is balanced on the S. side by one of Bishop Tanner of St Asaph (d. 1735). next on the S. is a tablet to Dean Aldrich (d. 1710), with medallion head, and beyond this the large canopied pulpit, early 17th c. and well in keeping with the building. The throne opposite is the vice-chancellor's, largely of the same date.

Return finally to the W. vestibule; on the left facing the bookstall is the tall white marble monument to Bishop Fell (d. 1686), with no effigy. The door ahead leads through the new principal entrance built under Bodley in 1872–3, and out into Tom Quad.

Paisley, St Mirin (Roman Catholic, Strathclyde)

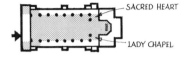

The church of 1808 was replaced in 1930–2, in the strange sort of watered-down medieval style which one associates with Methodist buildings of the period. The architect was Thomas Baird. It became the seat of a bishop in 1948.

In a very practical way the aisles are reduced to narrow passages without seating. The arcades, Norman in character with scalloped capitals, support plain moulded arches and an extremely wide barrel-vaulted plaster ceiling which is broken into (rather unevenly) by little transverse vaults from the tall clerestory of twin openings. The slender chancel arch also attempts flimsy Norman detail, and the last clerestory windows before it suggest a kind of transept effect by extending just a little higher. In the polygonal apse the upper windows come in threes and have coloured saints in their glass.

The white marble font stands now at the E. end of the S. aisle. The carved stone pulpit with wooden canopy is wrapped round a nearby column of the S. arcade. The quire, extended forward with a white marble floor, has a black and white marble altar rail and a fine octagonal baldacchino with upper 'templum', cantilevered from gilded pilasters and square columns. From this end of the building can be seen the organ on its very plain gallery.

Outside, there is space all round, but nothing of interest beyond the dressed-up W. front with its meaningless battlements.

Peel, St German (Church of England, Isle of Man)

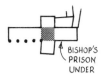

BISHOP'S
PRISON
UNDER

A tradition that St Patrick came in the 5th c. and set up a see with St German as first bishop cannot be substantiated, but a small Celtic monastery almost certainly existed on St Patrick's Isle in the 8th c., before the Norse invasion of Man. By the 10th or 11th c. it had become Irish in character, as is evidenced by the round tower of the ruined St Patrick's church. St German's cathedral, also on the Isle, was begin *c.* 1226 to serve Man and the Hebrides, together known to the Norsemen as the Southern Isles or 'Sudr-eyjar'. This became corrupted via medieval Latin to Sodor, and to this day the diocese is called Sodor and Man, though the Hebrides had ceased to be part of it by *c.* 1400. The bishop's full official title, creating as many doubts as it resolves, is 'of the Isle of Man, of Sodor, of Sodor and Man, and of Sodor of Man'.

The cathedral quire floor was raised *c.* 1300 to accommodate a higher crypt, and the nave floor raised correspondingly. A S. arcade was added in the 14th c., but subsequently much damage was done in invasions, and the upper parts of the tower and N. transept and the whole S. transept were rebuilt *c.* 1400 by Sir William le Scroop, who was given a licence to build a castle on condition that he repaired the cathedral. A fortification, however, had existed at least for a century in the wall overlooking the harbour, and, as at Old Sarum, there were squabbles between clerics and soldiery in the confined space; here they went on till the 18th c.

Long periods of neglect and spasmodic repairs culminated in a re-roofing with slate *c.* 1695, the old lead being used in 1714 for a new church of Patrick. In spite of the building of a causeway connecting the Isle with the mainland in 1750, the cathedral ceased to be used about that time. The last enthronement there took place in 1773 and the bishop's prison in the crypt was last used in 1780. It then fell to ruin. As a parish church it had already been superseded by a new church of German in the town of Peel, *c.* 1600. The bishop's throne is now in the 19th c. chapel of Bishop's Court at Kirkmichael (where the bishops had had a palace from the 13th c. onwards); major

Cathedral from SW., Peel

ceremonies are, however, held in St George's, the largest church of
the capital, Douglas.

Except for the S. aisle, the walls are reasonably complete, but they
are no longer considered strong enough to support a roof without
drastic reconstruction. Cathedral and pro-cathedral are both owned
by the Manx Government; the latter, which was so designated in
1895, is only open for Sunday worship, and the former is subject to
the same visiting hours as the castle.

Inside the castle gatehouse, the cathedral stands immediately to
the right. The 14th c. red sandstone S. arcade, and the 68 ft tower
and prominently embattled low S. transept (both virtually rebuilt
c. 1400) are seen first. Inside the **nave** there is no evidence of there
ever having been a N. aisle (only a blocked doorway in the 13th c.
N. wall); indeed, it is not clear whether the S. aisle was actually
built, for till about a century ago the whole arcade was blocked (as
its E. bay still is) with a wall containing 14th c. windows. Plain
corbel stones which supported the roof brackets can be seen, also a
small opening in the W. wall very doubtfully called a lepers'

window. The **W.** arch of the **tower** is 13th c.; the other three date
from the rebuilding of *c.* 1400. Under it is the tomb of Samuel
Rutter (d. 1662), the last bishop buried here, with a jocular Latin
inscription on brass referring to his abode shared with the worms.
The **N. transept**, of which all but the upper part is 13th c., has no
special features. The **chancel**, all 13th c. except that the E. wall with
its three lancets has been reconstructed, has the plain tomb recess of
Bishop Simon the founder in its N. wall and a piscina in the SE.
corner. The unnaturally low windows result from the raising of the
floor for enlarging the crypt. Just inside the **S. transept** on the left is
a statue bracket, facing a secondary doorway with a holy water
stoup.

Go through this doorway and bear left around the transept to
reach the narrow stair to the **crypt** prison, a dark chilly chamber
barrel-vaulted with pointed ribs early in the 14th c. Another stair on
the further side opens into the prison yard.

The E. wall of the cathedral, which is continuous with the earliest
part of the main defensive wall, the Red Curtain, can only be seen
from outside the castle. The N. side is reached by passing right
round Half Moon Battery and its projecting wall which meets the
W. end of the nave. Straight ahead, i.e. N. of the quire, is the ruined
Lord's Residence, largely 16th c. walling overlying earlier buildings.
There is much else of interest in the castle, particularly the Round
Tower (*c.* 1000) and the ruined church of St Patrick (*c.* 1100).
Another small ruin N. of St Patrick's and NW. of Half Moon
Battery has been said to be a chapel to the cathedral though for
what purpose is not clear.

Perth, St Ninian (Scottish Episcopal Church, Tayside)

Like the little cathedral at Millport, St Ninian's owes its inception
both to the Earl of Glasgow and to William Butterfield who built
the quire, transepts and one nave bay in 1849–50. It was the first
new cathedral built as such in Scotland since the Reformation.
Largely because of dissensions within the Church, work was not
resumed till 1889 when the nave and a temporary W. end were
completed. Further additions by F. L. Pearson were finished in
1901; these included the E. bay of the quire, its aisles with organ
chamber and Lady chapel, and the 'cloister' with chapter house and
vestries. The W. end in its present form (without the intended tower)
was finished in 1910.

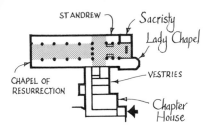

The porch in North Methven Street leads by a long arched passage into the end of Pearson's main 'cloister' walk. Doorways to the right lead to the chapter house (not open to the public), vestries, etc. and that at the end goes into the S. nave aisle.

The **nave** has unusually high and wide arches to its aisles and a small high clerestory above which the roof framing continues vertically before its steep slope begins. Its cusped braces make a strong brown and white pattern far overhead. Behind the temporary-looking nave altar and rail is a three-arched stone screen by Sir Ninian Comper with typical blue and gold cresting and Rood over. Comper also designed vestments, plate and banners for the cathedral. At the other end of the nave is the very tall arch of the intended tower; under it stands the fairly plain marble-shafted octagonal font (1853) with, however, a towering pinnacled Gothic cover of c. 1920 by Comper. The attractive W. window of deep browns and mauvish tones is of 1890, i.e. contemporary with this end of the building.

The little chapel of the Resurrection to the S. of the baptistry contains a Risen Christ statue and a tablet, both in memory of Robert Pullar (d. 1930). The canopy across the arch behind the altar is by Comper.

At the W. end of the **N. aisle** is a showcase of books, plate etc. The big round pulpit with carved scenes in niches is of 1901. Past this is the N. transept, from which one can look across to the organ in the S. transept and to the rose window curiously off-centre to the arch in front. The architecture is indeed mismanaged at this junction, the arch seeming to be uncertain whether to be a special transept arch or merely part of the main arcade.

At the NE. is **St Andrew's chapel**, part of the 1901 additions, though the present panelling, altar and communion rail are of 1950. On the S. wall is the crozier of Bishop Torry, the first bishop, whose memorial may be seen set into the grey Aberfeldy stone wall-arcading near the NE. corner of the **quire**. The High Victorian baldacchino is actually as late as 1910, also grey but of Cornish stone and inlaid with gold and other mosaic. The wine-coloured carpet-tiled floor enhances the greys of the stone as well as the browns of the pinnacled stalls and the canopied bishop's throne. The E. window is of 1876. On the S. side of the sanctuary, opening into the Lady chapel behind, is the tomb canopy of Bishop Wilkinson (d. 1907), with his over-large kneeling bronze figure by Sir George Frampton.

The apsidal, wooden vaulted **Lady chapel**, by Pearson, is entered through an iron screen of 1931. From here, go back to the S. transept, past the brass lectern and with perhaps another look at the W. window, to the cloister door. A complete circuit of the outside can be done (preferably from the opposite sides of the streets), starting at the North Methven Street porch which adjoins a former school building on its S. side, now a retreat and conference centre. The SE. view shows mostly Pearson's work, though the transept and flèche are Butterfield's. In Atholl Street, along the N. side, gates lead at the W. end into a rear drive from which access can be gained back into the cloister.

Peterborough, St Peter, St Paul & St Andrew (Church of England, Cambridgeshire)

One of the six abbey churches made into cathedrals by Henry VIII, it was founded about 655, ravaged by Danes in 870, refounded under Benedictine rule in 972, and badly damaged by fire in 1116. Rebuilding on a much bigger scale began in 1118 with the chancel, and by the end of the century had reached the W. end. The W. front and towers were completed by 1238 and the porch added in the 14th c.; during this period, too, the majority of the windows were enlarged and provided with tracery. The fan-vaulted retro-quire was built in 1496–1508.

Much internal spoliation occurred in the Civil War, and thus Peterborough is not rich in ancient monuments or fittings. The central tower with its piers (in its upper parts a 14th c. remodelling) was rebuilt in 1882–6 under J. L. Pearson, and the quire fittings largely renewed in the 1890s in their former position (in the 1820s the quire had been pushed wholly into the space E. of the crossing). At that time the foundations of the 10th c. church were found beneath the S. transept, in a position indicating that the new

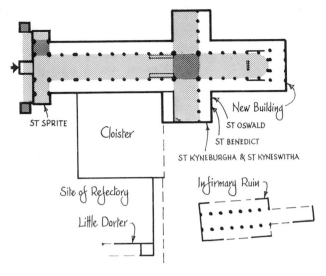

ST SPRITE

Cloister

ST OSWALD

ST BENEDICT

ST KYNEBURGHA & ST KYNESWITHA

New Building

Site of Refectory

Little Dorter

Infirmary Ruin

Norman chancel and tower were built completely clear of it.

The dramatic three-arched E. front is difficult to understand without first examining the inside, and will therefore be left till last. Entry is by the 14th c. **porch**, two-storeyed but dwarfed by the giant arches. The upper storey contains the cathedral library, with doors on both sides just inside the 18th c. iron gates. The inner doorway has a central trumeau standing on a kind of inverted capital with a carving of a man upside-down (supposed to be Simon Magus) being tormented by demons.

The **nave** is an awe-inspiring procession of Norman arches in three high tiers marching to the E. apse, capped by a rich flat painted ceiling and broken by the crossing-tower and the new hanging Rood by George Pace; the aluminium Christus is by Frank Roper. This is one of the grandest Norman interiors in England, and its system of arcade, tall gallery and clerestory is typical of its period and hardly altered. The nave roof is of a century later and painted with a rhombus pattern containing all kinds of pictures of persons and animals. A trolley-mirror is provided for viewing it, and near the W. end on the N. side a coin box for illumination.

The whole W. end is made complicated by several changes of decision during building. It can be seen that the nave was at first meant to be only eight bays long, plus a tower over the ninth bay of

the aisle each side: the extra width of the arcade piers at the end of
the eighth bay and the extra thickness of the aisle wall in the ninth
bay show that clearly. But then it was decided to make the nave two
bays longer, viz. by the previous 'tower' bay and one more, and then
to build a W. transept, as it exists, with the towers two bays further
W. than originally and still over the aisles. All this started off in the
Norman style, including the very high tower arches right up to
clerestory height but then it can be seen that pointed arches crept in,
and Early English foliage capitals (it was then about 1180), and
finally in the W. wall there is little of round-headed work at all.
Only the N. tower was actually completed, for attention seems to
have been directed instead to the W. front, which was to have been
of seven bays: three for the main doorways, two for the spaces
between, and two for the transepts. All this will be seen later from
outside.

The nave W. wall has a quaint wall-painting and verse in memory
of the gravedigger 'Old Scarlett' (d. 1594): 'You see Old Scarlett's
picture stand on Hie . . .' This was discovered behind the oil
painting (1747) of the same man when it was taken down for
cleaning, and the two versions can now be seen on either side of the
doorway.

In the transept bay beyond the **NW tower** is the font, an unusual
bowl of undulating form on modern columns and base. The
character of the **N. aisle** is determined by the wall-arcading on one
side, the great nave piers on the other, and the ribbed vaults above.
It is enhanced by the great black cylindrical Gurney stoves, now
converted from coke to oil. Looking across to the S. aisle, one can
appreciate the great size of the gallery, a full-height extra aisle at
first-floor level. Just beyond the N. doorway is a quaint uninscribed
figure with skull and cross-bones and scythe. On the right, the
hexagonal classical pulpit with graceful stair and canopy is by Leslie
Moore (c. 1938); so is the lectern which balances it.

Because the E. arm was never lengthened, the enlarged choir
space needed in the later Middle Ages had to be accommodated
within the nave. The present stalls are entirely of 1894, also the
organ over their N. side and the bronze gates at their entrance. In
the N. aisle, at the back of the organ, is a lithograph of a painting of
the nave ceiling done in 1830.

The **N. transept** is architecturally similar to the nave, but plenty of
interest can be found in detecting the differences: one side aisle only,
shafts separating the bays stopped on lumpy extra brackets on the
main arch capitals, extra outer columns to the gallery arches, etc.

S. Aisle of Quire, Peterborough

The crossing arches with their supporting piers were rebuilt from their foundations by Pearson. The ceiling is again flat wood, with a marked rhombus texture but unpainted; it was much renewed in 1886. The nine Perpendicular-traceried N. windows and their glass are of *c*. 1850–65. By the altar is a 17th c. carved chair. The E. aisle, separated by 15th c. wooden screens, is now a vestry; the few monuments in it are unimportant. The first and third bays were chapels; the second led to a 13th c. Lady chapel, taken down after the Civil War to raise money to repair the cathedral. The fourth arch leads into the **N. chancel aisle**.

Here on the left are three minor wall tablets and a fine medieval traceried wooden chest. The effigy opposite, of local (Alwalton) 'marble' is said to be of Abbot Benedict (d. 1193). From this point the Victorian high altar and sanctuary can be seen, with typical late Gothic Revival baldacchino believed to be by Pearson, iron and brass communion rail, and proud marble and mosaic floor (1892) which stretches right back to the crossing.

The second bay of the aisle has three very good wall tablets including a classical one to Dean Duport (d. 1679) and an elegant flowery cartouche to Constance May (d. 1681). Beneath stands a model of the cathedral. The banners of England and Spain in the next bay indicate the grave of Catherine of Aragon: the black slab beneath the arcade was put in in 1895. The window on the left is by Wailes (1856). Next comes a short 13th c. bay which took the place of the original 12th c. apse; it has a quadripartite vault, and a beautiful little double piscina with Geometric tracery and a large wall tablet to Richard Tryce (d. 1767).

The rest of the 13th c. chapel has given way to a four-centred arch with clumsy fleurons lying in its deep moulding, leading into the Tudor retro-quire which is still called the **New Building**. The fan-vault here forms an astonishing contrast with the massive Romanesque apse it embraces, and it is fascinating to examine how the essentially rectangularly planned vault has been knitted on to the old curved E. end. The designer may have been John Wastell, who built the similar vaulting in King's College Chapel, Cambridge.

Just inside the New Building on the right is a restored 15th c. three-niched cenotaph, possibly the shrine of St Tibba, or of Abbot Hedda who was killed in the Danish invasion. A gate just beyond opens into the **chancel** apse, which has a small chapel backing on to the high altar. In the centre stands the so-called Hedda stone, now considered earlier than his time, perhaps about 800; its purpose is uncertain but the figures along the sides are probably Apostles. Here the chancel itself can be examined. It differs little from the nave except in the curved E. end where the bottom arches have been obliterated by filigree work in connection with the fan-vault behind. The wooden roof is 15th c., again partly flat, but with vaulted coves at the sides. The bosses are ancient but the colouring is 19th c. The Majestas painting on the flat part over the apse was designed by Sir George Gilbert Scott; the windows below have fragmentary 15th c. glass.

Now back into the New Building the same way. On the floor are innumerable ledger stones from the 17th c. onwards. The recumbent figure straight ahead is of Lewis Clayton (d. 1917). The classical monument on the apse wall, flanked by cherubs, is to Bishop Cumberland (d. 1718). Of several windows of 1860–1910 the most noteworthy is that at the S. end of the E. wall by Clayton and Bell (1861). The Gothic tomb near it, with white marble effigy, is of Dean Ingram (d. 1901). Facing that, on the apse wall, is the large white marble memorial with reclining effigy of Thomas Deacon (d. 1720), by Robert Taylor. Then in the last bay before the S. chancel aisle: on the left the presumed and much damaged effigy of Abbot Kirkton (d. 1528), and on the right what remains of an early 17th c. monument to Sir Humphrey Orme, put up in his lifetime 'to save his heir that charge and trouble' and, before he died, savagely treated by Cromwell's men. Below is a 13th c. coffin-lid.

Then comes a 13th c. junction-bay like that on the N., with another pretty double piscina and a good cartouche to Joseph Stamford (d. 1683). On the left in the **S. chancel aisle** another mutilated figure is probably Abbot Alexander of Holderness (d. 1226). Two Scottish banners and a modern plaque on the aisle pier indicate the original grave of Mary Queen of Scots. A second, unidentified, abbot is a splendid bearded figure with his staff in a dragon's mouth. Opposite him is the showy inlaid marble tomb-slab of Bishop Creighton (d. 1901). In the third bay is another abbot, and on the right the classical tomb of Archbishop Magee of York (d. 1891) with marble figure by James Forsyth. Finally, against the E. aisle of the S. transept, yet another abbot under a Norman arch, and two tablets of 1695 and 1730.

The **S. transept** differs little from the N. except that its aisle is still divided into chapels with stone walls between them, and 15th c. wooden screens. The first, St Oswald's, contains a stair probably serving a gallery for watching a relic, St Oswald's arm; it is now reserved for private devotion. The second, St Benedict's, has a shallow Norman wall-arcade on one side wall and contains a

window of 1958 by Carter Shapland. The third is dedicated to
St Kyneburgha and St Kyneswitha and contains a miniature
Annunciation in a mirrored case, by Alan Durst in memory of his
wife Clare (d. 1968). The lower left window in the S. wall is an early
work (1862) of William Morris. The 14th c. ogee-headed doorway
on the W. side leads to a late 12th c. vaulted vestry, not open to the
public. To the right is a little 8th c. panel with two saints.

On the SW. **crossing** pier is another coin-box, for lighting the
chancel ceiling, and as in the nave a trolley-mirror is provided. The
wooden tower vault is a Pearson reconstruction, with old bosses re-
used or copied. But what Pearson replaced was a 14th c. lantern
rather like Ely's; it seems that this had been put in because the
Norman tower was too heavy, and that at the same time the E. and
W. crossing arches were rebuilt in their present pointed form. They
were reproduced by Pearson but the lantern was not. The chancel
pulpit and the bishop's throne are of 1892. Westward is a second
view of the Pearson stalls. The brass eagle lectern is 15th c., a rare
monastic survival.

Next the **S. nave aisle**, where some Saxon stones are displayed on
the right. Just past the lectern is a bronze memorial to Edith Cavell
(d. 1915) and towards the W. end is the Bishop's door into the
cloister, which should be seen at this point. All the walks were
destroyed in 1651, but traces of the vaulting are left. The Norman
doorway on the W. side led to cellars. The specially rich Early
English opening at the W. end of the S. walk led to the refectory.
Then come five 15th c. bays of washplace, a range of Early English
wall-arcading, and another doorway towards the infirmary. From
this corner there is a good view of the whole S. side of the cathedral,
with the stump of the unfinished SW. tower and the rich wall-
arcading of the transept. Reverting to the S. aisle: this leads to the
space under the incomplete SW. tower where the projecting
transeptal bay is the **chapel of St Sprite**. The black and gold screen is
of 1920, and the seating by Pace, incorporating three ancient carved
misericords at an unaccustomed height on the back row. Here is
another little Geometric double piscina.

This completes the interior, and the **W. front** can now be re-
examined. As has been seen inside, the nave was lengthened as an
afterthought, and towers were planned at the W. ends of the
extended aisles. Only the N. one was actually completed and it
stands in a very odd position in any view of the façade. When the
idea of a grand covered portico was first conceived, it was to have
had seven bays, representing: transept, aisle, (blank), nave, (blank),

aisle, transept; with a separate vault over each bay. That is how the
inner W. wall was worked out. But in the end five bays took the
place of seven, the flanking turrets were added, and the three giant
arches and gables fail to express what lies behind them. Moreover,
the central porch is of an entirely different style and scale; possibly it
was added to strengthen a weakness in the great piers. The sense of
unease is increased by the rather arbitrary assembly of niches, wheel
windows and wall-arcading in the three gables, which try to be equal
though the arches are not. Some of the high sculpture has been
renewed by Alan Durst.

Finally, a clockwise round of the **Precinct**. On the left is the
Abbot's Gateway leading to the Abbot's lodging, now the bishop's
palace and diocesan offices. Straight ahead is the Outer Gate into
the Market Place, and on its right what remains of St Thomas's
Chapel. Go through the Tudor archway immediately N. of the W.
front and into the Layfolk's Cemetery which has some 18th c. tombs
and headstones. This side of the cathedral differs little from the S.,
except where traces of the Lady chapel can be seen on the E. side of
the N. transept. Beside the N. chancel aisle is a big flying buttress
put in in 1923. Then the outside of the retro-quire, with a pierced
parapet and weatherworn figures thought to represent Christ and
eleven Apostles. This part of the churchyard is called the Monks'
Cemetery; near its SE. corner is a fine group of 18th c. headstones.
To the S. lie the infirmary buildings. The lane leads right into their
13th c. arcaded hall, open to the sky but with houses built into the
aisles and chancel. From this part of the Precinct there is an
impressive view of the retro-quire and chancel apse, with S. transept
and central tower to their left.

Now one can either retrace the way back round the E. and N.
sides, or walk W. as far as the refectory wall which bars the way
ahead. To its right is the door to the SE. corner of the cloister; to
the left a lane which goes S. and then E., past some old barns and
into Bishop's Road.

Plymouth, St Mary & St Boniface (Roman Catholic, Devon)

Designed by Joseph A. Hansom in an Early English style, it was
opened in 1858; the steeple, however, was added later, with the
main entrance beneath it. This leads to a light spacious interior
with octagonal granite columns and trumpet-shaped capitals,
clerestory of twin lights, and high-pitched roof with slender black

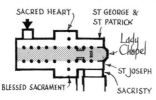

trusts and pale blue ceiling (note that sometimes only the rear door
into the S. transept is open). The crossing has tall arches to nave and
quire, the latter with a hanging Rood, and beyond is a tester over
the high altar. Stonework (except the columns), painted walls and
composition floor are all light buff. The W. window portrays the
story of St Boniface and below, between the twin doorways, is a
figure of the Virgin Mary: these are the cathedral's patrons.

The aisles have dark single-strutted trusses and white ceilings;
the Stations of the Cross are by Joseph Cribb. The N. aisle also
has a Pietà at the W. end. The N. transept, roofed like the nave, was
originally filled by an organ from St Martin-in-the-Fields, London;
its successor is confined to the E. bay, leaving space for the Sacred
Heart chapel. The N. quire aisle leads to the simple chapel of
St George and St Patrick; on its right is the richly carved chair used
as the bishop's throne, with a plain hanging as an effective canopy.

Behind the high altar is the Lady chapel, with double Gothic
reredos, recent window glass, and statue-niches between. From here
one can look back along the nave and up at the quire roof with its
stencilled enrichment. The simply furnished SE. chapel is
St Joseph's. In it is the door to the sacristy, where an ancient
Flemish Crucifixion painting may be seen on request.

Into the quire next, with polished marble columns and a carpet
strongly patterned with reds and green: then the S. transept, where
the Blessed Sacrament chapel is remarkable for its coloured and
gilded iron screen of quatrefoil patterns, continued as enclosing
gates over a matching communion rail. The S. window is a
memorial to William Vaughan, the first bishop (d. 1902): a brass
with his recumbent effigy is on the wall beneath. Finally, the S. aisle,
with a plain octagonal 19th c. font.

Outside, the little W. piazza gives a view of the very slender 205 ft
high broach spire and leads to an attractive garden behind, with
Cathedral House on its E. side. There is no way round, so the N.
and E. sides of the cathedral must be seen by retracing one's steps.
Tidy new paving and bollards add much to the unassuming exterior,
and the projection of the E. apse into Cecil Street gives it a
decidedly Continental air.

Portsmouth, St Thomas of Canterbury (Church of England, Hampshire)

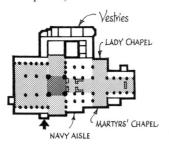

St Thomas's in Portsmouth was never monastic or collegiate. For over a century following its foundation late in the 12th c. it was not even a parish church, but merely a chapel to St Mary, Portsea. Yet having been built under the auspices of Southwick Priory, a few miles inland, it possessed from the start a special dignity.

After Civil War damage the nave and tower were rebuilt, the latter at the W. end instead of the crossing. It became a cathedral in 1927. In 1935–9 Sir Charles Nicholson built the first three bays of a new nave (thus making the tower central again), W. transepts, outer aisles to the old nave (which became the quire) and a suite of vestries and offices to the N. – all in a curious amalgam of Tudor and Romanesque.

The S. porch leads into Nicholson's aisles and nave. It is best to leave these till later, and first to turn right into the low vaulted space beneath the organ and tower. Looking E. from here it is easy to understand the original, medieval, form in spite of subsequent changes. The present **quire** was the nave. Its arcades of three bays plus one taller one mark respectively the original aisles and the square crossing where the first tower stood. The present arcades with their Tuscan columns are, however, of 1683–93 and the corresponding outer walls were pierced by Nicholson to lead into his new outer aisles. The blue ceiled wagon roof with its domestic-looking dormers is also 17th c. Beyond the crossing, the original chancel (now the presbytery) is little altered; the main arch and the plaster vault, however, are of 1843. The gallery, confined now to the W. end, extended in the 18th c. right along the aisles and into the transepts as well. The quire seating is a miscellany, largely of 1904. At its NW. corner is a little portable baluster font with gilded top, from a local hospital and probably 19th c.

Cathedral from NW., Portsmouth (Tower 17th c., nave 1935–9)

Now across to the **outer N. quire aisle**. The four banners are of
local militia and regiments and in the N. wall is the 1935 foundation
stone. A doorway leads to the 'cloister' of vestries and beyond is the
N. transept. Like the presbytery this is late 12th c., i.e. early Early
English. It was once vaulted; the present plain open roof is 17th c.
On the N. wall are three small 18th and 19th c. tablets. A screen of
1927 divides the Lady chapel from the remainder of the transept,
where on the E. wall there is a faded 13th c. wall-painting: a Host of
Angels with a Majestas above. More minor wall tablets are scattered
on both E. and W. walls and a fine shafted arch leads into the **N.
presbytery aisle**.

These E. aisles, with their original rib-vaults, are the least altered
parts of the medieval building, and have a pleasing variety of detail
in their supporting shafts and foliage capitals. The presbytery
arcades are unusual in having twin main arches within big
semicircular ones, the sort of treatment more usually found at
triforium level, and comparable only with Boxgrove Priory in
Sussex. There is no triforium but the clerestory has a walkway
within the wall thickness. The black shafts, once of Purbeck stone, are
now of Irish 'marble' and the vaulting, once of stone, is of wood and
plaster. Amongst many wall tablets in the N. aisle is a cartouche at
the E. end to Admiral Cleland (d. 1795).

Behind the altar a small ambulatory leads to the S. side. Below
the single narrow lancet window is the plain tomb of Benjamin
Burgess, a Presbyterian minister (d. 1673). In the **S. presbytery aisle**
the heraldic monuments, unconvincingly re-coloured, are to Robert
Moulton (d. 1652) and William Willoughby (d. 1651). Above these
are two tablets of *c.* 1800, and in the second bay two earlier
cartouches.

At this point the sanctuary can well be seen. Its marble paving is
of 1904, the communion rail, altar and tester by Nicholson (1939).
Facing it from the fourth bay of the aisle is Nicholas Stone's
monument to the Duke of Buckingham, murdered in a house nearby
in 1628. Another fine arch matching that on the N. leads into the **S.
transept**, part of which is the Martyrs' chapel. The statue of
St Sebastian is by John Philipson (1972) and the lower windows, by
Carl Edwards, are a post-war memorial to Sir Bertram Ramsay.
There is a miscellany of 18th and 19th c. tablets, of which the five
cartouches around the W. end are noteworthy.

Next, return to the pulpit, which is of 1693, octagonal and
dignified. The canopy with its trumpeting angel, however, is a
replica of the original, put up in 1904. The brass eagle lectern was

given in 1903 by King Edward VII. It faces the Corporation pew,
which is contemporary with the pulpit; the mayor's mace rest is 20th
c., but the stone royal arms of William and Mary are original and
specially fine.

Moving now W. down the centre, one passes on the left the
modest throne, a 20th c. oak version of St Augustine's chair at
Canterbury. Beneath the gallery (of 1706 but entirely reconstructed
by Nicholson and displaying a 19th c. wooden royal arms) turn left
to the **outer quire aisle** or Navy aisle. On the left pier at the E. end is
a fragment of Nelson's flag from Trafalgar. In the centre bay is a
tablet to Admiral Sir John Kempthorne (d. 1679); hanging above it
is a model of his ship *Mary Rose*. The aisle is Nicholson's and he re-
used the plain 17th c. window surrounds from what had been the
outer wall. The twin double arches are entirely his and so is the **SW.
transept** with its stair to the gallery (not open to the public). Besides
several more wall tablets there is a painting, 'The Miraculous
Draught of Fishes' by W. L. Wyllie; also a red velvet pulpit fall of
1695 in a glass case.

Under the tower is a plain oval tablet to the first bishop, Nevill
Lovett (d. 1936). Having returned to this point one can now look
out westwards at Nicholson's concrete-vaulted nave with its giant
stone columns and inner and outer aisles. The twin outer arcades
pick up in a strange way the theme of the Early English twin arches
in the sanctuary. It all stops short at a temporary brick wall on
which the former inner door frame of the tower (1694) is displayed.
Nicholson intended to continue in the same way. In the 1960s Seely
and Paget and Pier Luigi Nervi planned instead an arena-like
concrete-framed end in memory of the D-Day landings of 1944 but
that has not been realized.

Nicholson's **NW. transept** is the baptistry; the simple octagonal
font is 15th c. On the right, i.e. on the outer N. wall of the tower, are
a tablet to William Brandon (d. 1705) and a bigger one to Sir
Charles Blount (d. 1600). On the E. wall of the transept is a
beautiful della Robbia majolica Madonna, *c.* 1500. The altar frontal
in a case matches the pulpit fall in the opposite transept. More wall
tablets are on the N. and W. walls, the best perhaps being a
cartouche to Dorothy Baxter (d. 1711), over the arch to the **outer N.
aisle** of the nave. The gilded ship is the old cupola weather vane of
1710.

Now down to the W. end where flags of H.M.S. *Invincible* hang at
the sides, and in the centre an altar-like stone of 1966 'marks the
resolve' to complete the **nave**. Its height is explained by the fact that

N. doorway, Portsmouth (17th c., re-set in 20th c. wall)

the floor level is planned to be raised. This is the best point from which to see the organ case of 1718. It formerly faced E. into what is now the quire and was built by Abraham Jordan junior (his actual organ has not survived). The delicate carving of King David and cherubs may be by Francis Bird.

The **exterior** can well be seen from a circuit of the surrounding streets, for all the other buildings formerly crowded on to the site have been demolished; it is best to go into the High Street and turn right, thus starting with the Nicholson building and the late 17th c. tower, which contains ten bells; its cupola was added in 1703. Oyster Street looks on to the temporary brick end, into which the former W. window of the tower is inserted. The former W. doorway, also from the tower, and dated 1691, can be seen further round, from St Thomas's Street. Then come the N. entrance, and the vestries and so-called cloister. Beyond them is a good diagonal view of the N. transept with its Early English lancet windows, and from Lombard Street a similar view of the E. end. Round the corner, attached to the S. wall of the presbytery, the old vestry is probably 18th or early 19th c. The tiled and dormered quire (former nave) roof, a 'catslide' which spreads down over the aisles, retains something of the 'churchwarden' atmosphere which still lingers inside the cathedral in its older parts.

Portsmouth, St John the Evangelist (Roman Catholic, Hampshire)

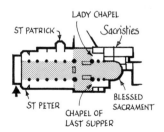

Portsmouth's first Catholic chapel was opened in 1792 in Prince George Street. St John's, which replaced it, was begun in 1880 on a site destined to be hemmed in by roaring streams of traffic; it was designated a cathedral in 1882. By then no more had been built than five bays of nave and moreover the architect, John Crawley, had already died. He had won the commission by competition and was succeeded by Joseph Hansom who built the crossing and transepts by 1886 and the chancel and apse by 1893.

In 1906 the high altar was brought forward from the apse to the centre of the chancel, a very early instance of a move towards present-day liturgical practice. At the same time the W. end was completed and the narthex added, but the SW. tower and spire envisaged by Crawley were never built. St Patrick's chapel on the N. side is of 1924–5. Extensive damage caused by a bomb in 1941 was repaired by 1950, and further re-ordering of the interior was done in 1971 under Austin Winkley.

The W. narthex, a curious lean-to addition designed, with the W. turrets, by Canon Scoles, covers the rather gaunt inner main doorway. This opens into the grand **interior**, essentially Geometric in style, with tall arcades on clustered columns and foliage capitals, tall clerestory, and a hammer-beam roof – boarded (contrary to Crawley's intentions), which gives it an unsatisfactory trefoil shape. The same kind of roof continues eastwards, even into the apse.

The Rood at the W. end is of 1897 and used to hang in the chancel arch. Below, to the right of the doorway, is a brass to Bishop Cahill (d. 1910), and nearby, centrally in the nave, is a splendid oval table, probably 18th c. The aisle doorways bear the significant dates 1882 and 1906. The semi-octagonal recess in the NW. corner was the original baptistry and it still has windows on that theme. These, like most of the other glass in the cathedral, are post-war replacements by Arthur Buss of Goddard & Gibbs. The Sacred Heart statue was originally in the SE. chapel.

Along the **N. aisle** are confessionals, as well as the vaulted St Patrick's chapel (1924–5) by James and Wilfred Mangan, with marble-shafted arch and decorations by Louis Beyaert.

The entirely redesigned sanctuary occupies the crossing, with the bishop's throne where the Rood once hung. Close to the N. aisle are the font (with flowing water) and Paschal candle, both by Fritz Steller (1971). The low Portland stone altar with ceramic figures, the candlesticks, the slender Tau Cross to the S. (capped with a figure of Christ) and the illuminating corona hanging above are all by Steller too. The bold brown and beige carpet enhances the general effect.

The **N. transept** window has three strongly coloured heraldic panels by monks of Pluscarden Priory in Scotland (1962). Beneath is a brass commemorating the consecration in 1887. The door to its right leads to the sacristy; to the right of that is the **Lady chapel**, with simple iron gates, marble and mosaic stepped floor, coloured

wagon roof and alabaster Madonna. From here the **quire** is visible.
On the other side is the rather over-exposed but musically
impressive organ, and behind that a big circular window with
flowing tracery based on the 'Bishop's Eye' at Lincoln. The quire is
flexibly planned with simple oak stalls and a fence-like screen behind
the bishop's throne.

Next the **Blessed Sacrament chapel** in the apse, which was the
original sanctuary. A rich decorative scheme by Nathaniel Westlake
provided a pronounced horizontality to counteract the high walls
and pipe-like columns, but all except a few angels has been painted
out because of war damage and general deterioration, and as a
result the three fine windows (renewed by Buss) seem too high and
disconnected to belong. The new reredos is formed of three brown
and green blocks and there is a delicate brass desk. The big statues
on each side are of St Joseph (under the Lady chapel arch) and
St John the Evangelist (opposite); in the back of the screen behind
the bishop's throne can be seen a panel from the former throne and
a record of bishops and their coats-of-arms.

The **Last Supper chapel** in the SE. corner, now little used, has
more of Westlake's angels – all that is left of another over-all
scheme – as well as an ornate reredos and some more Buss glass.
Directly outside the simple iron screen is a secondary porch to
Edinburgh Road. Then comes the **S. transept** with the organ, the
lower part being screened with a splendid curtain of nine bright
saints in appliqué work by Kathleen Isherwood (1969). The aisle this
side is unbroken by chapel or confessionals and leads to the SW.
chapel, altarless but with a lively statue of St Peter.

From the **outside** the W. additions by Scoles – the lobby, which
has a good carved tympanum, and the copper-capped turrets – seem
to harmonize better than they do inside. The materials of the
exterior are dark Fareham brick and Portland stone. No complete
circuit is possible because on the S. side Bishop's House (rebuilt
after bombing) abuts the E. end, and on the N. side a high wall is
followed by the Cathedral School buildings.

Ripon, St Peter & St Wilfrid (Church of England, North Yorkshire)

A monastery was founded at Ripon *c.* 655 and is believed to have
had a bishop's seat *c.* 681–6. The crypt of that period actually
survives. Though the church was subsequently only collegiate, it
developed on a moderately large scale. The chapter house building is

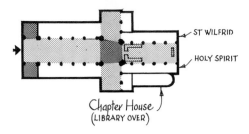

Chapter House
(LIBRARY OVER)

probably mid-12th c. and most of the remainder dates from between that time and 1300. Some reconstruction of and around the tower was done, however, in the 15th c. and the nave was rebuilt early in the 16th c. and aisles added. Further rebuilding stopped short at the Reformation, and the college of priests was dissolved. In 1604 the chapter was re-established, still within York diocese, and in 1836 the church became a cathedral in its own right. Restorations and alterations were done by Edward Blore in 1829–34 and, more extensively, by Sir George Gilbert Scott in 1862–70.

The centre doorway of the noble Early English W. front leads straight into the short wide **nave** which with its late Perpendicular arcades and big clerestory provides an immediate contrast of style. Vaulting shafts were prepared for a stone nave roof but the present ceiling is Scott's of 1868; only the aisles have stone vaults, and they are Scott's too. A much odder contrast stands ahead, where the round Transitional Norman crossing arch has begun to be replaced with a much taller one, not to conform with the nave but because the spire collapsed in 1450 and damaged the S. pier. It is not a handsome sight but very telling as an illustration of how buildings were altered and modernized piecemeal in the Middle Ages. What happened to the other crossing arches will be seen later.

Turning back now to the W. parts, the inner flanks of the Early English towers – a big arch, blank 'triforium' of four arches, and clerestory of three – are connected to the nave arcades each side by a curious part-bay with blank clerestory and 'triforium' extended downwards. This suggests that the earlier nave had no aisles or arcades. The W. window glass is by Burlison & Grylls (1886). The screened space under the NW. tower, at one time a bookshop, is not open.

At the W. end of the **N. aisle** the base of a former 15th c. stone screen forms a low enclosure which was used as a consistory court; in it a 10th c. column base is displayed. The fact that the towers

existed before aisles were added to the nave is confirmed here by the
appearance of the unarched E. side facing into the aisle, obviously
once external. Amongst the many minor wall tablets a cartouche in
the second bay to Ann Hutchinson (d. 1720), should be noticed. In
the fourth bay is some heraldic glass dated 1664. Turn aside into the
nave to look at the canopied pulpit of 1913 by Henry Wilson in a
rich Art Nouveau manner; an octofoil bronze-faced body with
triangular-headed ornament, standing on tall shafts of grey-green
Cippolino marble. Its four figures on fruity corbels represent Saxon
saints. This is an outstanding example of harmonious design in a
style neither Gothic nor Classical. Bay 5 of the aisle has a
swashbuckling heraldic window of 1840 by Ward & Hughes. The
blank early 13th c. walling on the right of bay 6 was left by the
builders of the later arcade as a buttress for the main tower.

The **N. transept** is of the earliest kind of Early English or late
Transitional, perhaps *c*. 1170, three-storeyed and with a well-
proportioned E. arcade. Variety is provided at both triforium and
clerestory levels by changing the contents of the bays on the N. and
W. sides. The aisle is vaulted but the high roof is flat wood of
Perpendicular type, painted brick red and with beams and bosses
coloured and gilded.

Now a closer look at the **crossing**. The rebuilding of the further
arch, to the S. transept, as well as that to the quire, was completed
in the 15th c. That to the N. transept remains in a lopsided state not
unlike that to the nave. In the Middle Ages little compunction was
felt about destroying old work and replacing it with new; now both
have become equally precious even in such an unhappy
combination, and it is difficult to conceive that this particular job
could ever be finished. A further peculiarity, incidentally, is that the
tower is not square, as may be seen from the ceiling panels above its
lantern storey.

The figure perched on a high column at the SW. corner of the
N. transept is of James I and was made at his accession for the
pulpitum of York Minster. On the W. and N. walls are more wall
tablets. The first window on the W. side contains various coats-of-
arms and small scenes dated 1664, re-made in 1815. Low down are
two brasses: a worn inscription to William Gibson (d. 1680) and an
ornate one in Arts and Crafts style to Canon Badcock (d. 1897).
Under these is a worn 13th c. coffin-lid and to the right (i.e. in the
NE. corner) a sadly damaged double tomb-chest with effigies of Sir
Thomas Markenfield and wife (d. 1497).

Between the bays of the E. aisle is the similar tomb-chest of a

14th c. Sir Thomas and wife: he in armour and she now headless.
Amusing corbel heads terminate the vaulting shafts behind. The
second bay contains a piscina, and window glass by Harry Harvey
(1977); just outside stands a battered but uncommon 15th c. stone
pulpit.

Part of the N. quire aisle is used for storage, so the **quire** itself is
taken next, by passing first through the stone pulpitum (late 15th c.
but with renewed statues). The organ case is by Scott (1860). On the
N. side the architecture starts (like the transept) not long after the
middle of the 12th c., with beautifully moulded piers and arches
supporting a blank triforium and a well-defined clerestory – each
with a round centre arch which betrays its early date, if it is to be
regarded as Early English. The corresponding bays on the S. were
converted to Perpendicular after the building of the nave aisles. To
add to the complexity, the three E. bays (both sides) are Geometric
Decorated of c. 1300, with a double clerestory. Even here the
triforium is not quite the same on both sides. The splendidly
Geometric E. window has glass mostly by William Wailes (1854).
The wooden vault is by Scott but includes some very fine 14th c.
bosses.

The stalls also owe a great deal to Scott. In their W. parts they are
essentially 15th c., but he had them restored and added the rest to
match. Notes on the unusually fine series of carved misericords can
be found on boards each side. The organ case should be looked at
again, for projecting from its E. front is a movable hand which can
be used for beating time. The brass eagle lectern is 19th c. At the E.
end the rich Gothic reredos is a war memorial by Sir Ninian
Comper (1922); its typical extravagance of gilding and figure-
carving compete too much with the E. window. The piscina and
triple sedilia are rich but restored early 14th c. work, and the simple
quire pulpit and scrolly brass communion rail 19th c.

Now into the **N. quire aisle** and chapel through the wooden
screen. The E. bays are Geometric like the quire and all are vaulted.
The reredos of the altar (St Wilfrid) is a triptych painting of the
Ascension. Cross the quire to the **S. quire aisle** and the chapel of the
Holy Spirit. Its furnishings (1970) are perhaps the most
controversial works in the cathedral. Some find the contrast with the
rest of the building disturbing and even describe it as 'jazzed up'.
Others point out that the nave pulpit provoked similar reactions in
its own day, and that one of the cathedral's features is that differing
styles are placed together without disguise or apology; to them
Leslie Durbin's metal work is a challenging present-day commentary

on the theme of the Creator Spirit. The altar rail and the hanging pyx in the form of a Cross are Durbin's work and the altar frontal (to his design), was made by Theodora Moorman. In the second bay is the damaged effigy of Dean Fowler (d. 1608) under a canopy – also two brass inscriptions of 1678 and 1710. Close to the doorway in bay 3 is an unusual medieval stone wash-basin. A flashy screen of aluminium, silver, black and brass, also by Durbin, leads out of the chapel into the aisle proper. A carved bracket on the wall depicts St Willibrord, and just before the main chapter house doorway are two croziers in a glass case.

Being used as a vestry, the **chapter house** is not open to the public but may sometimes be seen on request, together with All Souls' chapel in the crypt beneath. It is a vaulted and apsed room of c. 1200, i.e. earlier than the main building. The still older crypt on which it stands will be seen outside.

Above the arch into the **S. transept** are, on the aisle side, a 'skied' late 17th c. tablet and, on the transept side, three figures in niches, a memorial to Dean Owen (d. 1940). This transept differs in design from the other, chiefly in the alterations made to its two E. chapels in the 15th c. and subsequently. The first bay now contains a stone stair (re-formed by Scott) to the early 14th c. library (originally Lady Chapel) which forms a third storey of the chapter house building. At the bottom is a carved stone, part of a Viking cross. The second bay, called the Mallorie chapel, contains the upright memorial (without any effigy) of Sir John Mallorie (d. 1666), also a late 17th c. royal arms and a big 16th c. secular cupboard with carved panels. Various aumbries and other recesses can be seen in both bays, including one behind the monument to John Aislabie (d. 1742). The floor here is curiously set out in squares. Against the end of the transept itself it is arranged radially around an elegant memorial to William Weddell (d. 1789) – a bust by Joseph Nollekens under a semi-elliptical Composite canopy, for all the world as though it were a garden feature. Amongst numerous small memorials is a big brass inscription to John Crosland (d. 1670).

Now a look at the bay of the **nave** nearest the crossing. This has tall 'triforium' arches like that at the W. end. The oak nave stalls, including a small bishop's chair, are by J. Oldrid Scott (1902). On the N. side is a memorial to Hugh Ripley (d. 1637) with a bust. re-erected in 1730 after Civil War damage. On the S. is one to Charles Floyer (d. 1766); below that a piscina and the narrow stone stair to the 7th c. **crypt**. This is used as a treasury, so the fee enables one also to see a collection of church plate of the diocese in the two small and one big chambers. The big one, lying beneath the crossing, is believed to have contained a shrine.

The exit on the N. side, reopened in recent years, emerges under the pulpitum, so one must then go diagonally to the **S. nave aisle**, where there are small wall tablets all along. Those worth noting are: in bay 4 a nice cartouche to Hellen Bayne (d. 1695), and in bay 6 a brass to Evard Hodgson (d. 1705). The shape of the font, at the W. end of the aisle, suggests that it may be another post-Civil War renewal. In the window near it are 15 medallions of 14th c. glass.

Now back into the nave again (with more tablets on its blank bay) and into the **SW. tower** space. Here is a curious cartouche-like memorial to Emily Oxley (d. 1898), with a cluster of angels wearing family portrait heads. The giant monument with painfully reclining bewigged figure of Edward Blacket (d. 1718) has been moved here from the N. transept; who the flanking figures are is not clear. There is also another font, big, broken, 12th c., pieced together on a wooden base.

Outside, the W. front should be looked at again (preferably from well back) in the light of the history of the nave, which makes it surprising that the towers, suggesting in most great churches the terminations of aisles, seem in this case to have antedated their aisles by several centuries. The church's collegiate status must have necessitated enlargements of the E. parts long before the W. Scott altered the façade, changing the doorways, removing two-light tracery from the lancets, and reducing it all to rather bare essentials – Early English at its most severe. The central doors bear the date 1675 in studs.

Along the S. side Early English quickly gives way to the Perpendicular of the aisles with their heavy buttresses. The transept is 12th c. again: note the round-headed doorway with foliage caps. As a possible diversion, the sloping path down to the South Walk gives a good view of the central tower, Perpendicular in its upper parts. Next is the chapter house building, with library above and undercroft below, the last being perhaps as early as the 11th c. and now containing All Souls' chapel and a choir room. The apse at its E. end is a surprising feature, difficult to explain in this position.

The churchyard slopes away a great distance to the SE., but a way leads close under the big Geometric E. window to a gate in Minster Road. The change in the quire clerestory from Geometric to very Early English is readily seen, the latter continuing in the N. transept. The transept also has an unusual doorway with trefoil head inside a round arch. The attractive early 19th c. building opposite is the Court House; the older ones beyond belonged to the minster precinct and one now forms the cathedral shop.

Rochester, Christ & St Mary (Church of England, Kent)

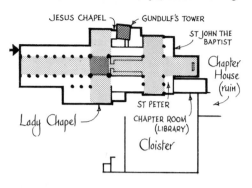

The bishopric dates from 604, and is thus the second oldest in England. Nothing is known for certain of the pre-Norman cathedral. It was rebuilt *c.* 1080–1130 but to a great extent again later in the 12th c. From the former period there remain the big detached Gundulf's tower on the N. side and a good deal of the walling of nave and quire. The E. parts were much enlarged in the first half of the 13th c., largely as a result of the setting up of a shrine of St William of Perth, murdered on his way to the Holy Land. This rebuilding proceeded as far as two bays of the nave before funds ran out. The Lady chapel, not at the E. end but S. of the nave, was added late in the 15th c. The central tower was rebuilt with battlements and pinnacles by Lewis Cottingham in 1825, and Sir George Gilbert Scott and J. L. Pearson did much restoration *c.* 1870–90. The tower was again rebuilt (reverting to the original design) by C. Hodgson Fowler (1904–5).

In its modest way the late 12th c, **W. front** is one of the most satisfying amongst English cathedrals, in its proportions and strength and in its honest expression of the nave and aisles behind. The sturdy outer stair-turrets, not at all alike in their upper parts, were rebuilt by Pearson. The big Perpendicular W. window inserted into the Norman wall-arcading echoes its general pattern in shape and scale and is typically English. The rich doorway below, however, might well have been transplanted from Poitou and has splendid individually carved voussoirs; the column-figures at the sides may be Solomon and the Queen of Sheba or Henry I and Matilda, and the tympanum is a Majestas, with Apostles on the lintel below.

Cathedral from SW., Rochester

Just inside the 14th c. NW. doorway the foundations of an apsidal church, probably the Saxon cathedral, are outlined by brass strips. The **nave** is Norman only in its six W. bays: the last two are 13th c. with pointed arches instead of zigzag-enriched round ones and, curiously, no triforium. The 15th c. clerestory and timber roof run over both without much respect for the bay spacing. The Norman piers are inconsistent in shape, too, so that although there is much of interest in detail the whole rather lacks coherence. The crossing arch was altered and provided with shafting in the 13th c. Beyond that is the pulpitum, mostly (including the organ case by Scott) 19th c.

Other points of interest are the successful pendant lights by Emil Godfrey (1957) and the dim remains of a medieval St Christopher wall-painting on the W. pier of the S. arcade.

The **N. aisle** – like the nave, never vaulted – has 17th c. walling in the middle part. In the last three bays, however, it is early Norman. Its W. window is by Charles Kempe (1898). In the first three bays are minor wall tablets; in the fourth, one to Francis Barrell (d. 1724), by Robert Taylor. Two bays beyond are cartouches to two more men named Francis Barrell (d. 1679 and 1772), and a clumsy tablet to Ann Spice (d. 1795). The pulpit is 19th c. The blank stonework on the right of the aisle is a tower buttress which would have been removed on completion of the new N. arcade; in it can be seen numerous pieces of early Norman interlace carving.

The **N. transept** is entirely 13th c. The vaulting is of French sexpartite type, one unit to two bays, with a ridge-rib added. Clerestory and triforium have lancet openings with very slender Purbeck or Petworth marble shafting and some oddly shaped arches with dog-tooth ornament. Though the lower windows in the N. wall are by Clayton & Bell (1859), the glass as a whole can hardly be said to enhance the architecture. In the little Jesus chapel on the E. side is a piscina and to its right a classical marble monument to John Parr (d. 1792).

An arch with dog-tooth ornament next leads into the **N. quire** aisle, with an eight-part vault. On the right is the solid, basically early Norman, N. wall of the quire, with a canopied tomb attributed to Bishop de Hythe (d. 1352). Opposite is a damaged wall tablet to William Streaton (d. 1609), with kneeling effigies. Up the so-called Pilgrims' steps and past (on the right) a white marble tablet to Augustine Caesar (d. 1677) is a double arch with black 'marble' into the **NE. transept**. Architecturally this is very similar to the main transept: sexpartite vault, 'marble' shafting and dog-tooth. The early 13th c. tomb on the N. side may be that of St William of Perth, whose shrine stood in the middle of the transept; the two-arched early Decorated canopied one (the effigy has been several times renewed) is that of Bishop de Merton (d. 1277). Then there is the tomb-chest of an unidentified prior.

The two E. bays of the transept were separate chapels but are now one, St John the Baptist's. The tomb-chest in the left arch is of Bishop Lowe (d. 1467). An interesting series of memorials inside the chapel is to clerical members of the Warner family: John (d. 1679), Bishop John (d. 1666) by Joshua Marshall, and Archdeacon Lee (d. 1698). The painting within the bishop's monument is Venetian of *c*. 1500, and depicts St Sebastian and St Roch. Under the arch to the presbytery is the effigy of Bishop John de Sheppey (d. 1360), with much original colouring though the canopy is a restoration. Some 13th c. tiles can be found under a rug near the way out of the chapel. The ironwork on the S. side of the Sheppey tomb (seen by going round the 19th c. pulpit into the **presbytery**) is 16th c.

The presbytery is a distinguished piece of Early English work, unusual in having neither triforium nor aisles but instead a series of bays which contain tombs. Again the vaulting is sexpartite. Much of the interior including the reredos is Scott's work (1883). The brass communion rail is fashioned like wrought iron. On the N. side the second tomb, with arcaded front, may be that of Bishop de Glanville (d. 1214). The third, with Purbeck marble effigy and heavy canopy, is probably of Bishop de St Martin (d. 1274). Those on the S. side begin on the left with a shapeless wooden effigy (possibly Bishop Gundulf); the next is that of Bishop Ingoldsthorpe (d. 1291). Below the late 14th c. triple sedilia is the late 13th c. coffin-lid of another bishop.

In the **SE. transept**, which repeats the NE., the first bay contains St Peter's chapel, the second the ambitious Decorated doorway to the chapter room (now library). Its sculpture is much renewed – prophets and teachers above, and on the jambs allegories of the victorious Church and the blindfold Synagogue. On the right pier of the arch leading back into the main transept is a framed 14th c. painted panel of a screen. The walls and columns here lean outwards considerably and Cottingham thickened the main S. wall (blocking the stair) to strengthen it. In the centre arch is a foliated coffin-lid; above is the kneeling brass figure of Dean Cane (d. 1913).

Now the **quire**, left till after the remainder of the E. end because its character is still so much determined by the solid early Norman walls each side, an unusual arrangement. But in the 13th c. the walls

were refaced, with high wall-arcading and shafted clerestory, and
more sexpartite vaulting. The unendingly repeated lions and fleurs-
de-lys were done in 1876 under Scott, copying some medieval
fragments that remained. At the NE. is a more genuine 13th c.
painting of the Wheel of Fortune. The bishop's throne is Victorian
and also the stalls (by Scott) but the latter include some early 13th c.
arcaded work in the back row (claimed to be the oldest stallwork
in England) as well as some panelled fronts in the middle row said
to be of 1541 and therefore equally unusual in date. On this side of
the pulpitum, too, there is some 13th c. wood arcading.

Back now via the SE. transept into the **S. quire aisle**, a strangely
planned space little more really than a big vestibule with flights of
steps. Half-way along is a big buttress to support the quire vault. On
the right the medieval wooden partitioning enclosed a vestry, and
(looking back towards the transept) on the E. wall are Hanoverian
royal arms. At the bottom of the first steps is a tomb recess, and
then another flight leads into the **crypt** through a 13th c. doorway.
Two groin-vaulted Norman bays remain under the E. end of the
quire, but otherwise the crypt is 13th c. and it extends under all the
E. part of the cathedral with varied round and octagonal columns.

To the left as one enters, i.e. in the Norman W. part, are a rather
inaccurate model of the cathedral as it was, and some Civil War
relics. There is also a ship model (the *West Kent*, 1838). The chapel
at the NE. is dedicated to St Ithamar and that in the E. part to the
Holy Trinity; an intricate piece of stone carving on the sill of the
latter is probably part of a screen. Various quaint medieval graffiti
can be found on the crypt walls and columns, and remains of wall-
paintings under the SE. transept.

Back in the **S. quire aisle**, the tomb recess on the right is of Bishop
de Bradfield (d. 1283), but the badly damaged effigy in it is said to
be rather older. Here is the cathedral shop, and on the W. wall a
blocked 13th c. doorway. On the right, before the arch into the main
transept, are some modest memorials to cathedral vergers, organists
and others.

The **S. transept** differs considerably from the N. The vault, for
example, is of three bays, not sexpartite, and of wood. The windows
are different in number and type, the lower main ones having 'Y'
tracery, an indication of later date. This seems to have been a
favourite part of the cathedral for memorials, and the following are
the principal. On the W. wall: Sir William Franklin (d. 1833), with
white marble bust by Samuel Joseph; and Sir Richard Head
(d. 1689), said to be by Grinling Gibbons. In the centre of the S.

wall: the jack-in-a-box type of bust of Richard Watts, a 1736 copy of a 16th c. original, and below it a poor brass to the novelist Charles Dickens (d. 1870). On a free-standing tomb is the white marble effigy of Dean Hole (d. 1905), by F. W. Pomeroy. On the W. side of the transept, the screen to the Lady chapel is of 1928. The medieval wall-paintings high on the E. wall should also be noted.

Next a closer look at the **crossing**, where the flat panelled wooden ceiling has some remains of old colouring. The pulpitum as seen from this side is entirely of 1888.

The S. nave aisle has a separate, late 15th c., arcade to the **Lady chapel**, with a low stone screen. The ugly monument between the first and second bays is to county regiments in South Africa (1903). The chapel entrance is in the third bay; but first notice the 13th c. foliage carving incongruously done on a Norman-type capital of the main arcade at the point where rebuilding petered out. The chapel roof is a 19th c. copy and the glass is of *c.* 1890–1920. In the floor are two deeply engraved 18th c. black ledger stones. Continuing down the **S. aisle**, the outer wall is early Norman. The very large monuments on it are to Ann Henniker (d. 1792), with Coade stone figures of Truth and Time by Thomas Banks, and to Lord Henniker (d. 1803), with two more female figures by John Bacon junior. Then a 17th c. and an 18th c. tablet, and on the right the round marble font by Thomas Earp (1893). The Norman doorway to the SW. stair turret has somewhat unusual Greek key ornament, and on the W. wall the Norman arcading encloses mosaic war memorial panels of which the less said the better.

The **outside** walk has to be in two parts, of which the S. with the cloister is here taken first. The S. aisle wall is late 11th c. with later windows and parapet, and the clerestory 15th c. Then comes the Lady chapel which may be as late as 1510. Further up the road is the 15th c. Prior's Gate. Turn left instead into the churchyard and pass the early 13th c. S. transept and Cottingham's big flying buttress against the quire aisle, to reach the cloister which lies, unusually, beside the E. end instead of the nave. Only low walls remain on the W. side, except for a small gateway at its far end. The entire S. side is Roman wall, on which the refectory was built; the two arches towards its W. end were the washplace. On the E. side is early 12th c. wall-arcading all along, with openings and once-fine carving marking the chapter house entrance and, to its right, the way to the dormitory. Beyond is the former Deanery.

Starting again at the W. front: the gatehouse to the N. is College (or Cemetery) Gate, and the church is St Nicholas'. The road beside that leads to the Deanery (or Sextry) Gate, passing (between the transepts) the stump of the late 11th c. Gundulf's tower. Its top storey was removed in the 18th c. To the left are war memorial gates and a view into the High Street, and on the right the N. side of the quire with its crypt and finally (seen from the garden) the E. end, much remodelled by Scott, with the chapter room beyond.

St Albans, St Alban (Church of England, Hertfordshire)

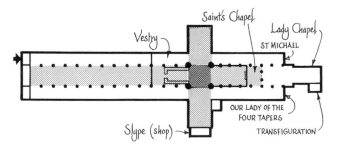

Like Brecon and Southwark, this is a purely monastic church which survived the Reformation, became a parish church, and was only created a cathedral in recent times (1877). The date of the original church, built on the site of the martyrdom of St Alban, is unknown but a monastery is supposed to have existed in the 7th c., and by 1163 it was recognized as the premier among English abbeys. The present building was begun in 1077 and completed in its initial form about 1089. It consisted of the present tower, crossing and transept, with nave and aisles three bays shorter than now, quire with three-apsed end extending as far as the present ambulatory, and two more apses to the east of each transept.

Late in the 12th c., lengthening of the nave by the three extra bays was begun, the westernmost Norman bays (one on one side but two on the other) being rebuilt at the same time, as well as parts of the S. presbytery aisle. For lack of funds, this nave work was never vaulted, and the new W. front, lacking its intended towers, was not finished till about 1230.

Soon after that, in 1257, a complete rebuilding of the E. parts was begun in a style which, by the time the Lady chapel was finished early in the 14th c., had progressed from Early English to Decorated. Hardly was that achieved when, in 1323, five bays of the

S. arcade collapsed: these were rebuilt to harmonize with the Early
English W. bays, by then outdated. Unfortunately the work never
proceeded further than funds and absolute necessity dictated, and so
the St Alban's nave was left with its extraordinary lack of balance
between N. and S.

With the Dissolution all the monastic buildings were swept away,
except the great gatehouse. The Lady chapel became a grammar
school, the ambulatory a thoroughfare, and a dwindling portion of
the remainder a parish church which was always far too big to be
maintained properly. Restoration, long overdue, was commenced by
Sir George Gilbert Scott in 1856 but later both financed and
designed by Lord Grimthorpe, a lawyer and amateur architect. At
the time of his taking over, in 1880, the building had recently been
designated a cathedral. He provided a complete new W. front and
new ends to the transepts and made the entire building secure. What
he did was and still is fiercely criticized on aesthetic grounds.

Entry into the S. quire aisle is often possible, but the main way in
is at the W. end, where the impact of Lord Grimthorpe's W. front is
inescapable. Its chief faults are its lack of harmony and sympathy
with the mellow building behind – hard stone against the older

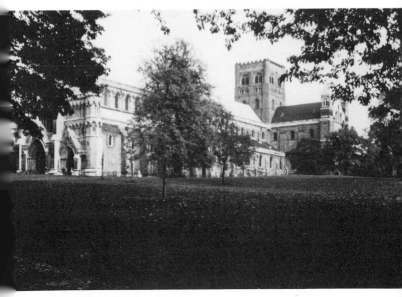

Cathedral from SW. St Albans

medley of reds and greys. Wherever he found Perpendicular work he
eliminated it in favour of his own version of Early English. Scott
had already raised the flat nave roof to a steep pitch, as well as the
first four bays of the S. aisle. Lord Grimthorpe built a new W. gable
to accommodate them and continued to raise the aisle and transept
roofs to about their original height. Far behind, but dominating the
cathedral even from this angle, is the great Norman central tower,
built almost entirely of Roman bricks salvaged from the city of
Verulamium. It once had a tall steeple and later a traditional
Hertfordshire 'spike' which was finally removed in the 1830s. Like
the inside brickwork it was plastered.

Lord Grimthorpe's features are perpetuated on the traditional
allegorical angel of St Matthew, to be seen in one of the spandrels of
the wall-arcading inside his central W. porch, on the left-hand side.

Inside, it is best to start by going up the steps and sitting near the
back of the nave. Looking E: the stone screen forms a very definite
break three bays before the crossing; those three bays, which are the
quire, are Norman and from this distance hardly visible. On the N.
side the six bays W. of the screen are Norman too. Then come four
Early English bays. These represent the late 12th c. extension which
was never properly finished, nor vaulted. On the S. side the same
extension shows as five bays (at the W. end); then there is a break
and finally five more bays back to the screen, more or less matching
the first five. This is the part that was rebuilt after the collapse of
1323. The ceiling throughout is plain flat wood, except that beyond
the screen it is painted. The wall-paintings on the E. parts of the N.
arcade are also prominent. The aisle vaults and windows are 19th c.
Behind, the W. window glass is by Sir Ninian Comper, a 1914–18
war memorial.

The rigid internal divisions rather restrict circulation, and the
following route will be found similar to that marked by blue and
yellow signs, which are however changed according to
circumstances.

In the **N. nave aisle** the classical black and white marble font with
three-tiered columned cover was designed by Randoll Blacking
(1933). The traceried door standing against the wall, and another in
the S. aisle opposite, are late 14th c. from the former W. entrance. In
the aisle wall are slight traces of another arcade that opened into a
chapel of St Andrew; the doorway in the fifth bay led to it. Further
along the N. aisle are the great Norman piers: in front of each must
have stood an altar and above each altar site is a 13th c. painted
Crucifixion with one or more figures of saints below. The arch soffits

are painted with patterns, fragments of a decorative scheme that once covered the whole church, making the architecture much less severe. It is probably the use of Roman bricks that caused these arcades to be even more gaunt and unrefined than is normal in work of this early period: they look in fact little more than openings carved out of a massive wall and are hardly arcades at all in the true sense, though towards the screen there has been some attempt at chiselling rude pilasters. The triforium and clerestory are not in their original form but were altered in the 15th c. when the roof was lowered.

Stepping into the **nave** past the fourth Norman pier, one can see more wall-paintings facing outwards. These are 14th c. The simple nave stalls are the work of George Pace. A 19th c. traceried oak pulpit has replaced Lord Grimthorpe's giant, and the altar rail is simple 20th c. The stone rood screen, forming a reredos with two doorways, is late 15th c.; the statues originally in the niches have gone.

This is also the point to examine the Early English arcades and to compare the 14th c. work with the late 12th c. bays which it so consciously imitated. The differences are fairly subtle, though quite obvious in the triforium: cinquefoiled arches, foliage ornament instead of dog-tooth, and portrait-heads as label-stops where previously it had been intended to bring down vaulting shafts. The odd thing about the earlier triforium (that of the W. bays) is the unorthodox way in which the enriched moulding of the inner twin arches runs into an identical moulding of the outer arch instead of being set back in a different plane.

Back in the **N. aisle** the wall-paintings continue. On the left are various monuments to the Hertfordshire Yeomanry, and a book of honour. The altar, with its four statues, stands in front of a 19th c. continuation of the screen, which forms another reredos concealing the vestries behind. So to reach the quire it is necessary to cross to the S. aisle, go through the wooden screen, and turn left beneath the organ.

From its W. end the **quire** is like a magnificent cruciform church in itself. Essentially Norman except in its E. bay, the severity of its architecture is tempered by the splendour of its fittings. The reredos and the four great tower arches, each 55 ft high, dominate it, and light streams in through both transepts. The flat wood ceiling of the quire proper, painted with coats of arms and sacred monograms, is late 15th c. That of the presbytery, continuing beyond the reredos and over the Saint's chapel, is a 13th c. wooden vault painted in the

15th c. and restored in recent years. More wall-paintings are prominent: more arch patterns for example, and two painted saints high on the N. side. The rich stalls, as well as the bishop's throne by the SW. pier of the crossing, are by John Oldrid Scott (1905–8). The organ case is mostly his too, but the more classical centre section is by Cecil Brown (1962).

The **crossing** itself contains the 19th c. quire pulpit of stone and grey marble, and the bronze eagle lectern. Above the great arches are, in effect, a triforium and clerestory and above that another flat ceiling, painted early in the 16th c.

Next the **presbytery**, E. of the crossing and up five steps. Though the 13th c. rebuilding started here, the first five bays are still Norman at the base. They are virtually solid walling with Early English detail applied. The triforium and clerestory are quite different from those of the nave. To the left of the sanctuary is the chantry of Abbot Ramryge (d. 1519), the latest and most elaborate of the pre-Reformation monuments; it is fan-vaulted within. The great reredos with its three tiers of very richly canopied niches is of about 1490, but all the figures are replacements of 1884–90. The Resurrection panel immediately over the altar is by Sir Alfred Gilbert of Eros fame. To the right is the chantry of Abbot William of Wallingford (d. 1492), which is entered from the aisle.

Amongst the unusual embossed tiles on the presbytery floor are numerous tomb-slabs with brass matrices and some with actual brasses (the best are protected by rugs). Towards the NE. of the main floor is that of Abbot Stone who d. 1451 (a fine canopy, but little else); just S. of it, Brother Robert Beauver, *c.* 1460 (a figure in gown and cowl); and S. of that again, Sir Anthony Grey (d. 1480), richly accoutred in mail. Then just W. of the last, but a fragment of the marginal inscription only: Abbot John de Berkhampstead (d. 1302).

The Norman purity of the **N. transept** has been shattered by Lord Grimthorpe's so-called Bankers' window, with circles of different sizes representing coins. Otherwise the transepts closely resemble those of St Etienne at Caen (the first Norman abbot was Paul of Caen). The design is less austere than the Norman nave arcades and includes in the triforium some Saxon balusters re-used from the previous church. Starting from the corner nearest the organ, there are, first, doors to the vestries, capped by a crown, lion and unicorn removed from a former mayoral pew. The marble tomb-chest is that of Bishop Claughton, the first bishop (d. 1895). On the N. wall is a tablet to Christopher Rawlinson (d. 1733). The glass in the two small windows above is 19th c. but one has medieval vine pattern on the arch. The openwork tomb-chest is that of Bishop Blomfield (d. 1894). In the window to the right is a little ancient glass. Then come two old chests and a white memorial to Frederica Mure (d. 1834), by Sir Francis Chantrey. To the left of the N. presbytery aisle arch is an elaborate 15th c. painting of Doubting Thomas.

Next, through the wrought-iron gates, the **N. presbytery aisle**. The first bay has a groined Norman vault, but the rest is 13th c. and has a wall-arcade. Over the doorway to the right is a painted panel from the tower ceiling, renewed in 1952. Further on, beside the steps, are royal arms of about 1700 and two nice cartouches of the same period. Next comes the Ramryge chantry, already seen from the presbytery side. Facing a 15th c. doorway in the outer wall is one of the entrances to the Saint's chapel, and in the centre of the aisle floor at that point is a worn brass to Thomas Fayrman (d. 1411) and his wife. Then on the left is the 14th c. shrine of St Amphibalus, built up from shattered fragments, and opposite it the back of the watching chamber, to be seen presently from the Saint's chapel. The carvings of rural scenes and pastimes are interesting; they continue on the S. side.

The chapel at the end of the aisle is **St Michael's**, restored and refitted as a World War I memorial. These two bays, together with the chapel of Four Tapers opposite and the retro-quire between, were the last part built before the Lady chapel.

Three large moulded arches separate the retro-quire from the **Saint's chapel** and mark the E. end of the 13th c. building. The centre one forms the main entry to the chapel; from inside the chapel can be seen the extraordinary bits of miniature tracery above the capitals and, down in the lower left corner, behind protective glass, a medieval painting of Archbishop Fitzherbert of York. The further end is enclosed by the back of the great reredos, resurfaced this side, and in the centre of the chapel stands St Alban's shrine, early 14th c. but completely reconstructed in 1872 after being found in 2000 pieces. The spiky black and gilt kneeling rail, Cross and candlesticks and pendant light are recent work by George Pace. On the N. is the wooden loft, *c.* 1480, in the upper level of which a custodian always kept watch. In the base are cupboards with various museum pieces, and a narrow stair. Opposite is the chantry of Humphrey Duke of Gloucester (d. 1447). Richly panelled and niched in its upper parts, it is open at floor level like a triple triumphal arch so as not to impede the view of the shrine; the grille now closing it is a rare example of 13th c. ironwork and does not belong.

Now back to the retro-quire and the **Lady chapel**. The last part of
the cathedral to be built, and the most lavish in detail, it is early
14th c., Decorated. The ball-flower ornament round the windows is
typical. The tiny saints in niches in their reveals are much less usual.
The stone vault and foliage corbels are 19th c., also the present wall-
arcading. A blocked opening between the piscina and sedilia in the
SE. corner opened into the tiny chapel of the Transfiguration; this
was rebuilt by Lord Grimthorpe and is reached by a doorway to the
right of the sedilia.

Sometimes the Lady chapel seats are reversed to face a platform
in the retro-quire, where the shrine of St Amphibalus originally
stood. To the left is the SE. **chapel of Our Lady of the Four Tapers**,
which is 13th c. The wall-arcading, richer than elsewhere, is much
renewed, and there is a three-arched piscina. On the right is a
pieced-together armoured figure of an Earl of Huntingdon.

This leads into the **S. presbytery aisle**, architecturally the most
complex part of the cathedral, for so many building phases are
intermingled. In general it is evident that the walls and vaults are
earlier as one moves W. The openings and arches in the outer wall
were connected with chapels that are now gone. On the right is the
Gloucester chantry again and then, just past the doorway to the
shrine, three memorials to the Maynard family: Radulph (d. 1613)
wholly painted on the wall, with kneeling figure; Raffe (d. 1613), a
wooden tablet; and Charles (d. 1665), a more orthodox tablet
beneath. Beneath again is a quite plain tomb-chest, and under a mat
in the aisle floor close to that is the brass of Ralph Rowlatt (d. 1543)
and his wife.

Down the steps on the right is the Wallingford chantry, already
seen from the presbytery. This is now furnished for private prayer as
the Blessed Sacrament chapel and the minor brasses formerly
displayed in it are now in a vestry. Its former attribution to Abbot
Wheathampstead is now considered incorrect. Its vault and
ironwork are specially noteworthy.

The aisle vaulting changes from quadripartite to groined in the
last two bays, which are Norman. On the left are some exposed and
restored pieces of Norman arches which had been obliterated by
later work. High on the right is a quaint painted memorial to a
Dutchman, John Hylocomius (d. 1595); then a poor-box with a 17th
c. wooden figure above it, begging for alms. Still on the right are
two stone coffins and a 16th c. panel from the N. transept roof
painted with a representation of St Alban's martyrdom.

The **S. transept**, much of which is a sales area pending completion of the new chapter house and visitors' centre, is like the N. transept but its five lancets, again by Lord Grimthorpe, form a less ugly termination. In the triforium some of the brick arches and spandrels have been restored and left exposed. The richly carved doorway in the N. wall is basically Norman, later than the transept itself, though its inner arch is a 19th c. embellishment intended by his lordship to confound his antiquarian critics. It leads to the slype, the passage between the transept and the (destroyed) chapter house. The slype itself is rebuilt and is now used as a shop; it contains numerous fragments of Norman and later carving. On the W. side are displayed a collection of roof bosses, three 16th and 17th c. bread cupboards with balustered fronts, and the magnificent brass of Abbot de la Mare (d. 1396). This is of Flemish workmanship and one of the largest and most elaborate in existence.

Finally the **S. nave aisle**, back to the W. end, the first three bays being those alongside the quire and thus Norman. In the first bay is the rich doorway to the vanished cloister, later 14th c. with a niche each side and traceried doors. On the right are some museum cases, with a list of bishops, deans, etc. Next on the left is the canopied tomb of two hermits, Roger of Markyate and Sigar of Northaw (c. 1330), followed by a memorial with busts of John Thrale (d. 1704) and his wife. Opposite is a good tablet of standard 18th c. type to William King (d. 1766). The next five bays, alongside the nave proper, are part of the 14th c. rebuilding and have their original vaults, but those of the last five are 19th c.

The abbey gatehouse lies straight ahead as one leaves the W. entrance; the extensive domestic buildings lay to the left of it. It is late 14th c., and survived through being used as a prison. The grammar school was moved to it from the Lady chapel in 1871.

The N. side of the cathedral is rather featureless, and interest centres on the tower and N. transept, red with Roman bricks: but the smooth-faced ones in the transept ends are Lord Grimthorpe's. He added the transept turrets and, further round, he virtually rebuilt the outside of the Lady chapel. The area SE. of the cathedral is called Sumpter Yard: approach from this direction leads to the aisle doorway already mentioned, which is not always open. The great cedar tree was actually brought from the Lebanon. Past this, a new chapter house is being built on the site of the old.

Hardly a vestige remains above ground of the monastic buildings which stood beyond. From the arcading on the S. wall beyond the transept, however, it is clear where the cloister stood. It is the city's good fortune that the great sweep of land from here down to the abbey fishpond in the valley and beyond has hardly been built on.

St Andrews, St Andrew [Scottish Development Department] (Fife)

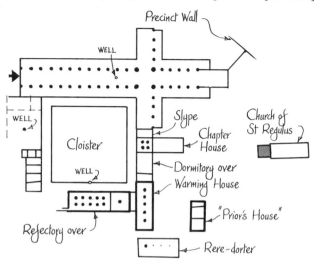

St Regulus is said to have founded a monastery, probably in the 8th c., around the relic of St Andrew he had brought from Greece. The bishopric was transferred from Abernethy in 908. During the 12th c. the Augustinian order gradually displaced the Celtic, and the church of St Regulus (most of which still stands) was enlarged to serve as a cathedral.

The great new cathedral, which was also the church of the priory, was begun about 1160. It was the largest church in Scotland and at one time the longest in Britain except Norwich. The quire was completed by 1238; the whole building was consecrated in 1318. A serious fire about 1380 occasioned extensive rebuilding, which was not completed till 1440. An archbishopric was established in 1472. After the Reformation the usual desecration, pillaging and theft of materials occurred. The cathedral ruins were taken over by the Barons of the Exchequer in 1826 and the priory buildings by the Ministry of Works in 1946. Admission to the churchyard and ruins is free during the usual Scottish Development Department hours, but a charge is made for entry to the museum in the priory warming-house.

From the NW. gate of the churchyard the general layout is easily

Nave and Quire, looking towards E. gable, St Andrews

grasped. On the left the E. gable is prominent, and on the right, close to the road, the W. front. In between stands the whole S. nave aisle wall, curiously intact; behind that were the monastic buildings. The **W. front** should be examined first. Following storm damage this was rebuilt two bays inwards about 1275 and a galilee porch built outside; parts of its side walls and vault corbels are visible. After the fire a century later it was removed and the upper part of the front, above the wall-arcading, rebuilt.

Within the **nave** it is just possible to imagine the former grandeur, though so little is left but marked-out column bases. In the S. wall, however, even the windows are fairly complete; the change from round-arched late 12th c. work to two-light 13th c. windows is misleading, for all but the two W. bays are really 12th c. and the later windows indicate a partial rebuilding which probably included the vaults also. Their springers and wall-shafts can be seen. Further E. in the nave is a deep well believed to have been originally put in for masons' use.

Continuing E., the **N. transept** has little left but foundations, but its three E. chapels are clear enough. In the **S. transept** the 12th c. W. wall is nearly complete, with intersecting wall-arcading at its base; much of the remainder is early 15th c., again with three chapels. In its SW. corner is the night stair that led down from the dormitory. Of several floor-slabs one has been identified as that of Canon Cathall (d. 1380).

Next the **quire**, where the bases of several clustered piers remain (late 12th c.). Tomb slabs here include the great Tournai marble one set up on medieval stone coffins at the top of the sanctuary steps, roughly where the high altar once stood. The E. wall can now be clearly seen to be almost entirely 12th c. but with a 15th c. window inserted. Originally there were three rows of round-headed windows: the second is clearly delineated, the third less obvious.

Now the monastic buildings, commencing to the SE. of the S. transept with the clearly defined **chapter house**. It has several medieval coffins in the floor and on its S. wall retains the wall-arcading that backed the seats. This and what is left of a splendid doorway are clearly 13th c. Going next towards the cloister: there is a vestibule which was the original chapter house; this has a triple doorway to the cloister, with nail-head ornament. Another arch, closer to the transept, led to the slype. Above all this range was the dormitory.

The **cloister** walks have gone but the layout is clear enough, with doorways at the NW. (13th c.) and NE. (12th c.) into the S. aisle. The well in the centre of the S. side served the washplace. The S. range, the undercroft of the refectory, was virtually rebuilt in the 19th c. The W. range, standing to the full height of its lower storey, was used for storage. It is a good idea to pass round to the back of this, thus seeing the inside of the priory's outer wall, and then to go along the outside of the S. range: the bulbous projection, preserved in the restoration, was the support for the refectory pulpit. A doorway at the end leads back into the cloister, but beyond is a projecting wing, the end of the dormitory range with the (restored) vaulted warming-house in its undercroft, now the museum. To the right of the roadway the room with a single standing column was the rere-dorter; the main priory drain passes along its further side.

On the left of the road is another building, called the Prior's House and now a store for post-Reformation tombstones. The priory wall here has a re-entrant angle, and it is best to follow it to the N. and then to turn W., back into the E. walk of the cloister; the museum entrance will be found in the SE. corner passage. Displayed here are numerous carved memorial stones, many being of the 8th, 9th and 10th cc., as well as some medieval fragments.

The church of St Regulus or Rule, just to the E., should certainly

be included in a visit, since it was the cathedral's immediate
predecessor. It is remarkable for its 108 ft tower and is thought to
date from the 1070s and to have been extended E. and W. *c.* 1130 to
serve as a cathedral. The roofless walls E. of the tower represent the
quire; beyond that was a 12th c. sanctuary which has disappeared.
The nave, the 12th c. addition W. of the tower, has also gone; the
stair was put in in 1789. Remarkable resemblances have been found
between this church and those of Wharram-le-Street in Yorkshire
and Aubazine in Aquitaine. In the churchyard are countless post-
Reformation grave-stones and memorials of great historical and
artistic interest.

The 14th c. priory wall was strengthened about 1516 and was
about a mile long. Most of it can be followed, but the following
circuit takes in only half. It starts with the 14th c. main gatehouse
called the Pends, SW. of the cathedral. The road passes through it,
and then roughly bisects the former precinct. Leaving the cathedral
on the left, it leads down the hill to the harbour gate, called Mill
Port. By turning left beyond that, a path can be followed just
outside the wall, leading along the cliff top, past the exposed
foundation of the 12th c. church of St Mary of the Rock, and either
back again to the end of North Street or on to the castle, which was
the bishops' and archbishops' residence.

St Asaph, St Asaph (Church in Wales, Clwyd)

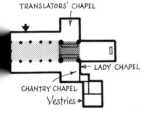

As elsewhere in Celtic Britain, church history is here inextricably
mixed with legend. A date in the 6th c. is accepted for the setting up
of a monastery here by the Scottish bishop Kentigern, and Asaph
was his successor. After that very little is known for seven whole
centuries, half the entire life of the settlement. That hardly a
fragment of Norman work survives, and nothing at all of earlier
date, cannot be unconnected with St Asaph's vulnerable position on

the coastal plain. It is surprising that so small a cathedral establishment held its ground at all. When eventually the building was destroyed by the Earl of Warwick's soldiers, a plan was approved for re-erecting it by the castle at Rhuddlan. That of course never happened, for other counsels prevailed.

Thus the cathedral as it stands is mostly of the 14th c., and it was probably complete by 1380. In 1402, however, it suffered again, along with much of its property, during Owain Glyndwr's rebellion, and the present nave clerestory and the roofs date from the subsequent restoration. A consequence of the periods of neglect and vandalism of the 17th c. was that the chapter house on the N. side of the quire was demolished in 1779. Worse, the nave roof was taken down in 1811 and worship thereafter was confined to the quire.

An extensive restoration under Sir George Gilbert Scott took place in 1869–75, and many of the furnishings and fittings date from those or subsequent years. The quire in particular was virtually rebuilt.

The usual **entrance** is by the N. doorway (there is no porch), and the first impression is that this is like a fairly large parish church – though cruciform churches in Wales are not exactly frequent. The low 14th c. arcades carry their mouldings right to the floor without any capitals; the clerestory was built (or rebuilt) after Glyndwr's activities, and the timber 'vault' is Scott's work. The grey stone walling which dominates the interior must originally have been plastered and painted.

In the **N. aisle** stands a fine iron chest made in 1738 for the cathedral plate and now used as a collecting box. Past a number of minor wall monuments is the entrance to what is now called the Translators' chapel in the N. transept; it is set aside for services in Welsh and for private prayer. The name recalls the men who, from the Reformation up to 1630, worked on the translation of the Bible and Prayer Book into Welsh and who were nearly all closely connected with St Asaph diocese. Here are two more 18th c. tablets.

Next the **crossing**, with choir stalls. The wooden 'vault' above is Scott's work of about 1870. The canons' stalls are in the **presbytery**, with the bishop's throne at the far end on the right. A large part of this woodwork, with its bold crocketed pinnacles, is late 15th c.: many layers of paint and grime had to be removed in the 1870 restoration. Scott's work in the presbytery amounted to a virtual rebuilding in Early English style (except for the E. window) which is at odds with the rest of the building. His is the inappropriate reredos of Derbyshire alabaster, and his the restoration from fragments of the sedilia and piscina. The glass in the great E. window is a memorial to Bishop Carey.

Now back to the nave, past the brass eagle lectern (another Scott fitting) and into the **S. transept**, where there are two altars and two quite separately fitted out chapels side by side. The left one, with a heraldic window over the altar and a wrought-iron screen beside it, is the Lady chapel. The other, with a stone altar and black and gold pews, is merely called the Chantry chapel. Though modern in their furnishings, these chapels perpetuate in their names a tradition dating from 1336. A doorway in the SE. corner of the transept leads to the new vestry block by E. A. Roiser (1956).

Finally the **S. aisle**. Amongst the monuments are one very new – a slate tablet to the explorer H. M. Stanley – and one very old – the effigy of the second Bishop Anian (d. 1293) under whom much of the present cathedral was built. The font at the W. end is of standard 15th c. design, but largely modern owing to Civil War damage.

In the SW. corner of the churchyard, beneath the building that now houses the diocesan registry, is a small museum which the verger will open on request. It contains various archaeological and documentary relics and should certainly be visited by anyone making a detailed study of the district. Closer to the N. side of the cathedral is a pinnacled memorial of typical Victorian outline commemorating (like the chapel inside) the 16th and 17th c. Translators.

The tower is best appreciated from this angle. The line of the old presbytery roof can clearly be seen on its E. face, and at its NE. angle is a stair turret that sweeps without a pause from the ground to the battlements.

Passing round the E. end, perhaps regretting Scott's harsh mechanical detailing, one comes to the outside of the 1956 vestries. Facing them on the other side of the road is the Dean Williams Library, founded in 1893. Completing the circuit past the S. side and W. front: the only objects of special note are the two conspicuous matching table-tombs outside the W. doorway, commemorating Bishop Barrow (d. 1669) and Bishop Vowler Short (d. 1846).

St Davids, St David (Church in Wales, Dyfed)

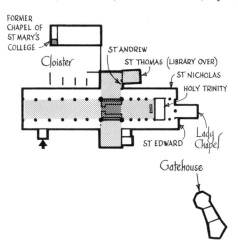

St David's is reputed to be among the oldest surviving cathedral foundations in Britain, but its real origins are lost amidst the tangle of early history and legend. St David (Dewi) lived in the 6th c. and little is certain about his life except his saintliness and his rule of this, his monastery. The Celtic Christian church, vigorous and independent, was to maintain its position here until long after the Norman Conquest. Eventually it was subjugated, the organization brought into line with English secular cathedrals, and the cathedral itself rebuilt. Visits by Henry II and a great influx of pilgrims to St David's shrine meant that within 50 years (by about 1180) a more ambitious rebuilding could commence: that is the basically cruciform structure which exists today.

In 1220 the tower collapsed and was rebuilt; also St Thomas's chapel was added E. of the N. transept. Next the E. end was extended by piercing the walls and prolonging the aisles eastwards clear of the E. wall, linking them with an ambulatory and then, around 1300, adding the Lady chapel at the extreme E. Then the NE. and SE. chapels were added.

In the next phase of work, around 1330–45, much of the main walling (including the tower) was raised in height and larger, Decorated, windows inserted. A chapter house was built over St Thomas's chapel, and a treasury on top of that, the Lady chapel

was rebuilt, and the S. porch added. Within the cathedral the
pulpitum was rebuilt, while beyond the stream to the W. the
Bishop's Palace was enlarged. A college of priests was founded later
in the century and a cloister built for them adjoining the N. side of
the cathedral.

In the 15th c. many of the main roofs were reconstructed because
they and the walls supporting them had become unsafe. Early in
the 16th c. yet another stage was added to the tower, and numerous
improvements and additions were made to chapels and chantries
throughout the cathedral, including the construction of the fan
vaulted Holy Trinity chapel where hitherto there had been an open
area.

After the usual sorry story of abandonment of the chapels and
subsidiary buildings and centuries of semi-neglect, John Nash of
Regent's Park fame made an ill-judged remodelling of the W. front
in 1793, and eventually Sir George Gilbert Scott carried out a
proper programme of repairs including the securing of the
remaining Norman tower arch, a more harmonious reconstruction
of the W. front, and the provision of a drainage system to prevent

Cathedral from SW. St Davids

further settlement of the old walling.

The way from the village passes beneath the octagonal gatehouse-tower, Porth-y-Twr. Only in this century has this been given its intended ring of bells. From here is the best general view of the cathedral with its basically Norman cruciform arrangement and its central tower, 16th c. in its top stage, 14th c. in the 'lantern' and 13th c. in the lower parts. Of the main clerestories the nave is Norman and the presbytery Early English, but most of the other windows are Decorated insertions more or less contemporary with the Lady chapel on the far right. Over to the left stand the extensive ruins of the Bishop's Palace.

A long flight of steps leads to the 14th c. porch. Inside the **nave** the alternation of round and octagonal columns in the powerful Norman arcades is disguised by their attached shafts. The arches themselves have a diversity of moulding and ornament and support only one further storey of arcading, within which the triforium and clerestory are both contained. This is an unusual arrangement, and surprisingly it is roughly contemporary with the early Gothic work at Wells – which shows what an impediment distance could then be to the spread of new ideas. The crossing-arch ahead is the only remaining one of the four under the tower which is still Norman in style – though it was in fact rebuilt by Scott. The richly panelled wooden ceiling represents the final stage of the general 15th c. reconstruction of roofs: obviously lower than the original, its essentially simple system of main ties and cross-beams was given a remarkably ornate, almost Moorish, appearance by the pendants and the delicately carved spandrels connecting them. Completing the eastward view is the rich but oddly asymmetrical 14th c. pulpitum, topped by the comparatively new organ case and hanging Rood (the organ itself is largely 19th c., but some parts are earlier).

In the **N. aisle**, the elegant internal flying buttresses inserted as part of the 15th c. operation to secure the main arcade and clerestory from further movement are prominent. The aisle roof has been reconstructed; the wooden 'vault' of the **N. transept** is 19th c. too. The E. arcade of the transept is 13th c. Within its central arch is the altar of St Andrew. The left arch leads into St Thomas's chapel. The library now housed there, open at advertised times, is reached by a stair from the N. quire aisle; it was originally the chapter house and treasury. Beneath the crossing-arch on the S. side of the transept are the shrine of St Caradoc and the effigy of a priest. Above is part of the organ case, and above again an oblique view into the tower, the 14th c. lantern storey being readily distinguishable. Its richly coloured 15th c. wooden vault features the coats of arms of former bishops.

Next the **N. quire aisle**. On the right is the plain back of St David's shrine, with holes for pilgrims' offerings, and this is followed by a 13th c. stone knight in armour. Further along, through a small doorway, are several other worn effigies, and then in the NE. corner of the cathedral the chapel of St Nicholas. Here two separate starts at stone vaulting can easily be seen, the actual roof of timber is quite recent, and the memorial E. window of this century is praiseworthy for its scale and lightness.

Before passing through the double Early English arch into the ambulatory, go back a few paces and through the early 16th c. stone screen into the little fan-vaulted **Holy Trinity chapel**, or Vaughan chantry. In another pilgrims' recess beneath the main E. window, in what was at first an external wall, rests a modern reliquary containing what are considered to be bones of St David himself, found in this wall during Scott's restoration in the 1860s. Over the altar opposite, the five reredos carvings are 14th c. and the niches each side 16th c., but the statues (of Bishop Vaughan the chapel's founder, and Giraldus, d. 1223) are modern. The style and quality of the fan vault show how much the interchange of ideas had quickened by the end of the Middle Ages.

Now return to the ambulatory, which leads through a glazed wrought-iron screen (1978) filling the double arch into the **Lady chapel**. Here the style is Decorated: the lierne vaults were built afresh about 1900, though their springer stones are ancient. The triple sedilia and the two tomb canopies (one with an effigy) have all suffered from this chapel's long state of ruin.

Another double arch leads to the SE. chapel, St Edward's. Here again there are vault springers but a modern timber roof. The alabaster effigy is of Viscountess Maidstone.

The return westward along the **S. quire aisle** leads past the stone screen at the S. end of the Trinity chapel, as well as a case with various relics of Queen Victoria's coronation, the back of the wooden sedilia of the quire, numerous medieval stone effigies (some of bishops, some unknown), and a stone with mitre and crossed croziers which came from Nash's W. front of 1793. But before passing through the Transitional arch into the S. transept, turn right into the **quire**.

Here the arches are pointed and therefore slightly later than the nave. There is no triforium, but evidently vaulting was intended. The present wooden roof, lavishly painted and gilded, is a reconstruction by Scott, who replaced the late Perpendicular E. window with a row of lancets (the three lancets below, rather strangely filled with Murano mosaics by Antonio Salviati, had already been blocked when the Trinity chapel was roofed in, and form a rather sombre backing to the high altar).

From the quire space itself the inside of the tower lantern is in full view. The stalls within the crossing-space below it are separated, unusually, from the presbytery by a light wooden parclose screen. They are also unusual in including places for the Bishop and for the Sovereign: the Bishop has, as well as his canopied and pinnacled throne, a stall just inside the quire on the S. side, while the Queen, who by tradition is a member of this and of no other chapter, has one in the SW. corner. Beneath the seats are fascinating miserere carvings of the first quality, and above is rich panelling capped by an openwork parapet. All this is late 15th and early 16th c. work.

In the centre of the presbytery is the tomb of Edmund Tudor (d. 1456), brought from the Greyfriars' church at Carmarthen by command of his grandson Henry VIII; the brasses in its upper slab are modern reproductions. On the N. side the triple arches at two levels are the late 13th c. front of St David's shrine; beyond is the tomb of Treasurer Thomas Lloyd (d. 1613). Opposite are the sedilia. Wooden sedilia are of considerable rarity, and these are most delicately carved; their beautifully embroidered backs are, of course, modern.

Now go on into the **S. transept** and look back at the arch from the S. quire aisle. Its curious buttress-pillar was probably part of Scott's programme of strengthening the tower. Much of this transept, lit by three stages of Perpendicular windows in its S. wall, is taken up with library and vestries, and these are supplemented by 19th c. additions on its E. side. On the E. wall, readily visible through the door in the first panelled screen, is the Abraham stone, a memorial to the sons of an 11th c. bishop. The reredos painting behind the small altar in this transept is apparently of Greek origin, the altar stone being an early portable one, perhaps dating from the time of St David himself.

Now pass across the end of the S. aisle and back into the nave, and stand before the pulpitum. Bishop Gower, who built it *c.* 1340, rests in the richly carved cinquefoil-arched chantry at its S. end. The niche between it and the archway leading to the quire contains a modern statue of St David with symbolic dove on his right shoulder Some of the ornamental features of the pulpitum must have been re used from the previous screen: this may help to explain the curious

lack of symmetry, which is largely disguised by the delicate rhythm
of the wooden rood-loft, echoing the parapet around the inside of
the quire. The other little chantries within its considerable thickness
are of unknown priests and have remains of original colouring.

Back in the S. aisle, the floor slope towards the W. is very
noticeable. Against the W. wall is a stone with a hollowed-out top
which, it is argued, could have been the font used by St David. The
present font close by is probably late 12th c., an octagonal bowl of
standard design on nine round columns.

Above the font the 'misplaced' round window is a visual reminder
of how far the design of the Nash W. front, of which this is a relic,
had strayed from the Norman original which Scott subsequently
endeavoured to restore. After going out of the S. door, turn right
towards the tiny river Alun. This favourite spot for visitors has
views of the W. front as well as the Palace ruins and St Mary's
College Chapel. This chapel, recently re-roofed for cathedral use as
a meeting hall, is not normally open, but anyone can wander into
the little walled garden at the back. In front of it lay the small
cloister, made even more confined by the great buttresses put in to
prop the N. side of the cathedral in the 15th c.

After walking past the E. end of the cathedral and back up to the
gatehouse, it is then possible to make a longer circuit down the hill,
past the Deanery (the white house near the bottom), and either to go
further afield to the remains of the medieval city wall, or to make
for the Bishop's Palace, now a state-conserved ruin.

St Paul's, St Paul (Church of England, London)

The first cathedral of London is said to have been built in 604. This,
or its successor, was burnt down in 1087 and replaced by the
Norman building which has become known as Old St Paul's. The
quire of this was rebuilt in the 13th c. to provide more space, the
total eventual length being 585 ft, 10 ft more than the present
cathedral. The spire added to the central tower in 1315 was 489 ft
high; there were also two W. towers and a detached bell-tower.
After the Reformation neglect set in and when the spire was
accidentally burnt down it was not renewed.

In the 17th c. Inigo Jones, commissioned to improve the
cathedral, refaced the nave and W. end in classical style with a
grand portico, just as he had seen churches in Italy transformed.
After the Commonwealth Wren made ready to continue hiding the

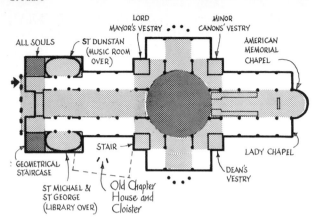

'Gothick rudeness of the old Design' by casing the inside of the nave
with Renaissance detail and by building a great dome over the
central crossing where the spire had been. These plans were abruptly
terminated by the Great Fire of 1666.

Not until 1675 was a scheme for complete rebuilding finally
approved. Wren had made several other designs, including that
illustrated by the so-called Great Model still in the cathedral. When
it came to actual building, he insisted on having a much freer hand,
and the cathedral seen to-day bears only a family resemblance to the
approved or 'Warrant' design. It was completed in 1710, when Wren
was seventy-eight.

From the outside, two of the most familiar features of St Paul's
are misleading. First of all, the outside dome is not the inside one: it
is many feet higher above the ground, leaving space between the two
for a great hollow cone of brick. This cone is the real supporter of
the stone lantern that seems to stand on the familiar hemisphere of
lead and itself carries the golden ball and Cross 365 ft above the
ground.

The other deception is in the outer walls. Built as two distinct
storeys, they suggest that the whole interior is as high as that. Inside,
however, the arrangement is a traditional high nave flanked by low
aisles. Wren adopted the medieval device of flying buttresses to
carry the thrusts of his nave vaults to the outer walls, but instead of
displaying the buttresses in the Gothic manner he screened them by
doubling the height of the outer walls – thus forming big hidden
open areas above the aisle roofs.

St Paul's Cathedral from SE., London

Inside the W. doors the first impression is one of spacious, but cool, grandeur. Fundamentally the plan is like those of most other great cathedrals, except for the wide expanse beneath the dome, a space so often severely constricted by the giant piers of a central tower. The pausing area at the W. end of the nave is flanked by oval chapels N. and S. Then there are arcades and aisles of three bays, leading to the dome space. Beyond that lie the quire and its aisles with arcades of three more bays, culminating in the great baldacchino.

This is a Baroque building, with an inventiveness of detail not to be found either in ancient classical buildings or in later Renaissance ones. Wren was an engineer as well as an architect and many of the apparent idiosyncracies in his designs can be traced to structural necessities. In addition he had the devoted and in many cases lifelong collaboration of many of the finest craftsmen of his time, in stone and metal and wood, and after one has either been overwhelmed by the building, or perhaps by long acquaintance come to terms with it, it is in the end their work as much as Wren's own which attracts and commands wonder and respect.

The quality of the monuments however ranges widely, and the selection here, out of the vast number to be seen, is dictated as much by notability or sheer size as by artistic worth. The clockwise sequence differs somewhat from the guided tours: they omit the upper galleries but include certain other parts not normally open to visitors.

Under the **NW. tower**, the chapel of All Souls contains the memorial to Lord Kitchener, carved by Sir William Reid Dick (1925). Next to it is the oval chapel of St Dunstan, reserved for private prayer. It has a marvellous screen with Corinthian columns, made by Jonathan Maine *c.* 1700.

Continuing along the **N. aisle**: the first prominent monument is of Lord Leighton (d. 1902), by Sir Thomas Brock. Next is that of General Gordon (d. 1885) by Sir Edgar Boehm, and under the arcade (better seen from the S. side) is Alfred Stevens's huge monument to the Duke of Wellington (d. 1852). In bay 3 the memorial of William and Frederick, Viscounts Melbourne (d. 1848 and 1853), by C. Marochetti, takes the form of Gates of Death guarded by angels.

At the corner of the **N. transept** the statue of Sir Joshua Reynolds (d. 1792), by John Flaxman, is one of four similar figures of Benefactors of the English People (the other three are by John Bacon); till these figures were put in, the cathedral had only the few

NW. Tower, St Paul's (1706–8)

monuments saved from the old building in 1666. The huge font of 1727 stands within a recently formed baptistry. Around it and along the N. wall are three big monuments to soldiers killed in the Napoleonic wars, and in the NW. corner the Middlesex Regimental chapel, with a 16th c. altarpiece (the Virgin with St Luke, possibly by Titian), and an altar on transparent plastic supports by Bernard Feilden. On the door of the aumbry in this chapel is a pelican in her piety carved by a cathedral craftsman in 1978. Two other large monuments to soldiers of the 1790s fill the flank walls on either side of the main transept area. The saucer dome above was badly damaged by one of the two high-explosive bombs which directly hit the cathedral in World War II.

This is a good point to go and sit somewhere in the vast space beneath the **dome**. Its breadth is that of nave and aisles together and the whole area comfortably seats more than 2000 people. In front is the quire, the vault mosaics of which were done in the 1890s by Sir William Richmond; the main subjects of the three saucer domes are the Creation of animals and trees, fishes and birds.

The great canopied oak pulpit, the fourth at least that the Wren cathedral has possessed, is by Lord Mottistone (1960). The bronze eagle lectern is of 1720. Overhead around the base of the dome is the Whispering Gallery, and above that the inner dome painted with scenes from the life of St Paul by Sir James Thornhill (1716–19). Lower down, the mosaics are 19th c.

The **quire** is not normally open to the public (except for the special tours) but most of it may be seen from either end. The grand baldacchino designed by Stephen Dykes Bower and Godfrey Allen stands close to where a bomb pierced the roof in 1940. The quire stalls are amongst the most splendid work of Grinling Gibbons, rich with columns and little cupolas, garlands and cherubs. Over their western end, half on each side, is the organ, its case equally richly carved; in Wren's time it stood at the quire entrance, with the stalls 'returned' under its E. side, as in a Gothic cathedral. Lately its mechanisms have again been altered, and a new series of trumpet pipes is prominent at the extreme W. end of the nave. Jean Tijou's beautiful wrought-iron screens are also in this part of the cathedral, though some have been moved about at various times. There is no finer craftsmanship of its kind anywhere in the world.

The right-hand (E.) side of the N. transept is not open to the public, but on the left, opposite the door to the Minor Canons' vestry, a bronze memorial to Sir Arthur Sullivan (d. 1900) by Sir William Goscombe John can be glimpsed; and, to the right of the door, a tablet to Sir John Stainer. The statue near the **N. quire aisle** entrance is of Dr Samuel Johnson. Within the aisle are two large copper candlesticks, the original of which, made for Wolsey's tomb, were sold by the Parliamentarians to the church of St Bavon, Ghent, whence these casts were obtained. Past them is a Tijou screen at the side of the sanctuary, and at the end the chapel of Modern Martyrs. From here steps lead up beside the high altar and baldacchino to the **American Memorial chapel**, with a roll of honour behind the high altar. (A copy of this roll, containing the names of all Americans who died in World War II, can be inspected in the S. aisle on request.) In the chapel windows is almost the only stained glass in the cathedral, by Brian Thomas.

The E. end of the **S. quire aisle** is the Lady chapel and has against its side wall a Madonna by Josephena de Vasconcellos (1957). Also on the left are monuments to Bishop Blomfield (d. 1857), by Richmond; John Donne (d. 1631), by Nicholas Stone (a macabre upright figure in a shroud, the only pre-Fire monument above the crypt); and – opposite – Bishop Creighton (d. 1901), a standing bronze figure by Sir Hamo Thornycroft.

The benefactor at the corner of the S. transept is John Howard. Round to the left is a bronze plaque to Captain Scott (d. 1912), and then the entrance to the **crypt** (a charge is made for admission).

Historically the crypt is the chapel of St Faith because St Faith's parish church was demolished in 1255 to make way for the quire extensions. The part beneath the quire is now largely taken up with the chapel of the Order of the British Empire; W. of it, the centre of the dome area is marked by a circle of Tuscan columns in contrast with the heavy piers elsewhere, and beyond is the nave crypt, some parts of which are in occasional use for exhibitions. The transept crypts are not open to the public, though there are plans for a treasury and a visitors' centre.

Go first along the right side of the S. aisle. In the first bay is the recumbent effigy of Bishop Jackson (d. 1859), by Thomas Woolner. In bay 2 the central tomb is of Thomas Rennie (d. 1821), the big kneeling figure is Bishop Heber of Calcutta (d. 1826) by Sir Francis Chantrey, and the memorial to Sir Edwin Landseer (d. 1873) is by Woolner. Bay 3 contains the famous simple tablet to Sir Christopher Wren himself (d. 1723): LECTOR, SI MONUMENTUM REQUIRIS, CIRCUMSPICE. In the floor are tomb-slabs of himself and his great-granddaughter, and of Sir John Millais and Lord Leighton (both d. 1896); on the E. wall is an unusual horizontal cartouche to the Holder family. In the end recess: a pretty classical monument by Sir

Alfred Gilbert to Randolph Caldecott (d. 1886), and one to Wren's daughter Jane (d. 1709) by Francis Bird. To their left are memorials to Wren's wife, Maria (d. 1712) and William Blake (d. 1827). Facing these are memorials to artists, including a modern tablet to Antony van Dyck.

Going W. again: the prominent floor-brass is that of Sir Lawrence Alma Tadema (d. 1912). On the side piers (mostly) war correspondents are commemorated, and, in the next bay on the right Walter de la Mare (d. 1956) and E. V. Knox (d. 1971) – by excellent slate plaques typical of the present generation of memorials. Opposite these: persons connected with St Paul's; on the next pier, Edward Bulwer Lytton (d. 1891), by Gilbert; and, in the last bay, a completely unsophisticated tablet to John Wasdale (d. 1807), in the company of soldiers and statesmen.

Across now into the main aisled area, passing on the left a memorial to Ivor Novello (d. 1951), and turn left through the gates. Dominating the centre is the Duke of Wellington's sarcophagus of Cornish porphyry by F. C. Penrose. Around it are ten tablets of 1979 t field marshals of World War II. Beyond is the dome area with Nelson' tomb in the place of honour, a black marble sarcophagus designed by Benedetto da Ravezzano for Cardinal Wolsey's body at Windsor and left unused for three centuries. Under the arch to its E. is Florence Nightingale's memorial (d. 1910).

In the eight bays around Nelson are commemorated very many other sailors and soldiers; for example – SE., Lord Jellicoe (d. 1935) and Lord Beatty (d. 1936) both floor slabs, and Admiral Codrington (d. 1851); S., Lord Collingwood (d. 1810); SW. Lord Napier (d. 1890); W., (by the younger Bacon) Captains Duff and Cooke, both killed at Trafalgar. Along the S. side of the nave crypt the first (deep) bay has a bust of George Washington; the bronze head of W. E. Henley (d. 1903) beside him is by Auguste Rodin. Further along is Penrose's pulpit of 1861, now discarded: then big memorials to Lord Rodney (d. 1792) by J. F. Rossi; Dean Milman (d. 1868), – a tomb-chest; Lord St Vincent (d. 1823) with standing figure by Baily; James Watt (d. 1819), with seated figure; Sir William Ponsonby, killed at Waterloo (Baily); and Mountstuart Elphinstone (d. 1859), by Matthew Noble. At the W. end is the great gun-metal funeral carriage of the Duke of Wellington, weighing 18 tons and made in 18 days by 100 men working in shifts.

Back along the N. aisle are memorials to Lord Duncan (d. 1804), by Sir Richard Westmacott; Captains Mosse and Riou (d. 1801), by Rossi; Henry Hallam (d. 1859), by William Theed; and then a group of battered medieval effigies salvaged from Old St Paul's, all labelled

and none of much merit. Next: General William Napier (d. 1860)
and General Charles Napier (d. 1853), both by G. G. Adams; and
Admiral Malcolm (d. 1838), by Baily. Till recently all these big
memorials from Rodney's onwards were in the N. transept.
Following the N. aisle, one then comes to the sumptuous mayoral
floor-brass and wall memorial of George Nottage (d. 1885).

In the remaining radiating dome bays are more memorials: NW.
to Lawrence of Arabia (d. 1935), and Commonwealth statesmen;
NE. to soldiers. Now go back into the centre aisle, re-passing
Wellington's tomb, and turn left into the inner N. aisle beyond. In
the W. recess is Sir Jacob Epstein's bust of Sir Stafford Cripps
(d. 1952). Further along are commemorated Sir Alexander Fleming
(d. 1955), and a group of architects and artists, with on the pier a
big bronze Crucifix by John Sargent (d. 1925). In the floor are the
tombs of Sir Arthur Sullivan and Sir Hubert Parry (d. 1918). Over
the N. side, not accessible at close quarters, is a monument to John
Martin (d. 1680), with kneeling figures.

Beneath the sanctuary of the quire is the **O.B.E. chapel** (1960),
designed by Lord Mottistone within the whitened piers and vaults,
and rich with wrought iron, painted glass and crimson velvet.
Finally in the inner S. aisle facing the chapel 'nave' is a group of
memorials to eminent sculptors.

Back at main floor level, continue around the **S. transept**, which
has a marvellous display of early 19th c. memorial sculpture, most
of it naval and military. In its E. aisle: General Jones, d. 1843 (by
William Behnes), Sir Henry Lawrence, d. 1857 (by J. G. Lough),
Lord Howe, d. 1799 (by Flaxman), and at the S. end Lord
Collingwood, d. 1810 (by Westmacott). Within the arch into the
transept proper: J. M. W. Turner, d. 1851, and Lord Heathfield,
d. 1790 (by Charles Rossi). At the S. end is a magnificently carved
doorcase, made up of parts of the organ screen discarded when it
was rearranged. Left of it is Westmacott's memorial to Generals
Pakenham and Gibbs, killed at New Orleans in 1815. Looking
towards the dome: on the left is Nelson's statue by Flaxman, on a
big circular pedestal with Britannia presenting two young sailors to
him; opposite is Lord Cornwallis (d. 1805), by Rossi. Under the
arch to the W. aisle is Sir William Hoste, by Thomas Campbell
(1833), and in the W. aisle (starting at the S. end): Sir John Moore,
died at Corunna 1809 (by the younger Bacon); Sir Astley Cooper,
d. 1842 (by Baily); and Sir Ralph Abercromby, d. 1801 (by
Westmacott). Under the arch towards the dome: Lord Lyons,
d. 1858 (by Noble), and William Babington, d. 1833 (by Behnes).

Facing the dome from the SW. corner is a memorial to Sir William Jones, the orientalist, and on the left is the doorway to the upper galleries, to see which a charge is made. These and the crypt are open on weekdays between 10.30 a.m. and 3.30 p.m. A surprisingly gentle circular stair (the lift is not for public use) leads to the internal Whispering Gallery. From this height there are fascinating views of the quire and transepts and nave, changing as one moves round, and a new conception is gained of the system of construction – the massive dome resting on the windowed 'drum' whose walls by intention lean somewhat inwards, and all this supported on the eight great arches below. Even the arcades of the nave and quire receding into the distance seem from this viewpoint to be playing their part in holding up the dome. Here too Thornhill's paintings can be examined more closely, and someone may be demonstrating the famous acoustic effect whereby a voice whispering very close to the drum wall can be clearly heard around its perimeter.

The narrowness of the upper stairs necessitates a one-way system, and having reached the Whispering Gallery on the S., one leaves it on the N. to climb to the external Stone Gallery. There the wonderfully intricate W. towers can be appreciated in a way that seems impossible from the ground, where the eye is distracted by the dome. Also one can look down into the spaces above the aisle roofs, behind the screen walls. There are bird's eye views of many of the Wren parish churches, such as St Bride's to the W., the brick St Benet's, Paul's Wharf, to the S., St Vedast's to the NE., and the ruined Christ Church Greyfriars to the N.

The finest vantage point is of course the Golden Gallery, reached by more stairs and passages in the hollow between the outer dome and the brick cone. The stairs down from the Stone Gallery are on the S. side again, rejoining the upward route at the top of the main wide staircase around the lift shaft.

On the right of the **S. nave aisle** hangs Holman Hunt's famous painting 'The Light of the World', a replica of the original in Keble College, Oxford, and along the wall are big memorials to Captain Westcott, d. 1798 (by Banks); Thomas Middleton, first bishop of India, d. 1822 (by Lough, behind the bookstall); and Richard Burgess, killed 1797 at Camperdowne (Banks). The oval chapel on the left is that of **St Michael and St George** and contains the stalls and banners of the Order of that name and a Sovereign's throne at the W. end. Its woodwork, partly of Wren's time and partly of 1932–3, includes work by Grinling Gibbons taken from the quire stalls in the 19th c.

Cross on top of Dome, St Paul's

Finally (though at present normally only opened at the start of guided tours) there is the famous Geometric Stair in the SW. tower, a tour-de-force of construction in which each step is a stone slab cantilevered from the cylindrical outer wall and supported on the edge of the step below. It leads to the library above the S. aisle and at the bottom is the Dean's Door, to be seen later from outside.

Outside the W. portico is the restored monument to Queen Anne. To the N. is Wren's red brick chapter house (1712–14). Resembling a domestic building and thus totally unlike the medieval conception of a single polygonal hall, it was gutted by bombing and afterwards restored. It contains the cathedral offices and meeting rooms and is not open to the public.

The N. transept pediment sculpture is by Grinling Gibbons, whose work is more familiar in wood. Beyond is a newly repaired and realigned length of the famous churchyard railings, made at Lamberhurst in Sussex before the age of coal. Then a stretch of real churchyard containing Paul's Cross (1910); the nearby site of the original preaching cross is marked. E. from the cathedral is the modern Choir School, incorporating the restored tower of the former church of St Augustine (its graceful steeple is now of glass-reinforced plastic). To the S. are more railings, enclosing (W. of the transept) some remains of the 14th c. chapter house and a modern interpretation of Becket by the sculptor Bainbridge Copnall. The S. transept pediment by Caius Gabriel Cibber cannot be properly seen without standing further back. At the base of the SW. tower is the Dean's Door, over which is the weeping cherub, long forgotten till the cathedral stonework was cleaned in the 1960s.

Going back to the W. portico from its S. side, look at the upward curvature of its steps – a classical design refinement to correct the podium's tendency not to seem level, which sometimes leads visitors to think the towers are sinking. The W. pediment sculpture and the sadly weatherworn statues above are by Bird. The NW. towers contains the famous peal of 12 bells (1878), while in the SW. tower are the clock and bells, including 'Great Tom' which stands in for 'Big Ben' whenever the need arises.

Salford, St John (Roman Catholic, Greater Manchester)

Begun in 1844 and opened in 1848, St John's church became a cathedral only two years later when the diocese was created. The architects were Weightman and Hadfield.

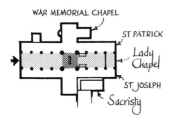

WAR MEMORIAL CHAPEL

ST PATRICK

Lady Chapel

ST JOSEPH

Sacristy

The street doorway brings one in centrally at the W. end. The entire design of the nave is based on that of Howden church in Yorkshire (c. 1300), with clustered columns, and a clerestory of twin windows repeated on the inner face. The open main roof and the lean-to aisle roofs are now white with blue panels, the latter being divided into conspicuous squares. The baptistry, in the N. aisle, has a slightly traceried stone screen and plain octagonal font.

Next the **N. transept** and a view of the newly re-ordered sanctuary (1973) with buff marble floor. The twelve-sided hanging metal tester, ornamented with corn and grapes and with corner lamps, was designed by Edward Blackwell. The reredos-like structure at the end of the transept, with paintings of the life of St Peter, has at its base the effigy of the founder, Bishop Sharples (d. 1850). Flanking this are simple tablets to later, diocesan bishops. The side bay is the War Memorial chapel, entirely floored and panelled in marble.

In the **quire** the Decorated architecture is based on Selby Abbey, with quatrefoil columns and foliage capitals, niches over the columns, clerestory, tierceron vault and, most notably, the E. window of flowing tracery which here has glass by Hardman (1854). The Selby details are somewhat simplified, especially those of the clerestory. The vaults have white ribs and yellow panels, those of the aisles being quadripartite. The NE. chapel, St Patrick's, is the Lee chantry, the canopied monument being that of Daniel Lee (d. 1877). The Lady chapel is central, and flanked by screens like the baptistry. Balancing the Lee chantry on the S. side is the Leeming chantry (St Joseph's) with tablets to that family and the canopied tomb (with a brass) of John Leeming (d. 1847).

Now the quire itself, entered from its S. aisle through another light screen. Straight ahead is the clumsy, dark bishop's throne; to the left are simple Gothic stalls, and to the right the niched and pinnacled reredos. Of more artistic value, perhaps, is the fine mosaic floor with central coat of arms.

The **S. transept**, all marble and mosaic and entered through an inelegant iron screen, retains the former sanctuary and altar of the

Blessed Sacrament (the Sacrament is now reserved at the high altar). The pulpit, on the right of the S. aisle and facing into the nave, is Italianate on brown marble columns but with a Gothic traceried balustrade.

Outside, the W. front is impressive in a modest way, with good main doorway and window and four turrets – all unashamedly copied from Howden. On the N. side is a passage with a disused porch; on the S. a spacious courtyard with Cathedral House forming two other sides. This offers the best view of the splendid tower with broach spire and four tiers of lucarnes (a replica of the upper part of that of Newark) – also of the corbel-table of the S. transept with carved animals. Another good view can be had from the otherwise depressing estate of flats at the rear.

Salisbury, St Mary (Church of England, Wiltshire)

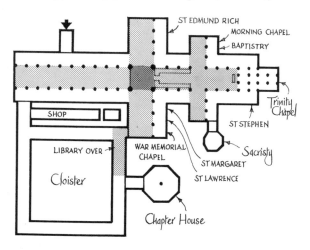

The cathedral establishment was moved early in the 13th c. from Old Sarum on its hill-top a mile or so to the N. As a result Salisbury is the most uniform in date (and therefore in design) of English medieval cathedrals. It was begun in 1220 and consecrated in 1258. Building continued however, the non-monastic cloister and chapter house being begun *c.* 1270 and the heightening of the steeple not till 1334. Two little chantry chapels, one each side of the E. end, were

Cathedral from SW., Salisbury

added in the 15th c. and removed by James Wyatt who also (*c.* 1790) took down a detached 13th c. bell-tower (rather like that at Chichester) and 'tidied' the whole interior with regrettable thoroughness. A more scholarly restoration began under Sir George Gilbert Scott in 1863.

Salisbury is celebrated as the textbook example of Early English perfection. Its plan shows exactly what was needed in the 13th c. for congregational and clergy seating, side chapels, and processional ways, and above all a sense of order and dignity. Its elevations and its massing (audaciously perfected by the spire) express the separate parts so clearly that here, if anywhere, one should enjoy the exterior first – and last – in one of the memorable views across the Close from NE. or NW. Such articulation is specially English: the main transept coming forward from the tower, the E. transept projecting less far from the quire (each transept with an E. aisle only, to provide side chapels), the tall quire with its aisles and 'Lady' chapel (the whole cathedral is Our Lady's, so the E. end is really the Trinity chapel), and the nave and aisles with the W. front extended as a continuous corner-turreted screen across them. Except in the tower and spire, which are full-blown Decorated, the windows are lancets in twos and threes and with tracery limited to the simplest kind – just a hint here and there of the coming Geometric style. The general effect is cool and precise.

The tall **N. porch** is typical in its internal details: Purbeck 'marble' shafting, two stages of wall-arcade, springing foliage capitals, big outer arch, and a smaller inner doorway with a restored Majestas in the vesica panel over it.

During the summer a charge is made to enter the **nave**. Go to the centre first to see the general design system: clustered columns with attached Purbeck shafts, triforium arch uncomfortably spread over two twin openings, double clerestory of lancets with walkway, and simple quadripartite vault. Purbeck stone is used profusely and there is more in the aisle vault-shafts and window shafts. The crossing vault is of lierne type, 14th c. Even from here the piers of the crossing can be seen to be bowed under the weight of the steeple they did not expect to bear. Beyond is the quire, similar to the nave, and beyond that the Trinity chapel – an uninterrupted vista without Scott's reredos and quire screen (removed in 1959–60 amidst much controversy).

The W. wall, with lancets containing much 13th c. grisaille glass saved from Wyatt's destruction, is criticized for its failure to link properly with the main arcades – a difficult but not insoluble design

Interior looking W., Salisbury (early 13th c.)

problem. Now return to the **N. aisle** and walk E. from the entrance
door. Wyatt lined up all the effigies from the Trinity chapel and its
chantries under the nave arcades. The first is probably 15th c. –
nameless, having lost its brasses; the second is of Sir John de
Montacute (d. 1390), in armour and very worn. The brass beneath
the next arch is a replica, made for the purpose of rubbing, of the
splendid 14th c. Wyville brass in the NE. transept; on the wall
opposite is a tablet to 28 people killed in 1906 in a railway accident.
In the next bay is a floor brass to Sir Giles Hungerford (d. 1685); on
the wall are a tablet to the third Earl Nelson (d. 1913) and Allan
Wyon's bronze bas-relief bust of Sir George Harper (d. 1922), and
under the arcade the double tomb-chest of Walter Lord Hungerford
(d. 1449), with indents of brasses. The well-preserved alabaster effigy
under the last arch is of Sir John Cheney (d. 1509).

In the **N. transept** the 15th c. traceried strainers across the crossing
arches are prominent: much less so the diagonal buttresses inserted
into the triforium and clerestory all round the crossing. One only
needs to look up one of the tower piers from its base to understand
past concern over stability. At first sight the transept matches the
nave; in fact, the main piers and triforium differ in design. The big
N. wall is a splendid sight with its three tiers of lancets (their
grisaille glass is 19th c.).

The transept W. wall, having no chapels or arcade, has pairs of
giant lancet windows instead. Along it are a large 18th c. tablet to
the Harris family; a brass to the antiquary John Britton (d. 1857); a
big iron-bound chest; a tablet to James Harris (d. 1780) by John
Bacon, with medallion head; a 13th c. cope chest; the reclining
figure of James Earl of Malmesbury (d. 1820), on a monument by
Sir Francis Chantrey; the bearded bust of the writer Richard
Jefferies (d. 1887); two more ancient chests; and above the last a
female allegorical figure and Good Samaritan scene by John
Flaxman in memory of William Earle (d. 1796).

Close to the triple-arched tablet to John Peniston (d. 1858) on the
N. wall is a beautiful plaster model of the cathedral made *c.* 1825 by
Sir James Pennethorne. The central canopied tomb is of Bishop
Blyth (d. 1499); on the wall each side is an original coloured
consecration cross (19 of these remain, inside and outside, out of
24). Then the seated figure of Sir Richard Hoare (d. 1838) by R. C.
Lucas and a classical tablet to Sir Edward Hamilton (d. 1915). Of
the former E. chapels the first contains organ works, so Flaxman's
memorial to Walter Long (d. 1807) cannot be seen. The second is
St Edmund Rich's and has a coloured Gothic reredos, and the third

is dedicated to St Thomas à Becket.

19th c. gates lead to the **N. quire aisle**, with the backs of the stalls and organ on the right. On the left is the big plain canopied tomb of Bishop Woodville (d. 1484). In bays 3 and 4 on the right are two 16th c. cadaver effigies, the first of Archdeacon Sydenham (d. 1524) and the second (in a canopied tomb) of Precentor Bennett (d. 1558).

Then the **NE. transept**, very like the main transept but altogether smaller in scale; the architecture needs no further comment except for the big strainer arches (like those of Wells), probably put in in the 14th c. It is entered through a plain 15th c. wooden screen. On the W. wall the mid-13th c. wall-arcading with exquisite carving is in fact the original rood screen; the central doorway, however, came from the 15th c. Beauchamp chapel destroyed by Wyatt. The left (Morning) chapel has a double aumbry and an enriched Gothic reredos. The other is the baptistry. The unusual trough on the E. wall, late 14th c. with a vaulted canopy, is not an immersion font but a basin moved from near the vestry; the real font in front is of *c.* 1850. To its right is a tall double piscina. On the floor near the screen is the splendid and extraordinary brass of Bishop Wyville

W. gable and Tower, Salisbury (early 13th c.)

(d. 1375), his praying effigy set inside a stylized fortress. The smaller one is of Bishop Guest of Rochester (d. 1578).

Now across the aisle into the **quire**. Here again the architecture is similar to the nave. The three E. arches and the variety of refinement of the Purbeck shafts should be specially enjoyed; to go into more detail would make a tedious distraction from its beauty. The vault painting is a 19th c. restoration and the glass of the upper three E. windows dates from 1781. The tombs around the three E. bays will be seen later from the aisles: taken clockwise, they are of Bishops Roger de Mortival, Audley, Bingham and Kerr, Lord Hungerford and Bishop Simon. The slate tablet to the left of the opening to the S. quire aisle is to Henry Earl of Pembroke (d. 1600).

The ornate bishop's throne and stalls are Scott's. The stalls do however retain 14th c. work at the base of the two rear rows, and a number of misericords; the canopies are of 1913–14. The Purbeck floor was laid in 1960. Scott's octagonal stone and marble pulpit, just outside where his screen stood, is of 1877. Back in the quire, the wooden pulpit on the N. side is by Randoll Blacking, c. 1950. Beside it is the way back into the **N. quire aisle**. The glass ahead in the NE. transept is by Burlison & Grylls, c. 1887.

Moving E. again: on the left is a tablet to John Lord Castlehaven (d. 1769), and on the right the high canopied tomb of Bishop Roger de Mortival (d. 1329); it has a brass indent and remarkable miniature angels perched like crockets on its arch. Next, the splendid fan-vaulted chantry of Bishop Audley (d. 1524), with an open stone screen. His tomb occupies its SE. corner close to the high altar, and behind its own altar is a little 15th c. Florentine Assumption painting. In the next bay, on the left is a bronze bas-relief of Bishop Donaldson (d. 1935), by Wyon: on the right the well-preserved effigy of Bishop Bingham (d. 1246), under a rebuilt canopy. The plain canopied tomb next on the left is of Bishop Longespée (d. 1297), with a window of c. 1920 above, by Edward Woore.

The E. end of the aisle is dominated by the showy tomb of Sir Thomas Gorges (d. 1635), with two fine effigies and a canopy on extraordinarily unsafe-looking twisted columns. The window behind is by Christopher Webb. On its left are some medieval tiles and a double aumbry: on its right an 18th c. Snetzler organ (its case of c. 1960 by Lord Mottistone) and under the arcade the effigy of Bishop Wordsworth (d. 1911), by Sir George Frampton.

The E. or **Trinity chapel** is probably the most beautiful part of the cathedral, with delicate Purbeck columns, single and slender or (at

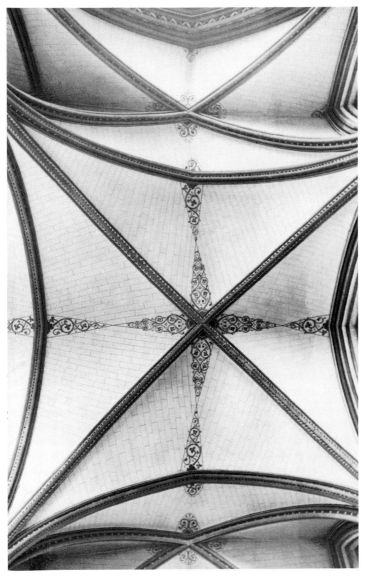

Trinity Chapel vault, Salisbury, as seen from below (early 13th c.)

the W. end) in fives. It has its own narrow aisles, and little 15th c. fan-vaulted recesses added along each side. The side windows are by Clayton & Bell; the E. are largely 13th c. grisaille but with some 16th c. glass in the centre and a 14th c. Annunciation at the base of the far left window. Turning about, one can look through the open scrolly screen down the whole length of the cathedral.

Under the E. arch of the **S. quire aisle** is the plain coffin-lid of Bishop St Osmund, first builder of Old Sarum cathedral (d. 1099). St Stephen's chapel at the end of the aisle houses the giant memorial of Edward Earl of Hertford (d. 1621), with lavish architectural decoration right up into the crown of the window, and effigies on shelves; the kneeling figures under the side canopies (each a sumptuous enough monument in itself) are his sons. The modest tomb-chest on its right is of William Witton (d. 1523). Another Webb window is behind. In bay 2 is the canopied tomb of Bishop Moberley (d. 1885), designed by Sir Arthur Blomfield. Bay 3 has a pretty tablet to Susan Wordsworth (d. 1894) with a floral mosaic, and, opposite, the effigy of Bishop Kerr (d. 1869), by R. Pleydell Bouverie. Next is the big chantry of Walter Lord Hungerford (d. 1449), made of iron, with a flattish coloured wooden ceiling and pendants; it came from one of the chapels demolished by Wyatt. Opposite is a tablet to Archdeacon Rolleston (d. 1766). Further along the wall are two 17th c. memorials (one a heraldic painted board) and the canopied tomb of Bishop Giles de Bridport (d. 1262), with Purbeck effigy and two bays of exquisite Geometric arcading. Opposite lies Bishop Simon of Ghent (d. 1315), with a brass matrix and a big canopy.

This brings one to the **SE. transept**. Its 20th c. screen has panels of Indian origin and encloses a vestry, not open to the public. There can however be glimpsed the canopied tomb of Bishop Burgess (d. 1837), on its left an Art Nouveau tablet with an angel, and in the SE. corner a double piscina. The monument to Bishop Seth Ward (d. 1689) cannot be seen. The S. windows all have 13th c. grisaille glass, easily visible over the screen. Opposite, the statues over the quire doorway are memorials of the 1930s.

The next aisle bay has on the left a big tablet to Bishop Davenant (d. 1641), and on the right the tomb of Bishop Capon (d. 1557). Lastly on the left is the splendid canopied tomb of Sir Richard Mompesson (d. 1627), fully coloured and gilded and with two recumbent effigies. Beyond it, i.e. against the first chapel of the **S. transept**, is another canopied tomb, of Bishop Mitford (d. 1407). The almost exact symmetry of the cathedral continues here. The S.

windows have more grisaille glass but only the top centre one is
ancient. The first chapel, St Margaret of Scotland's, has a 17th c.
Spanish altar frontal. The elaborately arcaded tomb-chest on its
right is by G. E. Street to J. H. Jacob (d. 1862). Beside the next
chapel, St Lawrence's, is another canopied tomb, with mitre, Bible
and crozier in place of an effigy: that of Bishop Fisher (d. 1825).
St Michael's chapel, reserved for quiet prayer, has an elaborate
Gothic reredos (*c.* 1925), a display case of old books, a double
piscina, and a tablet to Bishop Ridgeway (d. 1921), with bronze
bas-relief by Wyon.

Follow next the end wall of the transept, past the modest tablet to
Bishop Hume (d. 1782), and the big Gothic canopied monument
(1817) of Bishop Poore (d. 1780) and his family (flanked by two
more consecration crosses), to the **library** door. The library is open
on weekdays except Thursdays from 10 a.m. to 12 noon and from
2 p.m. to 4 p.m. for a small charge. It was built in 1445 over the E.
cloister walk (this upper floor originally ran its whole length) and
contains many valuable documents including from Lacock Abbey
one of the four original specimens of Magna Carta.

In the W. wall of the transept is a door to the cloister (an unusual
position, the N. walk being spaced away from the aisle). Then come
several wall tablets and the distinguished bust of Sir Robert Hyde
(d. 1665), in an oval medallion.

The **S. nave aisle** is taken bay by bay and alternately left and right
as follows. In bay 1 a classical tablet of 1960 to Bishop Burnet
(d. 1715), and a 17th c. cartouche; on the right the splendid mailed
figure of William Longespée (d. 1226), on a wooden tomb-chest with
arcaded sides (this is the oldest soldier's effigy in England). In bay 2,
interesting tablets to Elihonor Sadler (d. 1622) and Sir Henry Hyde
(d. 1650); on the right the worn figure of Bishop de la Wyle
(d. 1271). In bay 3 three 18th c. tablets and, under the arcade, part
of the shrine of St Osmund, with foramina or holes into which
diseased limbs were pushed for cures. In bay 4 tablets to Mary
Cooke (d. 1742) and John Priaulx (d. 1674); on the right the fine
effigy of Robert Lord Hungerford (d. 1459). In bay 5 two 17th c.
tablets on the wall, and the tall tomb-chest (not originally his) of
Bishop Beauchamp (d. 1481). In bay 6 one 18th c. wall tablet; some
more in bay 7 and on the right a nameless tomb-chest of *c.* 1500. In
the next bay some more small wall tablets and above them some
excellent 14th c. glass, originally part of a Jesse Tree in the W.
window of the nave; on the right are effigies of Bishop de Bohun
(d. 1184) and Bishop Roger (d. 1139), both brought from Old Sarum

and of great artistic value. At the end is another door to the **cloister**.

Go through this, passing (or visiting) on the left the shop and refreshment room, and turn left along the N. walk. The cloister was begun *c*. 1270 and is thus Geometric in style, quite distinct from the rest of the cathedral. The quadripartite vault has bosses progressing in date and style around the four walks. A number of small tablets and servicemen's crosses line the walls and there are several cusped doorways, some now disused. From the E. walk a vaulted lobby leads through a double doorway (all much restored) into the **chapter house**. This splendid octagonal room is Geometric too, with marvellously big bar-traceried windows, central pillar and vault, and wall-arcading with carved capitals, heads and spandrels a good deal renewed. The patterned glass is 19th c., the circular table probably 13th c.

Continue down the E. walk and along the S., where the two cedars frame the view of the S. transept and library and the steeple. At the SW. corner are remains of the former central column of the chapter house; the capital and base placed together look like a font. Along the W. walk are a collection of carved stones, coffins, etc., and four ancient bells.

Back now into the cathedral. Under the W. bay of the S. arcade is one more plain tomb, nameless. In the **nave**, left of the W. doorway, is Michael Rysbrack's big memorial to Thomas Lord Wyndham (d. 1745), with seated figure of Hibernia. Over the doors is another consecration cross, and to their right the monument of d'Aubigny Turberville (d. 1696). The tomb-lid under the W. arch of the N. aisle is also unnamed. In bay 3 stands a working 14th c. clock originally in the detached bell-tower; its has no face but now sounds the hours on a bell in the triforium. Under the arcade is the mailed effigy of William Longespée junior, killed in Egypt on a crusade in 1250. The curious tiny figure beside him may denote the heart burial of Bishop Poore (d. 1229). Lastly, in the bay beyond, is the plain tomb-chest of William Geoffrey (d. 1558); the banners on the wall are colours of the 2nd Wiltshire Regiment.

A circuit of the exterior must start with the W. front, somewhat disappointing either as an expression of the nave and aisles behind or as a fully considered design in its own right. The curious half-arches each side of the main W. window, the half-hearted buttresses on the end turrets, and the squashed-in aisle portals are perhaps its most obvious faults. It is of 1258–65, and the figures are nearly all 19th c. renewals by Frank Redfern.

The houses in the Close are probably the finest such group in

England, far too many and too diverse in dates to describe here, and
it would be invidious to single out any. A longish but worthwhile
walk takes one S., past the cloister wall to Harnham Gate, then left
along de Vaux Place outside the precinct wall and left again up
Exeter Street (with a good SE. view of the cathedral where the wall
gets lower), past the 14th c. Bishop's Gate (to the school in the
former bishop's palace), through the 14th c. St Ann's Gate into the
Close again, and down the E. side of the cathedral to the school gate
to see the palace (partly as old as the cathedral) and chapter house.
From here one can cross the churchyard wall by steps and follow
the E. and N. sides of the cathedral back to the N. porch – noting
the web of flying buttresses propping the base of the steeple and its
surrounding parts, and finally the intricate gablets and corner
turrets and the banded spire itself soaring to a height of 404 feet.

Sheffield, St Peter & St Paul (Church of England, South Yorkshire)

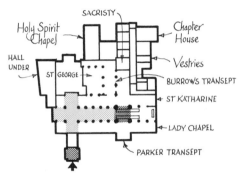

Before becoming a cathedral this was a typical parish church of a
prosperous town. Much of the plan of the 12th or 13th c. building
survives, but little or none of its actual stonework except possibly in
the chancel walls. The whole was rebuilt in the 15th c., and the S.
(Shrewsbury) chapel added about 1520. Extensive alterations were
made in the late 18th c. and the entire nave was rebuilt about 1804;
only the E. walls of the chancel and chapels survive from that
period, for the nave was again rebuilt, together with the transepts
and E. windows, around 1880 under William Flockton.

The diocese was formed in 1913. The years of indecision and
frustration that followed have left an interesting architectural tangle.

A first extension scheme by Sir Charles Nicholson was abandoned.
A start was made on his second in 1936; it involved a turning of the
axis of the building so that a new nave would stand to the S. of the
old and a new chancel to the N. By 1939 the suite of vestries and
chapter rooms was completed. The chapel of the Holy Spirit at the
far end of the intended quire was started, and the new nave
foundations laid, before work was again abandoned in 1942. After
the war the chapel was finished. When Nicholson died, his
conception of the whole project was re-worked by George Pace in an
effort to reduce the cost, but eventually it had to be given up
altogether, and the remainder as subsequently built to the original
orientation is by Arthur Bailey. St George's chapel now stands
where the quire was to have been, the nave was slightly extended to
the true W. with a new crossing-lantern and a porch-tower, and the
chapel of the Holy Spirit was left in a rather odd relationship with
the rest of the building. The new work was completed in 1966.

Bailey's porch-tower marks the way in from Church Street.
Trying simultaneously not to be Gothic and not to be not Gothic, it
nevertheless harmonizes in scale and material with the older building
and makes no attempt to compete with the simple 15th c. tower and
crocketed spire. Two sets of glass doors lead to the new **W. crossing**,
a stone framework capped by a lantern-turret with stripy glass and
strange pendants symbolic of the Crown of Thorns. The large N.
window immediately ahead contains the glass from the former W.
window by W. E. Dixon (1881), supplemented in the lower part by
some of 1899. On the left is the font, grey granite with bronze figures
(also 1881). The reveals of the new W. window behind contain a
group of wall tablets and well-lettered bronze plates from the old
building, as well as the bell of H.M.S. *Sheffield*. The best of the
memorials here is that to Archdeacon Blakeney (d. 1895), with bust
by Onslow Ford.

The **nave and aisles** of 1804 were to have been replaced by a
bigger nave, crossing them at right angles. The slender octagonal
piers, embattled capitals, clerestory and low-pitched roofs (with
gilded bosses in the nave) are a convincing imitation of
Perpendicular. The tower arches are early 15th c., and on the W.
face of the tower can be seen marks of the two previous nave roofs.

A triple arch and six steps in the N. aisle lead to **St George's
chapel**, the chapel of the York and Lancaster Regiment. It stands
where the new quire and sanctuary were to have been. Behind its
altar another triple arcade marks the limit of Nicholson's building;
beyond that, at a lower level, can be seen his chapel of the Holy

Spirit, intended to be in the traditional position of a Lady chapel. On either side of the way in from the aisle are statues of St George and St Michael as soldiers. To the right is another Nicholson arcade separating what would have been the S. quire aisle (now called the Burrows transept), and to the left a series of Bailey windows with indifferent glass portraying military insignia. The ceiling is a strange drooping pattern of truncated pyramids, echoing the effect of the numerous hanging banners. The seating, consisting entirely of stalls with hollowed-out backs, provides another rather worrying pattern. Two further statues each side of the sanctuary represent St Oswald and St Martin.

Under the sanctuary is the vaulted crypt **chapel of All Saints**, used as a columbarium. It is reached by going into the Burrows transept and turning left and left again down the steps. To the right of its altar is a sparkling window by Keith New. More steps lead down to the lower entrance hall. Opposite the crypt entrance, however, is the enriched doorway to the **Holy Spirit chapel**. An ante-chapel with a small organ introduces the blue and white canopied screenwork and chapel-wise seating by Sir Ninian Comper. The big *Te Deum* E. window with its upper tracery like a dove is by Christopher Webb (1940), and the elaborate reredos with Christ and the Apostles by Temple Moore. The stone carving of the aumbry and piscina and of the roof bosses is noteworthy.

Back now to the **Burrows transept**, passing on the left a slate tablet by Pace to Bishop Heaslett (d. 1947). The N. window (above the stair) contains 14th c. glass, possibly part of a Spanish Jesse window. Going towards the nave again, the organ screen on the left with gilded finials is by Pace, and just past it is a tablet by David Kindersley to Bishop Burrows, first bishop of the diocese (d. 1940). The comes the former **N. transept**, containing the S. face of the organ and a window with soldiers in memory of Bernard Firth (d. 1938). The altar of St George's chapel was to have been here, and the body of it would have extended right under the tower to the S. transept. Under the organ is a splendid illuminated display of cathedral plate.

The simple 16th c. oak screen that divides this transept was originally in the Shrewsbury chapel. Beyond it is the organ console and its enclosure (by Pace) and the NE. **chapel of St Katharine** is then on the left, through a blue and gold screen by Randoll Blacking (1937). This chapel was formed in 1914 on the site of an 18th c. vestry and fitted in its present form in 1935. The E. window is by Webb, and one in the N. wall by Harry Harvey (1948). On the right is a large tablet to William Jessop (d. 1734), and below it a 15th c. canopied oak triple seat used as movable sedilia, a rare piece. The large floor brass commemorates the Rev. Thomas Sutton (d. 1851). The candelabra are modern.

Next the **chancel**, largely 15th c. but with earlier work in its walls. The hammer-beam roof is original, but the wings of the gilded angels are recent additions. The E. window is by Dixon (1854). Restored wall-arcading on the N. side of the sanctuary contains three tablets to vicars, the centre one of which, to James Wilkinson (d. 1805), was the first work of Sir Francis Chantrey. Opposite, in front of the canopied tomb, is a carved seat by Blacking. The brass beside it is all that remains of a monument to Elizabeth Lady Mountjoye (d. 1510). The simple light oak quire seating (by Temple Moore) extends back into the tower space; the bishop's throne, marked by a pinnacled canopy, is by Nicholson (1937). On the piers at the W. end of the quire space are several more tablets and brasses.

The **Lady chapel** is unusual in that its E. bay, being for centuries the resting-place of the Earls of Shrewsbury, was to all intents and purposes Roman Catholic. In 1935 it was restored to church use. The chapel dates from about 1520 and its arcade was probably Flockton's model for the nave. The reredos (1935) stands on a medieval altar, repaired and painted. On the left the canopied tomb already seen from the chancel side is that of the 4th Earl of Shrewsbury (d. 1538), with alabaster figures of himself and his two wives. Facing this on the S. wall is the 6th Earl's monument with another effigy in armour; he was husband of 'Bess of Hardwick' and died in 1590. Further W. the bust in front of an obelisk is that of Thomas Bamforth (d. 1739). On the floor is an unusual brass to Martha Lister (d. 1663), in the same manner as Gothic canopied brasses but with a classical architectural surround complete with Corinthian capitals, keystone and coat-of-arms. On the chapel floor and on the wall by the Bamforth monument are many smaller brasses.

The S. transept is part of the 1878 building. It is known as the **Parker transept**, being a memorial to the surgeon Samuel Parker (d. 1876). The windows show scenes of healing. Amongst the memorials is one by Chantrey with a bust of the Rev. Alexander Mackenzie (d. 1816).

The oak pulpit is of 1886. In the **S. aisle**, which is lit by four rather dark 19th c. windows, is another Chantrey monument, to Thomas Harrison (d. 1823).

A rightward turn outside the main doors takes one into St James
Row; from this alley the Bailey W. end can be seen, and there are
steps to the basement hall and to the car park behind. The
juxtaposition of Nicholson's Gothic chapel of the Holy Spirit and
Bailey's chapel of St George is decidedly curious, particularly as the
'modern' work is the nearer to the old building. From the lower
road, Campo Lane, gates lead back into the churchyard at the N.
end of Nicholson's vestry block. The 18th c. tomb stationed between
the vestries and the Holy Spirit chapel is an unused one removed
from the Shrewsbury chapel. The path is paved with richly lettered
headstones. The statue on a granite pedestal opposite the NE.
corner of the cathedral is of the poet James Montgomery (d. 1854);
the main E. window commemorates him too. Further S. are four
isolated gate piers which led into the churchyard. Beyond them, near
the line of bollards, is a good spot to turn round and look back at
the older parts and particularly at the tower.

Shrewsbury, Our Lady Help of Christians & St Peter of Alcantara
(Roman Catholic, Shropshire)

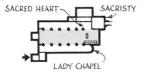

The first Catholic chapel in the town was built in 1774. The diocese
was one of those established in 1850 and after a double false start,
first with Augustus Pugin who died in 1852 and then with his son
Edward who at first designed a church too for the site, the
present building was begun in 1853. Its site is indeed cramped, close
to the town wall and without even a pavement outside. Though
towerless and only the size of a parish church, its relative height
gives it dignity and it has been little altered. The SE. Lady chapel is
by Edmund Kirby.
    Inside the SW. porch the seventh of Philip Lindsay Clarke's set of
Stations of the Cross is prominent. The arcades are of Early English
type with springing foliage capitals on octagonal columns. The high-
pitched nave roof rests on posts and corbels, the aisle roof on single-
strutted trusses. The shallow chancel still contains the original altar
and reredos but under the large chancel arch, which is flanked by

statues in niches, a nave altar has been discreetly added.

The font at the W. end of the N. aisle, dated 1856, has a marble-shafted stem and simple iron railing. Along the aisle, past the confessionals, is the sacristy door and just inside are two memorials older than the building – on the right a brass to William Berington (d. 1766) and on the left a tablet to Samuel Jones (d. 1833) – as well as four floor tiles from the medieval abbey. The NW. chapel of the Sacred Heart has an ornate Pugin reredos and a good brass communion rail which continues across the whole church, though moved one bay W. in front of the **quire**.

Here the timber roof, pointed in form, has painted panels with emblems. The E. window is by Hardman (1862), not specially attractive, but the side windows by Margaret Rope, narrative in content and traditional in style, are excellent. On the S. side are triple wooden sedilia and a marble-shafted arcade to the **Lady chapel**. Inside, this is richly arcaded at upper level too with brown-veined marble shafts, and has a star vault with central boss. The circular pulpit is also largely of marble. From here there is a good view of the splendid W. window, also by Margaret Rope, and of the gallery with its unhappily placed organ.

The outside can be viewed closely only from the road or from the high walk opposite, though its grey stone façade and bellcote are prominent from the public park below the town wall.

Southwark, St Saviour (Church of England, Greater London)

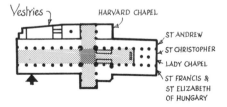

One of the many monasteries in and around the City of London, the Augustinian priory of St Mary Overie ('over the river') held a unique position close to the S. end of London Bridge. A church stood here before the Norman Conquest, but it was re-founded in 1106 under the auspices of the Bishop of Winchester, who also built himself a palace nearby, accompanied by a prison (called the Clink) to assist enforcement of his authority in the area. Early in the 13th c.

much of the church was rebuilt after a fire, but work of various kinds went on long afterwards, interrupted by another fire about 1385 and by the collapse of the nave vault in 1469. The great reredos and the completion of the tower about 1520 owed much to Bishop Fox of Winchester.

After the Reformation the church of St Mary Overie became the parish church of St Saviour Southwark, and the extensive monastic buildings were dismembered. The retro-quire was turned to other uses. Decay, neglect and maltreatment in the three succeeding centuries followed their usual course. At the beginning of the 19th c. several half-hearted attempts at partial repair were made, but then matters were brought to a head firstly by the rebuilding of London Bridge in 1823–31 in a position much nearer the church and secondly by the removal in 1831 of the nave roof, condemned as unsafe. In the disagreements that followed the retro-quire, too, was threatened with destruction. The nave was rebuilt in 1838–41 under George Gwilt. Meanwhile the railway arrived, perched on a viaduct scandalously close to the church.

The rapid expansion of Greater London led to moves to establish a diocese separate from Winchester and Rochester. The associated building work (here consisting in the main of another, this time more authentic, reconstruction of the nave), unlike that of so many other new cathedrals, preceded the enthronement of the first bishop (1905). It was done in 1890–7 under Sir Arthur Blomfield.

The cathedral's intensively commercial surroundings are surely the least beautiful in Britain. Approached from London Bridge, the 15th c. tower is prominent (the pinnacles are a late 17th c. addition). A little footbridge leads across an old cobbled street to the churchyard, now 15 ft below main road level. The E., Early English, parts come first. Behind railings against the S. quire aisle stands the tomb of George Gwilt, architect of the 1840 restoration. Just beyond it the start of the Blomfield building is obvious from its smooth facing: this is the organ chamber, built partly on the site of a big projecting chapel demolished in 1822.

The main entrance is the S. porch, leading straight into Blomfield's **nave and aisles**. Typically harsh and mechanical in their detailing, their arcade, triforium and clerestory are probably nevertheless a fair representation of the general appearance of the 13th c. building. Their least beautiful feature is the strong over-regular stone patterning in the vault spandrels and other plain areas. Eastwards is the 13th c. quire with its stone reredos; in between, the crossing with its hanging candelabrum.

At the W. end, two angels and a figure of David with a harp on the top window sill came from a 17th c. organ case. Unusually, there is no W. doorway. In the **N. aisle** a collection of carved wooden bosses on the W. wall came from the nave roof which stood from 1469 till 1831. To its right is the 16th c. stone 'cadaver' of a canon; then a much restored Norman arch which led into the cloister. The glass is of the same period as the building; much of it is by Charles Kempe and devoted to local historical subjects, but the W. window is a Creation by Henry Holiday (1893). Towards the end of the N. aisle is the tomb of the poet John Gower (d. 1408). His head rests on his three principal books. The brilliant painting and gilding are entirely modern. The Norman doorway beyond it is more convincingly ancient, particularly when seen from the other side where there are also remains of a holy water stoup.

Now the **crossing**, and a closer look at the splendid brass candelabrum, given as a memorial to John Applebye (d. 1680). It is remarkable for the wrought ironwork surmounting it. The embellishment of the tower ceiling is modern (by Ronald Sims), using gilded 15th c. bosses from the nave with applied ribs of red, green and gold. Also by Sims are the raised crossing floor with nave altar, Cross, candlesticks, seats, desks and remodelled pulpit. The E. and W. crossing arches are unusual in resting on completely plain areas of wall, with only small (and unequal) corbels at the top. The N. and S. arches are 14th c., on earlier backings. In the sanctuary is a Jacobean chair whose back tilts forward to form a table top.

In the **N. transept** the W. and N. walls are Norman at the base and the remainder mostly 13th c. Working clockwise: there is first a strange monument by Nicholas Stone to Joyce Austin (d. 1626), with harvesters and an allegory of Agriculture. In the second bay are two 18th c. tablets and then a robust hexagonal 18th c. pulpit relegated to a corner (the one in use is of about 1900). On the N. side is the agonized effigy of Lionel Lokyer (d. 1672), on a couch; the inscription includes 'his virtues and his PILLS are soe well known'. Then a most unusually elaborate early 18th c. altar table from St Thomas's church with twisted legs in groups of four, and behind it a sword rest of 1674 from St Olave's, and a hatchment. In the next bay is the wigged bust of Richard Blisse (d. 1703).

The E. side has two arches to the **Harvard chapel**, filled with glazed screens by George Pace; the left opening shows traces of having led into a Norman apse (as will be seen outside). The chapel itself was converted from a sacristy in 1907 and has recently been reorientated and its vault cleaned. Entrance is now from the N.

quire aisle through a 16th c. studded door. The octagonal altar, processional cross and stalls are by Pace, also the stone setting for the jewelled tabernacle by Augustus Pugin (formerly in St Augustine's, Ramsgate). The glass of the E. window is a memorial to John Harvard, earliest benefactor of the U.S. university, who is believed to have been baptised in the church in 1607. Round to the right, i.e. in the S.E. corner, is a 16th c. Pietà by Garofalo.

From here on, back to the S. transept, all is effectively 13th c. The **N. quire aisle**, entered by an awkwardly shaped arch, has two hatchments and many minor wall tablets. Noteworthy are a wooden one in the third bay to John Gawen (d. 1647) and a neat heraldic one to John Morton (d. 1631). Almost embarrassingly bright is the new colouring, gilding and silvering on the bigger monument to John Trehearne (d. 1618) and his wife. Further on are two foliated arches, one with the plain tomb-chest of Thomas Cure (d. 1588), and the second with a late 13th c. knight's effigy in oak. On the right of the aisle is a fascinating model of the whole priory as it was in its heyday; then a monument of triumphal arch type with kneeling effigies of Richard Humble (d. 1616) and his two wives.

Black and gilt gates next lead into the **retro-quire** with its four chapels. The division into four instead of three is unusual and emphasizes the breadth. This is regarded as one of the purest expressions of Early English architecture, but restorations have left too little that is original. Just inside on the left is the Nonesuch chest, with astonishingly elaborate architectural detail, given in 1588. Beyond, at the entrance to St Andrew's chapel, is a model of a Dutch ship of about 1700. The second chapel is St Christopher's. The screens between all four are by Sir Ninian Comper; so is the war memorial on the W. wall of the retro-quire, with its lively medallion of St George and the Dragon. Above it, backing the altar screen, is a curious area of shallow blind tracery.

The other two E. chapels are dedicated to Our Lady, with altar and riddel-posts by Comper, and to St Francis and St Elizabeth of Hungary. Until 1830 the former extended two bays further E. The seat and table against the S. wall of the retro-quire are the 18th c. consistory court.

In the **S. quire aisle**, through another set of gates and backing on to the high altar, is the four-poster tomb of Bishop Andrewes of Winchester (d. 1626), largely a modern reconstruction by Comper. Next on the right is the bronze effigy of Bishop Talbot, first bishop of Southwark (d. 1934), by Cecil Thomas. Opposite is the one panel of ancient glass in the cathedral, a royal arms of Elizabeth I.

At this point one can step into the **quire** itself, also early English but showing slight French influence in, for example, the continuation of the vaulting shafts right to the floor. The alternation between round and octagonal columns is hardly noticeable. Between the N. and S. sides there are differences in detail even more subtle. The vault and most of the clerestory are modern restoration.

The altar screen was added about 1520 by Bishop Fox; the statues are of 1905. The colouring at the base, and the altar with its reredos and riddel-posts, are by Comper and have tended to change a rich effect into an overcrowded fussy one. The blue window above is by Comper too (1950). The bishop's throne (by G. F. Bodley) on the N. side of the sanctuary, as well as the stalls throughout the quire (by Blomfield), and the eagle lectern, are no older than the formation of the diocese. The great 17th c. candelabrum is still prominent, and so are the tombs each side of the sanctuary: Humble on the N., Andrewes and Talbot on the S.

Now back to the **S. quire aisle**, with the organ on the left and a ramp on the right leading down to the crypt. Set into the aisle floor is a small piece of tesselated Roman pavement found in the churchyard.

The **S. transept** repeats the N. in all its essentials, but is 14th c. rather than 13th and thus offers interesting comparisons; the main shafts, for example, are stone, not Purbeck marble. The main S. window is 19th c. On the E. side is the display face of the organ. The coloured coat-of-arms on the column beside it is that of Cardinal Beaufort (d. 1447). Of the monuments on the S. and W. walls the following, in clockwise order, are of more than passing interest: to Thomas Cole (d. 1715), a refined specimen of a very standard type, with three cherubs' heads; to Thomas Jones (d. 1710), with his bust; to John Bingham (d. 1625), with half-figure high up; to William Emerson (d. 1575), with a tiny effigy; to Sir Frederick Wigan (d. 1907) a cathedral benefactor; and to Richard Benefeld, with another 17th c. bust.

Just inside the **S. aisle** on the left is a canopied monument with reclining effigy of William Shakespeare, carved in a strangely textured stone – not, of course, his tomb, though his brother Edmund was buried in the church in 1607. The font and cover at the W. end of the aisle are by Bodley. In the W. bay some 13th c. wall-arcading forms the base of Blomfield's outer wall.

Finally the remainder of the **outside**. A good general viewpoint is the SW. corner of the churchyard, i.e. half right outside the S.

porch. The W. end is overshadowed by warehouses. There is a way round the N. aisle, past the vestries huddled against it. The N. wall of the N. transept has been refaced, but just past it is a piece of rough masonry that begins to curve back into the building: this is part of the Norman apse which stood in the place of the present Harvard chapel. The E. end can then be inspected from the lower road, from which there are ways back either to the S. porch or to London Bridge.

Southwark, St George (Roman Catholic, Greater London)

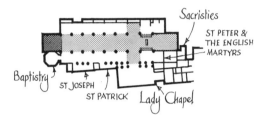

The first Catholic chapel in Southwark was founded in 1786, a room in a house. Within a few years a proper chapel had been built near the Elephant and Castle. In 1838 Augustus Pugin designed an over-ambitious scheme rivalling Westminster Abbey in size, but lack of money forced him to reduce it drastically. Dedicated in 1848, it became a cathedral in 1850 when dioceses were established.

Having been severely bombed in 1941 and 1944, it was extensively restored in the 1950s under Romilly Craze. The arcades, clerestory and shallow transepts are his, as well as the Lady chapel and undercroft and the baptistry.

The first impression is of pleasant clean Caen stone and yellow brick, coupled with a sense of disappointment at the unfinished tower (not entirely a war casualty, for it was never completed by Pugin). The main entrance leads beneath it to a light airy interior of light stone and plaster, an amalgam of Pugin and a style somewhere near Perpendicular: white composition floor, complex columns with shafts to nave and aisle and double shafts for the arches, no triforium, clerestory with curious semicircles superimposed on the tracery, and stone-arched steep timber roof with painted panels. The main E. and W. windows are very rich and dark.

The aisles have skeleton vaults, Bristol fashion, supporting flat ceilings and cruciform light pendants; their red, white, grey and gold colouring is typical of much of the restored interior. In the **N. aisle** are the tombs of the founder, Thomas Provost Doyle (d. 1879), and Archbishop Amigo (d. 1949), contrasting Victorian richness with modern dignity. Then on the left is Pugin's little vaulted Knill chantry, a fascinating miniature chapel richly but not excessively coloured and gilded; the 'aisled' treatment of its sides, and the canopied Adoration of the reredos are specially noteworthy. The NE. chapel of the Blessed Sacrament has a gilded iron screen and a stone reredos which was unharmed in the bombing.

Now back to the '**crossing**' which Craze formed by raising a bay of each aisle roof and bringing the altar further W. The communion rail is plain unpierced marble, the bishop's throne and stalls simple Gothic, and the temporary wooden nave altar very plain by contrast with the richly curtained high altar and its gilded angels. The arched and panelled presbytery ceiling is painted, like the nave, with a variety of sacred emblems.

Beyond the red and gold screen to the right is the chapel of St Peter and the English Martyrs. Then a double arcade with little traceried screens between the bays, and in the centre bay the Petre chantry. This arcade leads to the **Lady chapel**, its main body entirely by Craze and distinguished by large windows of Elizabethan type. The new altar is central on the S. side, the old E. sanctuary with a wooden star vault and rich blue circular window being visible through a silver screen.

The chantry of Edward Petre (d. 1848), is another work of Pugin, notable for the rich carving and gilding of its altar and reredos. The fan vault, too, is gilded but rather oddly, in its panels instead of its ribs.

The **S. aisle** is similar to the N., but instead of being lined with confessionals (which on the N. occupy the areas between the buttresses) it has two chapels: first St Patrick's, distinguished by its green carpet and by the addition of green to the colour scheme of its flat ceiling, and then St Joseph's, vaulted in two parts of differing heights.

Finally the **baptistry**, another addition by Craze, with silvered iron gates and a plain octagonal 'tub' font with a silvered saucer-cover. It has an ingenious double-cross vault with four pendants where the ribs cross and a higher, red, centre section.

Outside, the W. front flanked by the baptistry is imposing in spite of the tower's being stunted. For the rest, a perambulation is not greatly rewarding. Going anti-clockwise: the passage down the S.

side leads to the entrance to the undercroft beneath the Lady chapel, normally locked when not in use for functions. However, the exterior of the chapel with its handsome W. doorway and windows is attractive. From there it is possible to walk through the car park, round the rather depressing multi-storey brick block of diocesan buildings, and back to the S. side of the cathedral, which is best appreciated from the other side of Lambeth Road.

Southwell, St Mary (Church of England, Nottinghamshire)

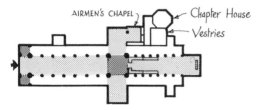

The title Minster here indicates a college of priests, not a monastery – but with such independence from the diocesan authority of York that in the Middle Ages it had its own chapter and influence similar to a cathedral's: however, it became the seat of a bishop only in 1884. The earliest documentary record refers to a date near 956. Slight remains of the Saxon church exist, but it is thought not to have survived the Conquest. A complete rebuilding was begun about 1108, and of that church the greater part from the crossing and transept westwards survives. The E. parts were rebuilt to a much extended plan in the years 1234 onwards. The chapter house with its approach was added in the last decade of the 13th c. and the great W. window was put in in the 15th c. Subsequent work included major restorations following damage in the Civil War and from a fire in 1711, and in 1880 some re-roofing and alterations to the tower tops under Ewan Christian.

The bold **W. front** with its twin towers makes this one of the least English-looking amongst cathedrals; yet its pyramidal steeples represent much more accurately the original appearance of major Norman towers than most others which have either lost their steeples or have been given some quite different termination. Here the tops were rebuilt in 1880. The central doorway of four orders is original, and so are the doors themselves with their splendid scrolly ironwork; but the very large window above is, of course,

Perpendicular. Before its insertion the **nave** and aisles must have been extremely dark.

Inside the W. doorway the first impression is of the strong rhythm of the 12th c. arcades marching towards the crossing arches, which frame the pulpitum and organ. The barrel roof with its prominent tie-beams is of 1880; the aisles have their Norman rib-vaults. Compared with many, the arcades are not tall. The triforium seems almost as tall; each arch of it was meant to be subdivided with a little central column and two smaller arches in the normal way, but apparently with the addition of a little upper column resting on the lower and going up to the crown of the main arch where a stub to receive it can be seen. The clerestory is unusual too in that the actual windows are circular, though that is only obvious from outside. The two W. towers are inconspicuous inside because the three storeys run on across them with just a wider pier at the junction.

The **N. aisle** has little of interest: some matrices of brasses in the floor, an incised effigy beneath the first arch of the arcade, a cross-slab in a recess in the N. wall, and the doorway to the N. porch (the inner lobby of which is by Ronald Sims, 1978). The glass in the W. part was shown at the Great Exhibition of 1851 and is by O'Connor. E. of the porch the window pattern changes to Perpendicular.

In the **nave** the canopied pulpit with figure carving, the eagle lectern and the bishop's throne are all 19th or early 20th c. Going back into the aisle to pass the nave sanctuary, one comes to the **N. transept**. The crossing arches, N. and S., are of exceptional majesty, with cable ornament and quite tiny capitals. All is still Norman, and similar in design to the nave. But in the NW. corner the stair turret doorway has a primitive lintel that could be Saxon: on its left are David with the lion and lamb, and on its right the dragon, with winged St Michael in the centre. The large alabaster tomb in the NE. corner is of Archbishop Sandys (d. 1588). The eight steps beside it lead into the vaulted Airmen's chapel, all early Decorated and with extraordinarily acute arches.

On the E. wall of the transept are some minor tablets, also the bronze bust of Bishop Hoskyns (d. 1925). Then the **N. quire aisle**, through gates and up a step. This is where the Norman building gives way to Early English, but it is best to wait till the quire itself before looking closely at its design. For the moment the odd irregularity of the aisle vault should be noticed – determined by the problems of joining on to the earlier building. On the left is a door to a stair leading to the library over the Airmen's chapel. Then

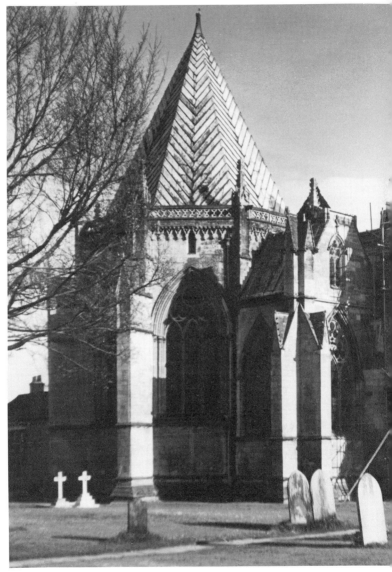

Chapter House, Southwell (late 13th c.)

comes the **chapter house** doorway, a marvellously enriched double arch with leaf carving on the capitals. Four steps lead down to an arcaded passage containing various exhibits, and on the right are vestries where originally was a little open court. Then on the right is an even richer double opening with Purbeck marble shafts and foliage carving of the utmost delicacy and beauty. It is no exaggeration to say that this is one of the finest doorways in the country. Through it lies the chapter house itself, fairly small, but the only one in England vaulted without a central column. Here too the foliage carving is justly famous.

In this room lies the inspiration for so much 19th c. ornament: yet its tenderness is the antithesis of almost anything the Victorians could achieve. Least damaged and restored, and least easily seen, are the window-capitals, and the bosses of the star-vault. The scattered fragments of coloured glass are mostly Flemish of the 16th and 17th cc. The big brass of which a rubbing is displayed is not in the cathedral but at Bottesford in Leicestershire.

Back in the **N. quire aisle**, the vestry door is on the left, and then the tiny E. transept which is a chapel reserved for private prayer. Its W. wall is arcaded too, with delicate leaf carving, and the windows are of about 1910, memorials to the Maltby family. The chapel at the E. end of the aisle itself has similar glass.

Now go in to the **quire**, past the showy quire pulpit of *c.* 1890. Here the arcade system is two-storeyed, i.e. the triforium and clerestory are combined beneath one tier of arches, which is very unusual. The sombre, stately nave and the tense, striving quire seem to need the pulpitum to keep them visually apart, so great is their emotional contrast. The date of the quire is 1233–48, the style pure Early English, the scale small compared with, say, Lincoln or Salisbury, but the design quality first-rate.

The pulpitum is another *tour de force* of medieval carving, this time of about 1320–30. The two-storeyed E. face is extraordinarily rich with crocketed gables and pinnacles and carved heads, and the niche behind the archbishop's stall is distinguished by an all-over diaper pattern. The stalls themselves are all 19th c. but the six return stalls have 14th c. misericords and the splendid brass eagle lectern between them is of about 1500 and came with two brass candlesticks from Newstead Abbey, where they had been thrown into a pond at the Dissolution.

The eight lancet windows in the E. wall follow the two-storeyed scheme of the rest of the quire. The glass in the lower ones is 16th c. and came in 1818 from the Temple church in Paris. To their right, the piscina and the rare five sedilia are contemporary with the pulpitum, equally rich but rather more heavily restored. The kneeling effigy under the E. arch of the S. arcade is of Bishop Ridding, first bishop of the diocese (d. 1904); his monument is by W. D. Caröe.

The **S. quire aisle** follows the pattern of the N., and its little transept has glass of *c.* 1906 like that opposite. It also has a big cope chest of 1961. The next aisle window contains a jumble of ancient glass.

The wood sculpture just inside the **S. transept** on the right is the Kelham Madonna (1952) by Alan Coleman. In design the transept is like the N. but its E. chapel (which in both cases was apsidal) has gone altogether, leaving blocked Norman openings. Below the larger of these is a model of the cathedral. On the walls are a few minor memorials, and on the floor quite a number of small brass plates, mostly shields. On the W. side are two rows of 15th c. 'bread pews'; beneath their front row is a trapdoor through which can be seen a piece of tesselated paving, probably the floor of the Saxon church using Roman materials.

From the **crossing** the W. side of the pulpitum can be seen more closely. It is rather less elaborate than the quire face. Within are miniature vaults with flying ribs that connect the two sides. Architecturally the crossing has much of interest, in the great arches and their carving, in the zigzag mouldings of the second stage arches (reputed to be amongst the earliest examples), and in the primitive figure carving of the capitals high up on the E. arch, believed by some to have belonged to the pre-Norman building.

The **S. aisle** windows repeat the arrangement of the N. aisle. Towards its W. end is the font of 1661, one of a large local group installed after the end of the Commonwealth. Its cover is of the same date.

On the **outside** wall close to the W. doorway is a quaint little tablet to George Chappell (d. 1679). A short way up the path stand four small headstones of the same period, with good lettering. Next, the N. side of the cathedral. The porch, very much a part of the original Norman design, is remarkable specially for its barrel vault: also for its two big pinnacles (the W. one of which is a chimney) and the rich internal wall arcading and inner doorway. Then the outer elevation of the nave and aisles with its wavy (in heraldic terms 'nebuly') corbel-tables and circular clerestory windows, and the N. transept, the gable of which is filled with a repeating zigzag pattern. Next comes the chapter house.

Facing the E. end is Vicars' Court, an attractive group of plain houses of 1780 with The Residence (provost's house) at the end. Further round, opposite the S. side of the quire, is the Bishop's Palace, a house of 1907–9 by Caröe within the ruin of a far larger palace built by the archbishops of York in the 14th and 15th cc. It is not open to the public.

In general the S. side of the cathedral repeats the N. The rich 12th c. segmental-headed doorway of the S. transept, however, should not be missed, and further on is an opportunity to study the central tower with its tiers of plain and intersecting arcades; no doubt it too once had a pyramidal roof. Finally the green slope up to the 15th c. churchyard gateway, from which the W. front is again in full view.

Truro, St Mary (Church of England, Cornwall)

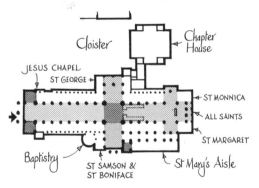

The Celtic church in Cornwall had its origins long before the Anglo-Saxon foundation of the see of St German's – which was formed out of that of Crediton *c.* 931 and re-united with it in 1043. The county remained linked with Devon as part of Exeter diocese from 1050 until 1876. When in the latter year the Cornish see was revived, Truro gained favour over Bodmin, which as the county town was the more obvious choice, because the latter was handicapped by having rejected the railway.

There was a typical two-aisled parish church; the S. aisle, now called St Mary's aisle, was retained as an integral part of the new cathedral, designed by J. L. Pearson and built between 1880 and

1910. His son Frank Pearson completed the nave and towers. Of the intended cloister, one bay was built in 1935. The chapter house, designed by John Taylor, was completed in 1967.

Pearson's style is Early English, but his silhouettes and massing are more French in character. Apart from keeping St Mary's aisle he made no concessions to Cornish traditional design; his soaring concept was inspired more by the busily enclosed site, and it is remarkable that a building of this size could have been fitted into the centre of such a close-knit town.

The double W. portal leads first to a vaulted area under the W. gallery. Ahead, the **nave** has arcades on clustered columns with the logical but unorthodox addition of a vaulting shaft continued down their main face. The triforium bay design of four lancets and a quatrefoil under one arch is unusual too; the clerestory of two twin lights is double, with a walkway. The vault is sexpartite (i.e., French in character), so the shafts already noted are alternately plain and clustered. The aisles have quadripartite vaults and tall free-standing wall arcades, forming an extra walkway against the outer wall. The slight twist in the alignment of nave and quire is due to the lines of the adjacent streets.

Under the NW. tower is a triple 19th c. monument in Jacobean style with busts of the 17th c. Sir John Eliot, Sidney Earl of Godolphin, and Sir William Molesworth. The first bay of the **N. aisle**, screened off as a chapel, has a reredos painting of Christ blessing Cornish industry. Further on, on the left, is a simple tablet by Allan Wyon to Sir Arthur Quiller-Couch (d. 1944). Under the arcade is the splendid brass lectern: an eagle trampling on a basilisk, flanked by candlesticks and with Evangelists' figures below.

The chapel opposite, in the aisled **N. transept**, is St George's, with numerous tablets on the W. wall, mostly to the Vivian family and some of them 'skied'; in its sanctuary is one to Richard Pendarves (d. 1667). The architecture is like the nave but with quadripartite vaulting; across the N. side is a gallery arcade slightly less tall than the main one. Under this are a classical tablet to Francis Burges (d. 1684) and the large canopied memorial of John Robartes (d. 1614), with two reclining effigies on shelves. To their right is the doorway to the chapter house, occasionally open in summer for refreshments but normally only to be seen from outside. On the transept E. wall is a tablet to the astronomer John Couch Adams (d. 1892).

Now into the **crossing**: by its NE. pier is Pearson's pulpit. The tower lantern has an impressive radiating vault on a square plan. On the left of the entrance to the **N. quire aisle** an ivory staff is displayed, then a marvellously detailed terra-cotta panel by George Tinworth and on the right an altar frontal chest of 1887. A floor brass is to Canon Donaldson (d. 1903). On the right can be seen the quire behind fine wrought-iron screens.

St Monnica's chapel in the NE. transept is entered through a wooden screen; all three E. chapels are intended for private prayer. Steps on the left lead to the crypt (not open to the public). Turn right instead by the altar, to **All Saints' chapel** behind the high altar, partly within the shallow two-storeyed easternmost bay. Either side of its pinnacled reredos are bronze plaques of 1910 to Bishops Wilkinson and Gott. The SE. chapel, St Margaret's, has brasses set in its wall-arcading, demi-figures of Canon Mason (d. 1884) and Canon Worlledge (d. 1919). Through the screen, in the floor of the S. quire aisle, is another of Bishop Frere (d. 1935).

Next, up the black steps into the **quire**, which is of more elaborate design than the nave. Triforium and clerestory are both double, the former with three sub-arches, the latter with twin plain lancets, and all enriched with dog-tooth ornament. The pavement is patterned with marble. The bishop's throne and stalls are by Pearson – of teak, apart from the prominent little statues below the canopy work which are oak. Turning E.: his elaborate but rather flat reredos is flanked by six Decorated-style sedilia each side, continuing on the N. with a throne and on the S. with a double piscina.

Return now to the S. quire aisle and pass beneath the extra outer arcade, down again into an ambulatory. On the left is another stair to the crypt, and ahead through an iron screen lies St Mary's aisle. On the left of the steps down into its W. end is a carving of St Nicholas from Brittany, *c.* 1500. The aisle is of 1504–18, typically Cornish in its ceiled wagon roof, simple clustered piers and wide arches, but less so in the close-packed pairs of windows. On the left is a bulbous 18th c. inlaid pulpit, and beyond it an organ said to have been intended for one of the Chapels Royal. A double piscina is in the sanctuary. The glass along the S. side is by William Warrington (that in the main building is by Clayton & Bell). Under Pearson's vaulted tower at the W. end of the aisle is a 19th c. font; also slate headstones on either side of the S. window, that to Owen Phippen (d. 1636) having a quaint account of adventures in Turkey. Nearby are pictures of the old church, a 16th c. poor-box, and an early 17th c. brass to George Phippen, rector.

The **S. transept** is like the N., but shorter and without a gallery. Round to the right is the staff of Edward Benson, first bishop and later Archbishop of Canterbury; round to the left on the E. wall is his simple memorial brass. Past the S. door are tablets to three others intimately connected with the building: Archbishop Temple, William fourth Earl of Mount Edgcumbe, and Edmund Carlyon. The adjoining chapel of St Sampson and St Boniface has a floor brass to Archbishop Benson; beyond is the baptistry, best seen from the **S. nave aisle**. Here Pearson has compressed his interpretation of Early English into a tight circular space and enriched it with shafts of Cornish serpentine. The font is mostly of red porphyry, with a pinnacled oak cover.

On the aisle wall are tablets by Wyon to two later bishops, 1949–50. One of the piers of the main arcade, of granite instead of Doulting stone, contains the foundation stone laid in 1880 by the future King Edward VII. On the left, a war memorial recess contains a Pietà, a book of remembrance and a marble tablet to Captain Thomas Agar-Robartes (d. 1915). Then the disused S. porch door and the bookstall, and the SW. tower which (unlike the NW. which has a wooden ceiling) is open upwards. It contains a large Boer war memorial and one to Edward VII.

Outside, look first at the W. front, from the little square called High Cross. The towers, completed in 1910, were called after King Edward VII and Queen Alexandra; statues of them and other monarchs and of notable persons connected with cathedral and county can be identified on the portal buttresses. On the N. side a cloister was planned: the former cathedral school (now offices) on the far side of the churchyard marks its extent, and one bay was built against the N. transept in 1935. Look up at the central tower, and pass under the chapter house (1967), concrete-faced and in quite a different idiom from Pearson's building but sitting happily in its shadow. Old Bridge Street gives a close view of the E. front with its crypt vestries, and leads to St Mary's Street alongside the old S. aisle. Externally this is more ornate than most late Perpendicular Cornish churches; amongst its carved work the (restored) Tudor arms with greyhound supporters on the E. wall should be noticed. At its W. end Pearson gave it its own tower, copper-capped, which assists the transition in scale between church and cathedral. Beyond are the big S. transept portal, rich with figure sculpture, and the plainer, now disused S. porch.

Wakefield, All Saints (Church of England, West Yorkshire)

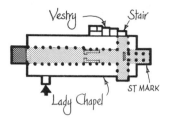

Wakefield was created a bishopric in 1888 and its ancient parish church a cathedral. Mostly Perpendicular at first sight, it is really a little more complex. Parts of the nave piers are in fact Norman. The arcades and aisles were gradually extended; the present chancel and its arcades are 15th c., as well as the nave clerestory and the tower. The S. aisle was rebuilt in 1724 and the N. aisle not long afterwards. Sir George Gilbert Scott rebuilt the spire and much of the exterior in 1858–74. The E. extension with retro-quire was added by F. L. Pearson in 1904.

After centuries of encirclement by noisy streets, the building is now virtually isolated from wheeled traffic. First to catch the eye inside the S. door are the tall arcades, the gilded Rood and angels (by Sir Ninian Comper, 1950) and the many 19th c. traceried pew-ends. The round piers of the N. arcade are 12th c., but were originally not so tall. Their tops and ill-fitting capitals and the other piers are 14th c. and so are the arches themselves. On the S. side the piers seem to be 13th c., of assorted sections, and the arches again 14th c. The W. bays and the tower with its tall arch are 15th c.; so is the clerestory, though that and the nave and aisle roofs are largely Scott's work, with old bosses re-used.

Most of the glass in the **S. aisle**, and indeed in the cathedral generally, is by Kempe, from the 1870s onwards. At the W. end of the S. wall, however, is a strange 19th c. window in purples and reds by Barnett of Newcastle. The unusually proportioned font is dated 1661 and has the churchwardens' initials on the bowl; the tall pinnacled cover is new. Into the **nave** now for a better view of the roof and the 17th c. rood screen, and then into the tower where two banners of the King's Own Yorkshire Light Infantry are framed on the N. wall. Three 18th c. memorials are also visible there; two more are 'skied' and like a number of others in the cathedral might be of interest if they could be seen.

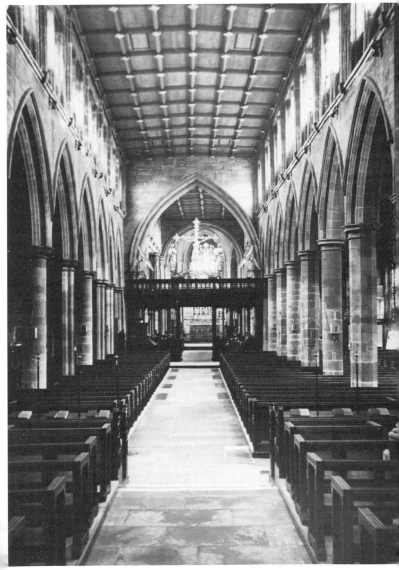

Cathedral interior, Wakefield

In the **N. aisle** is more Kempe glass; also a fine royal arms of
George III over the N. door and tablets to John Cookson (d. 1779)
and Samuel Disney (d. 1741). On the right, the square pulpit is all
that is left of a 'three-decker' of 1708. The carpeted nave sanctuary
has a 17th c. altar-table and three old carved chairs. A closer look at
the unusual screen shows that the lower part may well be older than
the delicately carved main arches and thin columns, which are
known to be of 1635. The chancel arch is 14th c., i.e. the same
period as the nave arches.

In the **N. quire aisle** is a display case of plate. Beyond it stands a
fine organ case of 1743 with cherubs and gilding. Other furniture
here includes a carved cupboard, two chests (probably 17th c.) by
the doorway to the vestries, and in the centre of the aisle a
magnificent rococo marquetry cabinet. At this point the Pearson
extension commences: a small E. transept with its own arcades and
a short retro-quire with incredibly slender columns supporting a
lierne vault. On the N. wall of the easternmost bay is a neat classical
tablet to Edward Green (d. 1865). This is the War Memorial chapel,
dedicated to the Holy Trinity. Through the screen is **St Mark's
chapel**, reserved for private prayer. The glass is contemporary,
c. 1905, but the canopied altar is of 1943. The communion rail is by
Thomas of Kilburn and bears his 'mouse' trade mark.

In the SE. chapel are two tablets to bishops, and in the S. transept
a Gothic tomb with white marble effigy by James Forsyth of the first
bishop of the diocese, Bishop How (d. 1897). Near it stands a replica
of the Saxon Wakefield Cross; the original is in St Mary's Abbey
Museum, York. The **Lady chapel**, within the old building, is still
where it was founded in 1322. It contains several 18th c. wall tablets
to the Pilkington family and two medieval stone coffin-lids. The very
large monument with reclining effigy is to Sir Lyon Pilkington
(d. 1714).

Now pass through the wooden screen into the **quire**, which is
15th c.; the roof lines of the 14th c. chancel can, however, be seen on
the E. face of the arch to the nave. Inside on the left is the bishop's
throne of 1974 by George Pace; its tracery has a curiously shaved-
off appearance. The elegant wall tablet on a column is to John
Ingram (d. 1841). The stalls and the screenwork behind are partly
15th c. (particularly on the S. side), with some old poppy-heads and
animals on the ends, and some misericords. In the sanctuary the
altar, reredos and stone sedilia are all by Pearson (1896–1912).

Back in the Lady chapel, the angled wall formerly contained a
stair to the rood loft. Memorials worth noting are to Janet Munro

(d. 1824), Elizabeth Maude (d. 1766) and Priscilla Smith (d. 1730). The last is of cast iron and may not have been meant for wall display.

The screen to the **S. aisle** was formed from the doors of the main chancel screen. In the corner by the chancel arch pier are another ancient coffin-lid and one discarded medieval bench-end.

Finally the outside, with a pause in the S. porch to look at the good wrought-iron outer gates. On the aisles, the curious tassel-like crockets on the buttresses and pinnacles are no doubt an authentic restoration by Scott of the late medieval appearance – likewise the panelled parapets and the 247 ft spire, the highest in Yorkshire – and there is now no obvious sign of the 18th c. rebuildings. Past the tower and down the N. side a narrow stepped passage leads into Teall Street below; Pearson's E. end towering above is as intricate outside as in, and can now be seen to be two-storeyed, with a crypt containing vestries and chapter room. A churchyard path leads back to the S. porch, passing the foundation stone of 1901 on the S. transept, as well as an ancient sundial.

Wells, St Andrew (Church of England, Somerset)

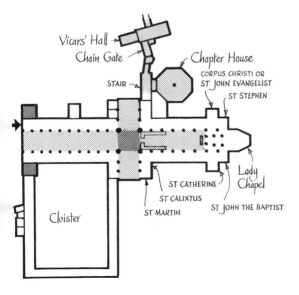

The diocese was founded in 909. The inclusion of Bath in its present name Bath and Wells is a legacy from the Middle Ages: until the dissolution of Bath Abbey the bishop had a throne there too and was elected by both chapters. It is said that the first collegiate church was built at Wells in 705. Nothing of that survives, nor of early 12th c. building work which is recorded.

The present cathedral was begun about 1180 and consecrated in 1239, but there was an important second phase of work in about 1290 to 1340, comprising the chapter house, the E. end with its Lady chapel and transepts and the quire vaults, and the upper part of the central tower and the stiffening of the lower parts. The W. towers were not finished till 1436; the central one was altered again *c*. 1440 and there were extensive alterations of parapets and window tracery in the same period. The cloister buildings are substantially 15th c.

Most people start at the famous 13th c. **W. front** and it can well be examined before the interior, to which it bears less relation than those of most cathedrals. This is chiefly because the towers stand clear of the aisles, and the nave-and-aisles shape is not expressed but takes second place to treatment of the whole façade as a display space for sculpture. Now bare Doulting limestone with the carving ravaged by destroyers and the weather, it once was coloured and gilded, at least in the niches and on the actual statues. Some idea of its quality can be gained from recent work on the N. tower where the carving has been cleaned and consolidated. A guide to the subjects can be bought, and it must suffice here to mention only a few, starting at the very top with the stump of a seated Christ. Below are the twelve Apostles (these are not 13th c., but of about 1400). Immediately over the main W. windows and running to left and right and all round the buttresses are niches with scenes of the Resurrection of the Dead. Over the main doorway is a very small Coronation of the Virgin, and in the tympanum a seated Virgin. The figures least accessible to iconoclasts are of course least damaged – e.g., around the N. tower. The upper parts of the towers, flat-topped and unassuming, are 15th c., and so are some of the lower windows.

Entrance is by the left-hand doorway, typically English in its human size. The **nave** is dominated by the giant X-shaped structure stiffening the crossing arch. This was put in in 1338 onwards because the tower had shown alarming weaknesses. Everything else is of *c*. 1200: fairly low arcades with exquisitely moulded arches and piers, and continuous shallow triforium not subdivided into bays at

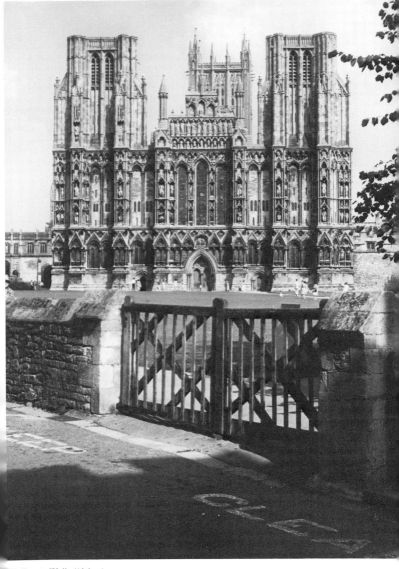

W. Front, Wells (13th c.)

all (the vaulting corbels come no lower than the clerestory). The painted foliage on the vault is a 19th c. restoration.

Walk E. three or four bays and look back to the W. window. The centre glass is by A. K. Nicholson (1931) but the remainder of 1670; the arches have dog-tooth ornament, coloured. As building work progressed westwards the foliage on the corbels and capitals became richer; a distinct break can be detected about half-way along the nave where the stone blocks become bigger and the head stops above the main arches die out. Other irregularities may be noticed: two big heads over the third and fourth piers of the S. arcade (originally intended to support an organ), and a 15th c. balcony right up in the clerestory of the sixth bay. Every part of Wells Cathedral is to be lingered in for the sake of its carving and this is truer of no part more than the nave.

The recommended visitors' route is anti-clockwise, and thus continues in the **S. aisle** where several windows are of *c.* 1900 by C. E. Kempe. Towards the end is the Sugar chantry. Hugh Sugar, cathedral treasurer, died in 1489 and his chantry balances Bishop Bubwith's on the N. But Bishop Knight (d. 1547) altered it to provide access to the remarkable early Renaissance stone pulpit which he gave and in which he himself was buried. From here is a nearer view of the stiffener arches and of the Rood put in in 1924 where one had stood originally.

The design of the **S. transept** is as the quire was, or was intended: arcades much as in the nave, triforium definitely divided into bays (except at the end where in both transepts it is continuous like the nave), clerestory and plain vault. There is much superb carving in capitals and corbels; on the capitals of the W. arcade are two of the cathedral's most famous sculptures, medieval equivalents of cartoon strips: 'the fruit thieves' and 'ailments'. The arch to the S. nave aisle was strengthened *c.* 1320 with an extra inner arch rather to the detriment of these carvings; similar extra stonework was added at the end of the nave arcade, and on the N. side, but it seems that the weakness was still evident and so the 'scissors' arches were inserted. This whole system of muscular tower stiffeners can now be seen at closer quarters, and above them the fan vault of the crossing, late 15th c.

The small round lightly arcaded font in the centre of the transept is probably of the same period as the building; its cover is 17th c. In the SW. corner is the entrance to the extensive 15th c. library building over the E. walk of the cloister. This was re-equipped in 1686 and may be seen on Mondays and Thursdays in summer.

Alongside it is a way out to the cloister. The two memorials on the
S. wall are not definitely identified: an elaborately canopied tomb
with fine effigy, believed to be of Bishop le Marchia (d. 1302), and a
chantry altar containing the brass of Joan Countess de Lisle
(d. 1464). The various carved heads around the former seem to be
unexplained. Under the E. arcade are 14th c. stone screens to two
chapels reserved for private prayer, each with 15th c. iron gates
made from the railings of the Bekynton chantry. The first, with a
brightly coloured reredos and a county roll of honour, is
St Martin's; the tomb here is of William Byconyll (d. 1448), and
there is some old glass. The left-hand chapel, St Calixtus', contains a
15th c. tomb with alabaster carvings: whose it is is uncertain.

   Now through the screen into the **S. quire aisle**, mostly a
continuation of the 1180–1239 building though the lierne vaults, of
an odd pattern without diagonal or ridge ribs, are of a century later.
A charge is made at this point to enter the E. part of the cathedral.
Just inside the screen is the alabaster effigy of Bishop Harewell
(d. 1386). Against the back of the quire stalls are the first three of a
series of effigies of Saxon bishops – all made in the early 13th c. and
entirely conjectural, but nevertheless valuable sculpture of their
time. Then three misericords (two medieval and one a 17th c.
imitation), the lightly incised tomb-slab of Bishop Bytton II
(d. 1274), the white marble effigy of Bishop Hervey (d. 1894) on an
alabaster tomb, and (on the left) a floor brass to Bishop Lake
(d. 1626). On the left is an opening into the **quire**.

   Architecturally this is perhaps the least successful part of the
cathedral, partly because of its mixture of dates and styles and
partly because of its irrational vault pattern. In the three E. bays,
which are early 14th c. and built after the work further E., the
triforium gives way completely to an array of delicate niches, very
vertical in form and feeling; in the three W. bays a similar treatment
was implanted on the earlier work, which must originally have
looked (at that level) like the transept. The three arches behind the
altar frame a glorious view of the E. end: the window above, like the
niches (the statues in which are a World War I memorial), is on the
verge of being Perpendicular in style instead of Decorated. It and
two windows each side (five in all) contain 14th c. glass, the main
one with a Jesse Tree being one of the best examples of the period in
England. The first and seventh windows of this group are of *c.* 1850.
The quire furniture also largely dates from Salvin's restoration of
1848–54. The sub-stalls however are 14th c. with a host of original
misericords, many of animal subjects. These can best be studied in

the comprehensive booklet of photographs on sale. The rich needlework on the stalls is of 1937–49. The pulpitum is 14th c., but Salvin altered it by projecting the centre part on the nave side to help carry the organ (the present organ case was completed in 1974).

Now back into the **S. quire aisle**, with some 15th and 17th c. glass (heraldry and scenes) in the windows straight ahead. On the left is the chantry of Bishop Bekynton (d. 1465); this has an effigy and cadaver, an elaborate altar canopy and splendid ironwork. In the next bay is another Saxon bishop's effigy. The following one opens out into the retro-quire, but first, on the right, is St Catherine's chapel with, at the entrance, the tomb of Bishop Drokensford (d. 1329), which has original colouring. The E. end of the cathedral was built in his time. In the chapel windows is some 16th c. Dutch glass from Rouen, and on the W. wall two small brasses of 1573 and 1618; the latter, to Humphrey Willis, is quaintly amusing. The tomb under the S. window is of Dean Gunthorpe (d. 1498).

St John the Baptist's chapel within the E. end of the aisle has a jumble of early 14th c. glass fragments; the tall canopied tomb with high pinnacled gables to the left may be that of John Martel (d. 1341). Beyond is the **retro-quire**.

This and the Lady chapel form a supreme masterpiece of Decorated architecture, and they need to be understood together. Except that the E. end of the Lady chapel is polygonal, all is rectangular in outline. Yet the Lady chapel contrives to be a graceful elongated octagon which visually merges with the retro-quire but really stops at two big clustered columns at its W. end. W. of those, stretching from aisle to aisle, is an even more elongated hexagonal shape bounded by the two columns and four more. The ingenious vaulting patterns and the placing of the columns give an endlessly fascinating interplay of diagonal vistas and lighting effects. Add to this the stone carving, colouring on the Lady chapel vault (done by T. H. Willement in 1845), and much original glass, and the result is indeed a masterpiece.

In the retro-quire are a 14th c. chapter chest and a great part-circular cope chest of the same date. In the Lady chapel the sedilia are by Benjamin Ferrey (1843). The glass is largely 14th c. and, though fragmentary, has many details to examine and enjoy.

The chapel in the E. end of the **N. quire aisle** (which virtually mirrors the S.) is St Stephen's and has furnishings by Sir Ninian Comper: altar with riddel posts, and a side screen with his typical gilded cresting. Its E. window is made up of medieval pieces. The projecting side chapel to its left is of Corpus Christi or St John the

Evangelist, and set aside for private devotion. Its columned wooden screen is partly 16th c. Under it is the tomb of Dean Godelee (d. 1333). Within the chapel are effigies of John Middleton (d. 1337) and Bishop Creyghton (d. 1672), the latter in alabaster on a bulging tomb-chest. The N. window above is of 1902 and on the E. wall is a 15th c. stone Ascension.

Continuing W. along the N. quire aisle: on the left is another Saxon bishop; on the right a window with some medieval glass. In the next window is more old glass and opposite it the alabaster effigy of Bishop Ralph of Shrewsbury (d. 1363) on a modern tomb. The window in the next bay has glass dated 1537; opposite are steps to the quire pulpit and a doorway into the quire. Next comes the plain tomb of Bishop Berkeley (d. 1581), and the last two of the series of Saxon bishops. A door on the right leads into a passage and thence to the undercroft of the chapter house; these are not open to the public.

Now into the N. transept which architecturally differs little from the S. Turn right first however along its E. aisle and through the medieval door ahead. It reveals the **chapter house** stair, one of the most beautiful parts of the cathedral and one of the loveliest staircases anywhere. It was completed in 1306. The worn steps lead straight ahead by a bridge (the 15th c. Chain Gate) over the road to the Vicars' Hall, and half-way up branch off to the chapter house itself. The Vicars' Hall, an unspoilt little 14th c. dining hall, is not normally open, but it is worth going as far as the door to enjoy the completely medieval atmosphere of the enclosed high passage, and then to go down and up again to the chapter house.

The vault is the glory of the chapter house. Thirty-two shafts radiate from its central column and nine more, palm-like, from every corner shaft, all meeting amongst a wealth of foliage bosses. The windows have 14th c. glass in their tracery, and their arches are lined with ball-flower ornament. More ball-flower runs round the stone stall-backs, which have portrait-heads between. Above the bishop's stall are the arms of James I.

On the left of the stair on the way down, near the bottom, is a particularly endearing carving of a gentle pilgrim stuffing his staff into the throat of a dragon, typical of Wells's rich leavening of religion with fantasy and fun. Back in the **N. transept** aisle, immediately on the right is the canopied tomb of Bishop Cornish (d. 1513). Against the E. wall is a monument to Bishop Kidder (d. 1703) with a reclining female allegorical figure, and one to Bishop Still (d. 1607) with lying effigy and original colouring.

In the N. transept itself, reached through the unusual 14th c. screen, is more superb carving in capitals and corbels. A charge is made to see the clock on its N. wall. A descriptive pamphlet explains the complex dial, the jousting knights that revolve above it, and Jack Blandifer who sounds the quarters at the far end of the triforium. The mechanism of *c*. 1390 was renewed in 1838 and again in 1880, the original (still working) being in the Science Museum at South Kensington. The W. aisle, behind the clock, is closed off with a stone screen; the Risen Christ, of yew-wood, is of 1955.

Then W. again along the **N. nave aisle**. On the left beside the nave altar is the Holy Cross chapel, or chantry of Bishop Bubwith (d. 1424), six-sided to fit between the arcade piers; it can be entered from the aisle and has an alabaster Ascension panel. Just beyond is the lectern or 'brazen Deske' of 1661, so inscribed and given by Dean Creyghton as a thank-offering for his return from exile. It is very like those at Canterbury and Lincoln.

Finally the exterior, and the lierne-vaulted **cloister** which can be reached by turning left and left again outside the W. front. Straight ahead through its porch one can enter the Palm Churchyard enclosed by the three walks, and this gives a fine view of the externally simple Early English nave and S. aisle (the windows are Perpendicular alterations) contrasted with the rich W. front treatment returned round the S. face of the SW. tower, and with the typically Somerset lacy 15th c. top of the central tower.

The W. and S. walks are late 15th c.; over the W. one is the Singing School. The tower doorway which it leads to has fine foliage carving. Most of the monuments in the cloister were taken out of the cathedral itself in the 1840s. Near the S. end of the W. walk are a seated figure of John Phelips (d. 1834), by Sir Francis Chantrey, and a memorial by John Bacon junior to John Burland (d. 1804). An over-large monument to Bishop Hooper (d. 1727), has been put at the SW. corner. In the S. walk the following are worth a glance: a memorial to Abigail Hooper (d. 1726) and two foliated medieval coffin-lids in the first bay; a nice cartouche to Samuel Hill (d. 1716), in the second bay; and four empty stone coffins. The SE. corner is dominated by an inelegant cherub mourning Peter Davis (d. 1749); just beyond it is another cartouche, to Sarah Keen (d. 1701). At this point is a way out towards the beautiful moated Bishop's Palace and the gateway called Pennyless Porch which leads to the Market Place.

This E. walk, which has the library over, is early 15th c. Towards the N. end on the right are some pieces of 15th c. carved stone from Bishop Stillington's chapel. This projected E. from the cloister on the site of a Norman Lady chapel but was destroyed in the 16th c. On the wall just beyond is a wrought-iron peacock as a common memorial to people associated with the cathedral. Back in the centre of the walk is a way out to the SE. churchyard, with views of the E. end. Note the clear break between the two phases of work on the quire – all to the E. including the Lady chapel being early 14th c. A path (not a right of way, and therefore sometimes locked) leads round the Lady chapel into St Andrew Street, past the house called The Rib. The chapter house is then on the left, and Vicars' Close immediately opposite. Past the Chain Gate, the building opposite the NW. tower is the former Archdeaconry, now the Cathedral School music department; beyond that is the Deanery.

On the N. transept of the cathedral are two 'quarter-jacks' in armour, connected to the clock inside. Finally there is the N. porch, really the principal entrance and worth special examination inside and out. It is Early English work, unaltered except for the parapets and treated with a rare degree of enrichment and fine detail. The E. capitals of the outer doorway portray the martyrdom of St Edmund. Above the inner doorway, which is double, is a rather surprising piece of Norman zigzag ornament.

Westminster Abbey, See note on page 447.

Westminster, The Most Precious Holy Blood, St Mary, St Joseph & St Peter (Roman Catholic, Greater London)

Westminster is unique amongst major English cathedrals because it is Byzantine in style. Historically it is also unusual because of the long period of preparation before it was built at all. The archdiocese was one of the original thirteen Catholic sees founded in 1850, but building its cathedral was placed so low on the list of priorities that it did not commence till 1895. A project for an Early English style building had been rejected so as to avoid competing with Westminster Abbey, and the architect John Francis Bentley drew his inspiration instead from Italy (especially Venice and Ravenna) and, no doubt, from what he had studied though not seen of churches of the Near East.

Externally its detailed appearance is not unrelated to that of the then fashionable streets that hemmed it in. Only in recent years has it been opened out to the hurly-burly of Victoria Street, with the

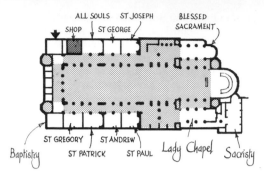

ALL SOULS   ST JOSEPH   BLESSED
SHOP   ST GEORGE   SACRAMENT

ST GREGORY   ST ANDREW
ST PATRICK   ST PAUL   Lady Chapel   Sacristy
Baptistry

kind of piazza that Bentley would have wished. So the first view now
takes in most of the W. front as well as the great campanile, 284 ft
high. The fusion of Italian motifs into the Byzantine form is at once
evident. The horizontal banding of stone and brick is derived from
Italy (Siena Cathedral for example). The great portico with its finely
fluted columns and medallions is Italian too, and was completed
after Bentley's untimely death by J. A. Marshall. But the receding
planes behind the façade, the domes behind those, and much of the
tracery and other details are reminiscent of St Mark's, Venice, and,
before that, of St Sophia in Constantinople. The structure is entirely
of brick, with no steel reinforcement anywhere.

The usual visitors' entrance is by the NW. porch, that is, beside
the base of the campanile. This leads into the narthex or W. aisle.
On the right are the formal W. entrance porches, and on the left
perhaps the most awe-inspiring church **interior** in Britain, framed by
two great columns of polished brown Norwegian granite, with white
capitals. Its particular atmosphere is due partly to its great width
and height – each of the three nave domes spans 60 ft and rests on
arches 90 ft high – and partly to the fact that it is unfinished: the
wonderfully varied marble facings (there are over 100 different kinds
of marble in the building) only reach to half the height and above
that is bare rough brickwork which in places is only dimly
discernible and has a primeval air that will be lost if the intended
mosaics are ever completed.

Beyond the vast nave, the fourth dome over the sanctuary is a
lantern of slightly smaller span, with piercings which admit a dim
light to the great hanging Rood (by Christian Symons) and the
baldacchino below. Down both sides are high galleries on arcades
with green Thessaly marble columns. Behind those is a complex

structure of buttresses and vaults which support the thrust of the
main domes and enable the side façades to be practically flat, unlike
a Gothic building where so much of the buttressing is external. The
existence of transepts is disguised, for they are not N. and S. of the
lantern-dome but one bay further W., and the galleries continue
across them as bridges. Facing W. on the main piers, and clumsily
breaking their proportions, are some of Eric Gill's series of Stations
of the Cross (1913–18); these bas-reliefs are considered to be
amongst his finest work. Then there are the great net-like pendant
lights, wholly Byzantine in feeling but in fact Bentley's very early use
of the newly available electricity.

Looking back into the **narthex**, on the W. wall is a perspective
drawing of the completed interior. The floor, like most of those
throughout the cathedral, is of patterned marble.

In the **N. aisle** the first doorway on the left leads into the
bookshop beneath the tower. On the right, within the NW. angle of
the nave, is a big bronze figure of St Peter. Not all the chapels are
fully finished with their marble walls and mosaic ceilings. The first
on the left, that of Holy Souls, is. Its gilt-iron screen, light pendants
and other furnishings are all by Bentley. The dull silvery vault
mosaic, on the theme of mourning, is by Symons. The next chapel,
St George's, has a similar screen and an English theme in many of
its details. The centrepiece of the floor is a rose, the marble generally
is red and white, and above the altar is Eric Gill's last work, a large
bas-relief of the Reigning Christ. The figure of St George on the N.
wall is by Philip Lindsay Clarke. On the S. side is the shrine of John
Southworth, martyred in 1654. The third chapel, St Joseph's,
contains a big model of the entire cathedral and has balustered pews
with figure carving in the ends. A cardinal's red hat hangs above the
tomb of Archbishop Hinsley. In this chapel the gilded screen, by
L. H. Shattock, occupies both arches, and the marble panels within
are particularly fine.

Next comes the **N. transept**. A bridge continues the line of the
gallery front, and on the left is a porch. Through the arches, and on
the left again, is the St Thomas's chapel or Vaughan chantry, with
its delicate bronze screen and columns of black and white marble.
The monument within is that of Archbishop Vaughan (d. 1903); a
cardinal's hat hangs above, though he is not buried here.

E. of the transept is the **Blessed Sacrament chapel**, reserved for
private prayer. The altar, rails and screen are by Marshall, and the
mosaics, which are complete, by Boris Anrep. On the left of this
chapel is the small Sacred Heart shrine, with interesting decorative

mosaics and light fittings. In the niches on either side of the arch
leading back into the transept are representational mosaics of a
peacock and a phoenix.

From here one can cross the E. end of the nave and take a closer
look at the very large **sanctuary** with its dramatic double arcading
each side and its triumphant baldacchino – all part of Bentley's
design though completed posthumously. The four columns of yellow
Verona marble each side of the altar are arranged in such a way that
they carry the thrust of the arch above without artificial aid – typical
of the constructional honesty of the whole building. Above hangs
the Rood, and high above that the mysterious blackness of the
fourth dome, with a great mosaic by Gilbert Pownall on the E. arch
below it. The reverse side of the Rood carries a painting of Our
Lady of Sorrows. On the left of the sanctuary is the archbishop's
throne, modelled on the papal chair in St John Lateran, Rome. The
E. apse is occupied by choir and organ.

The **Lady chapel** is reached through the S. transept. A good place
from which to see it is the aisle running along its S. side which leads
eventually to the sacristy. The marblework and mosaics are
complete, and the whole chapel is probably the richest in the
cathedral. The best of the mosaics are the reredos figure of Our
Lady and the Prophets in niches in the four corners: these are by
Anning Bell. The golden vault is by Pownall (1931–2). Its intricacy
seems to show little feeling for Bentley's conception of simple
grandeur.

The **S. transept** is like the N., but different in its details. On the W.
side of the central pier of the crossing, below Gill's XIIIth Station, is
a 15th c. English alabaster figure of St Mary. Within the crossing,
like a great peninsula amongst the seats, is the pulpit, made in Rome
in 1899 and much enlarged and raised on its twisted columns in
1934. The custom of leading an archbishop in procession into a
pulpit accounts for its great size.

Now the chapels leading off the **S. aisle** – four since there is no
tower this side. The first, St Paul's, is distinguished by the curious
mosaic vault representing a tent canopy. The floor is a reproduction
of one of the so-called Cosmatesque floors of churches in Rome,
and the balustered pews are like those in St Joseph's chapel
opposite. St Andrew's chapel, which is next, has a mosaic vault like
golden fish-scales and a silvered screen to the aisle. The marble floor
has a pattern of fish, and as well as references to St Andrew as a
fisherman there are allusions to Scotland and to Constantinople.
This is the only chapel fully furnished in Byzantine style, and its

ivory-inlaid stalls and kneeling desks by Ernest Gimson are superb in design and craftsmanship. In the third chapel, St Patrick's, which is predominantly green, many of the decorative marbles are Irish and there is a group of other, rarer, kinds displayed on the back wall. St Gregory and St Augustine's chapel, the last in the S. aisle, is all to Bentley's design and has complete mosaics; their theme is the early missionaries and saints. At the back is a screen to the baptistry which is, however, better viewed from the aisle. The very large font is also by Bentley.

At the time of writing the campanile is closed for repairs. Normally it is possible to go to the viewing gallery near the top by a lift which starts from the N. porch; as well as views of much of London this gives the opportunity of seeing the cathedral itself from a revealing angle.

Out in the street again, it is worth turning right along Ambrosden Avenue and walking round the whole block. The cleaned brick and stone wall on its granite plinth is impressive at close quarters. A gateway leads into a yard which allows a close view of the apse and the bridges that connect it with the Archbishop's House and the sacristy with Clergy House. Beyond them is the choir school playground. The crypt chapel of St Peter, which is signposted, is not normally open except for certain services. In a secondary chapel attached to it are monuments to Cardinal Wiseman and Cardinal Manning.

Back in the street, the Cathedral Hall, Archbishop's House and (round the corner in Francis Street) Clergy House are by Bentley too. The next right turn, Morpeth Terrace, affords beautiful glimpses of the cathedral through plane trees. Passing the modern primary school, and then the conference centre with bookshop beneath, one regains the piazza.

Whithorn, St Martin [Scottish Development Department] (Dumfries & Galloway)

Tradition says that the original monastery was founded by St Ninian, that he was born in the middle of the 4th c., and that he was buried in his own cathedral here in 432. About 727 a Northumbrian bishopric was established, and about 1128, after a period of Norse rule, the monastery was re-founded as a Premonstratensian priory with the church as cathedral. This 12th c. cathedral was cruciform; it was rebuilt much bigger in the 13th c.

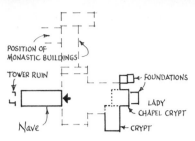

POSITION OF
MONASTIC BUILDINGS

TOWER RUIN

FOUNDATIONS

LADY
CHAPEL CRYPT

CRYPT

Nave

with aisled transepts and probably an aisled quire, and a cloister N.
of the nave. The nave, which never had aisles, was also extended
westwards. A big chapel S. of the E. end was added about 1500.
After the whole had fallen to ruin in the 16th c. the nave was
repaired about 1635 to serve as a Protestant cathedral. It later
became a Presbyterian parish church, but was again abandoned
after a new church was built in 1822.

The approach to the **nave** is from the S., and the entrance,
confusingly, is in the E. wall. This with its window is 17th c. and the
actual doorway 18th c. Inside, the present grass floor is two feet or
so above the original, as can be seen from the two empty 14th c.
cinquefoil-headed tomb recesses on the right. Remains of a third
one are on the left, i.e. S. of the doorway, and a fourth is near the
middle of the N. wall. The prominent W. gable is 18th c., rebuilt (E.
of its original position) after the tower had collapsed. The N. wall,
on the right, has no windows because the cloister adjoined it; the
three big windows in the S. wall were 15th c. but have lost their
tracery. The many 19th and 20th c. memorials are of little interest.

Now the **outside**, taken clockwise. The shafted doorway at the E.
end of the S. wall was made up of 13th and 15th c. work in the
1630s. The unusually rich Norman doorway near the W. end may
have been re-set there when the nave was repaired c. 1610. The
ruined walls beyond belonged to an early 17th c. tower. Near it are a
number of interesting tombs, including a 'table' of 1790 on Ionic
legs.

Looking along the N. side: the church of 1822 is on the left.
Straight ahead, the terrace and reconstructed low wall represent the
E. end of the cathedral, probably the Lady chapel. Further on and
below more masonry can be seen: this is a modern marking-out of
foundations that exist below the surface, possibly of St Ninian's
original church. It can be reached by turning towards the
churchyard gate and then taking the path on the left. On the left

first, however, is a long low vaulted chamber, the crypt of the SE. chapel. Further on, under the terrace, is another crypt and beyond that a small re-roofed 14th c. building which may have been a sacristy. The key to these crypts, which contain many carved stone fragments, can be got from the museum, which is on the left of the lane leading back to the burgh. In the museum, too, are numerous interesting crosses and carved stones from this and other sites.

Winchester, Holy Trinity (Church of England, Hampshire)

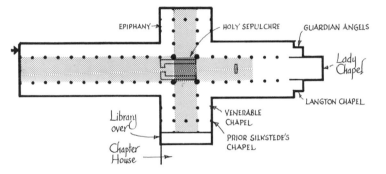

Long before the Norman Conquest three minsters stood here close together in a single precinct. The Old Minster (founded about 645) was immediately N. of the present cathedral nave, the New Minster (founded in 903) N. of that and almost touching it, and the Nuns' Minster (founded about 890) considerably further N. Much of the substructure of the first two has been revealed by excavation and now lies again hidden beneath the churchyard grass.

The present cathedral, the successor of the Old Minster, was started on its fresh site in 1079 by Walkelin the first Norman bishop, and completed within 20 years – that is, earlier than most of the major Norman churches that remain, and substantial parts of it do still exist. In 1107 the central tower collapsed and had to be rebuilt along with the adjoining parts of the transepts. In 1202 the extreme E. end was taken down and a complete new Lady chapel and retro-quire built – preserving the Norman crypt beneath. Next, a century later, the quire itself was rebuilt, over another part of the earlier crypt. When, in the latter half of the 14th c., resources enabled the nave to be improved too, this was done not by wholesale reconstruction but by remodelling and encasing it bay by bay in the new Perpendicular style and by crowning it with a rich vault. The W. end was shortened and a completely new W. front built.

Subsequent changes were less far-reaching: about 1490–1500 the extension and remodelling of the Lady chapel and the little SE. chapel, about 1505 the rebuilding of the upper parts of the quire and its aisles, and in 1635 the new (wooden) fan vault of the tower. The cloister, which was Norman, was destroyed in the 16th c., but parts of the surrounding monastic buildings survive amongst the houses of the Close. This summary omits any account of the chantries and furnishings, which are more important and numerous than in almost any other English cathedral. Major restorations were by William Garbett (1812–28), John Colson (1874–91) and Sir Thomas Jackson (1906–12). The last involved the celebrated underpinning of the whole of the foundations which had become waterlogged, a fact still brought home by the regular closure of the crypt for many months each year because of flooding.

The main entrance is by the NW. door in the W. front. From the centre of the **nave** near the W. end it is the great length combined with verticality that impresses most. At the crossing the semicircular Norman tower arches can still be seen, unaltered. The late 14th c. transformation of the entire nave from the Norman to Perpendicular style was a master-work of ingenuity, and only gradually can it be realized that much of what is now visible is still basically robust Norman. No real Perpendicular structure is so heavy, but the heaviness is disguised by the multiplicity of vertical mouldings and the retention of the main shafts running right up to the vault. The triforium disappeared altogether in the remodelling, and was replaced by a small gallery. This enabled both the main arcades and the clerestory to be heightened. The vault, of a graceful and complex design peculiar to Winchester, is of lierne type and is unusual and probably rather unscientific in having no continuous diagonal ribs.

Behind, as one stands at the W. end, is the great W. window filled with a jumble of ancient glass; below it are war memorial panels and books and some records of past repairs. The big bronze statues are nothing to do with either, but came from a former rood screen designed by Inigo Jones and represent James I and Charles I. Other relics of the screen are in the Museum of Archaeology at Cambridge. The present screen, which breaks the length one bay W. of the crossing, is entirely by Scott (1875) and the two prominent

chantries beneath the S. arcade, best examined later, are those of
Bishop Edington near the screen and William of Wykeham half-way
along.

In the **N. aisle** are more war memorials and other monuments, as
well as many fragments of old glass in the tops of the windows. The
Jane Austen memorial window (1901) is in the fourth bay, and
beneath it a brass plaque: her actual grave-slab (1817) is close by.
Beneath the fifth arch is the famous 12th c. black Tournai marble
font, one of only seven in England. On the sides of the bowl are
scenes from the life of St Nicholas, and even the top is carved. From
this point there is a good view of the Wykeham chantry opposite.
Then on the left of the aisle the coloured memorial of Edward Cole
(d. 1617), and in the seventh bay the banner of the famous soldier
Lord Wavell, with memorials to him and to others of his family.

This is a good place to turn aside into the nave again to see the
Scott screen more closely, also the nave altar and Jacobean pulpit,
some finely carved chairs, and the Edington chantry opposite. The
pulpit was made for New College Chapel in Oxford.

Back in the N. aisle there is an abrupt and quite startling change
to early Norman work, and here at the junction with the N. transept
can be seen the actual process of transformation, arrested at a half-
way stage: delicate Perpendicular panelling and mouldings and
pointed arches being overlaid on or cut out of the sombre masonry
of three centuries earlier.

No doubt the plan was to treat the transepts and the tower in the
same way, but it was never done. So stepping into the **N. transept** is
like stepping into a different age. The floor is a marvellously
irregular mixture of ledger stones and plain flags; the arcades, tall
gallery and clerestory have an awe-inspiring simple grandeur; and
the plain flat roof contrasts eloquently with the elaborations of the
Gothic vaulting elsewhere. Unfortunately the ugly back of the organ
does nothing to enhance it.

The little Epiphany chapel on the W. side of the transept,
separated by a modern screen, is reserved for private prayer. The
groined vault (i.e. without ribs) is additional evidence of the early
date. Specially attractive are its four Morris windows (1909) with
richly coloured scenes and gentle backgrounds of patterned foliage.

Between the N. transept and the quire, i.e. beneath the N. tower
arch, is the tiny chapel of the Holy Sepulchre. Though it is usually
kept locked, much of it can be seen through the side openings. The
vault is ribbed, for this is later Norman work subsequent to the
collapse of the earlier tower. Both it and the walls are enriched with

early 13th c. paintings. A foliated cross-slab outside the chapel marks the tomb of a priest.

Now the remainder of the transept. The two prominent memorials beneath its N. arcade are of General Buller (d. 1908) and Prebendary Iremonger (d. 1820). In the NE. corner is the striking memorial to Canon Cunningham (d. 1944), a plain stone block with a representation of the Annunciation in carved wood by Alan Durst. The SE. window has an interesting jumble of old glass. Near it is the door to the crypt, and from there is a better view of the junction with the N. nave aisle, where the transformation to Perpendicular reached triforium level but not the clerestory. However, the clerestory throughout the N. transept itself is of three-light Perpendicular windows.

The **crypt** is open to guided tours at advertised hours, but is liable to be closed in winter through flooding. Consequently nothing of value except a collection of old carved stones is kept there. Its plan preserves that of the early Norman E. end of the cathedral itself and dictated the layout of what took its place. The entry is into its N. ambulatory, a horseshoe-plan vaulted passage around an apsidal space beneath the former quire. At its E. end is a smaller apse-ended chamber called the Trinity crypt, lying beneath what was the Trinity chapel; extensions to the N., E. and S. of that represent the retroquire and the various added chapels above. Like most crypts of such antiquity, this is eloquent architecture, unchanged and uncluttered.

Next the upper parts of the E. end, a complex building with unparalleled contents. After the 11 steps from the transept to the **N. quire aisle** it is the floor that first catches the eye – encaustic tiles recently re-laid in large patterned rectangular bays. Then the window-glass – medieval pieces in all the heads and tracery lights. The windows themselves, and the vault, are early 16th c. like the nave aisles. On the right, the presbytery arcade is early 14th c. with richly clustered mouldings, but the stone screen is again early 16th c., showing more than a hint of Renaissance detail. The strange mortuary chests perched on top contain the bones of Anglo-Saxon kings including Canute and his wife; also early 16th c., they more than anything else give this part of the cathedral the feeling of an ancient engraving come to life. Behind this screen is the high altar. Further on, again on the right, is the Gardener chantry, marking where the building style changes again, back to Early English. The chantry is of 1555, i.e. well after the Reformation and well into the architectural early Renaissance. It is a strange combination of Gothic and Classical – Perpendicular windows but triglyphed frieze,

N. Transept arcade, Winchester (late 11th c.)

quatrefoiled vault but Ionic-columned reredos. In the flank wall is
the bishop's cadaver effigy, and within the chantry the chair in
which Mary Tudor sat during her marriage in the cathedral to Philip
II of Spain.

Back in the aisle the vaults change from lierne to quadripartite.
This is the retro-quire, begun in 1202. All about now are medieval
floor tiles in splendid variety, extending right across to the opposite
aisle, the largest area of such tiling in the country. This is a good
point to step into the central part of the **retro-quire**. Only a little
taller than its aisles, it is Early English at its purest, with typical
Purbeck marble columns, shaft-rings half-way up, and varied stiff-
leaf capitals. But more monuments rather distract attention from its
beauty. Immediately E. of the screen which shuts off the quire is the
feretory, or raised platform, where St Swithun's shrine stood. There
is also an effigy of Bishop Sumner (d. 1874). Then on either side
looking E. are the ambitious chantries of Bishop Waynflete (N.) and
Cardinal Beaufort (S.). Between them is the new St Swithun's shrine
(1962), a draped metal framework marking the grave which became
a resort for pilgrims throughout the Middle Ages and which
contributed in no small measure to the richness of the cathedral.
The Beaufort chantry is of 1447 but its effigy (with cardinal's hat) is
late 17th c., for Cromwell's soldiers wrought havoc with all these
memorials. It is unlike the other chantries, its centre being screened
only by a low balustrade. Waynflete's is equally richly pinnacled and
vaulted and has its original effigy.

Back in the N. aisle of the retro-quire the shafted windows and
the wall-arcading should be specially noticed. Close to the N. wall is
the early 14th c. tomb with stone figure of Arnold de Gaveston; his
chain mail has the rare feature of 'ailettes' on the shoulders. Then
comes a 13th c. bishop in Purbeck marble, and on the E. wall an
unusual vesica-shaped panel denoting the heart-burial of another
13th c. bishop. An arch opens into the little **Guardian Angels' chapel**,
with original (13th c.) painted angels on the vault, 15th c. niched
reredos and above it a medley of ancient glass. Inside on the right is
the splendid bronze-effigied monument to Lord Portland (d. 1634),
looking stylistically much later: Pevsner remarks that of its date
'Westminster Abbey has nothing to vie with it'.

Next is the **Lady chapel**, with a screen that is largely 19th c.
restoration but contains some 15th c. fragments; the stalls behind it
are similar. The reredos is a memorial to Charlotte Yonge (d. 1901)
and the glass is mostly of the same period, though a few 16th c.
figures remain in the E. window. The whole E. bay of the chapel and

the rich stellar vaulting throughout date from the remodelling of about 1500 and contrast interestingly with its W. bay which is three centuries earlier. The 17th c. communion rail was originally at the high altar. But the Lady chapel's most interesting and unusual feature is the series of early 16th c. paintings of scenes associated with Our Lady, done virtually in monochrome straight on to the stonework. A full printed description is provided, and reconstructions on hinged boards cover the originals.

Back in the retro-quire and continuing S.: the simple tomb of its builder Bishop de Lucy (d. 1204) lies straight ahead. On the left, at the entrance to the **Langton chapel** is a statue of William Walker the diver, who did more than anyone to secure the foundations in the 1906–12 restoration. The chapel itself is wholly taken up with the tomb of Bishop Langton (d. 1501) and its rich screen and stallwork; the equally intricate stone roof is not quite a true fan-vault.

The **S. retro-quire aisle** is architecturally similar to the N. and has some 13th c. glass that came from Salisbury. The prominent standing effigy on the left is of John Clobery (d. 1687). On the right is the Beaufort chantry, followed by a tomb attributed to Prior Basynge, 13th c., and then the Fox chantry matching Gardener's opposite. The bishop's effigy (he d. 1528) takes the form of an intentionally horrifying cadaver, dwarfed by the size and scale of the late Gothic screenwork. The complex vaulted ceiling has a pelican emblem amongst its bosses; most of its figure sculpture, however, is either late Victorian restoration or is missing altogether. The Fox and the Gardener chantries both have little subsidiary chambers adjoining on their E. sides, perhaps as vestries or for private meditation.

The stone screen to the **quire** echoes that opposite. It is only on passing through it that the upper parts of these four bays can be clearly seen to be not 14th c. but, like the aisle vaults, early 16th c. – large Perpendicular clerestory windows with some 15th c. glass, and a wooden vault like the stone vault of the nave and extending to beneath the tower. A canted mirror on a trolley enables the bosses to be viewed in comfort: they mostly portray heraldry and Passion emblems. The tower vault is very unusual in being a 17th c. fan vault.

Just to the left inside the quire is the bishop's throne, of the time of Garbett's early 19th c. restoration of the cathedral; just W. of it is the Winchester Madonna, a stone fragment of unknown origin. The canopied stalls were begun in 1308 and have excellent foliage carving, and in their misericords a whole host of animals and human

figures. The organ towers above them at the sides, and on the W. is
the Scott screen. The extraordinary quire pulpit, so busily carved
over every inch of its surface, has a flavour of early 19th c. Gothic,
but at least its body is of about 1510 and its bears the name and
silk-skein emblem of Prior Silkstede. The great stone high altar
screen with tier upon tier of niches is of the same period, but all its
statues are 19th c. The communion rail and the matching stall-fronts
are late 17th c. At the ends of the sanctuary steps are the 19th c.
tomb-chest of Bishop Courtenay (d. 1492) and a nameless 16th c.
one. The black marble slab on a simple plinth, also uninscribed, is
supposedly the tomb of William Rufus.

Back in the S. quire aisle, the kneeling white marble figure on the
right is Bishop North (d. 1820), by Sir Francis Chantrey. At the
head of the steps to the transept is a rare 13th c. wrought-iron grille
with repeating volutes.

Architecturally the S. transept is like the N. Visually it is more of
a muddle, largely because of the enclosure of its aisles for various
purposes. In the centre hangs a big brass 18th c. chandelier. Of the
monuments only two are specially notable: at the N. end that to
Isaac Townsend (d. 1731), and in the centre the ostentatious
canopied memorial of Bishop Wilberforce (d. 1873), designed by
Scott. On the E. side the left-hand chapel, called the Venerable
chapel, is for private prayer; it has a tall stone screen and many
minor memorials. The other, with an earlier screen, was Prior
Silkstede's but now it merely leads into vestry space; in it is the
Izaak Walton memorial window of 1914 (he is buried in the crypt).
Rearranged 16th c. screenwork and seats partition off the S. and W.
part of the main floor, and behind it a stair leads to Bishop Morley's
library. This is open to the public on weekdays from 10.30 a.m. to
12.30 p.m. (except Mondays) and from 2.30 p.m. to 4.30 p.m. It has
splendid late 17th c. bookcases which were originally in Farnham
Castle, and is believed to have been in continuous use as a book-
room since the 12th c.

Finally the **S. nave aisle**, like the N. aisle and again with much old
glass. On the right is the back of Bishop Edington's chantry, one of
the first (1366) and simplest, in effect an enclosure without a roof.
His alabaster effigy is damaged but is still a fine piece of sculpture.
Under the next arch is the alabaster tomb of Bishop Browne
(d. 1891). Over the S. doorway is a memorial window to King
George V, which can be compared with the glass opposite in the N.
aisle commemorating King George VI's coronation; these are by
Hugh Easton. Amongst many more wall-monuments is that of

Cathedral Library, Winchester

Bishop Willis (d. 1734), with reclining figure. Then beneath the arcade the Wykeham chantry: Bishops Edington and William of Wykeham (d. 1404) were the two men chiefly responsible for the nave as it exists today. The Wykeham effigy, unlike many others, is virtually undamaged; the three little men at his feet were probably his clerks, and two angels guard his head. Under another arch is the roll of honour of the King's Royal Rifle Corps, and lastly on the left before the postcard area an interesting John Flaxman monument to Joseph Warton (d. 1801), headmaster of Winchester College, with four boys and the heads of Homer and Aristotle.

In the W. bay of the N. aisle is a **gallery**. This is used for exhibitions of plate and other precious objects and has modern showcases and lighting. It is normally open in summer from 11 a.m. to 5 p.m. (2.30 p.m. to 4.30 p.m. on Sundays).

Now the **exterior**, starting with the W. front which is somewhat tame and unworthy. This is 15th c.: the Norman W. front which had towers stood further W. The following tour is anti-clockwise, i.e. commencing with the S. side of the nave which is reached by a small arch to the right of the W. front. The spectacular row of flying buttresses spanning the walkway was put in by Jackson about 1910. The space opens out into what was the cloister. The rather scattered buildings around, mostly of monastic origin, constitute the Close. The five ruined Norman arches straight ahead mark the chapter house, and to the right of them is the Deanery, originally the Prior's house. The passage between the S. transept and the chapter house passes under the library. Ahead is a brick house of 1699 and on the left the windows of the cathedral crypt come into view.

This SE. viewpoint is perhaps the best of all because it summarizes so much: early Norman the triforium of the transept, later Norman the clerestory above and the central tower, Early English the retro-quire on the right, Decorated the two lower right-hand windows in the E. wall of the transept, and Perpendicular the window to the left of them as well as the whole S. quire aisle with the clerestory of the presbytery behind and above it.

The path can still be followed eastwards, now between high walls. It turns left and leads into the street, past a water-garden with a glimpse of the E. end of the cathedral. The way back to the W. end is then through the churchyard by the path along its N. side. This gives a marvellous impression of the long low length of the building, which is in fact the longest cathedral in England and in the whole of Europe.

Worcester, Christ & St Mary (Church of England, Hereford & Worcester)

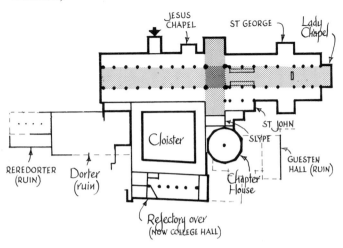

The bishopric was created *c.* 680; the first cathedral, St Peter's, probably stood N. of the present College Green. Bishop Oswald founded a Benedictine monastery *c.* 983 and his seat was moved to it. In 1084 Wulstan (the only Saxon bishop to retain his office at the Conquest) began rebuilding and the big surviving crypt and much of the transept walling were completed before his death in 1095. Of later Norman (12th c.) work the chapter house is the principal part remaining. About 1175 the two W. bays of the nave were rebuilt in a very odd version of Norman Transitional style. A few years later the central tower collapsed and in 1202 there was a fire.

From 1224 onwards the whole E. end was rebuilt, commencing with the addition of the Lady chapel. The remainder of the nave followed in several phases during the period 1320–70 and the tower *c.* 1375. The Victorian restoration of 1855–74 was under A. E. Perkins and Sir George Gilbert Scott; it involved almost complete re-facing of the exterior.

The two-storeyed **N. porch**, said to have been added in 1386, is now mostly 19th c. outside. Its tierceron vault is original; the inner doorway, though also 14th c., retains two slender Norman columns. Inside, the **nave** is less uniform than at first appears, and may be summed up as follows. First (looking W.) there are the two bays built *c.* 1175. Outside they look Norman; inside, the main arches are Transitional, i.e. of Norman clustered type but pointed. But the triforium design is most extraordinary, with two tall pointed bays each containing three thin Norman arches, all sprinkled with rosettes. The clerestory has a big round-headed arch flanked by pointed ones. The vault is late 14th c., not fitting the earlier wall-shafts. The W. window and doorway are 19th c., the glass on the Creation theme being by John Hardman.

Now, looking E.: the rest of the nave is early 14th c., though in general form so closely following the Early English quire that it might well be thought much earlier than it is; there are two twin triforium openings with Y tracery, and a stepped clerestory not unlike the W. bays. Closer examination will show subtle differences not only between N. and S. but also in the last two 14th c. bays on the N.; these suggest that work proceeded from the E. along the N. side with one or two interruptions and then similarly along the S. Finally the vault was added for the whole length including the two W. bays rebuilt earlier. Eastward, the crossing arches are late 14th c., with Scott's iron quire screen occupying the further one.

Turn now to the W. end of the N. aisle. Under the second arch is the mutilated canopied tomb of Bishop Thornborough (d. 1641), and at the extreme W. end the seated white marble figure of Bishop Philpott (d. 1892), by Sir Thomas Brock. On its left is a simpler memorial to Bishop Hurd (d. 1808). The 17th c. wall monument in bay 1, with cadaver and Greek inscription, has lost its name. By it is a memorial to the Worcestershire Regiment in India, 1845–6, by Richard Westmacott junior. In the second bay the little kneeling effigy beneath a canopy is of Abigail Goldisburgh (d. 1613); just past this may be found a simple dignified tablet to Sir Edward Elgar (d. 1934). The canopied monument in bay 3, with a kind of miniature fan-vault, has kneeling figures of John Moore (d. 1613) and his family. Of the three little 17th c. tablets in the next bay that on the right to Canon Bright is specially attractive. Under the arcade and past the N. doorway is the splendid tomb-chest of Sir John Beauchamp (d. 1388) and his wife, their coloured effigies resting on black swans. Then on the left the unattractive Boer War memorial of the Worcestershire Regiment; above it are worn late 17th c. royal arms, brought in from outside.

At this point a sally may be made into the nave to see the diagonal buttresses inserted into the triforium and clerestory when rebuilding of the tower began in 1374 – also the simple nave altar and choir desks and Scott's very elaborate pulpit of alabaster and green marble, carved by James Forsyth.

Back in the **N. aisle**, the little Jesus chapel (reserved for private prayer) has a stone screen of *c.* 1895, a 14th c. octopartite vault, a rich 19th c. Gothic reredos, and glass of 1849 by William Wailes. In the last bay, part of the nave organ stands on the right in a trellisy case, and on the left is the effigy of Bishop Bullingham (d. 1576), with a great block of stone round his middle. The glass of the 1860s in the window above, by Lavers and Barraud, is considered to be amongst the best in the cathedral.

The arch into the **N. transept** is early 14th c., and the transept itself Norman, though much altered: the vault is thought to be 13th c., the stone panelling over the arches to the nave and quire aisles is late 14th c., and the big Geometric N. window with its glass is of 1865–6. Memorials worth noticing are (starting at the left of the W. wall) to Mrs Henry Wood d. 1887 (bas-relief marble bust), Sir Thomas Street d. 1695 (classical canopy and flying cherub, made *c.* 1780), Bishop Stillingfleet d. 1699 (N. wall, to the right of the prominent stair turret), Bishop Fleetwood d. 1683 (a giant tablet of standard type), and Bishop Hough d. 1746 (by Lewis Roubiliac, with effigy precariously on a sarcophagus guarded by a mourning woman). The plain Norman arch in which the last one stands led to a chapel which has disappeared; that to the N. quire aisle has some remains of patterned wall-painting round it. Normally there is no way through here, so one must turn S. through the **crossing**, with a look upwards at its unusual late 14th c. lierne vault and a closer view of Scott's quire screen, into the **S. transept** which is dominated by the organ.

Though also basically Norman, this transept differs a good deal from the N. The vault is late 14th c. like the crossing, and thus of the same date as the applied wall panelling which here is more fully developed. The arch to the former E. chapel on this side has richly foliage-ornamented capitals.

A charge is made to enter the E. parts. Behind the desk at the **S. quire aisle** gate is another Westmacott junior memorial, to William Burslem (d. 1820). The large one opposite to Margaret Rae (d. 1770) is by I. F. Moore. The aisle then opens out into the two-bay St John's chapel, very dignified Early English with shafted triple lancet windows, quadripartite vault with whitened plaster panels, and 19th c. screen. It is a fitting introduction to the splendour of the **quire** itself, entered on the left through another 19th c. screen.

The quire with the Lady chapel and the E. transepts forms virtually a big cruciform church in itself. Begun in 1224 at the Lady chapel end, it is Early English at its finest, with typical and lavish use of Purbeck marble in the shafts. Clustered columns with excellent springing foliage capitals support another unusual triforium with a second arcade behind and out of step with the main one; in the outer spandrels are carved figures, too high to see properly without field glasses. The clerestory is double too, with a walkway between and stepped again like the nave. The paintings on the vaults are 19th c., by Hardman.

The furnishings of the quire, largely by Scott, are particularly splendid. Starting beside the S. entrance, the bishop's throne is his. So are the stalls, but the back row incorporates an excellent series of late 14th c. misericords; the most sumptuous canopy work is in the W. corners. The screens in the W. bays, intricate gilded ironwork, are by Francis Skidmore. The iron and marble quire screen, already seen from the W., is Scott's again, also the organ cases against which are more recent decorative hangings depicting St Oswald and St Wulfstan. The brass eagle lectern just inside the screen is 19th c. Opposite the bishop's throne are an 18th c. mahogany chamber organ and the quire pulpit, 'Gothic Survival' of 1642 but much renovated in 1874.

In the centre of the quire stands the tomb of King John (d. 1216); the chest is of *c.* 1530, the beautiful Purbeck marble effigy of 1232. The ornate brass and iron communion rail and the richly gilded reredos are again by Scott; the S. side of the sanctuary is enclosed by the chantry of Prince Arthur (d. 1502). This, with a simple central tomb-chest surrounded by rich openwork stone panelling, may be entered from the quire. Its shallow vaulted roof and the sadly despoiled reredos should be noted.

The **N. quire aisle** has a quadripartite vault like the S., with whitened panels. Turn W. first, past the regimental colours on the back of the organ case, to the giant memorial to Bishop Maddox (d. 1759). In contrast with Bishop Hough's in the nearby transept, this merely has a calm Good Samaritan scene on the sarcophagus. Moving E. again: high up on the left is the oriel window of the sacrist's watching chamber; next on the left are a piece of 19th c. Gothic screenwork and a carving of a towered New Jerusalem originally behind the pulpit. The bronze tablet beneath, to the second Duke of Hamilton, killed 1651 at the battle of Worcester, is 20th c.

Steps down at this point indicate the end of the crypt beneath. On the left is a 15th c. stone screen to **St George's chapel** in the NE. transept, a light spacious area where the clerestory reaches down and absorbs the triforium. Trefoil-headed wall-arcading begins here and continues all around the E. end; in the spandrels is a wealth of

sculpture, much of it 19th c. restoration but some original. The
chapel contains war memorials, colours and rolls of honour, and a
piscina in its E. wall. Reverting to the aisle, the two effigies straight
ahead cannot be identified but may perhaps be Bishop de
Braunsford (d. 1349), with ball-flower ornament, and Bishop de
Cobham (d. 1327). The adjacent walling was left unrestored by
Perkins and Scott to illustrate the former condition of the whole. The
three figures further E., a bishop, a lady and a knight, are all
somewhat earlier but unidentified.

In the NE. chapel the reredos Head of Christ is attributed to
Alessandro Tiarini. The seated marble figure on a couch under the
last bay of the arcade is by Sir Francis Chantrey, in memory of
Charlotte Digby (d. 1820). In the next bay the recumbent figure on a
rich Gothic tomb-chest is Lord Lyttelton (d. 1876), by James
Forsyth.

The general design treatment continues in the Lady chapel,
culminating in the superb E. window-wall with twice five lancets,
excellent but partially renewed spandrel carvings both between them
and above the continuing wall-arcade, and glass by Hardman. The
flat-looking effigy on the floor on the N. of the sanctuary is
probably of Bishop de Blois (d. 1236). On the wall behind is a pretty
tablet to Anne, wife of Izaak Walton, (d. 1662). To the right of the
altar, in front of the piscina, lies a more fully modelled effigy
attributed to Bishop de Cantelupe (d. 1266). Behind, the back of the
high altar reredos is inlaid with mosaic as a memorial to the wife of
Dean Peel (d. 1874); the tomb below is that of Prior Moore
(c. 1525).

Under the **S. quire aisle** arcade, corresponding with the Lyttelton
tomb, is that of the first Earl of Dudley (d. 1885), the effigy also by
Forsyth and the tomb to Scott's design. Now returning W., on the
left are a piscina and minor tablets and then the SE. transept or
Dean's chapel, also with its piscina. The central tomb-chest here is of
Sir Griffith Ryce (d. 1523); the brasses are 19th c. reconstructions.
On the S. side the mailed 13th c. effigy of a knight is thought to be
of Robert de Harcourt. A special treasure, in an illuminated case at
the NW. corner, is a Nottingham alabaster triptych of the Madonna
and Child.

Facing the chapel is the base of Prince Arthur's chantry,
containing the effigies of Bishop Giffard (d. 1302) and a lady of the
same period; the bishop was given this place because his own
chantry was considered an obstruction. Following the S. aisle
towards the main transept again, one comes to a modern wooden

Crypt, Worcester (late 11th c.)

stair to the **crypt**; beneath it are the remains of the Norman apsidal chapel. The crypt itself, almost all early Norman, is one of the most extensive and impressive in the country. On the left at the bottom of the stair are two 19th c. drawings done to aid the restoration appeal. Ahead is the double S. aisle and to the right the main 'nave' area, four-aisled with apsidal end – all with columns and capitals of the plainest kinds, and groin vaults. On the N. side (also double-aisled) are two stone coffins and a figure of Llewellyn ap Gruffydd, Prince of Wales (c. 1300). A fine 17th c. door with arched panels is also displayed.

The exit stair emerges in the **S. transept** beside the organ to the left of which is a nice tablet to Henrietta Wrottesley (d. 1719).

The **S. nave aisle** is unusual for its very plain early Norman arches or niches all along the outer wall: these are unparalleled in Britain. The numerous minor monuments cannot be detailed here but the following certainly deserve note: in bay 1 to Bishop Thomas, (d. 1689), large standard classical (by the cloister door); in bay 2 a 14th c. prior's effigy and in bay 3 the figure of Bishop Parrie (d. 1616), both in 13th c. recesses; in bay 4 a 16th c. tomb-chest and a memorial to John Bromley (d. 1674), tall and narrow to fit the space; in bay 5 one to Francis Mostyn (d. 1678), and under it an incomplete memorial to Robert Wilde (d. 1608) – also the tomb-chest of Sir Thomas Lyttelton (d. 1481), with edge brass, and a monument to a later Sir Thomas (d. 1650); in bay 6 to Bishop Freake (d. 1591), the canopy shaped to the Norman arch; in bay 7 by the cloister door (to be returned to later) to Bishop Blandford (d. 1675), large plain classical; in bay 8 to Col. Sir Henry Ellis, killed 1815 at Waterloo, with a spirited equestrian carving by John Bacon junior. On the right here, under the nave arcade, the black-robed figure on a four-poster tomb-chest is Dean Eedes (d. 1596). Lastly, in bay 9, are the late 19th c. font by G. F. Bodley and memorials to Richard Woolfe (d. 1877), of Italianate inlaid marble; Richard Solly (d. 1803), by John Bacon senior; and Bishop Gauden (d. 1662), with powerful bust. On the right at the W. end is Bishop John (d. 1774), by Joseph Nollekens, a design by Robert Adam.

Now into the **cloister** by the 15th c. doorway in bay 7. Though rebuilt in the 14th and 15th cc., it is basically Norman; the windows are Victorian renewals. The lierne vaults have fine bosses, differing in character in the four walks: in the N. walk they are angels and along its walls are animal corbels, the bays being out of step with the Norman buttresses. Near the E. end is a priest's effigy, time-worn into a sort of abstract form. The further doorway to the aisle is 14th c.

In the E. walk the vault bosses are smaller. On the left is the slype
or monks' parlour (used as a tea bar), groin-vaulted and with early
Norman wall-arcading, altogether not unlike the crypt. Next in the
walk are six bells of the 14th, 15th and 17th cc., then the late 14th c.
doorway to the **chapter house**, which may usually be seen on
request; on each side of its door are canopied niches. Internally it is
Norman, *c.* 1120, and most unusual in being circular. The two tiers
of wall-arcading are of special interest: the radiating vault even
more so. The windows are 14th c. enlargements.

Follow the E. walk towards the corner passage which leads to
College Green, but turn right along the S. walk which has the best
series of bosses, representing the descendants of Jesse. From close to
the big black Gurney stove there is a good view of the garth, and of
the central tower (1374) and the completely re-faced 14th c. flanks of
the aisle and gallery and the nave clerestory. The two Transitional
Norman W. bays stand out clearly. The doorway at the end of this
walk led to the refectory (now the hall of King's School) and round
the corner are two bays of washplace. The blocked doorway beside
it led to the dormitory, which extended to the W. from here and was
thus very unusually placed; some of its ruins will be seen. At the
NW. corner a late Norman pointed arch with zigzag leads into a rib-
vaulted passage with, on its right, a door to the 15th c. library over
the S. aisle.

An interesting circuit of the **exterior** can be made as follows,
starting from the terraces ahead of this passage, overlooking the
Severn, and remembering as one goes that the cathedral itself was
almost wholly re-faced by Perkins and Scott. Look back at the W.
front, and then walk S., past the complex but fragmentary ruin of the
dormitory and rere-dorter, through a garden and into the lower
parts of College Green. Here turn left. At the top of the hill on the
left is the refectory, 14th c. on a late 11th c. undercroft; it is now
called College Hall. At the end is the passage already seen from the
cloister end. Then the chapter house comes into view, the S. side of
the cathedral with its SE. transept, and what is left of the 14th c.
Guesten hall. Go straight on through the 14th c. gatehouse called
Edgar Tower, turn left along the alley called College Precincts and
return along the N. side of the cathedral past the transepts and the
Jesus chapel to the N. porch again.

Wrexham, Our Lady of Sorrows (Roman Catholic, Clwyd)

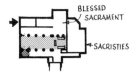

The diocese of Menevia was set up in its present form in 1898. It takes its name from the Latin equivalent of St David's; yet its cathedral is in the opposite corner of Wales. It is an Edward Pugin building with a modest stone-spired SW. tower, opened as a parish church in 1857. During the present century a NW. porch was added, followed by a N. transept and a link between the two, and lastly a new sacristy and suite of other rooms to the E.

The porch, a pale companion to Pugin's Gothic, leads into the N. aisle by the richly medieval-style tomb of Ellen Thompson (d. 1854); a dog lies at the feet of her marble figure and angels guard her head. From beneath the gallery most of the interior can be seen, Decorated in general style, with clustered columns and foliage capitals, round clerestory windows and a simple panelled roof now painted grey-green with white framing and brown principals. The lean-to aisle roofs are similar. Over the main arches Pugin has indulged in restless play with his hood mould, making it leap with a little arch over each column. His main E. window is odd too, for it is all tracery and lacks a lower part; below it the bishop's throne against a red curtain has replaced the reredos, and the altar has been advanced to beneath the chancel arch. The quire ceiling is also scarlet, with white framing.

At the end of the N. aisle the Blessed Sacrament chapel retains a white 19th c. altar with green marble columns, in a new setting with a green colour scheme. The transept added to its N. is connected by a vestibule to the porch, leaving Pugin's aisle buttresses inside. Through the twin arches the quire can be seen, with its 19th c. furniture re-set; the throne, however, has a new canopy.

Now back into the nave and across to the S. side, passing in front of the splendid brass communion rail with vine and wheat, St George, and a Pelican in her Piety. The small SE. chapel has a Pietà on the E. wall and the shrine of St Richard Gwynn on the W. Beyond it are confessionals and the way to the new sacristy, etc. Returning along the S. aisle, one can see the unremarkable W. gallery and window and organ. Finally, at the W. end under the

Cathedral interior, Wrexham (1857)

tower, is the octagonal font on five columns, within a simple iron railing.

Outside, the porch (unlike the vestibule) has the buttresses transferred to its outer wall. Beyond the transept is the new sacristy block, in brick on a stone plinth. There is a way round the house to the car park and back to the W. front and tower – the best view of which is from the other side of the road.

York, St Peter (Church of England, North Yorkshire)

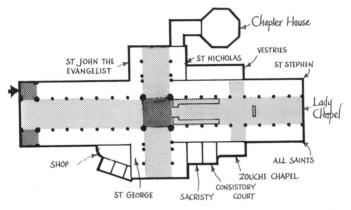

Under the Emperor Constantine there was a bishop at York at least by 314. King Edwin had a wooden minster built here for his own baptism in 627, under the guidance of Bishop Paulinus: that is the earliest record of an actual church. Below ground substantial remains can be seen of the Norman cathedral begun c. 1070, but of its immediate predecessor nothing remains.

The present building, in spite of its straightforward plan and appearance of unity, contains important work of every period from 1220 till 1472. The main transepts are mid-13th c. and the chapter house late 13th c.; the nave took the whole first half of the 14th c. to build, and the quire most of the second half; the central tower was rebuilt after a collapse in 1407, and the W. ones are later 15th c. Serious fires in 1829 and 1840 necessitated extensive renewals. G. E. Street directed a general restoration in 1871 onwards, and Bernard Feilden another, including major structural reinforcement, in 1966–72.

Discoveries during the recent underpinning of the central tower added greatly to knowledge of the Roman fortress building, across which the cathedral was built diagonally. Some of it can be seen at crypt level. The other supremely important feature of York (in its churches as well as its minster) is its glass, and much can be said in favour of a separate internal tour concentrating on that alone. A long spell of looking upwards can, however, be less than soothing to the neck muscles, and on balance it seems best to intermingle the description here (which has to be painfully abbreviated) with that of the architecture and fittings as usual. Those who wish to study it in the detail it deserves will find excellent illustrated guides readily available.

Inside, go first to the W. end of the **nave**. Begun in 1291 and completed *c.* 1340, it thus ranged from Geometric to the later, flowing, Decorated. The clerestory absorbs the triforium, or rather, the latter is disguised by the upper mullions being carried down across it, and by the main arcades being so high. The wooden vault, now painted white with gilded bosses, was renewed after the 1840 fire. The aisles however have quadripartite stone vaults, as well as quite elaborate wall-arcading which continues in a two-storeyed form on the W. wall and indeed right up and round the great window. A break in the upward progress of building is noticeable where the little arches change from the plain pointed of *c.* 1300 to the 'nodding' ogee type of *c.* 1330. On the trumeau of the W. doorway is a restored figure of St Peter. The little window above has 15th c. glass; that in the main window was given in 1338 and has eight archbishops at the base, twelve Apostles above, then two panels each of the Annunciation, Nativity, Resurrection and Ascension, then (below the tracery) the Coronation of the Virgin.

In the **N. aisle** the W. window was part of the same gift. The first N. one, under the tower, has some early 16th c. glass and a memorial to Captain Scott's navigating officer Captain Bruce. The second contains part of a 12th c. Jesse window (a precious relic of the previous building and said to be the oldest glass in England) and panels of several later dates. The third, fourth and fifth are all early 14th c., the last being called the Pilgrimage window: it has amusing animals at the bottom with a monkey's funeral. The wall-arcading is interrupted in the second bay by a doorway and in the third by a small 16th c. tomb. The S. clerestory windows are here more clearly visible: their heraldry is said to refer to the knights who rested on their way to Bannockburn in 1314.

The sixth bay contains the bellfounders' window with scenes of

Minster from SW., York

bell-casting and tuning and a border of bells, again early 14th c. On
the right, the nave pulpit is by Sir Ninian Comper (1948). Lastly
there is a window of *c*. 1308 with scenes from the life of St Catherine
and some fine heraldry.

Now the N. transept and a change to Early English style; about
1250 is its probable date. The piers are not unlike the nave, but the
upper parts are quite different – triforium with twin openings under
semicircular main arches, and clerestory of open and blind repeating
lancets. The vault is again of painted wood, but of *c*. 1400, and
springs from the base of the clerestory, which thus has a squashed
appearance. The aisle vaults are stone, quadripartite but with extra
ribs to meet the shafts between pairs of windows. The Purbeck
marble shafts and dog-tooth mouldings are of course typical of the
period. At the N. end is the Five Sisters window, largely with
original grisaille glass; in the bottom centre is an even earlier panel
showing Daniel in the lions' den. Before examining the transept in
detail it is a good idea to step aside into the **crossing**.

The great tower arches and lantern are early 15th c., and so do the
piers seem to be. Really they are casings round the piers of the
Norman tower, a fact which has necessitated major strengthening

work. The painted vault is like the nave but original; it and the heraldic glazing are 15th c. Beneath the E. arch stands the splendid and unexpectedly asymmetrical pulpitum, late 15th c. The standing figures are of kings from William I to Henry VI, all except the last being original. The organ case above was made after the 1829 fire; the wrought-iron gates are early 18th c. Turning to the nave, one can here enjoy its full splendour, especially the W. window with its 'heart' tracery.

Back to the N. transept and into the King's Own Yorkshire Light Infantry chapel (St John the Evangelist's); the iron screens are by Bainbridge Reynolds. The wall-arcading with springing foliage capitals is typically Early English and continues all round the transept; here each bay contains military memorials. The glass on the left is 14th c., from the church of St John, Micklegate. In the SE. corner, left on leaving the chapel, is the stone cadaver effigy of Thomas de Haxey (d. 1425). Go across the transept to the NE. corner. The big astronomical clock is a Second World War memorial to Allied air forces; Sir Albert Richardson and H. J. Stammers designed the case. Beside it is the chapter house entrance – delicately traceried twin wooden doors. A charge is made at this point.

The **chapter house** is believed to be late 13th c., and the vestibule to it is of the same date. Of this passage Pevsner remarks that it is 'the first English building whose design aimed at the total substitution of window for wall'. Most of its glass is early 14th c. Above its vault is a room which was used as a medieval masons' shop and still has incised setting-out patterns of tracery on the floor. In the passage are various cases of exhibits, and two cope chests. The beautiful Madonna on the trumeau of the actual doorway into the octagon is almost wholly a restoration. Inside, the eyes can easily be bewildered by the contrasting richnesses of the painted wooden vault (the pattern was re-done in 1844 and again in 1976), the glass (mostly of 1300–7 but with later additions), the busily canopied seats, each framed with Purbeck marble shafts in a singularly attractive way, and the patterned tiled floor (also of 1844). An excellent model demonstrates the complex hidden framing of the roof.

Back once more in the **N. transept** – the second bay on the left is the Children's chapel of St Nicholas and has an 18th c. wrought-iron screen. Inside on the right the canopied tomb of Archbishop Greenfield (d. 1316) has a brass. On the blank wall of the half-bay the clock with two 16th c. jacks was designed by G. F. Bodley

(1883); the memorial below is to Rear-Admiral Cradock (d. 1914).
Then come 18th c. iron gates in a 15th c. screen within the 13th c.
arch leading to the **N. quire aisle**. Suffice it for the moment to note
that this is the late 14th c. part of the building, with uncomplicated
vault and wall-arcading; the remainder will be best seen from inside
the quire.

On the left is the white marble effigy of Sir George Savile (d. 1784)
by John Fisher, followed by a very odd set of three shelves on little
vaults, one with the alabaster effigy of Edward III's son Prince
William (d. 1344). Opposite are the largest of the organ pipes. In the
second bay the backs of the quire stalls start: the recumbent marble
effigy is of Archbishop Harcourt (d. 1847), by Matthew Noble, and
the glass (in all the windows up to the NE. transept) almost all
15th c. The next low tomb is of the philanthropist Stephan
Beckwith, who d. 1843 (figure by Joseph Leyland). Opposite is a
museum-like model of a miner at work. The very large 'curtained'
marble memorial that follows is to Archbishop Sterne (d. 1683) and
may be by Grinling Gibbons. Opposite, Archbishop Musgrave
(d. 1860) is commemorated, the effigy again by Noble; behind him
are a number of 19th c. brass plaques. In the fourth bay are two
16th c. memorials robbed of their brasses. The double doorway
leads to modern staff rooms.

The fifth bay is the NE. transept, with high vault, clerestoried
sides, and window tracery double at the base. The glass is of 1422, a
magnificent series of scenes from St William's life. The kneeling
effigies of Henry Belassis (d. 1616) and his wife are by Nicholas
Stone. On the right is Archbishop Savage (d. 1507) under a canopy;
the wooden upper part, forming the chantry of God's Will, and
approached from the quire ambo, was restored by Richardson
(1949).

At this point are steps down to the E. crypt. This virtually repeats
the plan above, with extra piers. But it is much earlier. It carried
the late 12th c. quire and thus has stumpy Norman columns and a
rib-vault; confusing alterations were made in the 14th c. and after
the 1829 fire. Under the W. part of the quire, it was built around the
crypt of the 1070 cathedral; that part can be seen later, but within it
and behind the richly gilded font cover by Sir Ninian Comper (1946)
are a tomb and a chapel containing relics of St William's shrine.

Back in the sixth aisle bay, the white marble monument to Lord
Rockingham (d. 1723) is a rather unusual composition. Opposite,
and exactly a century earlier, are the kneeling figure of Henry
Swinburne, and busts of William Ingram and his wife. The window

is of 1405. Next is the ugly large monument of Mary Fenwick
(d. 1708); her father Charles Howard (d. 1684) has a floor-brass
below. The seventh bay has 14th c. glass and a marble bust of Vice-
Admiral Medley (d. 1747) by Henry Cheere. The last two bays, with
wrought-iron gates, are **St Stephen's chapel**. On the N. are a window
of late 14th c. glass and a 16th c. French one illustrating the life of
St James the Great. The E. window is 14th and 15th c., and the
reredos by G. E. Street (1879), with a Crucifixion scene in terra-
cotta by G. Tinworth. The memorials on the left are to Samuel
Brearey (d. 1735) and Lyonel Ingram (d. 1624). The tomb-chests on
the right are of Archbishops Scrope (d. 1405) and Markham
(d. 1807); the latter is one of many memorials remade after the 1829
fire.

On the E. wall of the centre bay, the **Lady chapel**, is a reredos by
Bodley (1905), flanked by monuments to Archbishop Frewen
(d. 1664) and Sharp (d. 1713), each with effigy typical of its time.
The great E. window above can be dated exactly to 1405–8. It is the
biggest single expanse of medieval glass in existence. Above the
gallery that runs across it are Old Testament scenes, and below it
illustrations of the Revelations of St John. A description can be
found by the arch into the S. quire aisle.

The tomb under the E. bay of the S. arcade, with an
extraordinarily high canopy, is of Archbishop Bowet (d. 1423); the
figure on the second tomb is all that survives of the monument of
Archbishop Matthew (d. 1628). The **SE. chapel**, All Saints',
honours the Duke of Wellington's Regiment and has another Reynolds
screen. In its far SE. corner are a little tablet to John Piers (d. 1594)
and a delightful alabaster bust of Anne Benett (d. 1601), by
Nicholas Stone. The much bigger monument on the right with two
standing figures is to the Earl of Strafford (d. 1695), by John Nost.
The E. window glass is 14th c.; the first S. one has 16th c. French
panels and the second is mostly 15th c. The third, in the **S. quire
aisle** proper, is late 14th c. Amongst many 18th and 19th c.
memorials is the brass demi-figure of Elizabeth Eynnes (d. 1585).
Then comes Grinling Gibbons's commanding marble figure of
Archbishop Lamplugh (d. 1691), followed by three attractive 17th c.
memorials with re-gilded lettering, and busts by Michael Rysbrack
of Henry and Edward Finch (d. 1728 and 1737). The glass in this
(fourth) window is partly 16th c. French and partly 17th c. Facing it
is Archbishop Dolben (d. 1686), welcomed by a galaxy of cherubs.

The fifth bay is the SE. transept, like the NE., and with 15th c.
glass depicting 75 scenes from St Cuthbert's life and intended also as

a tribute to Henry VI. Below it are two large 17th c. monuments, to Archbishop Hutton (d. 1605), and to William Gee (d. 1611), neither very inspired. Over the S. entrance to the crypt, opposite, is a tapestry of the Last Supper.

The sixth bay has a double doorway to the **Zouche chapel**, which is for private prayer. It is mid-14th c., i.e. earlier than the aisle it adjoins: its vault has segmental bosses fitting between the intersections of the ribs instead of concealing them. 15th c. cupboards line the N. wall. The two old stalls were saved from the quire after the 1829 fire. The E. window glass, also honouring Henry VI, is late 15th c.; in the S. windows many animals and birds can be found. In the SW. corner is a holy well, St Peter's. The little organ is of 1801.

Now cross the aisle into the **quire**. The part E. of the small transept was built first, before the Norman quire was demolished, and all was complete by about 1400. It differs surprisingly little from the nave in spite of the time-lapse – the clerestory windows are Perpendicular and the triforium more prominent – and the principal differences between the two halves of the quire can also readily be seen at those levels. The little transepts hardly show, for the main arches run right through, with bridges at triforium level. The lierne vault is again of wood but more complex than the nave. It and the whole of the quire woodwork were renewed by Smirke after the 1829 fire. The archbishop's throne, stalls and pulpit are probably close imitations of those destroyed; the organ case is of the same period and so is the stone reredos screen. The small ambo in the sanctuary, connected to the chantry in the N. aisle, is by Richardson (1951).

Back in **S. quire aisle**: the glass ahead (the next window W. of the little transept) is part of a late 14th c. Jesse Tree from New College Chapel, Oxford. Then comes an early 15th c. one with Biblical marriage scenes. Amongst many 19th c. monuments are a marvellously elaborate brass one to William Mason (d. 1854), made by F. A. Skidmore, and a regimental commemoration of the Russian campaign of 1854–5. The last window has various collected glass scenes. After a blank bay with organ both sides is the arch into the **S. transept**.

This is a little earlier than the N., and internally only differs in minor details. On the E. side against the blank bay the canopied tomb is of Archbishop Thomson (d. 1896). In the first of the other two bays stands the splendid tomb of Archbishop de Gray (d. 1255), with free-standing gabled canopy on slender Purbeck marble columns; the lower one is of Archbishop de Ludham (d. 1265). The tall one in the next bay is to Dean Duncombe (d. 1880), and was designed by G. E. Street. The lancet windows behind have old glass. In the S. wall the rose window is of *c.* 1500 and its pattern of red and white roses is thought to commemorate the marriage of the Lancastrian King Henry VII with Elizabeth of York. Those below are mostly 18th and 19th c.; the four lowest ones are by the 18th c. glass painter William Peckitt whose work occurs frequently elsewhere in the building. A model shows the layout of the new **undercroft** around the tower foundations and their relationship to the earlier Norman cathedral and to the Roman fortress beneath that. A new stair leads down to these spaces scooped out by the engineers and archaeologists (a fee is payable).

The showing of the authentic wall remains is confused by simultaneously treating them as exhibition galleries and bringing in for illustration purposes casts of carved heads, etc., found elsewhere. However, all is clearly labelled and there is no denying that seeing the 2nd and 11th c. masonry and the 20th c. concrete with stainless steel reinforcement is essential to one's appreciation of the building. What lies unknown under other cathedrals? In the largest gallery is even a large (reconstructed) area of Roman plastered wall with painted decorations. Further on are Saxon tomb-slabs, medieval carvings, a painted coffin-lid, and, best of all, the treasury newly formed within the earliest, W., part of the quire crypt to house plate and other precious objects. At its far end St William's shrine is again visible.

Back in the **S. transept**, the undercroft model will now be much easier to understand. In the SW. corner is the way to the tower stair, often open for a charge. This leads via the transept roof and a longer stair up the tower itself to the finest vantage point of the city. The W. aisle, enclosed by another heavy iron screen by Reynolds (1926) is the chapel of the Prince of Wales' Own Regiment (St George's); the glass in the two 15th c. lancet windows came from St Martin's church.

Lastly the **S. nave aisle**, with a double doorway in the second bay leading now to the shop, formerly the registry. Opposite stands an early 17th c. bread cupboard rather in the form of a grandfather clock. The window in this bay is in memory of Archbishop de Gray, (d. 1255); the next is also old but less distinct. The brass eagle lectern is of 1686 and has a more recent platform with lamps held aloft by cherubs. On the other side of the nave in the next bay to the W. a wooden dragon projecting from the triforium is thought to have been a suspension arm for a font cover. The third aisle window is 14th and 15th c. and has a school scene at the base. The following one was mostly renewed in 1907, the next is a 14th c. Jesse Tree, also much restored, the next is made up from fragments, and the last is mostly 14th c. The W. one, a Crucifixion, is a companion to the other aisle windows, i.e. of 1338. Near the end of the N. arcade is a splendid model of the whole cathedral, which should be examined before going **outside**.

In the W. front the change from plain to ogee Decorated occurs outside as within. The towers, however, are Perpendicular, the S. before 1450 and the N. twenty years later. Deangate passes between the S. aisle and the 16th c. church of St Michael-le-Belfrey and gives close views of, first the aisle with its gabled windows and the flying buttresses added early this century, then the choir practice room over what is now the shop, then the transept with restored S. portal and added 19th c. turrets. Across the road is a 2nd c. Roman column found buried in the S. transept. From there the central tower can be seen well. It was an early 15th c. replacement of one contemporary with the transepts, and its parapet is only 2 ft higher than the W. ones. Then the big Perpendicular quire clerestory, the aisle and the 14th c. consistory court, vestry and Zouche chapel buildings below, and the SE. transept.

Facing the noble E. front is St William's College, a mainly 15th c. house used by chantry priests. There is a way along the N. side of the cathedral, at first following Minster Yard with the chapter house on the left and the 17th c. Treasurer's House on the right. Gates lead into the park, with a curving path past the Five Sisters of the N. transept, back to the W. front. The buildings over to the right are the 13th c. chapel (now the library) and part of the cloister of the former archbishop's palace. As for the cathedral itself, its detail can be more quietly enjoyed from this side than on the S., and the towers especially are worthy of further study.

Greek Cathedral in London, St Sophia (Greek Orthodox)

There was a Greek church in Westminster as early as 1677. The community, however, increased considerably early in the 19th c. at the time of the Greek war of independence. A church was built in London Wall in the City in 1849. St Sophia in Moscow Road, Bayswater, was begun in 1877 and consecrated by the Archbishop of

Corfu in 1882. In 1923 it became the cathedral of a diocese
comprising the whole of Western Europe.

The architect was J. Oldrid Scott and the style Byzantine,
influenced surprisingly little by the tastes of the period. The simple
exterior of red and yellow brick gives little hint of the richness of
materials and carving inside. The orientation is turned, so that it is
the W. front which abuts Moscow Road, with two plain doorways
and an inscription on the sill above celebrating the Greek colony's
success in establishing the building. Inside the entrance porch on the
left is an inscribed stone of 1667 from the first church in Charing
Cross Road. The translation provided explains that it refers to
Charles II, and to Lord Henry Compton as Bishop.

Most of the domed interior can be taken in from just inside the W.
doorway. Ahead is the iconostasis or screen which completely hides
the E. end and altar except when the doors are thrown open during
ceremonies. Splendidly carved in walnut and inlaid with wood and
mother-of-pearl, it has paintings by Thiersch of Munich: those
along the top are scenes of the life of Christ. The high gallery to the
left, also of walnut, is for the choir. By the SW. crossing pier the
canopied square openwork wood pulpit on five marble columns is
by Scott. The delicate upright pews and the bishop's throne with its
open crown however mostly came from the former church of
St Saviour in London Wall. The mosaics and marble have been
gradually extended. Original are the green marbles throughout the
dado and main columns, the great traditional all-seeing
'Pantokrator' on the gilded dome, and the Apostles between the
lantern windows; they are by A. G. Walker, in a pre-Raphaelite
rather than Byzantine style. The scheme was completed much later by
Boris Anrep in a more appropriate idiom. His work includes the
prophets around the transept arches, birds and flowers around the
three doorways beneath the W. (visitors') gallery, and much else.
Apart from small areas of transept ceilings and the wooden
platforms under the pews hardly an area is left bare. The glass,
decorative outside as well as in, has leafy patterns in frosted
textures.

Near the W. end hangs a great hollow silver double Greek Cross
filled with little red oil lamps. The many lamps and the traditional

absence of carved figures accentuate the authentic character of this Eastern cathedral in a London setting.

It should be added that, unlike Anglican and Roman Catholic cathedrals, the building is not open at all times of the day.

Ukrainian Cathedral in London, Holy Family in Exile (Ukrainian Catholic)

The only British cathedral which started life as a Nonconformist church, this was the King's Weigh House Chapel, built in Duke Street in London's West End for the Congregationalists in 1889–91 and tracing its own history back to a chapel near the King's Weigh House in Cornhill in the City, burnt down in the Great Fire of 1666. The architect was Alfred Waterhouse.

The Ukrainian Catholic Church, a branch of the Eastern Byzantine-Ukrainian rite in union with Rome, first had its own place of worship in Saffron Hill, Holborn, in 1946. The Apostolic Exarchate or bishopric was set up by Pope Pius XII in 1957 with Cardinal Godfrey as first bishop and Augustine Hornyak as second, and the cathedral was consecrated in its new role in 1968. Though normally locked, it may be visited on application to the priest administrator at 21, Binney Street, London W.1.

A masterpiece of compact planning, with oval auditorium and gallery, it seats 900. The round-arched Italianate classical design, using hard brick and buff terra-cotta, is typical of Waterhouse, like his better-known Natural History Museum. The domed ceiling, a World War II casualty, has been restored; otherwise little has changed except for a remodelling of the sanctuary in 1904 under Sir John Burnet. He designed the towered organ case (the organ itself no longer exists), and Anning Bell the E. window glass; the reredos was designed by A. E. Henderson in 1927 and carved by Allan Wyon. Of Waterhouse's original details the embossed column facings, the curved wooden gallery front, and the Art Nouveau window patterns are specially noteworthy. On the ambulatory wall near the NE. entrance is a stone carving of the Holy Family salvaged from the Saffron Hill church and now a reminder of the cathedral's dedication.

As well as a crypt hall under the cathedral itself, there is an extensive suite of other rooms and halls adjoining, along Binney Street. Outside, the ingenious merging of oval and rectangle should be noted, also the dignified entrance portico and the impressive square tower over one of the twin gallery stairs.

Many ex-cathedrals (mostly in Scotland) are included in the main
text since they include substantial remains from the time when they
were cathedrals. The following, too, have at one time possessed
cathedrals and in a few cases slight fragments survive. The list is not
exhaustive.

Bath (Avon) A priory church which was a cathedral from 1088 till
the 12th c. Subsequently its chapter shared the election, and it still
shares the title, of the bishopric of Bath and Wells. The existing
church was built from 1499 onwards, smaller in extent than its
predecessor, much of the plan of which has been determined by
excavation. Above ground only one arch with a column can be
assigned to the Norman cathedral; this is at the E. end of the S.
quire aisle and led into the former transept.

Chester (Cheshire) The predecessor of the present parish church of
St John was a cathedral from 1075 to 1095. Nothing that survives
is older than the present nave, which is 12th c. The tower and the
E. parts, which were monastic, are in ruins. There was no
connection with the present cathedral of Chester.

Chester-le-Street (Durham) A see from 875 to 995. Site of cathedral
unknown.

Coventry (West Midlands) St Mary's priory church was a cathedral
from 1095 to 1129. Slight remains of its successor can be seen
close to the present cathedral (see main text). Coventry and
Lichfield were subsequently linked as a joint see like Bath and
Wells.

Crediton (Devon) A see from 909 to 1050, when the bishop moved to
Exeter. The present building was collegiate and is now a parish
church.

Denbigh (Clwyd) Leicester's church was begun by Queen Elizabeth's
favourite, Robert Dudley, in 1579 and was intended to become a
cathedral in place of St Asaph's. The nave had aisles; much of the
N. wall still stands as a ruin.

Dorchester (Oxfordshire) The seat of a great diocese once stretching
from the Thames to Lincolnshire. Its line of bishops begins in 634
and ends in 1072 with the transfer of the see to Lincoln.
Subsequently an Augustinian abbey was founded; the N. wall of
its church (now parochial) may possibly incorporate part of the
former cathedral.

Dumfries (Dumfries & Galloway) The seat of the Roman Catholic bishop of Galloway from 1878 to 1961 when the throne was transferred to Ayr; the pro-cathedral was burnt down the following year. The remains have been demolished.

Dunwich (Suffolk) Said to have been a see from 632 to 955 and, if so, the site of the cathedral founded by St Felix must now be under the sea with the rest of the ancient town; opinion, however, now favours Walton near Felixstowe as the correct location.

Everton (Merseyside) The church of Our Lady Immaculate was begun in 1856 with the intention of its becoming the cathedral of the Catholic diocese of Liverpool. The Lady chapel still stands.

Halkirk (Highland) Near Thurso, the seat of Caithness diocese in the 12th c. and till it was transferred to Dornoch in 1222.

Hoxne (Suffolk) A see early in the 10th c., its cathedral continuing in a subordinate role to North Elmham and then to Thetford.

Kinnedar (Grampian) Near Lossiemouth, the seat of Moray diocese for a short time c. 1190.

Leicester (Leicestershire) A see from 679 to 874. Site of cathedral unknown and not related to present cathedral.

Lindisfarne (Northumberland) A see from 635 to 875. Priory founded late in the 12th c., probably on site of cathedral.

Osney (Oxfordshire) An abbey church which served as the cathedral of Oxford diocese from 1542 to 1546 (see **Oxford** in main text). Of the abbey only one small 15th c. building remains.

Ramsbury (Wiltshire) A see from 909 to 1058 and then amalgamated with Sherborne. The cathedral became a parish church and was subsequently rebuilt.

Rosemarkie (Highland) The seat of Ross diocese in the 12th and 13th cc., after which it was moved to Fortrose.

St Andrews (Fife) The medieval kirk of Holy Trinity, subsequently much altered, served as a cathedral (much like St Giles', Edinburgh) during the years 1635–9 and 1661–88.

St Germans (Cornwall) A see from 941 to 1043. Subsequently an Augustinian priory was founded and the church rebuilt. It is now parochial.

Selsey (Sussex) A see from 680 to 1080. Site of cathedral probably now under the sea.

Sherborne (Dorset) A see from 705 to 1075, then removed to Old Sarum. Subsequently a Benedictine abbey was founded and the church rebuilt.

Sidnacester (Lincolnshire) The seat of Lindsey diocese from 678 until it was united with Dorchester. Attempts have been made to identify it with Stow, between Gainsborough and Lincoln.

Skeabost (Highland) On Skye, the seat of the Bishop of the Isles in the 15th c. before Iona.

Spynie (Grampian) Near Lossiemouth, the seat of Moray diocese from 1203 to 1224. The church was destroyed in 1736.

Thetford (Norfolk) A see from 1075 to 1091. Site of cathedral unknown.

Westminster (London) The Benedictine abbey's early history is obscure. Its church survived the dissolution of the monasteries through being the royal coronation and burial church and through being declared a cathedral by Henry VIII in 1530. Strictly speaking that qualifies it for inclusion in the main text even though it retained the status for only ten years.

CHRISTIAN, Ewan
  Carlisle, Southwell
CLARK, Michael
  Brentwood
CLEMENT, James
  Durham
COLSON, John
  Winchester
COMPER, Sir Ninian
  Aberdeen Ep, Derby,
  Durham, Ely, *Perth*, Ripon,
  St Albans, *Southwark CE*,
  Wakefield, Wells, *York*
COMPER, Sebastian (son of Sir
  Ninian)
  Derby, Northampton,
  Oxford
COTTINGHAM, Lewis
  Hereford, Rochester
COTTINGHAM, N. J. (son of Lewis)
  Hereford
CRAWLEY, John
  Portsmouth RC
CRAZE, Romilly
  Southwark RC
CROSSLEY, F. H.
  Chester
CROWTHER, J. S.
  Manchester
DAWBER, Sir Guy
  Ely
DENMAN, John
  Canterbury
DYKES BOWER, Stephen
  Bury St Edmunds, Carlisle,
  Norwich CE, St Paul's
EASTWOOD, J. H.
  Leeds
ELLIS, Alex
  Aberdeen RC
ESSEX, James
  Ely, *Lincoln*

FEILDEN, Bernard
  St Paul's, York
FERREY, Benjamin
  Wells
FLOCKTON, William
  Sheffield
FORSYTHE, W. A.
  Blackburn
FOSTER, John
  Liverpool CE
FOWLER, C. Hodgson
  Lincoln, Rochester
GARBETT, William
  Winchester
GARNER, Thomas
  Chichester, Lincoln
GIBBERD, Sir Frederick
  Liverpool RC
GIBBS, James
  Derby, Lincoln
GODFREY, Emil
  Rochester
GOLDIE, George
  Middlesborough
GRAHAM, James Gillespie
  (born James GILLESPIE)
  Edinburgh RC, Glasgow RC
GREENLANDS, S. K.
  Leeds
GRIMTHORPE, Lord
  St Albans
GWILT, George
  Southwark CE
HADDOW, T. Harley
  Edinburgh RC
HAMILTON, Thomas
  Glasgow CS
HANSOM, Joseph A.
  Arundel, Newcastle RC,
  Plymouth
HANSOM, Joseph S. (son of
  Joseph A.)
  Portsmouth RC

PACE, George
  Chester, Durham, Lichfield,
  Llandaff, Peterborough,
  St Albans, Sheffield,
  Southwark CE, Wakefield
PALEY, E. G.
  Lancaster
PALMER, John
  Blackburn
PEARSON, F. L.
  Perth, Truro, *Wakefield*
PEARSON, J. L. (father of F. L.)
  Bristol, Chichester, Exeter,
  Leicester, Norwich CE,
  Peterborough, Rochester,
  Truro
PENNETHORNE, Sir James
  Salisbury
PENROSE, F. C.
  St Paul's
PERKINS, A. E.
  Worcester
POTTER, Robert
  Chichester
POWELL, S. P.
  Birmingham RC
PRICHARD, John
  Llandaff
PUGIN, Augustus
  Birmingham RC, Chester,
  Leeds, *Newcastle RC,*
  Northampton, Nottingham,
  Shrewsbury, Southwark CE,
  Southwark RC
PUGIN, Edward (son of
  Augustus)
  Belmont, Liverpool RC,
  Northampton, Shrewsbury,
  Wrexham
PUGIN, Peter Paul (brother of
  Edward)
  Belmont, *Cardiff,*
  Motherwell

RAVEZZANO, Benedetto da
  St Paul's
RICHARDSON, Sir Albert
  Glasgow CS, *York*
RICKMAN, Thomas
  Blackburn
ROISER, Ernest
  St Asaph
ROSS, Alexander (& MacBeth)
  Inverness, Oban Ep
ROSS, Alistair
  Inverness
ROSS, Thomas
  Iona
ROSSI, A. P.
  Norwich RC
SALVIN, Anthony
  Durham, *Norwich CE, Wells*
SCOLES, Canon
  Portsmouth RC
SCOTT, George Gilbert junior
  Chester, Norwich RC
SCOTT, Sir George Gilbert
  (father of above)
  Aberdeen, *Bangor, Brecon,*
  Bristol, *Bury St Edmunds,*
  Canterbury, *Chester,*
  Chichester, Dunblane,
  Dundee Ep, Durham,
  Edinburgh CS,
  Edinburgh Ep, Ely, Exeter,
  Glasgow Ep, Gloucester,
  Hereford, Lichfield, Lincoln,
  Manchester, Newcastle CE,
  Oxford, Peterborough,
  Ripon, Rochester, St Albans,
  St Asaph, St Davids,
  Salisbury, Wakefield,
  Winchester, Worcester
SCOTT, Sir Giles Gilbert
  (grandson of Sir George
  Gilbert)

Chester, Liverpool CE,
Oban RC
SCOTT, J. Oldrid
(brother of George Gilbert
junior)
Bangor, Edinburgh Ep,
Glasgow Ep, *Hereford*,
Lichfield, Norwich RC,
Ripon, St Albans, *Greek*
SEDDON, J. P.
Llandaff, *Norwich CE*
SEELY & PAGET
(see Lord Mottistone)
SHATTOCK, L. H.
Westminster
SIMPSON, Archibald
Aberdeen Ep
SIMS, Ronald
Southwark CE, Southwell
SMIRKE, Sydney
Lichfield
SPENCE, Sir Basil
Coventry
STEWART, Duncan
Chester
STREET, G. E.
Aberdeen Ep, Bristol,
Carlisle, *Lichfield*, Salisbury,
York
TARBOLTON, Harold
Oban Ep
TAYLOR, John
Truro

TAYLOR, Robert
Peterborough, Rochester
THOMAS, F. G.
Liverpool CE
THOMAS, Percy, Partnership
Clifton
THOMSON & TURNBULL
Oban Ep
TORRY, John
Ayr
WASTELL, John
Peterborough
WATERHOUSE, Alfred
Ukrainian
WATSON, George Mackie
Kirkwall
WEIGHTMAN & HADFIELD
Salford
WHITE
Blackburn
WILSON, R. G.
Aberdeen RC
WINKLEY, Austin
Portsmouth RC
WOOD, John
Llandaff
WOOLER, John
Durham
WORTHINGTON, Sir Hubert
Manchester
WREN, Sir Christopher
Ely, *Lincoln, St Paul's*
WYATT, James
Durham, Hereford, Salisbury

Embroiderers, tapestry-makers, illuminators

DEAN, Beryl
  Chelmsford
ISHERWOOD, Kathleen
  Portsmouth RC
LAMB, Helen
  Dunblane
MARTIN, Iris
  Bangor
MOORMAN, Theodora
  Manchester, Ripon

RAYMOND, Carole
  Birmingham CE
SCOTT, Macdonald
  Glasgow CS
SMITH, Dorothea Nimmo
  Dunblane
WOOD, Malcolm
  Guildford

Furniture-makers

CHIPPENDALE, Thomas
  Lincoln
CURSITER, Stanley
  Kirkwall
GIMSON, Ernest
  Westminster

RUSSELL, R. D.
  Liverpool RC
THOMPSON
  Bangor, Wakefield

Glass artists

ARMITAGE, Robert
  Glasgow CS
BALLANTINE
  Edinburgh CS
BARNETT
  Wakefield
BELL, Anning
  Ukrainian
BOSSANYI, Erwin
  Canterbury
BROWN, F. M.
  Bradford
BURLISON & GRYLLS
  Ripon, Salisbury
BURMEISTER & FULKS
  Dunkeld

BURNE-JONES, Sir Edward
  Birmingham CE, Bradford,
  Edinburgh CS, Norwich CE,
  Oxford
BUSS, Arthur
  Portsmouth RC
CHAGALL, Marc
  Chichester
CHILTON, Margaret
  Aberdeen CS
CLARKE, Geoffrey
  Coventry, Lincoln
CLAYTON & BELL
  Bangor, *Bury St Edmunds*,
  Canterbury, Chelmsford,
  Chichester, *Durham*,

Glasgow CS, Hereford,
Lichfield, Norwich CE,
Oxford, Peterborough,
Rochester, Salisbury, Truro
COMPER, Sir Ninian
Canterbury, Sheffield,
Southwark CE
COTTIER, Daniel
Aberdeen CS, Edinburgh CS
DAVIES, A. L.
Bradford
DAVIS, Louis
Dunblane
DIXON, W. E.
Sheffield
EASTON, Hugh
Brechin, Durham,
Winchester
EDWARDS, Carl
Glasgow CS, Liverpool CE,
Portsmouth CE
EVANS, David
Bangor
EVETTS, L. C.
Newcastle CE
FORSETH, Einar
Coventry
FORSYTH, Moira
Guildford, Norwich CE
GIBBS, C. A.
Hereford
GRANT, Marion
Exeter, *Glasgow CS*
GULLAND, David
Aberdeen RC
HAIG, Henry
Clifton
HARDMAN (& Co.)
Arundel, Birmingham RC,
Bristol, Bury St Edmunds,
Cardiff, Carlisle, Gloucester,
Hereford, Lancaster,

Middlesbrough,
Northampton, Norwich CE,
Norwich RC, Salford,
Shrewsbury, *Worcester*
HARVEY, Harry
Ripon, Sheffield
HAYWARD, John
Blackburn
HEATON, BUTLER & BAYNE
Bradford, Chester
HEDGELAND, G.
Norwich CE
HENDRIE, Herbert
Brechin, *Glasgow CS*
HOLIDAY, Henry
Brechin, Southwark CE
HOLLAWAY, Antony
Manchester
HUTTON, John
Chelmsford, *Coventry,
Guildford*
JACKSON, Sir Thomas
Norwich CE
KEMP, Marjorie
Aberdeen CS
KEMPE, Charles
Bury St Edmunds,
Chichester, Dornoch,
Dunblane, Hereford,
Lichfield, Rochester,
Southwark CE, *Wakefield*,
Wells
LAVERS & BARRAUD
Worcester
LEE, Lawrence
Coventry
LUTTGENS
Nottingham
MAYER
Brentwood, Edinburgh RC
MOORE, Albert
Bradford

MORRIS, William (& Co.)
Birmingham CE, Bradford,
Chelmsford, Dornoch,
Edinburgh CS, *Oxford*,
Peterborough, Winchester
NEW, Keith
Bristol, Coventry, Sheffield
NICHOLSON, A. K.
Chelmsford, Lincoln,
Newcastle CE, Wells
PEACE, David
Manchester
PECKITT, William
York
PIPER, John
Coventry, Liverpool RC,
Llandaff, *Newport*
POWELL, Dunstan
(included in Hardman &
Co.)
POWELL & Sons
Liverpool CE
PRITCHARD, Sadie
Glasgow CS
PUGIN, Augustus
Newcastle RC
REYNTIENS, Patrick
Liverpool RC
RICHARDS, Ceri
Derby, Liverpool RC
ROPE, Margaret
Shrewsbury
ROSSETTI, Dante Gabriel
Bradford
RUTHERFORD, Rosemary
Guildford
SCOTT, Stanley Murray
Newcastle CE
SHAPLAND, W. T. Carter
Chester, Peterborough

SPEAR, Francis
Dornoch, *Glasgow CS*
STAMMERS, Harry
Canterbury, *Glasgow CS*,
Lincoln
STRACHAN, Douglas
Aberdeen CS, Brechin,
Dunblane, Edinburgh CS,
Glasgow CS, Iona
THOMAS, Brian
St Paul's
TRAHERNE, Margaret
Coventry, Liverpool RC,
Manchester
WAILES, William
Chester, Ely, Gloucester,
Newcastle CE,
Newcastle RC, Ripon,
Worcester
WARD & HUGHES
Lincoln, Ripon
WARRINGTON, William
Norwich CE, Truro
WEBB, Christopher
Chichester, Glasgow CS,
Lincoln, Llandaff, *Salisbury,
Sheffield*
WEBSTER, Gordon
Brechin, Dunblane,
Glasgow CS
WHALL, Christopher
Canterbury, Carlisle,
Dornoch, *Leicester*
WILSON, William
Aberdeen CS, *Brechin*,
Dornoch, *Glasgow CS*
WOORE, Edward
Salisbury

Metalworkers

ALDER, John
  Clifton
ATKINS, David
  Liverpool RC
BAKEWELL, Robert
  Birmingham CE, *Derby*
BLACKWELL, Edward
  Salford
CLARKE, Geoffrey
  Chichester, Coventry
DONALD, John
  Birmingham CE
DURBIN, Leslie
  Ripon
FEDDEN, Bryant
  Manchester

GOODDEN, Robert
  Liverpool RC
HADDEN, Thomas
  Dunblane, Edinburgh CS
HAYWARD, John
  Blackburn
REYNOLDS, Bainbridge
  York
SKIDMORE, Francis
  Chester, Edinburgh CS,
  Edinburgh Ep, Hereford,
  Lichfield, Oxford,
  Worcester, York
TIJOU, Jean
  Birmingham CE, *St Paul's*

Mosaic and ceramic artists

ANREP, Boris
  Westminster, Greek
BELL, Anning
  Westminster
BURNE-JONES, Sir Edward
  Llandaff
CLAYTON, J. R.
  Chester
COPER, Hans
  Coventry
KOSSOWSKI, Adam
  Cardiff
LOIRE, Gabriel
  Aberdeen RC

POWNALL, Gilbert
  Westminster
RICHMOND, Sir William
  St Paul's
ROBBIA, Andrea della
  Liverpool CE,
  Portsmouth CE
SALVIATI, Antonio
  Chester, Dundee Ep,
  St Davids
WALKER, A. G.
  Greek

Organ-builders

BEVINGTON, Henry
  Brecon
CASSON, Thomas
  Bury St Edmunds
HARRIS, Renatus
  Bristol
JORDAN, Abraham
  Portsmouth CE
LOOSEMORE, John
  Exeter

RIEGER
  Clifton
SCHWARBRICK, Thomas
  Birmingham CE
SMITH (Father)
  Durham
SNETZLER
  Norwich CE, Salisbury

Painters

ALBANI, Francesco
  Brecon
ALBERTINELLI
  Millport
BERNARD, Lambert
  Chichester
BEYAERT, Louis
  Edinburgh RC,
  Portsmouth RC
BORTHWICK, A. E.
  Edinburgh Ep
CEREZO, Matteo
  Edinburgh Ep
CLAYTON & BELL
  Chester
COTIGNOLA, Girolamo
  Middlesbrough
DEGASPERI, Ernst
  Edinburgh Ep
FEIBUSCH, Hans
  Chichester
GAMBIER-PARRY, Thomas
  Gloucester
GAROFALO
  Canterbury, Southwark CE
GRANT, Duncan
  Lincoln

HONTHORST
  Brecon
HUNT, Holman
  St Paul's
KEATING, Tom
  Bury St Edmunds
le MAISTRE, Roy
  Iona
MCCULLOUGH, Felix
  Aberdeen RC
MAZZOLA, Francesco Maria
  Edinburgh Ep
MILLER, Bernard
  Chester
NEEFS, Peter
  Canterbury
PHILIPSON, Robin
  Edinburgh Ep
PIETRO, Sano di
  Inverness
PIPER, John
  Chichester, *Newport*
RAEMAKERS, Louis
  Newcastle CE
RAPHAEL
  Chester

ROSSETTI, Dante Gabriel
    Llandaff
SCHWARTZ, Martin
    Norwich CE
SLACK, Brian
    Edinburgh Ep
STAMMERS, H. J.
    York
SUTHERLAND, Graham
    Chichester, *Coventry*
THIERSCH
    Greek
THOMAS, Brian
    Bangor
THORNHILL, Sir James
    St Paul's
TIARINI, Alessandro
    Worcester

TITIAN
    St Paul's
TOWER, W. E.
    Chester
TRAQUAIR, Phoebe
    Glasgow Ep
VANNI
    Leicester
WEIGHT, Carel
    Manchester
WESTLAKE, Nathaniel
    Portsmouth RC
WILLEMENT, T. H.
    Wells
WRIGHT, Austin
    Manchester
WYLLIE, W. L.
    Portsmouth CE

Sculptors

ADAMS, G. G.
    St Paul's
ADAMS-ACTON, John
    Carlisle
ALLAN, Maxwell
    Dunblane
ARMSTEAD, H. H.
    Carlisle
BACON, John
    Bristol, Leicester,
    Newcastle CE, Rochester,
    St Paul's, Salisbury,
    Worcester
BACON, John junior
    (son of above)
    St Paul's, Wells, Worcester
BAILY, E. H.
    Bristol, Manchester,
    Newcastle CE, St Paul's
BANKS, Thomas
    Rochester, *St Paul's*

BEHNES, William
    St Paul's
BEYER, Ralph
    Coventry
BIRD, Francis
    Portsmouth CE, St Paul's
BLAKEMAN, Charles
    Aberdeen RC
BOEHM, Sir Edgar
    Canterbury, Durham,
    St Paul's
BOUVERIE, R. Pleydell
    Salisbury
BOYD, Mary Syme
    Edinburgh Ep
BROCK, Sir Thomas
    St Paul's, Worcester
BRUMBY, Robert
    Liverpool RC
CAMPBELL, Thomas
    St Paul's

CAREW, J. E.
  Chichester
CARTER, Kenneth
  Exeter
CHANTREY, Sir Francis
  Bristol, *Derby*, Durham,
  Exeter, *Lichfield*,
  Norwich CE, St Albans,
  St Paul's, Salisbury,
  Sheffield, Wells, Winchester,
  Worcester
CHARTERIS, Sir Martin
  Norwich CE
CHEEVE, Henry
  York
CIBBER, Caius Gabriel
  St Paul's
CIMINAGHI, Virginio
  Liverpool RC
CLARKE, Philip Lindsay
  Shrewsbury, Westminster
COBBETT, John
  Guildford
COLEMAN, Alan
  Southwell
COLLINS, Alan
  Bradford
COPNALL, Bainbridge
  St Paul's
CRIBB, Joseph
  Plymouth
CROWE, Lesley
  Edinburgh Ep
DICK, Sir William Reid
  St Paul's
DRURY, Alfred
  Bristol
DUFF, Maxine
  Edinburgh Ep
DUNBAR, David
  Carlisle, Newcastle CE
DURST, Alan

Llandaff, *Peterborough*,
  Winchester
EARP, Thomas
  Rochester
EPSTEIN, Sir Jacob
  Coventry, Lichfield,
  Llandaff, St Paul's
EUNSON, Reynold
  Kirkwall
EVANS, David
  Liverpool CE
EVANS, George
  Lichfield
FISHER, John
  York
FITZGERALD, Clark
  Coventry
FLAXMAN, John
  Aberdeen Ep, Bradford,
  Chichester, Gloucester,
  Newcastle CE, St Paul's,
  Salisbury, Winchester
FORD, Onslow
  Sheffield
FORSYTH, James
  Manchester, Norwich CE,
  Peterborough, Wakefield,
  Worcester
FRAMPTON, Sir George
  Edinburgh CS, Iona, Perth,
  Salisbury
FRINK, Elizabeth
  Bury St Edmunds,
  Coventry, Liverpool RC
FRITH, W. S.
  Gloucester
GIBBONS, Grinling
  Canterbury, Rochester,
  St Paul's, York
GIBSON, John
  Durham
GILBERT, Sir Alfred